Into the Backing

Books by Lamar Underwood

On Dangerous Ground

Other Books Edited by Lamar Underwood

The Greatest Fishing Stories Ever Told
The Greatest Hunting Stories Ever Told
The Greatest War Stories Ever Told
The Greatest Survival Stories Ever Told
Lamar Underwood's Bass Almanac
Man Eaters
The Quotable Soldier

Into the Backing

Incredible True Stories
About the Big Ones That Got Away—
and the Ones That Didn't

EDITED BY
LAMAR UNDERWOOD

THE LYONS PRESS
Guilford, Connecticut
An imprint of The Globe Pequot Press

DEDICATED TO

Tom Paugh

Fine writer, superb editor of *Sports Afield* magazine, and the dear
friend who showed me the way to the greatest rivers of my life . . .
and who was with me on many of them.

The Lyons Press is an imprint of The Globe Pequot Press

Printed in the United States of America

10 9 8 7 6 5 4 3 2 1

The Library of Congress Cataloging-in-Publication Data

Into the backing: incredible true stories about the big ones that got away—and the ones
that didn't / edited by Lamar Underwood.
     p. cm.
   ISBN 1-58574-378-X
   1. Fishing—Anecdotes.   I. Underwood, Lamar.
   SH441.I58 2001
   799.1'24—dc21

                              2001050359

Dave Ames, "Ju-Ju Travel" from *True Love and The Woolly Bugger* (Helena, Montana: Greycliff Publishing Company, 1996). Copyright 1996 by Dave Ames. Reprinted with the permission of the author.

Ray Bergman, "Steelhead of the Umpqua" from *Trout, Second Edition, Revised and Enlarged*. Copyright 1938, 1952 by Alfred A. Knopf, Inc. Reprinted with the permission of Howard Christian, Jr.

Joe Brooks, "The Hat Trick" from *Joe Brooks . . . Greatest Fishing* (Harrisburg, Penn.: The Stackpole Company, 1957). Copyright 1957 by Joe Brooks. Reprinted with permission.

Mallory Burton, "A Guide's Advice" from *Green River Virgins and Other Passionate Anglers*. Copyright 2000 by Mallory Burton. Reprinted with the permission of The Lyons Press.

Christopher Camuto, Chapter 8 from *A Fly Fisherman's Blue Ridge* (New York: Henry Holt, 1990). Copyright 1990 by Christopher Camuto. Reprinted with the permission of the author.

John Gierach, "Headhunting" from *The View from Rat Lake* (New York: Simon & Schuster/Fireside, 1989). Copyright 1988 by John Gierach. Reprinted with permission of the author.

Harry Plunket Greene, "The First Trout in the River" from *Where the Bright Waters Meet*. Copyright 1925. Reprinted with permission.

Zane Grey, "The Dreadnaught Pool" from *Zane Grey: Outdoorsman,* edited by George Reiger (Englewood Cliffs, New Jersey: Prentice-Hall, 1972). Copyright 1972 by Zane Grey Estate. Reprinted with permission.

Sparse Grey Hackle (Alfred W. Miller), "Murder" from *An Honest Angler: The Best of Sparse Grey Hackle,* edited by Patricia Miller Sherwood. Copyright 1998 by The Estate of Alfred W. Miller. Reprinted with the permission of The Lyons Press.

Roderick L. Haig-Brown, "The Unexpected Fish" and "The Fish by the Cedar Stump" from *The Seasons of a Fisherman*. Copyright 2000 by the Estate of Roderick L. Haig-Brown. Reprinted with the permission of The Lyons Press.

Acknowledgments

Although it is not necessarily a requirement for achieving publishing excellence, any writer or editor who has his or her book under the guidance of a dedicated professional who happens to be a close personal friend is doubly blessed, in my opinion. Such is the case with my relationship with Jay Cassell of The Lyons Press, who has driven the wagon on this project from idea to printed page. Jay and I have been fellow troopers in both book and magazine publishing battles, and having him at my side has always made every project a rewarding experience.

In addition, I would like to thank the various contributors, their publishers and agents, for their participation in this collection. Also Fred Courtright for working with these fine people on the permissions.

Finally, a special nod for the talented Val Atkinson, whose photograph for the jacket truly takes us into the backing.

—Lamar Underwood

Contents

Introduction

Seen from a side angle, most fly reels offer a teasing, partial view of the backing as it rests beneath the colorful coils of fly line. The tight band of braided line arouses deep and irresistible passions in the fly-fishing faithful. Here are 250 yards of emphatic reminder of the possibilities of sizzling big-fish runs that await the skillful and enterprising angler. Indeed, the reddest and biggest of the famous "red-letter days," including the fish played again and again in memory and in good-hearted fish-war stories, are those that invariably include some form of the expression, "He was into the backing!"

For most of their time on the water, flyfishers are content to embrace the fringe benefits of their treasured activity. The day may have been a bust, with few or no fish hooked. On those too-frequent occasions, the returning angler is forced to retreat to a familiar fall-back position, uttering, "What a day to be out there. Fantastic. Absolutely fantastic!" The more loquacious of the brethren, from the time of the quill pen to today's laptop computers, are capable of describing what they saw, heard and felt in very readable prose, no less engaging from a lack of shrieking reels.

Consider, if you will, this pastoral scene from *Where the Bright Waters Meet* in which Harry Plunket-Greene is reminiscing about his beloved English chalkstream, the Bourne, as he knew it in the early 1900s:

> . . . when the mists begin to lift and the poplars to shine and the cock-pheasants crow in the beech-woods, the little Bourne will wake and open her eyes and find in her bosom again the exiles that she had thought were gone for good—the silver trout, and the golden gravel, and the shrimp and the duns—and smell the dust of the road, and see the sun once more, and the red and white cows in the grass, and the yellow buttercups in the meadow and the blue smoke of the cottages against the black elms of the Andover Hill—and me, too, perhaps, kneeling beside her as of old and watching the little iron-blue, happy, laughing, come bobbing down to me under the trees below the Beehive bridge on the Whitechurch Road.

Beautiful stuff, to read or actually experience. And the scene can be equally captivating in a variety of settings where the fish are not biting but the flyfisher's muse has compelled him or her to describe the setting. Starting with British chalkstreams such as the Bourne, to mountain cascades, to tidewater estuaries, angler-writers have rewarded their readers with landscape portraits that even on the bad-luck days of fishing make the location beckon like some distant El Dorado, a visit worth any amount of planning and loot from the old family exchequer. And the scribes are always right: The journey is the glory. Most of the time the fish would have been released anyway. We'll get some action another day. Hell, a lot of people who don't even fish like going outdoors. But they're from a different tribe and are hard to understand.

The flip side of the average flyfisher's propensity to look on the bright side of a dull day's fishing is a quite normal and healthy streak of realism: Too long a stint at taking fishing's consolation prizes can be tough on morale. There comes a time when we must, as the late Sparse Grey Hackle used to remind Nick Lyons, "Let the wolf out!" Or, as golfers say, "Let the big dog eat!" And nothing—nothing at all, mind you!—boosts a flyfisher's morale and let's the big dog eat like a big fish.

Thomas McGuane is a writer who has an unparalleled gift for capturing the essence of great angling places. Whether he's describing a tarpon flat near Key West or a salmon river in Russia, his prose always has me itching to buy a plane ticket, even when the action on the printed pages is slow. And when fate is smiling on McGuane, dealing him a winning hand, he knows exactly how to let you know what you missed by not being there. Here's an example from the story "Snapshots from the Whale," taken from McGuane's superb anthology, *The Longest Silence: A Life in Fishing,* published by Knopf in 1999. This encounter involves an Atlantic salmon on the Whale River in Quebec's remote North Shore of the St. Lawrence region. Tom tries several flies on a particularly difficult fish that teases him with its interest but will not take. Finally, he decides to try a smaller leader, six pound test instead of ten, and a small Blue Charm tied on in a riffling hitch to be worked across the surface, dragging a little wake. Here's an excerpt from what happened next.

> The fish went straight to it in a deep-bodied swirl. The line tightened on the water before me and I felt the weight in my left hand. I lifted the rod and the fish was hooked. I remember only my conviction that things were completely out of control. . . . The fish controlled the angles. I had to just stand there during the violent runs and ferocious, heedless jumps. It seemed marvelous that all the quasi-reasoning behind the fly changes, the fussiness over the line

mending and the constant revision of my views as the fish and I moved toward closure would end in such an uproar. . . .

Then, later:

Finally I worked the tired fish toward me, leading it through boulders and finally to the beach and the net. She was a powerful, heavy hen not long out of the sea, with subdued black dots on gunmetal and silver. I held her around the tail into the current, feeling the deep curve of belly and fat shoulders, running a finger over the small wonderfully shaped head. When I released her, she picked her way out among the boulders in unhurried progress to deep water. I found myself at a great altitude with yet all my life in which to come down. Indeed, as I write this years later, those moments are inescapable and vivid. What a thing to own.

How good is that? The fishing and the prose? The imagery McGuane shares here, achieving in his words the miracle the distinguished British novelist E. M. Forster called "A Felt Life," is the stuff that launches tackle catalogues, inspires phone calls to outfitters and airlines, sends SUVs grinding along remote trails. All card-carrying flyfishers long to "own" such rich moments, fill their mental scrapbooks with experiences to be savored again and again.

The memories are so strong because big-fish days are the exceptions. Most good days on the water can take other forms. A 12-inch brook trout taken in the Blue Ridge, in a remote pure stream deep among the shadows of the folded hills, isn't going to take you "into the backing" but is a true giant of a fish considering the circumstances. Yes, a trophy fish—for one's memory. And, as we have admitted, a day may pass without a fish at all, yet sparkle with jewel-like intensity as you recall the hours spent on the stream.

Even so, the big-fish challenge won't let go of us. Its siren call holds us hard, gets our blood up. We long to find Mister Big and take him on. "The big ones always get away!" the nonanglers chirp, mocking us. Oh, yeah? Well, just let *me* try for him!

Given a choice, which would you prefer: A three-day trip during which the action was fairly steady, and you landed and released 10 to 15 fish each day of average size for the water you are fishing? Or a three-day trip during which you had only three strikes and landed one fish of magazine-cover proportions?

Actually, deciding which of these two scenarios you would choose is a fool's errand, no doubt. First, you'll take what you can get, thank you very much! And there is another factor I have failed to mention: At different times in one's angling development, the choice might be for more action instead of trying for the infrequent big fish. Satiated on action, one might opt to have a go at finding and catching lunkers only. Such sentiments ebb and flow.

When the angler turns storyteller, the big-fish cards start hitting the table fast. Even a 15- or 20-fish day (I should be so lucky) only takes about two pulls on a bourbon and water to describe to our comrades. Introduce the chance to describe a truly big fish and we'll be off to the races—hands and arms gesturing wildly between gulps from our glass; voice crackling with an intensity as if we had just faced Armageddon, alone; eyes searching frantically to make sure everybody within earshot is getting the picture.

Make no mistake: Big fish are box office. They sell tickets. Excuse the gender metaphor here, but big fish are not like the famous "girl next door." They are the elusive drop-dead-gorgeous creatures of angling lore and myth. If you've ever had a date with one, that's the story your angling peers want to hear—about a very special fish that took you deep into the backing, a battle fought in desperation, with the sound of a whirring reel providing the background music.

You'll find many such battles—those won and lost—in the pages ahead. Best of all, it's not likely any of these tales could have taken place near your own backyard. To witness the frays, we're going places. Our guides are angling writers with the talent and sensibilities to describe what Papa Hemingway called "The way it was," sharing with us all the enchantment and exhilaration of fishing episodes that were anything but ordinary.

—Lamar Underwood
June, 2001

Encounter on the Flat

BY RENE HARROP

In this editor's very active fly-fishing fantasy life, one of the rivers that flows through my dreams is the Henry's Fork of the Snake in Idaho. Despite the number of articles I have read about the Henry's Fork—and sometimes edited for publication—I have, alas, never had a crack at its legendary fishing. I keep hoping that someday I will get my act together and head for this important destination. Until then, I will have to be satisfied with fishing the Henry's Fork in print. I can't think of a better writer to help me do exactly that than René Harrop.

René Harrop lives in St. Anthony, Idaho, about as close to the banks of the Henry's Fork as you can get without wading in, and is the owner of the House of Harrop fly-fishing supply company. He frequently shares his expertise on the finer points of choosing and presenting the right fly in articles in Fly Fisherman *magazine. And on occasion, he turns his talent and creativity to the role of story-teller. This piece from* Fly Fisherman *is one of my favorites.*

The long days of late spring and early summer can drive a fly fisherman to the edge of madness. Each year at this time I am overcome by a state of frantic urgency as I race around the Yellowstone area trying to experience everything that is happening. The streams have finally cleared in the high country and aquatic insects fairly bloom in the warm Western sun. It all seems to take place at once—salmonflies on the Madison, Pale Morning Duns (PMDs) on the Firehole, caddisflies on the Yellowstone; it goes on and on.

The Henry's Fork of the Snake is my home water and the aggregation of insect happenings on this stream alone can be almost overwhelming. From sunrise to pitch dark, there is almost always something going on. It is a constant distraction, and fishing is all I can think of. Fortunately, I have one stabilizing factor in my life; otherwise work, family, everything that resembles responsibility would undoubtedly go unattended while I chase trout. Like so many others who suffer from this affliction, it is my wife who keeps me in line, but luckily Bonnie loves to fish, too. Thanks to her, the bills get paid, the kids haven't starved, and I still get in more fishing than I deserve.

If you ask Bonnie where she most enjoys fishing, she will tell you without hesitation of a place in the interior of Harriman State Park, better known as the Railroad Ranch. There, where the Henry's Fork runs very slow, is a wide and shallow stretch she calls "the flat." She will also tell you of a 24-inch rainbow that she landed there several seasons back, and that she is certain there is an even bigger fish waiting there with her name on it.

Bonnie takes her fishing very seriously and is proud of her skills with a fly rod, so she is not likely to reveal that her real love for this special place is founded more upon the scenic splendor and abundant wildlife than the opportunity for a really big trout. I share her love of nature but not her patience, discipline, or energy, and I confess that I spend most of my time fishing the parts of the Henry's Fork that are quicker and easier to reach. It takes about 40 minutes to make the mile-plus hike, and if you take the trail near the river, there can be a lot of distractions that will slow you down or even prevent you from getting to the flat. Bonnie enjoys the walk and has no trouble resisting the temptation to stop and fish along the way. I, however, am a weak and undisciplined man who would probably never make it beyond the first big trout I saw.

The time and effort that are required to get to the flat probably account for the fact that this stretch of one of America's most popular trout streams is seldom crowded. Hatches are good there, but the flat does not always experience the heavy concentrations of emerging aquatic insects for which the Fork is so well known. Surface-feeding trout have a tendency there to seek isolated areas of the stream that offer shelter of some kind. They can be tough to find, if you do not know the river and what to look for. Mayfly spinner falls are a frequent exception. When hordes of dying insects collect on the water, trout are lured from seclusion and feed openly over the shallow weed-covered flat.

The big trout that cruise the weedbeds are veterans of many seasons. It takes five years or more for a Henry's Fork rainbow to attain a length of 20 inches. A trout this size or larger knows all the tricks, so you had better be good if you expect to fool one. The best anglers hook a few, but many who visit this demanding water hook none. No one lands very many.

Anglers who frequent the flat seldom arrive with great expectations. The anticipation of a truly exceptional trout is always there, however, and for some just the chance at one of those giants is enough.

Bonnie does not require a guarantee of success, which helps to explain why she is willing to forsake the more prolific water above the Ranch for a day on the flat. It was late June, and we had enjoyed several days of consistent, if not spectacular, fishing on the water between Box Canyon and the North Boundary of the Ranch. Mid-morning hatches of small- to medium-size mayflies were followed by a profusion of caddisflies in the early afternoon. The peak of the famed Green Drake hatch was well behind us, but there was still a scattering of the oversized mayflies, and the rainbows pounced eagerly on those that remained. That part of the river is always busy at Green Drake time, so I didn't resist too strongly when Bonnie, having had enough of the crowd, insisted on going to the flat.

The early summer sun and the brisk pace had me puffing and sweating in my neoprenes. Bonnie, who walks three miles every day, wasn't even breathing hard. We paused 20 minutes into our hike ostensibly to watch a hen mallard hurry her fuzzy brown-and-yellow brood away from the bank, but actually it was to allow me to catch my breath and roll down the top of my waders. A bit of snow still clung to the upper slopes of Mount Sawtelle, an inviting sight behind the placid river and seemingly endless acres of wildflowers. It was okay with Bonnie if I stepped into the water for a two-minute cooldown, but she insisted that I leave my fly rod on the bank with her. She, too, had spotted the big rainbow finning gently in the current near midstream.

With the flat now in sight, we continued along the narrow streamside path with Bonnie in the lead. She ignored the grumbled references to love, trust, and understanding that came from behind her.

A small bay near a string of islands is usually ignored by fast-moving fishermen who are headed for open water. We had found fish there in the past, so we decided to check it out. The slow current accelerates slightly over a gravel shelf, creating a long, shallow riffle. Big trout feed comfortably in this kind of water, knowing that the broken surface helps conceal them from danger.

We crouched in the tall meadow grass 20 feet back from the water and intently scanned the riffle. Two large rainbows fed almost imperceptibly in the thin water. They both were taking something on top, but their subtle rises barely pierced the surface. They would have been easy to miss without a very careful approach and the aid of polarized glasses. Bonnie had been first to spot the fish, so I left her to plan her strategy and moved downstream.

There were mayfly spinners everywhere—in the grass, in the air, and on the water. I eased into the waist-deep flow to examine the menu. The cool current tugged gently against my legs, bringing welcome relief to my overheated body. The small aquarium net I used to seine the surface revealed spinners in a mixture of colors and sizes, ranging from #24 Blue-winged Olive to

#14 *Callibaetis,* or speckled spinners. Pale Morning Duns appeared most numerous, so I selected a delicate PMD spinner that Bonnie had tied for me and clinched it to a 6X tippet.

Splashy rises of small trout dimpled the water around me, but I was looking for something better. I found it in the form of four blunt snouts that were punching distinctive holes in the glassy surface. They were all good fish, cruising and feeding a couple of hundred feet out and downstream from where I watched. Fighting the urge to hurry, I moved cautiously forward. My angle of approach was perfect, except for one critical mistake. I had forgotten the position of the sun. The 40-foot cast was good and my fly settled gently above the lead trout.

I had approached the interception point with the sun at my back, and the shadow of the line on the water was enough to alarm the fish; he bolted away. The other three trout vanished, too, and I cursed myself for being so careless. Upstream, Bonnie's bowed rod told me that her plan had worked much better than mine. I could tell from her position that she had chosen to approach her fish from downstream—a good choice, since neither trout in the bay was traveling as it fed. Failing to locate any other fish of significant size, I headed toward a high clay bank on the far side of the river for a better view of the flat.

From my perch 40 feet above the river, and aided by a small pair of binoculars, I was able to recognize most of the half-dozen anglers scattered about the stream. They were regulars, highly skilled individuals who love the river and can be found somewhere on the Henry's Fork just about every day of the season. It was a pleasure to watch them work and I almost forgot why I had gone there myself.

The dense carpet of mayfly spinners had tempted even the most reclusive trout into open water, and they fed aggressively over the shallow flat mostly in small groups of from two to six fish. Unfortunately for me, however, there did not seem to be a single opportunity to get in on the action without interfering with someone else.

The flat was empty a quarter-mile downstream, but the going is slow through the boggy meadow and the gentle puff of wind I felt on my cheek threatened to put an early end to the activity. There probably wasn't time to move to different water.

Wind on a Western trout stream is almost inevitable, but you learn to contend with it in most circumstances. Wind during a spinner fall is a different story, and if you are fishing spinners on flat water, it can be disastrous. The river there is only knee- to waist-deep in most places, and is close to 200 yards wide. When it blows, the wind rushes unobstructed across a broad, open meadow and the flats have neither the depth nor speed of current to prevent the water from being churned into a frothy turbulence. I thought about the blown chance at the four big fish earlier in the day and of my wife, who was now behind an upstream island and out of sight. The breeze had strengthened and I had decided to rejoin Bonnie when I spotted a huge rainbow.

He made a porpoising rise, slow and deliberate and clearly visible at 150 yards without the binoculars. His head was immense.

At first I was not certain I was actually looking at a fish, but then a broad dorsal fin came into view, followed by a tail as wide as my hand. The huge trout was above and well away from the other anglers, and he grazed slowly along a narrow patch of exposed weed. The aquatic vegetation provided just enough obstruction to create a slick on the wind-riffled surface. Each rise took him farther away, but if I moved quickly, I thought, there might be a chance to get a shot at him before the wind swept the remaining spinners from the water.

I raced up the bank to get above him, then stumbled clumsily down the steep slope to the river's edge. There wasn't time for the slow and cautious approach that is normally required, but the choppy current would help conceal my presence, so I moved quickly forward to where I hoped to cut off the huge surface feeder. He was coming up at about three-foot intervals and seemed to move through the rise in slow motion. His head came up first, followed by what looked to be more than a foot of spotted olive green. An equal distance separated the dorsal fin from his tail.

I quartered toward him and had closed to within 40 yards when a burst of wind destroyed the slick and he was gone. With my heart pounding from exertion and the urgency of the moment, I exhaled a long breath of resignation. He had been *so close.*

The wind dropped off a bit, but the anglers below me knew that the fishing was finished and were leaving the river. Within minutes the flat was empty. I still could not see Bonnie and thought perhaps she might have something going in the shelter of the downwind side of the island that concealed her from my view. All hope of seeing the monster trout again was gone, and I was about to cross back to the far side of the flat when he reappeared. Apparently enough drowned spinners remained to hold his interest, because he came up again 70 feet out and slightly downstream.

Several thousand days onstream and countless impressive trout have failed to temper the nervous excitement I always experience when a big trout is near. My hands trembled as I freed the #18 PMD spinner and rapidly tore 50 feet of line from the reel. My gear was set up for calm conditions; it would be tough to get the 16-foot leader to behave with a stiff right-to-left wind on my casting arm. Angling the rod over my left shoulder kept the fly away from my body, and with a back-hand casting motion, I began to extend line. It was a one-shot deal and I hauled with my left hand to speed up the line and punch the 5-weight across the wind. It was probably the best cast I had made all season—maybe ever.

The little spinner alighted amazingly close to where it needed to be, and I saw a glint of pale wing as my fly bobbed tenuously on the chop. It was a tremendously difficult presentation, and I had been very lucky. The spent-wing imitation had arrived on the water a dozen feet above the spot where the big bow had last shown himself. The take, if it came at all, could come soon. I stared at my fly, choked the rod handle, and waited.

I know better than to ever take my eye off the fly, or at least where I think it is, but when the fish failed to show I broke that cardinal rule.

He should be here by now, I thought, and my eyes searched frantically about the water. Now, when my attention returned to the fly I couldn't find it. Suddenly a dark snout materialized among the waves. Startled, I struck instinctively and very hard. Only the distance that separated us prevented the fly from being ripped away before the fish had a chance to close on it. The 60 feet of line and leader also helped to cushion the 6X tippet, which otherwise would have never withstood the shock of my overzealous reaction. My rod arched strongly against the weight. It was sheer luck.

He was an old fish and he reacted to the sting of the hook the way old fish do. No angry thrashing about the surface and no screaming power run. A hint of faded red along his dark sides showed faintly up through the foam and debris of the wind-whipped water as he turned toward the bottom. There was no movement at first, only a forceful side-to-side throbbing as the big rainbow tried to shake the irritation from his jaw. The movement, when it came, was slow but steady, and I could count the clicks as the line left the reel. The grating of the line against the dense underwater weed spelled trouble. This guy had been here before and he knew what he was doing.

The fly line was history now, replaced by a slender thread of white Dacron. It was apparent that this fish lived somewhere far from the middle of the flat and he was heading home. Normally I might have feathered the spool with my palm to apply a little extra drag, but not with a trout of this size. There was no margin for error, so I kept my free hand away from the reel.

The reel continued to purr as the backing melted steadily away, and then the fish stopped. A slight glimmer of optimism crept into my head, but I should have known better. The backing entered the water in a downstream direction, and if I hoped to retrieve any line, I had no choice but to follow. I had not made more than two or three turns on the reel handle when he came up far out across the flat and well upstream from where I stood. It was not a spectacular leap, but more a ponderous lunge that revealed only about half of the most massive trout I had ever encountered on the flat. The heavy resistance vanished with the wind-blown spray of his re-entry, and he was gone.

They say that a trout can't think, but you won't convince me that this crafty old veteran did not know what he was doing when he made his long, looping departure. The force of the current against 300 feet of fly line and backing was by itself enough to part the fragile tippet. I think that he showed himself above the water as an arrogant gesture of victory.

I know that hooking and losing big trout are part of the game on the Henry's Fork. Over the years, I have become accustomed to landing only a small percentage of the really large trout that I hook on light gear. In fact, I sometimes don't really try to land them. Still, I could not deny that I wanted to land that giant. As an adversary, he had me outclassed from the moment he was hooked, and I knew it. The disappointment I felt at not bringing him to net would disappear, but the memory of that encounter would remain for a lifetime.

The image of the great rainbow and that perfect cast played in my mind as I reeled back 300 feet of line and backing. The entire incident had lasted only a few minutes, but I was drained both physically and emotionally by the intensity of the experience.

The flat was empty now, and I stared out across the deserted water. A nesting pair of trumpeter swans passed low overhead, their broad, powerful wings pushing strongly into the midday wind. Downstream, a cow moose with her chocolate-colored calf plunged awkwardly from the bank and waded into midstream to feed. The rasping cry of sandhill cranes drifted out across the flower-laced meadow that seemed to extend all the way to the Teton Range etched faintly across the distant horizon. The fishing was finished for now, and I started wearily toward the far bank and the small, dark-haired figure who waited there. I had come to the flat at my wife's urging, and I needed to thank her.

The Last Pool

BY PATRICK O'BRIAN

Before he passed away in 2000, Irish writer Patrick O'Brian had achieved a towering international reputation as author of the Aubrey/Maturin seagoing epics set in the Napoleonic Wars. Most readers who have enjoyed the many novels of fighting men and ships such as Master and Commander, The Far Side of the World, *and* The Wine-Dark Sea *probably have little idea that O'Brian also wrote some of the finest short stories ever penned on fishing, hunting and nature. Several of these tales have been collected in the book* The Rendezvous and Other Short Stories, *published in America by W.W. Norton in 1994. I've often asked myself how I missed publishing such treasures as "The Last Pool" back when I was editor of* Sports Afield *and* Outdoor Life. *As I said in another anthology I edited, at least I'm not making the same mistake three times.*

This is the last pool,' he said again, as he stood by the side of it with the water running over the toes of his waders. He had said the same thing at each of the five pools below it, and he had meant that if he did not catch a trout he would go home. Each pool in turn had yielded nothing, not even a rise to save the face of his resolution. Each time he meant it more, and now he meant it entirely: beyond this pool was a long flat stretch of river, difficult to fish and notoriously barren; to circumvent both it and the small private lake beyond meant a tedious hot walk in waders already too warm for comfort.

The last pool was certainly the best pool for size and looks; it stood high above a series of chaotic rapids, and an almost unbroken rim of rock enclosed it. At the top end the river came clear over a wall of black basalt four or five feet high, curving over in green water before it broke into two main cascades that came down in foam to the pool. Even now, after weeks of drought, the top quarter of the pool was white, and the water had a menacing roar to it. The outlet was one single column of racing water, a broad mortal jet that came through a black gate of rock in the pool's lower rim; it was from this that it had its name of Goileadair, or, as some said, the Kettle. The sides of Goileadair were sheer-to, and down the middle of it was a shingle bed, piled there by the two competing falls above. The highest part of the shingle was out of the water now, and quite dry.

There was a sombre air about this last pool—little colour, for the valley just here narrowed to a gorge with a great deal of naked rock to its sides. The Scots pines that had taken footing in the crag to the left showed darkly above, and the flash of the falling water accentuated the black polish of the half-sunken rocks. In Conan's time they drowned lepers here.

The gorge was beautiful, this man, this James Aislabie, observed to himself; but it was a harsh, grim kind of beauty, God forbid. He sat down on one of the smooth rocks that marked the end of the pool, the edge of the cleft that let the water out; the river slid fast and silently between these rounded edges, its surface curved and tense. It ran over his dangling feet with an insistent pressure and a grateful coolness; and in ten minutes the all-pervading roar that filled the gorge no longer reached the threshold of his hearing.

At the top end a yellow wagtail perched on a flat stone and stood bowing there and bobbing, and as James Aislabie watched the bird—a fine bird in the glory of his feathers—a fish leapt out of the foam a little to the one side of it. It was a small white fish, a sea-trout of perhaps half a pound or less, but it was a sight pleasant enough to a man who had fished long hours in the heat of the day without the sight of a fish at all.

All day long the weary length of the river, with its difficult, reed-grown banks lower down, and the beat of the sun on his back: the disastrous lowness of the water, with its shining surface and his cast lying awkwardly curled upon it, and his hot boots and the grinding strap on his shoulder. The bad, short, laboured casts as his arms grew more and more tired, the glare on the water as his eye followed the place where his fly ought to be, and the swirling water. When he lay in bed thinking about fishing he did not recall these things, nor the flies cracked off, pulled off, dropped, lost high up in trees.

He considered the best way to fish this pool, and he thought about changing his fly. He had no confidence in the fly he was using and none in the only other fly he had left, which was far too big. However, he cut off the one and tied on the other: it was more a gesture of piety than anything else. The name of the fly escaped him; somebody's Fancy, or possibly Indispensable, he thought, as he pulled the knot tight round the black, shining eye. It seemed but decent to do the thing correctly, although his belief in his motions had almost wholly gone.

His faith in the day's fishing had gone in three stages. At first, on the flat, easy stretches of the lower river, he had been keenly expectant, had made each cast with extreme care: he knew that some fair sea-trout, two- and three-pounders, had been caught within the week, and he hoped with each new cast that he should see the white flash of a turning fish and hear the scream of his reel. Then as the hours passed he had begun to hope rather desperately for just one fish, one, to save him from the wretchedness of having nothing at all. He pictured to himself the beauty of the fish, its gleaming sides, its black spots, the square tail and the fine, strong head, the heft of a good one dead in his hand. The vision grew clearer and more desirable still as he became more and more certain that he was going to catch nothing. It seemed, towards the end of the day, so very unlikely that any fish should want to take an artificial fly tied to a piece of gut; it was so improbable that there were any fish in that river, that if it had not been for some nagging persistence in the back of his mind he would have gone home about tea-time.

The feathers were smoothed, the cast was tried; he stood up and worked out a good line, facing the falls at the top of the Goileadair. His arm was rested, and he cast well; the line shot handsomely through his fingers, and the new fly dropped into the eddy at the outer side of the right-hand fall. It settled for a moment while the current carried down the slack; Aislabie's hand, as though it had an eye, took the line and drew it in, while he stared after the racing spot on the surface that should cover his fly. He was just about to lift his line off the water when some tiny variation stopped him. Was the cast moving a trifle across the current? It was, and the movement increased. With a quiet, smooth firmness it glided across and then upstream: there was a swirl under it that checked his quick strike. Aislabie stood there with the coiled line in his fingers.

'Wait. Oh wait,' he whispered, and he let a coil slip out through the rings.

Then came the pull; a firm pull, rather than the jerk of a little fish. Aislabie struck, with a straight, tight line; he struck too hard from over-anxiety. He had not finished the lashing upward stroke before his rod sprang to violent life. The rod top whipped down to the water, and two coils of line shot from his detaining fingers, and the reel gave a flying screech. In the middle of a pool a huge fish flashed three-quarters of its length into the air: it shook its head, poised there for an instant and fell sideways. In that instant Aislabie had seen every spot on it—the impression burnt itself in as a flash of lightning does. A silver, fresh-run cock-salmon, the heaviest he had ever seen alive. He had even seen the gleam of his cast between the strong beaked jaws.

Before the splash had settled it leapt again, clear of the water this time, and stood on its tail, worrying its head from side to side. Aislabie dropped his rod top: his hands were trembling so much that he could hardly find the knob of the reel, and his heart hammered in the back of his throat. His mind was devoid of coherent, conscious ideas: there was only a sort of cold exultation.

Then came a period of short, frenzied rushes across and across the pool, while Aislabie did nothing but endeavour to keep a tight line. This was not too difficult, as the fish went to and fro across the middle water, keeping roughly the same distance from him. His sense returned, and with it the depressing certainty that he was going to lose his cast for sure and probably most of his line as well. His reason conscientiously told him that only a silly man would hope to land a thirty-pound salmon with a short trout rod and fifty yards of line, a 3X cast and a little fly that a salmon should never have touched.

A salmon had no right to be there: only three, and small fish they were, had been taken in the river in the past twenty years. The top of his desire had been a two- or three-pound sea-trout, weighed by a friendly scale.

His body and the rest of his mind fought the salmon with every particle of skill and resource he had. A wild hope began to glow there in his heart, he put a stronger check on the fish, and the salmon responded with a strength that made the running line bite into his fingers.

So far the salmon had made no attempt to run up or down stream, and at present the only danger lay in the long, dividing finger of the bank of shingle between the incoming falls: if the run took the cast across one of its stones and then the fish were to turn, the cast would surely break. He became aware of this at the same moment that he saw the salmon turn just below the surface at the right-band side of the pool and rush directly at the spit of shingle. Its shoulders were barely covered and he could see the wake it made, curving away right-handed to cross the tip of the spit. Plainly the salmon meant to go up into the deep hole at the foot of the left-hand fall. This would do two things: first, the curving rush would carry the line, if not the cast, over the bare rocks; and second, it would in all probability run the line clean off his reel, in which case it would tauten, stretch to the breaking-point in an infinitesimal fragment of time, break at the weakest point—he had a fleeting vision of the knot joining cast and line—and leave him with a still, lifeless rod.

As the wake neared the point, he leaned his rod out to the left horizontally and checked the racing line with all the force it could bear. The rod bent and quivered to the butt and the salmon's curve flattened perceptibly; it cleared the point several feet below the bare stones, but still the fish bore up right-handed. Aislabie could check no more. Suddenly he let go altogether, and his reel ran out free and screaming. He felt the knot between line and backing pass up through the rings, knocking as it went, and a bitter wave of disappointment welled up around his heart. There was very little backing—he had been careless—and that little was frayed and stiff. He could not gain any distance by wading into the pool; it was neck-deep a foot from where he stood.

The salmon took no notice of the slackened pressure; it sped on into the boil of the fall, to the topmost limit of the pool, and dived into the deep, slack water on the further side of the fall, the inward side under the falling water. There it lay, with its side and belly fins spread and its gills working violently: from time to time it worried, nuzzled against the water-worn rock, trying to dislodge the fly; but the hook was well home.

Aislabie stood there with a couple of yards of backing still on his reel, and for the first time he felt a reasonable hope. He had little enough ground for it, since the line was angled about a rock, and the salmon, should it wish to stay where it was, could not be moved. Still, ambition swelled up and took entire possession of him, so that he could hardly breathe. He saw the fish dead on the shore and wiped the loose scales from his hand—he would have to tail the salmon, for he had neither gaff nor net: he settled in his mind how to attach it to his bicycle.

The salmon, angered and disturbed by the thrumming that the taut line made in the fall, moved across the current and then quite slowly down into the quieter water. Aislabie left it alone until it was farther down than the shingle bed and then he bore gently on the line. The salmon, fiery as ever, hurled itself into the air twice, skittering along on its tail, and rushed straight across to the right-hand pool and back. It paused a moment, and then started a savage, exhausting series of short runs up and down the left-hand half of the pool. Had it not kept to the far side, right under the steep bank, the line would have crossed the middle bar every time, and it would certainly have parted. As it was, Aislabie, standing as high as ever he could, was just able to keep a straight line and a continual slight check on the salmon. Then, when the fish came over again to the hither side, he could bear more strongly against the pull, and now he felt that the salmon's first splendid flush of strength had gone.

His greatest fear was that if he should manage to tire the fish to a dangerous point, it would go downstream, through the pouring lip of the pool, down the strong column of water, and there, among the precipitous black rocks, he could not hope to hold it for a moment.

Time rushed by, marked only by the passage of crises; twice he had slipped on a mossy piece of stone, once the salmon had bored into the only small patch of weed in the pool, and many times his line had dragged perilously over the bare rocks. Long ago he had noticed, with a hurried glance at his top ring, that the sun had left the trees. By now he felt that he knew the fish intimately well, could fortell its reactions, could think in front of it. It was a stupid, angry fish, he thought, with little of the sharp wit of a trout; a clever fish would have been off in less than five minutes. His own reactions, the working of the rod, the instant reeling-in, the varied check, were quite automatic by now; he did not think of them at all. As the fish began to tire in good earnest, to make shorter rushes, he pressed it harder and harder, allowing no moment of rest. Often as it turned he saw the white of its belly.

'It will go down any minute now,' he said, and with half an eye he marked three loose stones. He shuffled one between his feet, and when the salmon turned heavily down the current he had it there to throw with his free hand. It was his one chance, a remote chance, but his luck was with him. The salmon was near the surface, just above the very strong rush of current, and the stone splashed six inches from its nose. It turned and ran upstream.

Quite soon after this the salmon began to tire so much that it was rolling in the water, and he could draw it towards him ten and twenty yards before it would run. At last he brought it into the side, curved with exhaustion and seeming half-dead. He towed it gently up the bank to the one place where the rock ran down to within a couple of feet of the surface. With slow, blundering haste he changed his rod to the other hand, knelt down, muttering 'Calmly, calmly . . .' and made a foolish, impetuous grasp at the salmon. His fingers slipped incapably on the scales, and the salmon shot away with enormous power. The rest and the touch of his hand had renewed its courage and strength. He had known it, he said, and a lowering premonition of failure had been upon him as he knelt.

It was a weary battle now; his strength seemed to have gone into the fish. The consciousness of his own ineptitude tired him more than anything else. He realized now that his arms were as heavy as they could well be, that his reeling hand was about to be seized with a cramp, that he was going to make some last fatal error.

With a headstrong wilfulness, he bore on the salmon, disregarding his frail, frayed cast. The fish sank in the depths, and he pumped it out with the force he would have used with tackle fit for a salmon. His foolishness answered; the salmon made a last flagging run, tried three leaps, each weaker than the last, and lay drifting on the surface.

Now that he could see victory, Aislabie's desperate courage left him; he wasted vital time gaping, tied in an agony of indecision. His body and mind were so tired that he could hardly think.

The salmon came drifting down on the current on the near side of the pool. It was not going fast, for it was not in the main stream, but to one side of it. The fish passed him, and he stood impotently staring: it was downstream of him now, drifting towards the outpouring fall, drifting faster. A queer eddy took the inert body, swirled it out of the current into the slack water of an overhung bay just to the one side of the fall's top.

With an awakening gasp he came out of his trance and ran heavily down the bank to the rock over the bay. He dared not draw the salmon along the bank now, so near the strong current, for he had left it so long that its strength might well be reviving, and one stroke of its tail would carry it into the run, over the edge and away. He knew that he must tail the fish there as it lay or lose it.

The rock on which he stood overhung the water by four or five feet; three feet down, below the usual high-water mark, a narrow sloping ledge jutted out. The fish was on the top of the water, filling this little cut-off basin, a demi-lune made by a backward swirl from the fierce stream that ran at right-angles to its mouth. He put his left foot down to the water-polished ledge— there was not an honest sharp edge of rock anywhere—put his right leg out behind and knelt on the smooth rock, facing up the pool. His right hand, holding his rod, stretched as far as it could over the flat top on which he had been standing.

He was oppressed by a sense of strong, present danger, and when he was in position he paused to collect himself. Peering down, he saw the fish from its dorsal fin to its tail; its head was under the rock and out of sight. It had sunk lower, and now lay in some two feet of water. Just above the tail fin he saw a faint band of lighter scales, the place where his hand had grasped before.

Now he let his arm down to the water, and as he touched the surface he felt his left knee move. There was a patch of dark wet moss under it, and the rubber of his waders was slipping gently on it, downwards. The movement was very gradual, but the slightest motion of his body increased it. He brought his hand back to steady himself, but all his weight was on his left knee, and his hand found no resting place to thrust upon. He put his rod down, quite gently, for any abrupt movement would be fatal, and sought with terrible eagerness for a hand-hold; there was none anywhere in the compass of his reach. His right elbow stayed him for a moment, and by a huge muscular contraction he seemed almost to recover his poise. But his elbow could not grip on the mossy rock; the tuft of moss and grass on which it relied slid from under it, and he felt his weight swaying over onto his unsupported left side. He knew he was falling then. It was quite impossible to get his balance again, and even the smallest movement made him slide a minute, sickening, irrecoverable distance. His right hand, as though working by itself, still searched every inch of the smooth rock for a hold. There was none. He slid further. His whole body was tense to the extremity of its power, and the tension was unbearable. It was a relief when he fell at last—he no longer had to do anything now; it was decided for him now. He observed that his reason was working perfectly well although he was terrified and sweating with the fear of death.

'Right,' he said aloud, and let himself go. His hand, already under water and within a foot of the salmon's tail, dropped right on to the lighter patch of scales: he gripped with a kind of furious reaction just as his face hit the water and his mouth and nose filled chokingly.

The salmon gave a vast, galvanic lunge which momentarily checked his downward fall so that his body was asprawl when it hit the dark racing water. His face was set in a horrible grimace, but his fragmentary thought 'Oh God, the speed . . .' had no horror in it.

It was like coming out of an anaesthetic. He was quite happy, and he was aware that he was conscious before he opened his eyes. As he had supposed, there were people around him, and they were talking, although at a great distance still. He looked placidly at the grey shingle alongside his cheek and somewhat out of focus because of its nearness, he saw the battered head of the salmon.

They were wrangling softly about where the priest was to be found, and Dr Niel said again, 'I tell you he will certainly be at Tobin's—we sent for him—my own patient, for all love. Hurry now, Jack, will you? You can take the poor man's bicycle from by the bridge . . . Surely to God it must be the biggest fish that ever ran up this river.'

Aislabie smiled secretly: a voice said, 'He has come to,' and another, so anxious and kind, 'Can we ease you, Mister, as you lie?' The doctor was speaking too in a professional voice; but Aislabie could not bring himself away from his deep innermost glow; he smiled again, and drew in the smell of the fresh-run fish.

Small Fly: Big Fish

BY VINCENT C. MARINARO

In the crowded elevator headed streetward from the Sports Afield *editorial offices, the man puffing on the big cigar was the target of daggerlike glances, even then, in 1974, long before smoking became a public sin. The man ignored the unspoken commands to "Stow the Stogie!" and continued to talk, gesture, and puff until we were out in the fresh air, headed for lunch. Vincent Marinaro was telling me about a manuscript he had been working on for some time, and his exuberance was not going to be tempered.*

In the Ring of the Rise, first published by Nick Lyons at Crown in 1976, was the first (and only, as things turned out) book by Marinaro since his A Modern Dry Fly Code *had become a fly-fishing icon in 1976. In June 1975,* Sports Afield *first ran excerpts of the text and several of the remarkable photos that made* In the Ring of the Rise *a second Marinaro classic.*

For Vince Marinaro, Pennsylvania's legendary spring creek, the Letort, at Carlisle, was more than a home stream. The Letort was a laboratory, photographic studio, and personal Camelot all rolled into one. Here, with his buddy Charlie Fox, Marinaro explored the mysteries and delights of learning what makes trout tick, and why and when they hit certain flies to the exclusion of all others.

This Letort big-fish episode from In the Ring of the Rise *is but a portion of the treasures that await the reader in Marinaro's two books.*

It is a hot day in September, the season called the doldrums when the water is low and clear and the overhead sun makes the sweat run into your eyes. You have come to the quiet meadow stream to capture a big handsome trout, bull-shouldered from spring and summer feeding.

The bold, slashing trout strikes of spring have died with the big mayflies. The trout is now a furtive creature who makes leisurely, inconspicuous rises, sometimes so fleeting and insignificant as to be almost invisible. He is the smart trout of late summer and early fall, feeding on the millions of tiny insects that now crowd the stream.

In your hand you have the most graceful and delicate of modern sporting weapons: a light, dainty fly rod (preferably of split bamboo) that may weigh as little as one ounce. Brilliantly conceived and executed, the rod has the romantic appeal and appearance of an ancient Toledo blade, responsive to your slightest wish, nodding and trembling with every movement of your hand. Yet, it can be powerful, capable of hurling a long cast, and conquering a creature a hundred times its weight.

Attached to that rod there should be as fine a reel as you can afford, with tension adjustments and a silky smooth operation. You will depend heavily on this reel for the delicate give-and-take required to protect the leader's end, a fine strand called a tippet with a diameter as little as .0033 inch—as fine as human hair—and a breaking point of only three-quarters of a pound.

To the tip of that leader is attached a dry fly so tiny the complete rig is often referred to as "something invisible attached to nothing."

There is no precedent for this minute artificial. We inherited our angling techniques from an older generation devoted to larger dry flies, 12, 10, 8, even larger. No. 16 flies have long been considered "small" and No. 18, "tiny." But the flies for what I call "midge" fishing are much smaller—sizes 22, 24, 26, and 28. A No. 28 dry fly is to a No. 12 as a mosquito is to a large grasshopper.

One of my most exciting experiences with this sort of tackle was on a stifling day in late August. I prowled one of the long meadows of the beautiful Letort River near Carlisle, Pennsylvania, pausing now and then to cool off under a shady tree, but always looking keenly for some sign of a rise. Then I saw it, a faint wrinkle in the glassy surface that was gone in a flash. It happened on the outside edge of a little backwater near my bank.

Up to this point I had stayed well back from the water's edge, looking from a safe distance (in smooth, clear water a trout can see you at least thirty feet away when you stand at water level—farther if you are on the bank). I knew I must avoid wading if at all possible, so I began to stalk the fish on hands and knees. Presently I could peer at him through streamside weeds from no more than five or six feet.

That fish was magnificent, and when I got my first glimpse of him I gasped a little. He was big-shouldered and heavy-girthed, with a broad tail that undulated with easy power every time he rose to take an insect. I estimated this brown trout to be between three and four pounds and more than twenty inches long. Every time he rose he drifted backward and lifted in that languid manner that often characterizes a big trout. At the end of each drift he turned away from me and faced the far bank as he picked off the insect. The interval between rises was something like one minute.

I backed off until I was a safe distance from the water, then sat down to ponder the situation and check my tackle. I peeled off fifty feet of line and quickly respooled it to make sure there were no kinks. My leader was a modern no-knot, continuous taper to 6X to which had been connected a thirty-inch tippet of 7X testing about one pound. After seeing the trout I promptly broke the 7X and replaced it with thirty inches of 6X, testing perhaps two pounds. I felt that I needed an extra margin of safety. (The no-knot leader is necessary on weed-filled streams like the Letort, as a conventional leader's several big knots pick and hold weed balls that are heavy enough to break a fine tippet.)

My rod was a seven-and-one-half foot, three-ounce bamboo on the stiff side. At that time of the year I needed length and stiffness to hold up my backcast above meadow weeds higher than my head. I tied on a No. 20 black beetle and hurried downstream to get below my fish, then approached the bank, crawling until I was about thirty feet below the trout.

Still crouched, I shook out the leader and some line to make sure everything was free and easy, then waited for the rise. Shortly it came and I marked its position in relation to a clump of grass on the bank. Now I began to extend line and leader until I had enough to make a pitch to the far bank, opposite the rise. Another pitch and shoot adjusted the length to put the fly two feet in front of the trout and a foot to his right, plus a float of at least six feet.

I slammed my pitch high and hard, deliberately overshooting so when the cast recoiled it came down just right, the loose, snaky 6X tippet settling softly on the surface. I could barely discern the little hump created by the tiny fly and noted with satisfaction it was floating freely on a true course. Now I saw the shadowy form of the trout beginning to lift, slowly undulating backward and upward, then turning to the right, and finally the little sip and the faint dimple on the surface.

The suspense created by the slow, deliberate, and visible rise of a big trout to your fly is agonizing. Only age and experience prevented me from jerking that fly from his open jaws or smashing the fine tippet with a violent strike.

Trembling, I lifted the rod gently and softly flexed the tip. Nothing happened and for a few long seconds time stood still. Suddenly the trout exploded in a furious dash upstream, plowing a long furrow in the water while my little reel chattered and whined. There were agonizing moments until he stopped short of a fallen willow. I looked down at my reel and noted with alarm that only a few turns of line were left on the drum, for I had no backing. (It would not have mattered anyway since there is no way to stop a big fish with midge tackle.)

I had put the rod tip down during that run and now I kept it low with the line hanging loosely. There was no pressure on the fish but he was still nervous, his head shaking in an effort to dislodge that passive but nagging irritation in his jaw.

Within a few minutes the trout became calm and I began the most delicate, tricky operation in midge fishing. I had to bring that fish back downstream, recover my line, and get him away from that fallen willow. One mistake and he would be into the willow with a jump.

I started by pinching the line with the thumb and forefinger of my free hand, drawing backward until I barely felt the fish. Then, increasing the pull slightly, I began to ease him toward me. I got him back a few feet before he realized what was happening to him. He got nervous again and I promptly released the line. When he had calmed I pinched the line and resumed; with several stops and starts, I got him back to his original position. But this was only the beginning.

I knew his kind—strong, wild, full of tricks. A smart trout that knew his ground better than I. His next maneuver was a familiar one that had lost me some fish in former years: He began swimming in a tight circle, slapping the leader hard with his tail. There is only one way to stop this—you must lift the rod high and parallel to the water, and with as much bend as possible.

When the trout found he could no longer slap the leader he became panicky, streaked downstream a short distance, turned upstream, and slithered into a big weed bed. I groaned. This is the safest refuge for a big meadowstream trout and he knows it. It would be a grueling contest after all.

I hurried downstream to get below him, put the rod low and to one side with as much bend as possible short of breaking that 6X point. You cannot drag a big trout out of a weed bed; you must hold him with a light but constant downstream pressure until he tires and backs out of his own volition. Sometimes this takes many minutes. It worked for me on this occasion and the trout did what I expected—he ran downstream again and burrowed into another weed bed.

Through sweat-blurred eyes I suddenly noticed that one of the dreaded weed balls was draped over my leader. A weed ball the size of your fist is surprisingly heavy; it can pop a fine tippet if the fish moves before you can free the weeds. I hurried downstream below the resting fish, plunged my rod tip into the water to force the floating line below or at least level with the weed ball, and swished the rod tip from side to side. Soon I had the weed ball slipping toward me, pushed along by the current and the rod movement. I quickly removed it.

The dive-into-weeds maneuver was repeated over and over, each stop becoming a little shorter. The contest was going my way and I felt good about it until the trout suddenly bolted downstream and started around a bend. Between me and the fleeing trout was a swampy section that I could not negotiate. I ran backward and headed for high ground, the rod held high to clear the meadow weeds, and dashed in a circular route after the trout.

We arrived at the end of the bend neck and neck, the trout still racing. Now I saw a final hazard that I did not anticipate—a small, midstream logjam with a clear channel on both sides. If he headed through the far channel, all would be lost.

He headed for the far channel. There was hardly time to think and my next act was pure instinct. I lifted the rod high with a lot of line bellying from the tip, then drew the rod back and hurled a high loop over the logjam. It cleared beautifully and fell in the far channel, running freely with the trout down the straightaway.

That was really the end of the fight. The trout's final defiant gesture was to push his head into a patch of watercress near my feet, leaving his body exposed. I netted him and carried him to a clear, shallow channel near the bank, then sat down to stroke him and help him recover.

What I said to this gallant fish during that rest period he probably never understood. If he had, I am sure we would have parted friends when, with a flick of his broad tail, he shot back into the safety of the Letort—after a contest that had lasted an hour and five minutes and had covered a quarter of a mile of stream.

When an angler new to midge fishing sees me land a trout like this, and I show him what I caught it on, the inevitable reaction is: "I don't believe it!" Not because the tackle is so delicate but because the fly is so tiny as to appear inconsequential.

Midge fishing differs from ordinary dry-fly fishing in two ways. Instead of doing everything possible to make one of the tiny flies float high by spraying it with a silicone solution and carefully snapping the water droplets from it, the fly is cast *into the surface film* so as to float flush like a drowning insect. This is a radical departure from standard practice. Also, you must never strike a fish in the conventional way with a sharp lift of the rod.

The bite of the tiny hook is only about $\frac{1}{16}$th of an inch, microscopically enhanced by bending the hook so the point is slightly offset to one side. As a result of this small bite, a midge fly is tricky to lodge in a trout's mouth, as I relearned one day last October when I located a really big trout feeding on tiny *Caenis* flies. I watched as the old boy tipped up and down with that easy, rocking-chair motion a big trout uses during a heavy hatch.

After surveying the situation I decided that the only spot where I could pitch to him without causing the fly to drag was directly across from him. I didn't like this, but I had no choice. Eventually I got a good pitch in front of him that he took. I lifted the rod gently. The hook, a No. 24 on a one-pound tippet, held momentarily, then popped out of his jaws.

I renewed my casting. Again he took my little *Caenis*. I lifted as gently as before and again the hook came out. Bitterly disappointed, I sat there berating myself for botching it. Then, to my amazement, that big trout began to feed again.

I made a good pitch and watched breathlessly as he tipped and sucked the fly. For the third time, so help me, the little fly came out of his jaws. When I lifted the rod to make a fourth try I couldn't get the cast away; my hand shook and I had to let the cast die.

Curious now, I crossed the stream below the trout and came back up, crawling close to his position. What I saw startled me—he was a hook-billed male with a big gap in his jaws! The fly had merely scraped past his teeth.

You must get that little hook into the soft, tough tissue in the corner of a trout's mouth. Once embedded, the fly will stay there and nothing can shake it loose. To accomplish this you must cast either upstream or across at a fish that turns away on the take so the fly catches at the jaw hinge. Then all you need do is tighten the line gently to sink the barb.

What makes midge fishing exciting is the challenge and the variety; each trout stalked poses different problems. One trout last season seemed almost impregnable, since his lair was only a yard beyond a hot cattle fence.

Cows had cropped the grassy banks as close as a putting green and there was no cover. Yet there was this eighteen-incher sipping *Caenis* spinners and there was that dreadful fence. I knew the trout would bolt downstream under the fence the moment he felt the hook.

I made a desperate plan. I put my landing net on the bank near a large bed of watercress. Then I crawled under the fence well away from the stream and inched toward it, pulling myself along by my elbows.

In position at last and still prone, I raised my right arm and cast. The trout took and shot under the fence. Keeping the rod low, I lurched up and ran to the fence and poked the throbbing rod under it. I was just able to reach across the fence and grab the rod with my other hand. Then I hurled the rod at the watercress thirty feet downstream.

Again I crawled under the fence. When I had dashed to the watercress and retrieved my rod, the trout was still on. I picked up my net, for the campaign was won. Some say trout fishing is a contemplative sport, but it never is when you stick a tiny fly into a big unsuspecting trout.

Two Episodes from
Fisherman's Spring

BY RODERICK L. HAIG-BROWN

In both the books and memories where great angling literature is stored, the names of a few writers have become icons. Roderick L. Haig-Brown has earned such a distinction by writing some of the most readable prose ever printed on the subject of fishing.

Whether he is sharing his expertise on gear, techniques, or fly selection, or describing memorable events that took place on the stream, Haig-Brown brings the ultimate in reader reward to every page.

Four of his most important works have recently been gathered into a single mammoth volume published by The Lyons Press. The Seasons of a Fisherman includes the Haig-Brown classics, Fisherman's Spring, Fisherman's Summer, Fisherman's Fall, *and* Fisherman's Winter. *The two selections presented here are both from* Fisherman's Spring *and show Haig-Brown at his best on streams in his beloved British Columbia.*

Born in Lancing, Sussex, England, in 1908, Haig-Brown first visited British Columbia in 1926 and moved there permanently in 1931. His most remembered works include the immortal A River Never Sleeps *and others available from The Lyons Press. Haig-Brown passed away in 1976.*

The Unexpected Fish

I nevitably there is great satisfaction in catching the exact fish one is fishing for; a big fish of his kind, yet not extravagantly big, rising or lying precisely where he should be, coming to the fly confidently and smoothly, fighting with anticipated vigor, sliding at last to net or gaff or beach in the calculated place. This is the reward of experience and performance, good to watch and good to achieve. Presumably it is the principal objective of going fishing. Yet the fish one remembers are not these noble creatures of orthodoxy and perfection but the unexpected fish, the almost impossible fish, that catch one with tackle and body off balance, and force improvisation and shocked, stumbling, cross-legged incompetence.

It is impossible to create such fish deliberately, by going out with inadequate tackle for instance, because their essence is to be unexpected. The closest one can come to it is to go out and fish calmly and conscientiously for fifteen- or sixteen-inch trout in a stream that also has a run of big steelhead or Atlantic salmon; but even this fails after two or three times, because experience steps in and makes the unexpected more than half-expected. One cannot do it with steelhead kelts in a spring trout stream, with a giant halibut or ling cod when looking for salmon or with an oversized Dolly Varden in a lake of small trout, because these are all pretty much undesirables and it is essential that the unexpected fish be very much desired. There is no harm in hoping, in an off-hand way, for an unexpected fish, but any too precise optimism will destroy him in advance by making him expected.

One unexpected fish that leaves me a little cold is the great, unyielding brute who takes a wet fly on 2 or 3X gut when it is at fullest stretch downstream, just as one starts to recover line; about all he adds up to is a solid pull, a lost fly and a moment of annoyance; one hasn't even time to blame oneself for heavy-handedness. His broad-backed brother, who shoulders suddenly out of a fast little run where a two-pounder should have been lying and seems to break 4X gut against the friction of the line on the water, is almost as bad. There is a limited hope that either fish may come again, but usually one can only mark the place and season for future caution. To resolve upon perpetual caution, a constant delicate anticipation of the unexpected, is to interfere too much with the easy pleasure of fishing though the shades of the mentors of one's youth will try to argue that this should be the lesson learned.

The first August steelhead I ever caught in the Campbell was the ideal of the unexpected fish. I was working a No. 6 Silver Brown with a 2X leader on a long slow swing across the tail of the Canyon Pool, expecting nothing more than a three- or four-pound cutthroat, secured in the expectation by the experience of six or eight seasons. The big fish took midway on the swing right at the surface, with a slash that sent a spout of water several inches into the air above the smooth pool. I let the drag of the line strike him and he ran upstream from the pull, keeping well to the middle, away from all trouble, wearing down his first surge of strength and giving me time to realize what it was all about. He could have broken me at any time during the first ten minutes and would have been well within his rights in doing so. After that he was under the control of the rod, though still dangerously heavy and strong. If he had flipped over and broken the gut as I beached him I should probably not have blamed myself much. He did not, and he weighed sixteen pounds.

I caught three or four more August and September steelheads of ten or twelve pounds in seasons after that before I realized that the river had a small late run of big summer fish. They are no longer altogether unexpected, but the run is too sparse for one to go out and deliberately fish for them. It is a time to look for two- or three-pound trout, with appropriate tackle, so the big fish retain many of the exciting qualities of the unexpected.

A fish need not be extremely large to qualify in the unexpected class. I shall remember a brown trout of my boyhood, not over a pound in weight, which escaped into a weed bed and broke me. He stayed where he was, head burrowed into the weeds and only an inch or two of his back showing intermittently as the long green strands moved in the current over it. I waded cautiously towards him from downstream, the net ready in my hand, though I hadn't any very clear idea of what I intended to do; I had tried and failed before to net trout out of weed beds. When I was still six or eight feet below him he came suddenly to life, darted out of the weed bed and a little way upstream. For a moment he rested there uncertainly, then turned and came downstream for his holt like a bullet. I thrust the net towards the line of his flight in a forlorn reflex action and felt a surge of astonished triumph as he thudded into it. He was my fish all right, with my little Ginger Quill trailing broken 4X gut from his mouth.

Last winter was cold, so cold that I shouldn't write of it in a book of springtime fishing. Towards the end of January I finished a book and felt I had to go fishing, though the weather was around zero and there was four feet of snow on the ground. Ann told me to be sure and get a fish because it was a long while since we had had one. I knew I shouldn't be fishing long in any sort of comfort, so I waded in a few yards above a good lie and began to work my fly out over it as quickly as possible. A fine fish took the fly almost at once, well out in the fast water, and ran strongly seventy or eighty yards downstream. There was ice in the rings of the rod already and when the wet backing began to come in I saw that it was coated with ice, so I began to worry a little and handle the fish carefully. The splice between backing and fly line jammed in the ice of the top ring, but I broke it through and felt a fine sense of relief when it came onto the reel. He took it out again twice and caused me plenty of other trouble and anxiety, but I had him at last within reach of the gaff and fairly quiet. I was standing among large boulders, in two or three feet of moderate current, but I knew I had to gaff him there because I dared not take him nearer the ice at the edge of the river.

I was standing awkwardly and the fish was lying awkwardly, head a little down and still upright. I judged him about fifteen pounds and thought several things one has no business to think when about to gaff a fish. I thought:
that hook's got a light hold. If I try to shift him he'll run again and he might
shake the hook or even get into the ice along the shore. I want him very much,
because it's going to be tough fishing from here on, with ice just about solid in
the rings and on the line, and forming faster than you can break it loose. With
him on the bank it won't matter much—at least I can relax and enjoy myself. . . . So I reached the gaff backhandedly over him and made the stroke. It
was a bad one, too far forward and not solid, but it pierced the gill-cover and I
lifted the fish, swung him across and started towards the bank, holding him out
of the water on the gaff. As I made the first step, the point of the gaff broke off
and the fish fell back into the water. I saw the gut was wrapped around the
broken hook of the gaff.

For one quick moment as I tried to free the gut, the fish was quiet.
Then he gulped water and expelled a cloud of blood from his gills, turned and
ran. I made one last move to free the gut, then it broke and he was gone.

In spite of my successive stupidities, I managed to feel quite sorry for myself, and at the same time disgusted. I knew from that cloud of blood I had killed
the fish—fish don't have much blood to lose. So he was wasted. And the chance of
another with the freezing line that would no longer shoot a yard was pretty small.

Out of my shame, in an unpromising attempt to reduce it a little, I developed the idea that I might find the fish if he died quickly. The river was
quite low and for a hundred yards or more below me the current set slightly
towards the bank, running at an uneven three to five feet among big boulders.
I started fishing again, but watched the water below me.

After about five minutes of fishing I saw a faint white reflection in the
water a few feet below where my fly was working. I lost it, then saw it again. It
was far too easy to account for—the white rock, I told myself, in the lower lie.
But I kept watching, and after a while it showed again, thirty or forty feet farther downstream. I admitted it was too far out to do me any good, but fished
on a little faster and still kept watching. It disappeared, showed again, disappeared again. I was casting in a sort of a way, but paying no attention to the fly
and hurrying over the big round boulders in a way that threatened to put me
off my feet at any moment. Then the flash showed again, still farther down but
close to water that might not be over my waders. I knew it was my fish now,
because I had seen the twisting shape of his body as he came up through the
water, and I knew it was my last hope, because the current set out again just
below where he was. I reeled up and hurried.

When I got to where he should have been there was no sign of him. I didn't want to be too hopeful, because the whole affair seemed moderately unlikely, but at the same time I was quite determined to stay with the fish as long as there was any hope at all.

He showed suddenly, starting from the bottom belly-up in a twisting effort that carried him almost to the surface, a few feet out from me and a few feet below. Then he sank slowly back and disappeared. I waded out and down, on tiptoe in the current, with an occasional flick of ice water slopping over the waders against my chest. I peered down into the water and saw the fish, right side up, curved against the upstream side of a rock, held against it by the current. Then I remembered the point of the gaff was broken off. I thought of lowering my fly down on the tip of my rod, decided against it and pushed the broken gaff towards him. It meant putting my arm in up to the shoulder but I reached him, got the remains of the hook well under him, and heaved. It didn't go home, but he came up on it almost to the surface, then slipped off. I raked the broken gaff along the length of him, hoping it might catch in the gills. It did. I lifted his head clear of the water, set my fingers in his gills and waded ashore. He weighed fourteen pounds, which is not large for a winter fish, and any triumph I could claim was born of clumsiness and poor judgment. But he rates high among my unexpected fish.

If doing the wrong thing can make an unexpected fish, it is far more certain that an unexpected fish can make one do the wrong thing. Not so long ago I was standing under April sunshine in a shallow, sandy slough at the head of a big lake. There were trout in the slough, handsome green-backed cutthroats up to two pounds or so, but they weren't moving much at that time of day. So I was wading cautiously along, hoping to see one against the pale sand. I was watching the edges of the slough mostly, expecting the fish to be close under the matted tangle of swamp brush that hung down into the water, so I did not see the big fish until he was almost opposite me.

He was swimming majestically, calmly, very slowly, right up the center of the slough. He was broad and deep and long, and I will say he weighed seven pounds, though I am quite sure he weighed over ten pounds. I have never knowingly put a fly over a cutthroat even nearly so big.

He passed me without a tremor of his fins to suggest he had seen me and I remained for a long moment in frozen hesitation. I thought of only two things: that I was going to put a fly over him and that I mustn't move to do so until he was far enough away. I did not manage to remember that I was fishing a No. 14 variant on 4X gut in my search for two-pounders, nor that the big fish was not trapped between me and the head of the slough, so that I could easily take time to change my rigging on the certainty I would find him again. I simply waited until his lazy swimming had carried him ten or twelve yards beyond me, then began to put out line in cautious but rapid false casts.

He was about sixty feet away when I gave it to him. I had the sense to set the fly to one side and a little ahead of him and the luck to make a shepherd's crook that kept the gut farther from him than the fly. As a cast, it was a pretty smooth operation all through—at one moment the flat, calm surface of the slough was empty, in the next my fly was there without a ripple to show how it had arrived. The big trout saw it and turned instantly towards it, probably wondering how the nymph had passed up through the water without being seen. There was no change of pace, only of direction. Very slowly he came, nudged the fly with his nose, took it down. I tightened on him and thought I was quite a fisherman.

Right in the second the little fly hit him, the fish knew he had no business in the slough and I began to suspect I had no business being hooked up to him. He was past me, trailing slack line, before I could turn around, and the line was tight again and the reel running before I could begin stumbling after him. Just for a moment he kept to the open slough and I kidded myself I still had a chance. Then the drag of the reel worried him and he cut over among the drowned tips of the swamp brush. The reel ran out a few more yards and stopped. I saw the flash of a broad, bright side in the brush, a splash and that was the end of it. I felt very lonely.

If they ever come to writing life insurance under water, the unexpected fish will be a pretty good risk. But I'd rather lose one honest example of the type than land a hundred orthodox creatures. It's nice to be reminded that one cannot put a line in the water without tempting the unknown.

The Fish by the Cedar Stump

The Cedar Stump Pool in the little river is a fine place to look for a steelhead in the winter, if you can get there. But that part of the river is a fifteen-mile drive over old logging grades from any traveled highway, and a foot or so of snow is enough to make it impassable; so in most winters the fish rest there peacefully, without the problem of deciding whether my flies should be intercepted or left alone.

By mid-March the snow is usually gone, or at least rotted down enough to give a car a reasonable chance. There may be a few alders and willows to clear out of the way or a wet spot to be filled in with cedar branches, but I like the pool and the other pools near it for a mile or so up- and downstream well enough to go in and look for the tail end of the winter run. In some years there are enough clean fish to make wonderful fishing; in others one releases everything that takes hold as too dark or too near spawning to be worth keeping. But that doesn't mean that the trip and its complications are not worthwhile.

The little river averages no more than fifty feet wide up here among the falls and sandstone ledges, so I take the ten-foot rod and hope the fish will not be too rough with me. In the big pool at the foot of the lower falls they usually are not. In the pool by the bridge, where they can run at once for the bad water at the head of the lower falls, I can rarely hold them. In the long series of pools below the upper falls a little effort and determination usually win out. In the Cedar Stump Pool, which is two or three hundred yards above the bridge pool, anything can happen.

It is a long, narrow pool, fast and quite deep. In normal March water, which is fairly high, one can wade the fast water under the left bank, but it is not too comfortable. The fish usually take opposite the big cedar stump, about two-thirds of the way down the pool, where the main current spreads and slackens a little, but only a little. The tail of the pool is short and still fast, tumbling over into a short broken rapid that twists awkwardly down through thirty or forty yards to a long, wide, shallow reach.

I got through to the falls reach in mid-March for the first time this year. There was still snow on the ground, but it was soft and rotten; the weather was almost mild, the stream at a good height and clear. A fish took me rather promptly in the pool by the bridge and was friendly enough to swim back up from the tail when I slacked line on him. For a foolish moment I thought I had a chance with him, then he got nervous and ran down fast under the bridge into the bad water above the falls. He jumped twice there and was free—fortunately he threw the hook, so I still had the fly. I judged him at about twelve pounds and he seemed very bright when he jumped, so I was encouraged.

I passed the Cedar Stump Pool on the way up, walking the top of the burned-off ridge and looking down into it, but seeing nothing, as always; the water is nowhere slack enough or shallow enough in the body of the pool to see bottom except in strong sunlight.

Up above, things went badly. The river was running higher than I thought and it was hard to get the fly down, and hard to wade in many places. One fish took me on the far side of the top pool, but he was chasing the fly as it came out of the slacker water and it pulled out of his mouth. I saw him as he turned back and thought he was dark. Another fish took beautifully in the pool on the flat, but he was already spawned and very sluggish; the weight of the current carried him a long way below me and I found myself blocked from following by the branches of a big alder that hung twenty feet out over the stream, so had to work him slowly and painfully back before I could release him. In the next two pools I found nothing at all, which was natural enough as the river was too high for them to fish properly from the side I was on. So I came to the Cedar Stump Pool, fishless and not too impressed with my choice of a day.

The pool fishes fast because it is so straight and so narrow. One wades in at the head, to get clear of the steep bank and the tangle of brush along it, makes a few short casts partially upstream to fish the head, and in almost no time the fly is hanging opposite the cedar stump, sixty feet below. That's probably just as well, because the head is never productive, and the suddenness with which the fly comes to the holding water makes one pause and work the cast again, just to make something out of the pool. I had a double reason for doing so on this day, because I thought I felt a faint pluck as the fly crossed by the stump.

I got the fly deeper on the second cast and felt the pluck again; almost a pull this time, but still something less than a definite take. I wondered about the possibility of a cedar limb wedged in the bottom, so that the fly just touched it on the swing. Twice more I cast and each time felt the faint interference. Then I let the fly swing over too far at the end of the cast and hooked a submerged alder limb. I could not free it from where I was standing, so went down.

When I had the fly again I stood for a moment wondering whether to go back up and try the lie once or twice more. I believed what I had felt had been a fish, but supposed my fly hadn't been working deep enough or slowly enough, so decided to make an upstream cast. I made an awkward roll to get out line straight in front of me, so that the fly landed on the far edge of the current, right in line with the stump, and whipped straight across. I could see it, almost dragging the surface, and I saw the fish roll easily up and take it.

It seemed the answer to a fisherman's prayer in such a place, because the strike came at once from the swinging line from downstream, and the fish went hard against it up to the head of the pool. I judged her to be a small female, not over eight pounds, and I had seen she was reasonably bright. She was holding now in mid-current, twenty yards above me, obviously swimming quite hard, so I kept a good strain on. It seemed reasonable to suppose she would tire enough to be content to stay in the pool and give me a chance.

I don't remember how long she held there or what started her down; probably I grew impatient and put on too much strain. She came suddenly, and very fast, right down the center of the pool. For a moment the line was slack, then she came hard against the reel and in another moment the backing splice went out. She was well beyond the tail of the pool now, but I still thought she might stop, and fifty yards of backing were gone before I began to stumble after her through the deep fast water. She was still taking line around the curve of the rapid when I came to a hanging alder and decided to ride past it on tip-toe. There was another alder below with limbs that pushed still farther out over the stream, but she was still running and the thin little spool of backing left on the reel gave line so unwillingly I had to help it with my hand; so I took a chance on the second alder and half-floated past that. I knew I had to get out then or swim a rugged trip through the rapid, so I struggled back towards the bank. As I got there I realized she had stopped running.

I rested for a moment on the edge of the stream because I was sweating and mildly winded. The thin backing stretched down into the broken water at a depressingly long angle and I warned myself that there was no reason to suppose it might still be holding a fish. I also decided I had grossly deceived myself about the size of this particular fish; she must be, I thought, all of fifteen pounds, and that was conservative. If the truth were known she was probably better than twenty.

There were alders fifteen or twenty feet high all along the edges of the rapid and for a moment I thought I must either break and lose my fly line, or else take the trip down the rapid after all. Then I realized that the bank sloped sharply up to a bench at least as high as the top of the alders. I climbed out and went up. By walking logs and climbing onto strategic stumps I managed to clear the line over the tops of the alders. The fly seemed to be wedged in something solid on the far side, just under the head of the long shallow reach. Things were easier now and I got downstream of whatever was holding the fly and went back to the river. Then I pulled quite hard. There was a great disturbance in the shallow water and I knew I still had my fish. I also supposed I must have been muddle-headed when the fish took, because the fish I had now was obviously red, and huge.

After the first plunge my fish went back to holding, so I waded out into the fast, even, two-foot depth of the shallow and put on more pressure. The fish came back, obviously tiring, but I knew my only hope of beaching her was on the far side, so I waded on across. Then I saw her, still very bright, an eight-pound female. And following her, in close solicitude, was an enormous, red-sided, hook-jawed male. She got below me again, of course, and made a clumsy affair out of what should have been a tidy beaching. And the male followed her, close around my legs, right into water so shallow he scared himself and started out again. But I could see him waiting no more than twenty feet away while I worked to free the hook. She was bright, and in good condition, and we needed fish at home. But with anthropomorphic sympathy I carried her back to the water and held her while she recovered. The male waited while I did so, swinging to within two or three feet of her without a sign of fear. And he followed when at last she swam away.

Tarpon Hunting

BY THOMAS MCGUANE

There are three of them—a triad of saltwater gamefish with the kind of power and elusiveness that anglers dream of encountering, and writers, photographers, and painters try to capture in works of art.

Perhaps the special attribute that has made flats fishing into an angling shrine is the fact that tarpon, permit, and bonefish come into water so shallow that sometimes it barely covers their dorsal fins. The thin, clear, tidal pushes of water over the flats give this fishing the visual drama of hunting. In a flats boat, gliding magically over the terrain of sand, grasses, and coral, poised with rod in hand as he watches intently for the sudden vision of fish moving, the angler hovers over the glassy surface like a gull or osprey ready to strike.

Another reason flats fishing is so seductive is because once these powerful swimmers are hooked, the life forces that sustain them past tides and predators are transmitted through an angler's rod hand in electric jolts and shocks, messages of uncontrollable fury, even anger. Every time I get a hookup with tarpon, permit, or bonefish, I somehow am struck by an immediate sense of inadequacy: Something tells me I'm going to screw things up for sure, that I never should have gotten into the ring with this guy, because he's definitely going to kick my butt!

But like everybody else who has ever tried flats fishing, I keep coming back for more. And that passion has fueled a very active desire on my part to read everything about the sport my eyes have clapped onto. Many of my favorite such pieces bear the words "By Thomas McGuane."

Beginning with the finest piece ever written on fly fishing for permit, "The Longest Silence," published by Sports Illustrated *in the 70s, and continuing through the present, Thomas McGuane has created a sparkling galaxy of fishing stories, set in places ranging from Russia to Tierra del Fuego to streams near his boyhood backyard in Michigan and his present-day ranch in Montana. While all this has been going on, he has authored original screenplays and novels and short stories published to critical acclaim that most serious writers would gladly open a vein to achieve.*

Happily for McGuane fans such as myself, all his fishing articles have been collected in a single volume, The Longest Silence: A Life in Fishing, *published by Knopf in 1999. "Tarpon Hunting" comes directly from McGuane's Key West experiences, the years when he lived there and the visits he and his friends have made since then.*

By March in the Keys you're thinking of tarpon. The fish have been around in small numbers all winter—not quite fishable numbers, somehow—when bonefish and permit have seemed the more logical subjects of attention. Night trollers and drifters have been taking tarpon in the channels and killing them for advertising purposes; they make the only sign a tourist will believe when hung up at the dock. The shrimp basin in Key West and the harbor always have quantities of fish, but these are domesticated brutes, feeding themselves on the culls of the commercial fishermen and rolling and burbling with the reptilian presence that half-tamed alligators used to have on Florida golf courses. We just stare at them unable to account for their feral behavior.

But usually, sometime in March, while permit fishing or bonefishing on an edge adjacent to deeper water, we spot the first string of migrating tarpon, often juvenile fish up to fifty and sixty pounds. Below Key West they inevitably appear to be travelers, pushing wakes and rolling with their eyes coming out of the water. You are absolutely sure they see you in the skiff, transfixed and watching. The whole mystery of their cycle seems contained in the absolutely deliberate way they travel, deliberate as caribou or spring warblers.

Mystery is not an altogether misplaced word regarding tarpon. Much serious research on the fish was dropped when schemes for converting these unparalleled creatures to fertilizer and cat food were abandoned. There seem to be vertical migrations of fish from deep to shallow water, in addition to the fish that appear to be traveling from the south, very probably Central America. But facing a lack of hard information, the angler feels the invitation to elaborate his own sense of the fish's presence. An awareness arises of the distinction between a species like the tarpon and the offshore pelagic fishes with which, as a game fish, the tarpon is often favorably compared. But in the tarpon, the aerodynamic profiles and chameleonic coloring of blue-water fish are replaced by something venerable; they are inshore fish, heavily scaled; they gulp air; and as if to seal their affinity for the land masses of the earth, they require fresh or brackish water to complete their reproductive cycle. They migrate, as many fishes do, and when we touch or intercept these migrations, we sense, subliminally, the dynamism of the earth: tarpon migrate by season, season is a function of planetary movement, and so on. Which is no more than to say you can face bravely those accusations of loafing when you have ruined a month chasing tarpon, racking your brain to understand their secret, sidling lives.

It is quite early in the morning. Not first light, because a higher angle of sun is required to see fish on the dark bottom we are working today. But it is early enough that as we cross Key West the gas stations are being swept down by sleepy attendants with push brooms, and the Cuban men are over on their end of Duval Street drinking cups of their utterly black coffee and eating *bollos*. In the still air you can smell the smoke from City Electric on the other side of town. The groundswell of Latinate noise—that first of all the things that make Key West another country—has not yet started, and as we go up Caroline Street all the side streets running down to the shrimp basin, marked for us because of the great trawling booms sticking up among the old wooden houses, are quiet. The shrimpers always line up first under the awning of the Fisherman's Cafe. No one there yet, though someone is arranging ship-to-shore radios and fathometers in the window of Key West Electronics across the road.

It feels like a tarpon day. Spring tides will give us a good push of water. The wind has swung almost into the full south and it's already hot. Up the keys the yellow mosquito plane will be skimming in over the mangroves, its cloud of spray hanging and settling in the windless air.

There are sponges drying on the balconies of some of the old wooden houses, and as if you might forget that the town is at sea, gulls and frigate birds soar high overhead. Next to Key West Oxygen Service, in an ugly asphalt parking lot that rivals the La Brea tar pits in midsummer, a bonefish skiff sits high on its trailer, bridging the imagination from the immediate downtown of Key West—both an outrageous honky-tonk and a memento of another century— to its gauzy, impossibly complex backcountry surrounds. When you're at the drive-in movie in Key West, watching adult fare with all the other sweating neckers, the column of light from the projectionist's booth is feverish with tropical insects blurring the breasts and buttocks on their way to the screen. At low tide you smell the mangroves and exposed tidal flats nearby, and you're within a mile of sharks that could eat you like a jujube. Once the movie is over and you've hung the speaker back on its post and are driving home, palmetto bugs and land crabs pop under the tires.

This morning, when we get to Garrison Bight, we turn off before the causeway and pull into the dry shed where my boat is stored. Across the bight at the ramp, a skiff is being launched behind a station wagon. I take out the binoculars and look. It's a Hewes guide boat. I see the chairs, the enormous engine, the push pole, the Teleflex steering up in the forward corner, and over me and my companion, Guy de la Valdene, comes that specific competitive tension you feel when another skiff is working the same country. If Saint Francis showed up with a guide boat behind his car, we would rather he stayed home. Every shallow-water fisherman down here is cordial on land, monstrous at sea.

It's not Stu Apte; his skiff has a center console. It's not Bill Curtis; his is yellow, and furthermore he fishes Key West mainly on permit charters. Woody Sexton is in Loggerhead today. Jim Brewer fishes out of a Fibercraft and this is a Hewes. Bob Montgomery has an offshore charter. Cal Cochran? He's supposed to have plenty of fish in his backyard at Marathon. Same with Steve Huff. Page Brown fishes out of a Mako and he would have told us if he was fishing Key West. It would be nice to know who it is so we could avoid running the same pattern. Possibly one of the sports from an angling club, chasing points, mounts, and records.

Richard, the manager of the boatyard, comes out and says, "Morning, Mister Tom," with that special look of philosophical resignation that is the hallmark of the Key West Conch. He climbs up on the forklift and heads into the shed for the skiff. I had it built right here at the yard only last winter, and the first rip of boat fever has not passed off. I love to watch the skiff come out on the fork so I can see the long, precise chine running from stem to bait wells. When the boat emerges, Guy says, "Yes, I know it's beautiful, but please don't say it again."

"I know, but—"

"Don't say it."

Richard rolls the forklift forward onto the concrete dock and lowers the boat into the slick water. To the untutored eye, nothing about the skiff is exceptional: bare nonfouling utility has been taken as far as the mind could create demands for the boat-builder.

The glass hull, brought down bare from the mainland, is white, low, and spare. From the side it looks like a simple linear gesture, the blade of a scimitar or an arrow. It is seventeen-feet, two-inches long, not counting the integral bait wells. The boat was built up from this bare hull with three-quarter-inch marine plywood, the arm-and-a-leg variety. From above, the skiff appears as a succession of bare surfaces over which a fly line can blow without snagging; the forward casting deck is continuous with the broad, flat gunwales. The aft deck is set slightly below the gunwales and, like the casting deck, overhangs the bulkheads by half an inch. Set into the aft deck are the lids of two dry-storage boxes, a battery box, and an insulated icebox. All topside surfaces are blue-gray.

The steering is forward and starboard, with the wheel set horizontal to the deck. Donald Duck's picture is in the hub; a pacifier hangs from the ignition. The throttle and gearshift controls are in a single lever, and there is a tachometer with which I pretend to monitor my engine's performance. I monitored my previous engine's performance, noticing not a thing right up until the idiot light turned on, a plug blew out of a cylinder and the whole thing froze like a tractor in quicksand. There is a toggle on the dash for the power tilt, the 125 Evinrude on the transom being too heavy for hand-tilting as frequently as flats fishing requires.

Guy is at the gas dock, filling the stainless forty-gallon tank under the casting deck. I get a block of ice and put it in the cooler with our lunch and twelve soft drinks. The rods go under the port gunwale, rain gear under the seat. The tackle box goes aboard with a couple dozen of Guy's shock tippets rolled like surgeon's suturing materials. And now we're ready, suddenly feeling the anticipation that is the result of the watching weather, reading the Coast and Geodetic Survey tide book, and listening to all the baloney and general hearsay from guides and other anglers about just where it is the tarpon might be.

Along the starboard gunwale, flexed tight against it, is the big kill gaff with its seven-foot hardwood handle, never to be used on a fish less than a world record, though Guy and I agree that the goal is to train oneself to release that fish, too. But at this early stage of development the gaff still goes along. Someday, when we have grown enough in the fishing, the gaff will be nailed up over my desk, with the stainless-steel gaff head that I wrapped and epoxied myself, a rather handsome old souvenir of barbaric times. On top of the port gunwale, resting in two teak chocks and secured with aviation shock cord, is a seventeen-foot push pole.

Choked and started, the engine idles on the transom; the boat trembles and laps gently against the dock. Guy slips the lines and pushes us away from the dock and I put it in forward, easing us out past the crawfishing boats and two or three sponge boats with tongs laid across the seats, then out into the basin in the low angle of light. Idling along, the boat rides low in the water with radically little freeboard. This is a skiff that will run forty miles an hour in less than a foot of water; offshore, it would be as reassuring as a waterlogged mahogany plank. Its design, derived from numerous other boats but primarily those built by Eddie Geddiman, is a pure, indigenous product of the fishing conditions of the Florida Keys. A fast, shallow-water boat.

We pass under the Garrison Causeway as morning work traffic is beginning to rush overhead. We can smell its exhaust with the same emotions with which we perceive the hamburger stands over by the charter-boat docks. Once on the other side, there's that damned guide boat we saw being launched, up on a plane now and way out at the front edge of a fan of wake. I hear the honking overhead and then a siren as a policeman runs down some sorry gob in a GTO. The brilliantly painted Cuban fishing boats are off to our left, gaudy as Arab smacks; behind them is the institutional slab of the navy bachelor officer quarters, built with the military's usual flair for grace in design.

By now the guide boat has upped and gone. We don't know where he could be and are just hoping that our two skiffs don't go wandering over the ocean making the same stops, tripping over each other as in some mis-timed, syncopated dance step.

I run it up to 4500 rpm. The bow lifts, then the stern comes up under the power and kicks the bow down. I slack off to 3600 and we bank and turn through the markers. Key West drops quickly behind and finally clusters at the end of our long arrow of wake. There is a sense of liberation as we run, civilization melting away while another country—mangrove keys, shallows, and open seas—forms around us.

When you pass them, the mangroves empty themselves of cormorants; the birds drop down slapping the water with their wing tips, then shudder as though it had been a close call. The backcountry is full of pelicans, frigate birds, ospreys, bitterns, egrets, and herons, not to speak of that mass of small shorebirds such as plovers, avocets, turnstones, surfbirds, and phalaropes or a number of glamorous "occasionals," as the bird books call them: ibises, eagles, and the utterly incredible roseate spoonbills, the color of a Miami street-walker's lipstick, that wheel out behind a sandy little key.

We stake the skiff in a small basin near the Northwest Channel. The shrimpers are coming in sporadically from the Gulf of Mexico, trawling booms swaying and diesel engines sounding like farm tractors at this range. We are watching for tarpon moving in the big channel to graze off or shortcut toward the smaller channels shoreward of us. We are staked—that is, tied to the push pole, which is shoved into the bottom along a sandbank that separates the channel from the basin, knowing it will deflect tarpon up into shallow water, where it is hoped they will be moved to take the fly.

We are using the big rod. It carries a No. 12 saltwater taper line and is a very effective rod for fighting a fish, if not exactly a wand to handle. It is powerful, with a second grip just short of the stripping guide. We have rigged a grizzly-and-orange fly on a 3/0 hook, using an 80 pound shock tippet. Ten inches above that, the 12 pound starts and it is this breaking strength that brackets what pressure the angler can put on the fish.

We take turns with the rod, watching for incoming fish that can appear and blow by too quickly if one's alertness flags. Very early on, some tarpon roll in the big channel. They are clearly travelers, though, and will keep right on going—to Mexico, for all we know.

After a bit, a good-size shark glides under the boat. Touched with the rod tip, he moves off in a surge. A little later a hawksbill turtle peers up at us from green water, then, frightened, races off at a speed one doesn't associate with turtles; his front flippers are a blur of effort, while the back ones cross and trail.

Guy stands up on one bait well and looks intently through the binoculars. "The damned guide boat," he reports, "is sitting on our next stop." Sure enough, the skiff is at Mule Key, exactly the place where we would be getting the phase of tide we wanted in another half-hour. "And you know what else?" The answer was posed in the tone of his question.

"Yes," I said ruefully, "he's fighting a fish."

We start looking at our watches. We're not getting any shots on this spot, have been cut off on the next, and when the men in the guide boat are done with their present fish, they very well might make a move to our next stop. Guy looks through the glasses.

"What's he doing?"

"He broke the fish off," Guy said. "There are two of them. They're sitting in the boat to rerig."

"I feel sort of frustrated here," I said.

"I do, too."

"If we don't crank up—I know this is irrational—if we don't crank up I'm afraid we're going to be following him all day long."

"Let's slip the stake," said Guy, "and blow all the way to Big Mullet before he gets his nose out of that tackle box."

I slip the pole out of the bottom, coil the line on the bow, put the pole on its chocks and secure it with the shock cord, then start the engine. I idle into Northwest Channel, then run it up to 5400 rpm, all the way to the stop, so that we are truly flying, running through the banks with a mean tide chop beating our back teeth loose.

We get two-thirds of the way across Northwest Channel and the rival guide sees the push pole on our gunwale and realizes what is happening to him. He quick-hands the rod he's rigging to his companion and starts the engine. Our problem is to hit the run-through channel in the Mule Key bank directly on the nose or else we'll be sawed off by our opponent.

The guide boat wheels around and things are still at the educated-guess stage. From here the bank looks solid and we appear to be heading on a collision course: running aground. Now the other boat is flying full tilt as well, on an interception course. It is sufficiently neck and neck that we'll have to find another place to fish if I'm forced to shut down the engine on the shallow bank and feel my way along for a place to sneak through.

But then a piece of the bank seems to peel away before our eyes and suddenly we spot a solid green creek running through the hard stuff. We cross the bank at 5000 rpm and shut off. In our new silence we hear the drone of the guide boat taper to an idle a short distance behind us.

"You look back," says Guy with a smile. We are both of us pretending to survey the basin as though we hardly knew another boat was anywhere in the country. I turn around and see the two men hunched in the idling boat, staring at us without love.

Alas, it is a far cry from the genial gatherings of anglers on the Test or the Itchen. When flats fishermen run into each other on the water, smiles and jolly waves notwithstanding, it is more like war. When information is asked for, a bum steer quite naturally springs to the lips. I rather suspect, though, that the true scoop on the Test and the Itchen would indicate that those anglers, tweeds and all, have the needle into each other as thoroughly as we do.

Soon the guide boat is running again, the big engine offering what we interpret as a mild trumpet of resignation. While we fully expect to see them at another stop, at the moment, we have the place to ourselves. Meanwhile, it is as quiet as can be, the water lapping gently on the sides of the skiff and pearly summer clouds resting along the horizon.

We tilt the engine and Guy begins to pole. He was a collegiate rower and poles better than I do, with a steady, persistent beat that is perfect for surveying an area when you are not absolutely sure of finding fish. Immediately we begin seeing life; clusters of spotted eagle rays bustle around like nuns, barracudas appear near the boat without ever having been seen in the act of swimming over, small sharks come, stingrays and houndfish. But not, for the moment, any tarpon. We're not talking very much. I feel the successive pushes of the pole and hear its steady rise and fall in the water. Occasionally we glide to a stop and I hear Guy lighting a cigarette behind me, and in a moment the boat surges forward again. The bottom is dark with turtlegrass and we look hard to penetrate its surface. At the same time we try to survey a wide range for rollers and watch the surface for the faint wakes that look like a thumbnail pulled gently along under a sheet of silk. What you see more than anything is movement; the laid-up or sleeping fish are the toughest to spot.

There is a little breeze now and a few horsetail clouds high in the sky, brilliantly white and lacquered. A radiant drop curtain of fuchsia light stands on edge from the Gulf Stream south of us. East across the channels Key West can still be seen, like a white folding ruler, in sections on the blue expanse.

Guy says "tarpon" so quietly that I wonder if he means tarpon in general, but with a certain dread I realize he has spotted fish and a moment later I see a large single swimming with easy sweeps, quite black and bulky looking, moving on a course we will easily intercept. This means it will be entirely up to me. I'm trailing enough line for my false cast and have already begun that rather tense process of trying to figure our range as it is modified by the progress of the skiff in one direction and that of the tarpon in another. That the fish itself looks about as manageable as a Cape buffalo is little help in the finer calculations of the mind. I know from experience that this peaceful meandering fish can offer a scarifying performance, calling into question (if usually theoretically) whether or not the angler is actually safe.

Guy poles to an interception point and turns the skiff in such a way we're at rest by the time the fish is in range. The pole is down and away from where my backcast could foul it. I roll my trailing line into the air, false-cast, shoot, false-cast again, shoot, get my range, and cast. The fly falls acceptably and I strip sharply once to get the fish's attention, continuing with a quick, jerky retrieve. Then the tarpon turns almost imperceptibly: the enthralling, terrifying moment when, unbelievably, the great fish alters its course, however slightly, to take the fly.

Now the fish is tight behind the fly, so close as to seem cross-eyed as he watches and follows it, a dense reptilian presence in pursuit of the streamer. Then comes his slight elevation and gain of speed, the mouth opening, and one last forward surge as the fly vanishes.

I strike him too quickly and feel little more than a bump as the fly comes free. The tarpon muscles about in confusion, making a depth charge of disturbance when he sees the boat, and turns over on himself clearing out. We should be fighting that fish now, one reflects gloomily. Yes, one is inclined to admit, one has blown off a good fish.

To seize the rod with a pontifical sigh and hand me the push pole would be Guy's every right, but he remains in the bow, camera around his neck, ready to record each new faux pas.

I return to my post in the stern with that special determination that surely prepares the angler for more garish errors than those which produced the determination. This is the vicious circle of angling, the iron maiden of a supposedly reflective pursuit.

We pole for a good long time without sighting another fish. We are beginning to lose our tide here, and the time has come to think of another move. We sit down in the skiff, drifting under the dome of unsoiled marine sky. Guy hands me a sandwich and we have our lunch, chewing and ruminating like cattle. We are comfortable enough together that we can fall silent for long periods of time. A flats skiff is a confined place and one in which potentials for irritation are brought to bear as surely as in an arctic cabin, but this comfort of solitude enhanced by companionship is the rarest commodity of angling. Pure solitude, nearly its equal, is rather more available.

Lunchtime, between tides, with the boat drifting before the wind: our piddling inclinations toward philosophy begin to emerge. My recent failure with the fly rod exaggerates my proclivity for higher things. We talk about "the meat bucket." Originally, the term indicated a particular place in the water that held fish in quantity. Then, gradually, it came to mean whole rivers or bays or banks that were good and, finally, states and regions where someone could live who could not live where the country was all shot to hell. In the end, the meat bucket was a situation of mind where everything was going to be okay. When you had gone and messed up your intelligence with whiskey or worse, jacked yourself all out of shape, the meat bucket was the final pie in the sky, the universal trout or steelhead or permit or what-all run, the place where you always threw the perfect loop and never had to live with righthand winds, cold rain, broken homes, failed religion, or long-distance releases.

The meat bucket was Bill Schaadt pantomiming coming up tight on a fifty-pound chinook on the Smith River, saying, "I'm into one!" loudly and reverently. The meat bucket was Russ Chatham making a precise delivery at a hundred feet with a hangover. The meat bucket was Jim Harrison screaming that his knees were buckling and "He's got all my line!" on his first hundred-pound tarpon. The meat bucket was Bob Weddell laying his ear to your Hardy reel that a twelve-pound steelhead was making scream, and saying with rapture, "They're playing our song!" The meat bucket was Bob Tusken's lead-filled Bitch Creek nymphs hitting you in the head when you tried to cast them, Guy de la Valdene skinny-dipping between two guide boats full of glowering anglers at Cutoe Key, Chico Horvath miming a gang bang in his waders on the banks of the Firehole, Rudi Ferris sleeping on the garage floor waiting for "the bite," Woody Sexton looking with horror at the bad housekeeping in my skiff, seawater and Lucky Strike wrappers in the dunnage box. In the end it was all the unreckonable fragments of the sport that became the reference points of an obsession that you called the meat bucket, or, among the archdiocese of angling maniacs you had come to know, more simply, the M.B.

The push pole is secured once more in its chocks; the engine is down and again we are running. This time we head southwest toward Boca Grande

Key. The light is so good we can see the stilt houses from where we ride. The spongers browse around in their little boats, standing in the bow and steering the outboard motors with clothesline tied to their waists, raking up sponges like oceanic gardeners.

We are heading for Ballast Key, where we expect to find tarpon and where I have every hope that I will not fall apart and bungle either the cast, the hookup, or the sometimes appalling fight that ensues.

The keys down here have a considerably less swampy character than those above us along the Gulf of Mexico. They are higher and, in some cases, have headlands, beaches, and woods. In the spring these are great meeting places for migrant warblers headed for cool northern forests.

We shut off next to an empty beach of wild palms amid clouds of wheeling white seabirds, and Guy begins poling down the face of Ballast. There is a wash here that raises and drops the skiff. The bottom is rock and packed sand, dotted with sea fans, a desperately difficult place to pole without falling out of the boat. When fish are spotted the poling is so noisy that the tarpon are often spooked, and the boat cannot be easily or quickly positioned for incoming fish. So you abandon yourself to the combinations and hope they come up in your favor.

Almost to Woman Key, we find tarpon: a string of fish, they are traveling on a bright sandy bottom, as distinct as fractured sections of pencil lead.

We are in good position and it is now only a question of waiting for them to come within range. At first we see them from afar, splashing and marking their progress purely in surface movement. At this remove, they are no more scary than a school of feeding jacks.

Then, as they approach, their above-the-surface presence of wakes and splashes is replaced perceptually by the actual sight of fish as specific marine entities, individual torpedoes coming at you. It is hideously unnerving, if you care about fishing.

I like my cast and at the first strip two fish turn out of the string to follow. Then one of them quite aggressively takes the fly and turns off to the side. I continue the strip I started with my left hand until I come up tight. Then, with the butt of the rod in my hip and the rod tip low and to the side, I hit two or three times hard.

The fish is in the air, upside down, making a noise that reminds you of horses, thunderous and final; your eye remembers the long white rip in the ocean. Then a short accelerated run is followed by an end-swapping jump by a game animal that has pulled all the stops. At the third jump the run begins. The fourth jump would be better observed through binoculars; the line no longer even points at the fish.

The tarpon has burned off a hundred fifty yards in such a way that the centrifugal surge is felt in the reel, shuddering my arm. Now he must be followed in the boat. The backing goes onto the reel at the expense of a painful swelling of the forearm and the shirt clinging wetly. After some time the fish is close enough that we can reasonably exert some pressure. Guy keeps the boat parallel to him, silver and brilliant in the deep green water, and the fight goes on, interrupted by inexorable fifty-yard runs from which we patiently recover. Now the fish makes a number of sloshing, head-rattling jumps, after which, in his new weakness, I can turn him slightly on his side.

In a moment he is beside the boat, bright and powerful-looking. I take the pliers and seize the shank of the hook, and with a twist the tarpon is free, though he is slow to realize it. I reach down and hold him for a moment, and I sense in this touch his ocean-traveling might. An instant later he has vanished.

Guy tells me firmly that it's my turn to pole.

August 25

BY W. D. WETHERELL

For those whose fly-fishing agenda for this year or next includes a trip to the Yellow-stone high country, my sincere congratulations and best wishes. For those whose calendar is barren of such anticipated entries, myself included, a remarkable consolation prize is immediately at hand: the prose of W. D. Wetherell.

In One River More, *his third book of fishing stories and essays, published by The Lyons Press in 1998, Wetherell includes some of the most detailed and engaging prose portraits ever written on what it's like to fish Yellowstone Park and the surrounding area. This particular chapter focuses on the Yellowstone River itself, in the Park, where we are about to wade in to try for the native cutthroat trout that are the river's treasure.*

Some jaded old hand might be muttering, "What's the big deal? Cutthroats never take you into the backing."

Wrong!

The Yellowstone is not only the most prolific trout river in North America but also the most intimidating, especially inside the national park. Above Yellowstone Lake on the Thorofare Plateau the wading isn't bad, *if* you can get there; it's a long hike in, from whatever direction, and the country is known for its quicksand and grizzlies. Just downstream of the lake is the notorious Fishing Bridge, where the trout butchers used to do their thing, but fishing is no longer permitted there, and with the river flowing at full breadth from one of the largest lakes in the country it wouldn't be any place to wade. The water in Hayden Valley is approachable and choice, but fishing isn't permitted there either, even though it's alive with feeding trout. Further downstream are the famous falls, among the highest on the continent; below these is a thousand-foot-deep canyon with precipitous walls of smooth and friable rock. Even at Tower Junction, where the river reemerges, the water flows past at warp speed, and this only gets worse further downstream in the hard-to-get-to, impossible-to-wade section known as Black Canyon.

If you do manage to find a place to fish you can sense all this wild and lusty exuberance working on you as you step into the water—the weight of Yellowstone Lake upstream, the giddiness of the falls just below. This is the longest untamed river in the lower forty-eight states, and the water, its very molecules, seem powered by this freedom, so they bear down on you with double the weight and energy of normal H_2O. This is water, cold water, that has been here a lot longer than man has and will be here rushing and tumbling and foaming downstream long after he is gone—and it's not above taking a sacrificial victim with it now and then to demonstrate this principle.

Between rapids and canyons and falls and regulations, there are very few stretches of the Yellowstone you can wade safely, let alone comfortably. One of these is called Buffalo Ford—*the* Buffalo Ford, famous for its cutthroats, pictured in all the magazines, the very epicenter of fly fishing's remarkable boom, and on a typical summer's day the most heavily fished pool in the world.

Not a place for the loner, the shy one, the fastidious. And yet on a warm and sunny late-August morning this was exactly who waded through the bright skipping water on its edge, stopped to look things over, stood rocking back and forth in his wading brogues, counting the number of fishermen he could see in the river, vowing that when he reached fifty he would turn around again and go back to his car. Something of an old hand now in this part of the world, a man who was taking a break from the family on what was otherwise a family trip all the way, he had deliberately avoided the Yellowstone on his two previous trips out West, scared off not only by the power of the water, but the power of that mob.

How many? Two fishermen just to the right of him, gearing up. Another straight ahead on the edge of an island, tight to a fish. A man and woman holding onto each other for balance, the current piling up in a golden *W* around their waists. Three scattered in the shallower water on the far and distant shore, one casting, one wading, one pointing a camera at the stolid echelon of buffalo grazing on the bank.

Seven fly fishers, not counting himself. Seven in a river that could swallow dozens and hardly show the strain. Whether because it was late August and the crowds had gone home, or because of some favorable, impossible-to-predict eddy in the current that compelled people to fish here, the fisherman had come on a day when for all intents and purposes he had the Yellowstone River to himself.

So, no excuses. He checked to see his wader belt was fastened, shuffled his boots against the pebbles on the bottom to clear them of weed, then slanted his way into the current, taking a line that would bring him above the island and into the slower water on the far side. Not hard wading, but not easy either—the Yellowstone may be fordable on four legs here, but two legs is difficult. Between the fast current, the bottom that alternates between pebbles and clay, the kind of moral vulnerability you feel when out in any big river alone, the fisherman was more than a little relieved when the bottom started shelving upward again, the pebbles came back, the water left off pushing solid on his waist and took to kicking broken on his shins.

Safe. He paused, feeling a certain triumph, then turned, startled, at a loud whuffing sound that was even deeper than the river's whoosh. Buffalo, another long file, coming into the river just behind him. They didn't seem to do this intentionally, with premeditation; they were grazing at the top of the bank, one or two stepped over, and before they understood what was happening the whole herd was caught up in a mindless inertia that carried them at a half-gallop into the river, where they stood snorting, coughing, and grunting, wondering why they were even there.

There was no exaggerating the fun of watching them. America is so full of place-names that no longer make sense—Trout Lake, with no trout in them; Cougar Canyons with no cougar—that it was good to be standing in a place that was literally being rechristened *Buffalo Ford* as he watched.

Where the bank jutted out into the river was another fly fisher, a woman this time. At this sport for well over thirty years, he'd only seen a woman fishing by herself three or four times, all on this trip, so it was clear the demographics were changing and changing rapidly. This particular woman was no beginner; she cast far and she cast fast, with nothing wasted in her motion. Stocky, she moved through the water with great delicacy and confidence, a disciplined skater in full command. With the sun behind her, the fly line decorating the sky overhead, the wind tossing back her hair, she managed in that beautiful landscape to take on a great deal of beauty herself; an old-fashioned poetical mind might have seen her as the very spirit of the river, and not be far wrong.

A few pleasantries—*How's the fishing? Fine! Three cuts!*—and then he was on his way again, climbing up onto the bank and taking off through the woods upstream. This was easier than forcing his way through the current, but not all that much easier, since blowdown pines were everywhere, and it was impossible to hike in a straight line.

Where to start? One of the conceptual tricks in fishing a big river is to try to break it up into smaller, more comprehensible channels within the expanse, not be overawed. This is hard to do on the Yellowstone—it sweeps impetuously along, with no thought for a fisherman's convenience—but not impossible. A hundred yards more of walking and the steep bank crumbled away, widening the river no more than eleven or twelve feet, and yet by this expansion making it lose several vital gallons per second of force. Some pines had fallen with the bank, and their roots were still strong enough to hold the trunks perpendicular to the current, breaking it up even more.

It wasn't long before he discovered the limits of this eddy; in tight by the bank all was fine, but eight or nine steps out it was a different story. The current was even faster and harder than it appeared from shore, so there was no going deeper than his hips without being bowled over. The bottom was tricky, too; a coating of pebbles and gravel gave good purchase, but mixed in were elliptical patches where the current had washed the gravel away, exposing the bone-white clay underneath—and to step into one of these clay patches meant a fast ride down toward Yellowstone Falls.

Things finally settled with his feet, he began looking about for trout. They were there all right—cutthroats of seventeen and eighteen inches right in front of him, though it took a few minutes before his eyes got accustomed enough to the water's glare to penetrate it, see beneath. Back in New England, where he did most of his fishing, you could go all summer without sight-fishing to a trout, so the experience was a new one to him and exhilarating. He was fishing an attractor pattern just attractive enough to make the trout, as it floated downstream, raise their heads a fraction of an inch, quiver in interest, then—the fraud becoming apparent—relax again in boredom and sink back to their original, tail-slightly-below-head position. The same happened when he fished a nymph, though this time they were interested enough to move laterally in the current to appraise it from the side, even bluff it with a little charge, before lapsing into that same irrefutable indifference.

He'd always heard these Buffalo Ford cutthroats were picky, and it gave him an odd satisfaction to learn the stereotype was true—it was like learning that all Parisians are indeed rude. It took three hours of hard work before he caught one. Tired of fishing upstream, he climbed back out onto the bank, switched to a sink-tip line, took a long detour inland, then balanced his way out along one of the fallen trees and roll cast a weighted stonefly into the current to let it swing down.

A fish was on it right away, an important fish. The fisherman was always somewhat casual in playing trout, but there was often one during a trip that he simply *had* to land, and this was one of those—the fate of the day was resting upon this. And he did catch it, but not without making a spectacle of himself. The fish continued upstream after fastening, but then balked at too much pressure and made an abrupt U-turn, not only stripping out line to the backing, but pulling the reel off the rod, so the fisherman had to grab for it in the current, hold it in his hand, and start down the shallows in pursuit—right onto one of those treacherous clay patches. When he got up again—when with some frantic screwing he got his reel reattached—the trout was still on, though an enormous distance downstream. His fall on the clay had muddied up the river, so it seemed the trout was fleeing the milky gray cloud as much as it was the pressure of the line, and by the time he caught up with it, landed it, photographed it, let it go, he was soaked through with river, sweat, and clay, and yet happy past all description.

Clumsy, but no fool, he'd packed along some extra clothes for just such an eventuality. Dry, somewhat composed, feeling stubborn, he hooked another cutthroat from exactly the same position, walked over to the bank, sat down on a rock, and played it in comfort, refusing to engage in any more shenanigans.

He ate lunch on top of the bank in what sundial-like shade a lodgepole pine casts. A nap would have been nice, but he got caught up in watching the pelicans, a bird he had always associated with Florida, not Wyoming. Squadrons of them flew down from Yellowstone Lake, much more graceful than the comic image you get from cartoons. Their whiteness, their airiness, did a lot to cool him off.

When he got his fill of these, there were buffalo, a few of them anyway. They seemed bewildered by the fallen timber, confused that there shouldn't be an easy way down to the river; with a few bothered snorts they wheeled around again and headed back to the ford that bore their name.

The fishing was better in the afternoon—rising trout now, coming up to those tiny *Baetis* that are everywhere in a Yellowstone August. This was sight-fishing again, at least toward the end of the rise, when a yellow-brown verticality would appear underneath the fly and slowly continue upward through the surface film, remaining there for a long and very visible moment before looping back down again. Hooked upstream, these fish were easier to land, and after three or four the fisherman decided there was nothing more to ask of the day. His total wasn't high, and yet the point had been made: yes, the Yellowstone was indeed the most prolific trout river in America, the breadth of it, the very substance of the water, alive with the presence of wild and beautiful fish.

He was taking down his rod on top of the bank when an invisible and yet very real force (strong enough to be felt even with the competition of the river) made him turn around. Where the bank dipped away to let a wet spot seep into the river was what he thought at first was a coyote. A second later it saw him and stopped; it was very obviously trying to decide whether to continue past him or change direction and retreat back into the woods.

The fisherman started to reach into his vest for his camera, then thought better of it. Coyotes were nothing new. Coyotes—why, they had coyotes right at home, trotting across their meadow in the course of their daily rounds. No, he wasn't going to waste film on a mere coyote.

Like a hungry and very gaunt German shepherd—that's how he described coyotes to friends who had never seen one. But then something in the animal's posture changed, some slight squaring readjustment in the way it was standing, and he realized it wasn't a gaunt German shepherd at all, but an extraordinarily healthy German shepherd, one with height and muscle, a princely attitude, and all the self-confidence in the world . . . that it wasn't a coyote at all, but the cherished object of a careful reintroduction campaign, a hero all the media was going nuts over, the subject of all those campfire talks by the rangers: a live and very real wolf.

A wolf, not ten yards away. There was no fear in this encounter, on either side. The fisherman looked at the wolf, childishly pleased that after hearing about them for so long he should actually be face to face with one; the wolf, for his part, stared into the man's expression with an alert kind of interest in which something was reciprocated, though it was impossible to say exactly what. Something mammalian at any rate; the wolf's alertness wasn't that different from the alertness of the trout, and yet that second, deeper something was much different, a consanguine kind of recognition nothing cold-blooded could ever manage.

There's no end to this encounter, not in dramatic terms. The lone wolf turned and walked unhurriedly along the riverbank; the lone fisherman turned and did the same in the opposite direction. When he entered the timber he stopped and looked back—but there they parted company, for that wolf, finding nothing remarkable in the encounter, trotted away without glancing back over his shoulder at all.

About Bonefishing

BY JAMES W. HALL

This selection finds us push-poling over the transparent shallows in search of the fish that really was responsible for getting the entire flats-fishing scene on angling's center stage back in the 1950s. Affectionately tagged with one of fishing writing's oldest clichés, the "gray ghost of the flats," the bonefish is a torpedo-shaped stick of pure dynamite that has set more reels singing and heartbeats racing than perhaps any other. Whether found in singles, doubles, small pods, or great schools of shapes and shadows cruising like a wolf pack, the bonefish is a fish to dream about, worth any amount of work, planning and your hard-earned bucks to have in casting range.

A writer who has woven his fascination with bonefishing into his prose is novelist James Hall, author of numerous flint-edged, taut novels of action and suspense, many involving the torrid darker sides of life in the Florida Keys. In his first novel, the critically acclaimed Under Cover of Daylight, *from which this selection is taken, Hall's leading character is Thorn, a young man with a passion for bonefishing with flies. Thorn later appears in other Hall novels, with other glimpses of flats fishing as seen from his point of view. All of Hall's books are superb reads, page-turners of the first rank.*

In this short excerpt from Under Cover of Daylight, *Thorn is enjoying a peaceful scene with his bonefish flies. To me, this "set piece" from Hall's novel catches the spirit, moods and mysteries of bonefishing better than anything I've ever read. This one isn't as long as most selections in this book. But don't be fooled by that. Good writers like James Hall aren't afraid to be brief!*

The Puff, the Hard Puff, Wild Harry's Delight, the Muddler, Improved Nasty Charlie, the Horror, Bonebuster, Purple Shadow.

Thorn sat at his rolltop desk and looked up at the cork board where his collection of flies was displayed. It was quiet, still an hour till daybreak. He could finish maybe three Crazy Charlies before the roosters started in.

There was an old rooster and a young one that'd recently begun to debate over a brood of wild hens that lived in the mangrove woods that bordered his house. The chickens provided him with feathers for his flies, and the crowing coaxed him back to an earlier day when the Keys were more a cousin of South Georgia than Miami's weekend playground and a tour stop on the Disney World circuit.

Captain Eddie would be showing up at dawn. Seven days a week he poled up to Thorn's dock, even at high tide, when there was water enough to use his engine, always wanting his half dozen assorted flies.

And after Eddie it would be Bill Martin, a retiree from Massachusetts, a professor of something or other who had discovered fly-fishing for bones and had acquired gradually the same reticence and sun-glazed stare of all bonefish addicts. And on like that all day, Thorn tying between their visits, never enough, always learning from them what was catching fish this week. And standing out on his coral dock, wondering with them why in the hell that little scrap of hokum brought those fish awake.

Crazy Charlie was the epoxy flat base fly he'd created in June. It skittered across the mud flats, trailing purple flasharoo, these Mylar strings that shook like tassels on a stripper's skirt. Silver beads from a key chain for eyes. A pinch of white squirrel fur for the body. Like a Martian roach. Glitter and flash, dressed for a twenty-first-century nightclub.

He had a desk full of animal fur, pelts, tails, whiskers, toenails. His friend Jerome Billings had a contract with the county to keep the dead animals off the highway. Thorn got his pick of the daily supply of highway cats and dogs, squirrels, raccoons, and rats. If the pelt were still fresh, Jerome would drop it by. Thorn gave him flies as payment, though he knew Jerome had never fished a day. Either Jerome sold them, or Thorn couldn't imagine, displayed them somewhere, used them in the bedroom? Scraping up squashed animals all day might have put a deep kink in there somewhere.

He laced the Crazy Charlie tight with the purple Mylar, tying a double turtle knot and leaving a single thread, something to attach the last of the squirrel fur to. All glitter and flash, but a bonefish might smack that thing and rip off a hundred yards of line in about four seconds. All torque, that fish wouldn't waver or jump, just burn those reel bearings, one long frizz. The pole straining. Heart crawling up into the esophagus. Thorn had been there; he'd been there and been there. And now he was here.

He loosened the vise a notch and rotated the Crazy Charlie. That vise had cost him a couple of hundred. It was a custom job he'd designed with a machinist in Tavernier. It had a needle-nose vise, rubber-coated gripping surface, and a largemouth vise with a fine-tune setting so he could hold a hook without marring the finish. Beautiful little tool.

The vise was about the most expensive thing he owned. His house. A few tools. A trickle of cash to pay the lights, and more anytime he wanted to speed up production. A library card. The land was his. Taxes paid from the trust fund Dr. Bill had left. A little cash left for gas for his rusted-out '65 Cadillac Fleetwood, his Keys Cruiser.

It'd been Dr. Bill's final car and had just enough life left to make the journey down to Islamorada once a month for Mexican food. It was about that often that Thorn wanted a break from snapper, grouper, trout, lobster, his payments, or gifts, from the guides who knew who he was, where he was, and what he did better than anybody else in the Keys.

All of his two dozen regular customers could tie their own flies, often bringing one by so Thorn could admire. But Thorn could do something else, some bright tiny nightmare magic he could bring to that chenille, that pipe-cleaner body, the flourish of calf tail or rabbit fur or cat. His flies caught fish. And not one of them looked like anything real.

Let it drift down into the murky dull mud of a salt-water flat, down into the drab world of bonefish, that little wedge of clear epoxy with bead-chain eyes and a flare of calf tail, and drag that fantasy through the silt anywhere in the peripheral sight of a bone and it'd smack that thing and run that zinging line to Bimini.

Bones ate like paranoid schizophrenics. Scared of food half the time. Offer them a jumbo shrimp, flicking away in front of their noses, snap, they'd be gone into the fourth dimension. But flicker one of those garish little gremlins nearby and they just might gulp a ton of them. You never knew. Not even the best ever knew.

Far as Thorn could tell, it was a kind of voodoo. He didn't have any picture in mind, but he'd sit there at that old railroad desk, start pulling scraps of fur from pigeonholes, badger, possum, raccoon, horse, cow, dog. Get his clear nail polish ready, his bobbin, his scissors, his hackle pliers, holding, tying, looping, imagining. Three-eyed Louie came in a frenzy like that. No plan. But it emerged, three silver eyes across a bar in front, and for one whole June in 1979 it caught bones every day from Marathon to Card Sound. Then poof, it was over. The guides standing out on the dock, shaking their heads, grinning at the bounty, frowning at the ongoing search.

That was the great pleasure of this for Thorn. The minor wacko variations. Permutations of eyes, head, body, tail. And always the barbless hook. There were a hundred thousand possible bonefish flies. Oh, hell, lots more than that. Nobody had found one that worked every time. Nobody ever would. The best bonefishermen in the world could go a week without having one on. They could pole across a hundred miles of flats, see a hundred tailing fish, lay a quiet line and a perfect lure right in their path, perfect presentation a hundred times, and that fish would rather starve.

Those guys were priests. They thought like priests. It meant whatever they thought they kept to themselves. When they did talk, they all talked alike, quiet as dust floating in church. And they had eyes burned hard and transparent by the sun off shallow water, from tracking ghosts with a ten-ton pull.

Thorn had been one of them for a decade. Back from his failed year at college, he'd started up. Nineteen and with about nineteen years of experience on the flats. Baptized out there. Knew how to be quiet and blend in. For ten years he tried to learn how to take money from strangers who knew how to do neither.

The lures, though, they were the real art. And as he moved through his twenties, he found it was tying flies, dreaming into life these surreal roaches, that sustained him.

At thirty he had quit guiding and started carving soap molds for his epoxy bodies, looking for the shape that slid across the bottom, glided and twitched with that rhythm he could picture but not describe.

Until Sarah had begun to change things, he'd been content with the hours of narrow focus. Willing to warm himself before these small, fiery creations. For years he'd stayed hidden away in the woods, the only action in his life happening deep inside. That had been enough. The silence. The reading. The food. The weather. The bonefish strikes. But now it wasn't. He was starting to feel a hunger. Lately he found his eyes drifting up from the desk, looking off.

God, Thorn couldn't believe it, but he'd even begun, at those moments, his eyes wandering out into the distance, to speak her name.

Thorn finished the Crazy Charlie. Set it beside the Flig and the Muddler he'd finished last night. Crazy Charlie—its knobby backbone was glossy purple. Iridescent trailers. Bug-eyed with a silver eyelet for a mouth. This one had a small disposition problem. Thorn noticed it now. One of its bead-chain eyes looked askance. Walleyed Charlie. It wasn't pleased, brought together like this.

Thorn broke the eye out of the epoxy body, touched the socket with another speck of clear nail polish, and reset the eye. There it was. A straight-ahead look. Smug, cocky even, but still vulnerable. Not an inch long, and nothing on it had ever met up with salt water before. But the thing would drift down to the marshy bottom and flicker into the dreams of the strongest, spookiest fish there was.

King Salmon

BY JOHN RANDOLPH

I had the great privilege of living in Alaska for almost two years when my father was stationed there during the Korean War. I graduated from Fairbanks High in 1954, when Alaska was still a territory. Being editor of the school paper, The Paystreak, *and working afternoons at Jessen's* Weekly *launched my career in journalism. Today I'm always fond of pointing out to people in the outdoor book and magazine publishing field that there aren't very many of us "territorial" school graduates around anymore.*

I have tried many times in my own writing to capture something of the grandeur and sheer exhilaration of the Alaska outdoors, including the novel On Dangerous Ground, *published by Doubleday in 1989 (now out of print). I always feel that I have not been very successful with my prose, because I know in my heart that the Alaska experience is just too vast for my limited ability to handle. That's one of the reasons I'm constantly on the alert to find good reading about the Alaska outdoors.*

This John Randolph piece has become one of my Alaska fishing favorites. As you probably know, John is the editor of Fly Fisherman *magazine. In that role he doesn't spend his days changing commas, but does what all great editors do: He finds things! Stories, pictures, ideas. He also is one heck of a writer himself, as you will see in this tribute to Alaska's biggest salmon, the Chinook, the King.*

I imagine that John came by his many talents through hard work, but I have to believe that some of his creative genes were there from his personal Day One. His father was the late, beloved Jack Randolph, for many years the caretaker of the widely read "Wood, Field and Stream" column in The New York Times.

Catching a Pacific-salmon grand slam (king, chum, sockeye, silver and humpy) is one of fly fishing's lesser known, and least attainable, holy grails. Lesser known because few of us have taken even one of the five Pacific salmon species on a fly, and most who have consider them to be dead-fish-swimming by the time they reach the headwaters of the Northwest rivers and the Great Lakes.

That makes the grand slam (taking all five species on a fly) a dream. And, with the destruction of the North American rivers, there are few places in the world where a salmon grand slam *can even be attempted*. Still there remains western Alaska, and especially Bristol Bay, the mother lode of Pacific salmon. It's possible to enter heaven on these waters, because in summer pinks, chums, kings, and sockeyes, run into the same or nearby rivers, and early-run silvers can provide a chance for a catch of all five species on one trip.

But there is a better goal. It's a cinch that if you catch all five salmon species, some of them will be logs, near the end of their run and approaching death. In some watersheds the runs overlap, but they are not simultaneous. Better to go for two or three of the salmon species near the salt, while they are fresh with sea lice still clinging to their sides. They are salmon that take you down into your backing and send you stumbling along rivers, dashing through a myriad of fish from seven in the morning until one the next morning. If you are one of those shuffling, half-crazed fly-fishing troglodytes, you should depart from Alaska with sated eyes and sweetly aching arms. You will be convinced that you are no longer an epigone, a second-rate follower: You have joined the Tenth Legion. There just remains that one hyperion fish.

There are a number of camps and lodges *near the mouths* of the great salmon rivers of the Bristol Bay–Kuskokwin area that have all five salmon species passing their doorsteps each summer. The trick is to hit the rivers at just the right time—when the right salmon are just in from the saltwater. They quickly turn color in the spawning rivers and their attention changes existentially, from moving and taking flies to regenerating their kind. The fresher the fish, the more savagely they take the fly.

Jim Teeny and I made plans to fish the Kanektok River, a tributary to Kuskokwim Bay on the edge of the great Yukon-Kuskokwim Delta. We would fish out of the Duncan camps on the lower river, 15 miles up from tide water. Our trip would begin on July 9, the tail of the king-salmon run and during the arrival of the chums and sockeyes. There would still be fresh kings in the river, and we would have leopard rainbows and Dolly Varden as finger food. The salmon would be sea-bright and full of fight and suckers for the fly.

★ ★ ★

Fly fishers are tackle junkies. In our quiet, reclusive hours at home we hallucinate the dreaded breaking of a knot, or being spooled by a mythic fish. We obsessively, secretively, rig lines to probe the watery depths, where no commercially made line can reach.

As my Alaska experience expanded, I had become increasingly paranoid about what I took for tackle and flies. I made special plans for this trip for giant kings and other strong salmon that seldom rise for the fly and the right lines and rods headed my list of weapons. I had learned through sad experience that when fishing for Pacific salmon you must fish bottom or a life trip can turn into exercises in frustration or, worse, panhandling companions for spare parts.

I spent days scheming the line strategy and rigging—a complete 10-weight shooting-head system from 200-grain to 800-grain, with the shooting-line rigged with a whipped loop for fast changes. To that I added a Teeny line system, from T-200 to T-500. To complete my sinking-line system, I added Uniform Sink 8- and 10-weights and two sinking-tips—one fast-sinking, the other slow-sinking. For fishing the surface, I included three weight-forward floating lines—two 8-weights and a 10-weight. Then I sat and carefully itemized the minimum line system I consider adequate for Alaska salmon fishing. I clucked "there" with self-satisfied approval. I tied and tested the backing-to-line and line-to-leader knots and clucked again.

King salmon are tough fish to beat on a fly rod. I estimated that I could survive with an 8-weight, 4-piece travel rod for the chums, the rainbows, and the sockeyes, but I'd need a three-piece, 10-weight for the kings, which would average around 20 pounds and run as high as 50. I knew that I'd break at least one rod, so I took two 10-weights, an 8-weight, and a 5-weight for grayling.

I also obsessed about my flies, and when Carl Richards described his near-birth experience with a lemming hatch on the Good News River, I added a dozen mouse patterns to my Clouser Deep Minnows, Teeny Nymphs, Woolly Buggers, egg imitations and Muddlers, all heavy-wire patterns except the mouse. I planned to fish on or near bottom 80 percent of the time.

Yes, I would need a quality reel with a good drag system and a minimum of 200 yards of 20-pound backing. I would still be taking a chance with a 50-pound king. A reel that would take 200 yards of 30-pound backing and the fly line would be ideal. It could handle all the salmon, and particularly the kings. I included in my gear two lightweight saltwater reels (one with 200 yards of 30-pound backing and another with 200 yards of 20-pound) and a 5-weight trout reel for rainbows and grayling.

★   ★   ★

When you fly over the Kilbuck Mountains, heading west toward the Bering Sea on Alaska's western littoral, the mountains fall away and a lake plain rises like a green carpet dotted with sapphires to meet you. In a small plane you feel diminished by the sight, and as you approach the Yup'ik village of Bethel, you realize just how remote from civilization you are. Down there a Stanley Kubrick–style hospital sits like a large, partially squashed, metallic yellow banana amidst a cluster of shanties. A lonely five miles of paved road runs through the village founded by the Moravian missionaries in 1884. Its buildings are constructed on posts to survive the permafrost. It looks healthy but tentative and alone, perched there on the edge of one of the world's largest river deltas formed where the 2,000-mile Yukon and the 800-mile Kuskokwim rivers become neighbors.

Life on the delta was always tenuous for hunter gatherers, but the lake-filled plain is one of the world's great waterfowl nesting grounds, and the salmon runs of the two rivers made life possible for the Yup'iks, who believed that the earth was created, or scratched, by a great raven who carved out the gorges of the Yukon and Kuskokwim rivers, lakes, and streams with its talons. About 10,000 Yup'iks, the largest ethnic native concentration in Alaska, inhabited the delta at the time of the arrival of the white man in the last century. Today 16,000 people live in Bethel.

The Kanektok slides out of the Kilbuck Mountains, across the ancient Kuskokwim flood plain and into Kuskokwim Bay. Its graveled runs are spawning grounds for all five Pacific salmon species. One hundred and fifty miles to the west lie Nunivak Island and the Bering Sea. The Duncans lease sport fishing rights on the river from the Yup'iks of Quinhagak, the native village near the river's outflow into Kuskokwim Bay.

In late June and early July, when the kings are in the river and the chums and sockeye are arriving, the Kanektok buzzes with urgent, purposeful life. The Eskimos pound up and downriver in family boatloads, netting and drying fish for winter food in their summer camps. They pass boatloads of white sport fishermen in search of fish for fun.

And the river is so full of fish. The long holes near the tidewater hold great congregations of silver salmon, all preparing for the move upstream to spawn and die. The kings are a dominant presence. They appropriate the water they want, and the smaller chums, newly striped with watermarks, move aside for them. The sockeyes, slim and shining like highly polished torpedos, lay up quietly in the sloughs and then swim upriver in great V-shape wedges in the half-light of the arctic summer nights. The fish are in and everyone is fishing, including the occasional bear, whose prints mark sandbars and whose scent turns the camp dog into a barking, schizophrenic canine.

There are so many fish and fishermen that you metamorphose into a round-the-clock predator, chasing them frantically until, exhausted, you drop. Then in a few brief hours you rise, eat, and go out again, hunting big, bright fish, fighting them passionately, searching for that obsessively imagined Great One. You see, sight-fishing to Pacific salmon is an intense visual and emotional feast for excited nerve endings, like sight-fishing to double-digit bonefish on an undisturbed ocean flat.

All the king-salmon pools are within 15 miles of camp, and where the salmon lie each year on their movements upriver is predictable unless the river floods in runoff and changes its familiar bottom geography.

You motor to the Ten Minute Hole and as the guide drifts the boat through, you stand on the deck and search for the large rust-green shapes of the kings resting on their upriver migration. You sight-fish to the shapes as you stand on the sand-and-gravel banksides and cast the heavy lines upstream of the brown-green forms barely visible in the green-gray water. Casting the lines is relatively easy; casting them long requires skill. The 27-foot tapers built into running lines must be slung with a smooth, high delivery, the excess line held in your line hand as loops that shoot as the heavy taper pulls them up into the guides. The head must be the right weight of sinking line for the speed and depth of the water, for when the head hits the water it must sink quickly through the current so the fly reaches bottom as it approaches the fish. The fly must bounce or crawl across bottom or the king will not grab it.

If your eyesight is good, and you use high-quality polarized glasses, you can spot the movement of the fish's head when it takes the fly and the line goes tight and you lift.

The king may hesitate momentarily, not realizing that it is hooked, or it may charge off and into the air or simply turn and begin a long, unstoppable run downriver, quickly into your backing. You yell "Boat!" and the guide kicks the broad, shallow-draft jet sled off the bank and the two of you chase the king through the long riffle water and into the next pool. Hopefully, if the fish is not too large and ocean bound, the fight will be waged there. With kings, as with tarpon, it's the size of the fight in the fish not the size of the fish in the fight.

When it is finally beached, the king will average about 20 pounds, but there are much larger shapes in the pools, and the shapes keep changing from day to day as newcomers arrive and depart for the upriver spawning gravel. When the shapes are of the brightest silver, and large as well, then the fishermen and guides become very excited: a large, bright king is the main event in this fly fishing.

★ ★ ★

Chum salmon come in two runs. The largest, the summer run (fish averaging seven pounds), arrives in early June and continues until mid-July when the fall fish (averaging eight pounds, with fish up to 15 pounds) arrive. In the long pools they occupy the same water as the kings, and when you fish for one, you fish for the other. And, like the kings, the chums take flies fished on bottom.

Chums are powerful fish for their size and when sea-bright they fight doggedly with vicious rolling and thrashing leaps. They take the same flies as the kings—brightly colored patterns (especially pink) tied on heavy wire. One day a green Teeny Nymph may work best, the next a pink deer-hair Polywog waked across the surface turns them giddy; then a black or red fly incites a suicidal grab. Which color today? Let's huddle and compare flies: only trial-and-success will tell.

The concentration required in this sight-fishing is exhausting. Haig-Brown described it in his book *A River Never Sleeps* as fishing to the ripples made by moving schools of fish. In the Kanektok and some other Alaska rivers, when the water is low and clear, you spot holding fish and fish to them. It's like saltwater-flats fishing, except you stand for long hours in one place working the fly carefully to one giant pod of fish. By noon your arms ache from maintaining a sustained predator's crouch and the fatigue of standing and fighting fish extends down your back and into your legs. Line burns crease your fingers; your eyes ache, and your forearms are tight from strain.

The right presentations require the utmost effort and attention, but the hookups and the fights are pure avoirdupois—dogged heavy-tackle battles between brute fish and man. For relief, you turn your attention to the gentle side-water, where the sockeyes are laid up waiting for the light to fall to begin their runs upriver. You creep along the banks and watch the bright finning salmon in the aqua-green, deep pools, knowing that tonight after supper you will fish for them on their migrations.

As the sun drops, the fish become more difficult to spot in the surface glare, so you fish carefully and instinctively to where they have been, and must still be. You fish urgently because the boat ride upriver for supper is approaching.

★   ★   ★

In the arctic twilight, the sun slides slowly toward the horizon and the salmon move. Below camp, where two flows converge, exhausted fishermen meet to fish the midnight run. Sockeyes ripple the surface in a long, slim backeddy. They are stacked in a little Grand Central Station of soft water, schools coming and going in a vast upstream evening push of fish. Jim Teeny waits for them and fishes a Nymph Tip line fixedly the way a pointing bird dog approaches a holding pheasant. The line moves imperceptibly in its quiet drift amidst the myriad sockeye, and he lifts and yells: "Fish on! Chromer!" In my half-sleep a half-mile upstream from Jim, I hear him exclaiming over another chrome-bright fish and I toss on clothes and stagger downriver to join the joyously atavistic hunt.

Some sockeyes leave the backeddy and, in schools, follow a leader over the four-inch-deep riffle bar. Standing at the head of the riffle, you can see them coming in a wedge-shaped ripple moving in the water's midnight surface glare. You cast with a sink-tip line, leading the wedge so the fly drops and intercepts the fish as they move upriver in the shallow water. The line hesitates, ever so slightly, and you lift and feel *fish*. A sockeye runs and jumps and jumps again and again.

You catch sockeyes there, with leopard rainbows and chums, until 1 A.M., until your arms and legs can stand no more. Only then, limp with the hunter's catch-sated fatigue, are your thoughts more on the cot in your tent than on fish. You must sleep. But . . . just one more tug.

★   ★   ★

The leopard rainbows are dry-fly light-rod candy in the rivers that drain to the Bering Sea. No one has explained why their markings are so brilliant. They are true river rainbows, not ocean-going steelhead. And they are suckers for the little lemmings, mice, and voles that inhabit the banks of their rivers and occasionally tumble in and struggle to swim.

Under pewter-gray skies, Brad Duncan skulls the boat driftboat fashion downriver, holding while we drift-and-shoot the banks with mouse patterns. The water is cold, about 50 degrees, and the rainbows are sluggish and strike short. We adjust—leaving the fly, twitching it—and they take.

"When the water temperature rises five degrees, they'll take hard and you'll have thirty-fish days," Duncan says.

The river braids and in the side-channels we walk and wade and work the alder sweepers, stalking the lemming hatch. When the rainbows come, they attack the fly, suddenly shooting out from under the brush, and are instantly airborne. After the large brutish salmon, they are luminous, like celestially marked rainbows leaping on dark Montana days.

★   ★   ★

The mind must slowly accept a return to civilization. The adjustment commences on the last day on the river, when you urgently search the holding runs for the largest king salmon you have ever seen. When the shape appears, unexpectedly where there had been no rust-colored apparition before, your stomach tightens and you peer hard at the image—disbelieving. It cannot be *that big*—one fish. Perhaps there are two there, side-by-side in a pair. No, no, it's one fish all right. But, God, it's got to be 50 pounds!

Wade close. Carefully. Get positioned just right, just downstream of the fish so you can hit the bucket, that sweet little slot in front of the fish's nose, with the first cast. Cast way upstream ahead of the fish so the fly will tick bottom as it approaches the shape. There! No, not quite right. Cast again. And again.

The minutes and casts string out. You are ready to resign—the ache in your arms and back is too much. One more cast.

There! There!

The head moves. The fly stops solidly. Then the bottom moves; the shape is underway. This weight comes from the center of the earth. Line peels off the reel. The fish runs away across the river. And then . . . Oh! leaps in a full-bodied, eye-level, Atlantic-salmon bravado.

"Is that your fish?" Roger yells. "He's big! Boat!"

We are in the boat and away . . . helplessly following. The fish leaps again; it drafts on the downstream currents backward into the lower end of the pool; it jumps again—it's a female! Then it turns and heads downriver. She will do what she will. There is no stopping his charge. We can only follow and re-gain backing when she—oh, please!—comes to rest with a pod of kings in the next pool.

She *does* hesitate and I can put pressure on her, standing back from the shore with the rod bent double, the line stretched taut like piano wire. She dis-likes the pressure and turns.

"Boat!"

Once she has her body into the current, the fight is all her way and we must follow—down into the next pool, and the next, and the next. She does not jump any more. She knows now that something serious has begun—a fight for survival. I can gain line when she holds, but I cannot turn her head or move her body weight sideways. I'm irritating her, and when she holds in the cur-rent, I can only sap her strength by pulling her hard sideways. I must not give her rest. She must *feel* defeated before she *is defeated*. She can sense my fatigue through the line. I can feel her existential determination, and when she sulks and rests, I can almost feel her heart beat.

I know her life history—her mother dropping an egg into the gravel to which she is now headed to drop hers; the egg hatching in early spring; her tenuous wiggle emergence as a fragile swim-up fry; her gradual metamorpho-sis into a gaily colored smolt; her joining with others of her kind, the cloudlike young-of-the-year school that will drift its way downriver to the sea; her two- or three-year odyssey in the sea; and her urgent return to her square-yard of clean gravel where this all began.

My odyssey as a fly fisher has taught me that the odds of her making it this far are in the millions to one. Now only I stand between her and her final genetic ritual, her grotesque physical deformation, and her death spasms in a quiet river side-channel, where only a hungry bear may notice, inspect her briefly and splash off in search of better fish to eat.

★ ★ ★

"You've got to beat her before she reaches those root wads. See them down there at the end of the pool?" Jimmy shouts. The fish is tired. I can feel her fatigue, and I can see that the shape flounders a little when I give her the butt and strain the line until it sings. Will the knots hold? She flounders back toward the current, and I lose 20 feet, then 50 more. She's going to make the root wads.

"Boat! Boat, now!" Jimmy yells. "Too late! She's gonna snag you! Boat!"

"Damn!, Jim, she's in the wads."

In the boat, beside the wads, I can peer down and see the line and leader all tangled in the roots. Frustrated . . . desperate . . . I plunge into the water and pull and lift on the line.

"No! No!, John. Do it from in here, in the boat. We can free it!"

It's hopeless. The line will not come free. In a last, desperate, effort, I wrap the line around my hands and haul with all my might. It comes free from the top roots, but there are others. I haul hard again.

"No! You've got her! That's *her* down there. See!" Jim shouts.

Deep in the blue-green water, at the base of a root wad, lies a shape.

"That's her there, John. Lead her downstream. Don't let her have her head or she'll dash in and break you off. We can land her there, on that beach down below. See it? It's just right!"

I lead her gently downstream away from the wads. She swims sluggishly toward the large flat. Her weight is still so heavy that I can only watch line peel off the reel again. But this time she turns into the quiet water beside the flow, and as I tumble from the boat, I know that the end is very close. "Please don't let the knot break now," I whisper. "It's been an hour and a half and a mile of river. How long can monofilament and a 10-weight three-piece last?" The truly large fish are usually lost with the leader at the tip-top.

Jim shouts staccato instructions. "She's tired. Get farther back on the beach! You can turn him now! Once he's turned, keep her coming. When she feels the stones on her belly, she'll bolt, so be careful she doesn't make a sudden move and break you off. If you get her far enough up on the gravel, she'll turn over on her side. Then she can't swim; we've got her. Keep backing up! Reel! Keep the pressure on her!"

She feels the pebbles on her belly, and she bolts in a weary, inertia-more-than-energy-driven dash for the main current. For the first time I can stop and turn her. She comes to me. She comes. The pebbles tickle her stomach, but she does not have the energy to turn and run. Her jaw slides up on the shallows and she tips on her side, and Jimmy and the guides and the other fishermen are with her. "There!"

I can touch her now for the first time. When I grasp the hard muscular wrist of her tail, my hand cannot completely encircle it. She is muscular, firm, full-bellied and cold in my hands. I can lift her only momentarily. She is the largest freshwater fish I have ever held. Her sides are already turning reddish brown. Her eye is a black onyx, celestial. As she revives in the current, I can feel her full strength . . . pulsing, reviving. Then I feel something tight within me release, as though a heavy stress had been lifted from my heart. I relax and exhale deeply.

She quivers anxiously; she needs to be off upriver. She is determined—strong again. It cannot be that she will spawn and quickly die. She seems immortal. I slowly, reluctantly, release my grip on her tail wrist. She senses freedom . . . and she charges away, sending rooster tails across the shallows as she heads for the main current.

She is gone, I have her here, still with me.

The Yup'iks believe that to fish for fun is a sin: Fishing must be for food. This is not sin. This is communion.

The Evening Rise

BY JOHN WALLER HILLS

*By sheer numbers of hours of enjoyment, reading and rereading, John Waller Hills'
classic* A Summer on the Test *ranks as my Number One choice of English chalkstream literature. As I said in introducing* A Summer on the Test *in another anthology, one reason I enjoy reading the book so much is probably because Hills does not
write in an instructional vein, but rather creates straightforward description of the fishing under varying conditions. When Hills takes to the stream, our spirits fall and rise as
his own. The pageant of the seasons, the off-again, on-again nature of the hatches, scroll
through* A Summer on the Test *like enchanting but mysterious dramas in which we
view our leading player, Mr. Hills, with empathy and hope.*

*A Summer on the Test was first published in a limited edition in 1924
and reprinted in a popular edition with new chapters in 1930. The book was repub-
lished by Nick Lyons in 1983.*

*In this chapter, John Waller Hills duels with the largest trout he has ever en-
countered while fishing a dry fly.*

Some time after mid-May the evening rise starts, and lasts till the end of
the season. There is a great difference between different rivers. On the
Test and Itchen you do not get it before May is well on its way, and the
same on the Hertford and Dorset streams: on Driffield Beck not till
June. On the Kennet, on the other hand, you get it from earliest times. I have
known it in April, and on cold nights, too. But it is nowhere in full swing until
June, and one part of it, the sedge rise, till July. It is an unsatisfactory thing, this
evening rise. You get fish, certainly, but you seldom get as many as you feel you
ought. And the mind is weighted with an unpleasant apprehension of finality.
Daylight has a definite end which nothing can prolong. A morning rise, starting at eleven, may last an hour or it may last five. It has the charm of uncertainty and of hope. But an evening rise has a fixed limit. There is no scope for

imagination or fortune, and the pleasures of fishing are mental. The trout, too, during an evening rise are always difficult and often exasperating.

But before discussing that, it is necessary to analyse the rise in rather more detail. When the hay has been cut, and wet places are golden with mimulus, and the pomp of high summer is reigning, there are three evening rises. The first begins some time between six and seven (ordinary, not summer time) and lasts till shortly before sunset. This I call the casual rise. The second starts after the last edge of the sun has sunk below the actual horizon and ends when it is too dark to see a small artificial on the water. This is the small fly rise. The third rise then opens and runs for something under half an hour, rarely longer. This is the sedge rise. The casual rise may begin any time after six. Trout move languidly, often taking spinners, but sometimes indecipherable insects. They are difficult, because at no time in the twenty-four hours are they so readily put down. A cast which would pass muster in the stillest noon sends them off like a shot. I suppose this is due to the slanting light. And it is not easy to see what they are taking. Altogether they are a high test of skill. But they can be caught. Try them with the prevailing spinner, or a fancy fly such as the pheasant tail. A blue upright sometimes kills.

The small fly rise has a very different appearance indeed. If it be a good one, trout rise not languidly but eagerly, sometimes madly. And it starts with all the unexpected suddenness of the morning rises of early May. I recollect particularly the 25th July 1918. I was strolling up the bank on a quiet, warm evening. A stile had to be crossed, and I remember stopping a minute or so before crossing it and watching the aquamarine sky and its reflection in the opal water. The stile lay a little back, behind a bushy willow, which shut out the water. Before crossing, not a ring was to be seen: when I had crossed, and cleared the willow, the surface was boiling. The movement had started as though on the stroke of a clock. And often this sudden beginning will come immediately after the last rim of the sun has disappeared.

During the casual rise fish are usually taking spinners, if spinners there be. On warm, still evenings, when the female fly can get back to the river to lay her eggs, there will be spinners. But if it be cold, and particularly if it be windy, the females are driven away, and none of them fall as spinners. Smuts, too, are often on the water at this time, or you may have a hatch of small sedges. If so you will find that trout take the artificial very well. During the small fly rise, trout may want either duns or spinners, or occasionally nymphs. It is often very difficult to see whether they are rising or bulging; or, if they are rising, what they are rising at. During the casual rise, too, the fish, though picksome and hard to please, are not particular about pattern: but during the small fly rise they settle down to one article and refuse everything else. Your fly must be exactly right, or you get nothing till dark. During the casual rise fish are often unapproachable; during the small fly rise they are easy to approach and hard to put down, but hard to catch. You no longer need crawl or kneel, you can stand up. As the dusk deepens, you can get nearer and nearer. Your hook can be a size or two bigger, your gut thicker: though, if you take my advice, you will never, even for mayfly or sedge, use stronger than finest natural, for on that you can kill the biggest trout that swims. But in spite of the advantage of ease of access, larger flies and heavier gut, trout are harder to get: harder than they are in the heat of noon, with 4x points and 000 hooks. They are hard because they take only one kind of food and because they demand a higher standard of imitation. You must copy what they are eating and you must copy it in a way they like.

As I look back over many evening rises, I get the impression of more failures than successes. Not absolute failures, perhaps, but relative; one brings away the sense of not having done as well as one ought. Fish rise so confidently and so often: there are so many: you do not put them down, for they go on rising: but though they are taking winged fly, you they will not take. Rivers differ greatly in the ease with which fish are caught in the evening, and so do different parts of the same river. The Test is easier than the Itchen, and the Kennet a good deal harder than either. But the Test can be difficult enough.

Even if you see what the trout are gulping down, your troubles are not over. A typical summer evening fly is the blue winged olive, and the best artificial is the orange quill. By the bye, never be afraid of a large orange quill, up to No. 1. But sometimes they will not look at the orange quill or at the coot-winged imitation, or at any olive or red or ginger quill that man's wit devised. Then you have an extremely difficult choice to make: are you to go on trying fly after fly, losing precious time in changing, and rattling your nerves, too, or are you to stick to what you think the best pattern? That is to say, are you to change your fly or change your fish?

Before answering that, let me ask you if you are sure that you know what trout are taking. Blue winged olives are floating down, certainly, and fish are breaking the water: but are they feeding on the nymph or the winged fly or the spinner? It is wonderful how hard it is to tell this, in the lessening light. Anyhow, if the winged fly is refused, do not hesitate. Try the hackle blue-wing first, then the sherry spinner, and then the nymph sunk. The pattern of a nymph is given in a later chapter. However, since fishing books should be definite or nothing, I will tell you exactly how I do behave, not how I should. I try first an orange or red quill, according to river, then a hackle blue-wing unoiled

and awash, and then probably a sherry spinner. After that, I should think it useless to go on changing, and certainly at some time or other I should go back to
the fly I thought best. Whether my final choice were an orange or red quill
would depend on the river: at Driffield a red, on the Test, Itchen or Kennet an
orange. In streams where you do not get much blue winged olive, such as those
of Dorsetshire or Derbyshire, my final selection, if all else failed, would be a
ginger quill. I kill more fish nowadays on the ginger than on the red quill,
whatever may have been the case twenty years ago.

Hitherto, I have been talking of nights when the blue winged olive
alone comes down: but they are rare, for you usually find a mixed mass of pale
watery and medium olive as well, and also their spinners, and perhaps that of
the iron blue. You can tell if the trout are taking pale watery, for their rise to it
is very different from the boil that they make at the blue winged olive, and you
can act accordingly. Again, you can sometimes tell when they are taking spinners, but in the dusk you cannot tell which. So you must try the sherry, yellow
boy, houghton ruby and Lunn's particular, all of them. But often you are
beaten, and then, as I say, at some time of the night, if nothing will induce them
to rise, go back to one fly and stick to it. Carry an electric torch, and then you
can change your pattern easily on the darkest night.

But here I must interpolate. On some evenings, and indeed some seasons, you get an early hatch of small sedges, and after them come the blue
winged olive and sherry spinner. The ordinary procession is reversed. Thus on
the 14th and 15th July 1928 there was a hatch of small sedge early and a fall of
sherry spinner after dark. On each night I killed on a sedge at about eight
o'clock and then on a sherry spinner and 3x gut after eleven o'clock had struck.

But now for the sedge proper. When it gets too dark to see a No. 0 fly
on the water, you can try a good sized sedge. It is little use before this, and little use after complete darkness. Do not change to sedge too soon, and if your
orange quill is killing well, stick to it. The time during which a sedge is taken
rarely exceeds half an hour and is usually only a quarter. Of all fishing the
sedge rise is the most uncertain. Not only may you have bad days, but bad
years. I am not sure, too, whether success is caused by the presence of sedges
themselves. Sometimes they are swarming in the reeds like bees and you cannot get a rise, while at others you may kill fish when there is not a natural fly to
be seen: but you do not usually do much with the artificial until the time has
come for the natural to hatch out, and it does not hatch in full force until July.
A warm, windless night is almost essential. The easiest fish to catch is one lying
close under the other bank, provided of course that it is within your reach. Get
straight opposite him, and cast two feet above him. Be quite sure that you are

reaching him; the tendency in the dusk is to cast short, particularly when you are throwing into the liquid reflection of the reeds. If he does not take, try this: when your fly is about to come over his nose, pull six or eight inches of line sharply through the rings with your spare hand: this has the effect of causing the fly to scutter over the water, and often makes the trout come at you with a glorious smashing rise like a sea trout. Pattern is not important, though size is. In the early part of the season do not go beyond No. 2: in July and August you can get up to No. 4 or 5. Always fish the sedge dry. I myself do not carry more than four patterns: small dark sedge, coachman, large hare's ear sedge, and cinnamon sedge. Of late I have unconsciously dropped the silver sedge, which I used to use greatly: I killed on it the biggest trout I ever got on the dry fly, as will be told later.

Sedge fishing is not scientific, though a good man will always beat a bad one. But fish are often simple-minded, and anyone can catch them, those great cunning creatures which defied the most skilful in daylight. You catch trout by throwing across, or across and down, and either pulling the fly intentionally, or letting the stream cause it to drag. This, though it looks like clumsy fishing, actually reproduces most accurately the path of the natural sedge. But curiously enough it only answers at night, for never have I known shy fish to take a dragging sedge by day. Some fishers despise the sedge: others regard it as the best part of a summer day. I express no opinion one way or another, but only mention three qualities which the sedge rise possesses. First, you may get hold of heavy fish quickly one after another, which is great fun. Second, you can redeem a bad day, and get even with those contemptuous, supercilious trout who have defeated you. Third, you have a chance of getting a real monster. On still summer nights, when not a leaf stirs, and in the pearly shadows you cannot see where the reeds end and their reflection begins, when the ghost moth is rising and falling over the damp meadow, and if you are lucky you may catch a glimpse of the graceful pink elephant hawk moth flying at the yellow iris flowers: when the great red sedge is flopping about in his feeble and aimless flight, and clouds of smaller sedges are flickering tirelessly up and down over the unbroken surface, perchance some dim memory begins to stir in the slow mind of the old trout. All the season through he has fed at the bottom, grubbing on shrimps and caddis and water-snails and minnows and even on his own relatives. But he recalls seasons such as this, far back in former years, when all was quiet and warm and peaceful, when the fat sedges would tumble clumsily on to the water, and in their efforts to escape would make a ripple and commotion spreading far over the placid pool, and he remembers how fresh and fair they were to eat. Then he forsakes his lair under the arched willow roots and rises to the top and takes up his old station in the shadow of the tussock, where he used to lie long ago in his active middle age, when he weighed a bare two pounds. Aye, he weighs more than twice two pounds now, perhaps three times or more, he is the prize of a lifetime—and perhaps as your sedge comes over him you will see a break like that of a big raindrop, a little circle like the palm of a man's hand, and when you strike you will think you have hooked the trunk of a tree. That possibility always gives an excitement to sedge fishing. You are on the edge of the mysterious and the unknown, and you feel as you do when fishing a salmon river in which forty pounders are not an impossibility.

For sedge fishing you must have a warm, still evening, and this is best for the small fly rise, too: but do not be driven home either by mist or cold or rain or wind. If it is cold and wet, spinners will not get on the water, what I call the casual rise will be blank, and you will do nothing till the winged fly hatches; but there is often a good show of this on inclement, tempestuous nights. Do you recollect that typical summer evening, 14th June 1907? It was shiveringly cold, there was a wild wind and pelting showers. When I reached Winchester by the evening train, the weather looked so bad that I only went out because I was too restless to stay in: and yet I got a brace before being driven in to the fireside. Or the 13th June 1922, on the Kennet, a vile day which got viler, until the rain hammered down and the bitter wind blew in your teeth? Yet blue winged olives hatched from eight to half-past nine and I landed ten takeable fish, of which I kept two brace. Or again, that other day in the same year, cold and wild and wet, 15th July 1922? There was a mighty hatch of the same fly just before dark, and I got six fish weighing nine pounds. Or the 23rd May 1924, wintry and wet, with half a gale? There was a splendid evening rise at Mottisfont right up to half-past nine. And perhaps the worst night I ever was out was 9th June 1928, at Stockbridge. So cold and wet was it, that two or three of us sat before the fire in the keeper's house debating whether we should go out. Yet there was a good hatch and we all got fish. I landed one of 3 lb. 7 oz. and broke in another which assuredly was bigger, on the sedge, too. No, never let weather keep you indoors, even on English summer nights. However, warm clear nights are of course the best. Black thunder clouds are very bad, in fact light is of great importance, and fish are often shyer on a cloudy than on a cloudless night. Fog is generally bad, but sometimes, if it is light and silvery, fly will hatch and trout will swallow them.

Many a bad day has the sedge redeemed. My most notable recollections of it, however, relate, not to the Test, but to the Kennet, which is the greatest of all sedge rivers. On 28th June 1914 a friend and I were fishing there. It was clear, summer weather, fair and hot, with an indeterminate breeze varying from south to west. Working hard till dark I got four fish of no great size, none of them on the sedge. Some time between nine and ten at night I reeled up and went in search of my friend. He had caught nothing till the last quarter of an hour; however, in that short space he had beaten my whole day's efforts, for he had taken four fish which weighed a great deal more than mine, all on the coachman. That is no unusual incident. On 26th July in the same year I toiled all day till tea-time for two fish which were only just over the pound limit, and at the small fly I failed to rise fish after fish: but in ten minutes with the coachman I rose all the six fish I tried for and got two brace. Again on 2nd August 1914, the last day's fishing before the war, I laboured unceasingly against a gusty wind for three fish, and once more made an utter mess of a hatch of blue winged olives; whilst in the magic fifteen minutes during which trout take the sedge I landed four out of the six I found rising, and kept three which weighed only a fraction under six pounds. That year, 1914, was a good sedge year, and such years are scarce and should not be missed.

A moon behind your arm, especially a full moon, makes fish nearly impossible to approach. They are put down far more easily than by the brightest sun. You may be rising trout regularly, when suddenly the first cast stops them, because the unnoticed moon has risen. It is an immense advantage to be ambidextrous, and fish underhand with the inshore hand.

Those who fish rivers where mayfly come will agree that, though with it you get a higher average weight, yet actually the biggest fish are killed on the sedge. 1903 on the Kennet was a great mayfly season for heavy fish, and a friend of mine who had the Ramsbury water got the truly remarkable bag of six fish in one day which weighed over nineteen pounds: and yet the two heaviest fish of the year were got on the sedge. I got the heaviest. It was the 26th July 1903, a cloudy, gusty day, with a downstream wind, and I was on the water from eleven till five without seeing a rise. My friend and I then had tea and walked up the river at a quarter-past six. Olives began to appear and trout to move; and suddenly a really large one started rising. We stood and watched, with growing excitement. He was taking every fly, in solid and determined fashion, and the oftener he appeared the bigger he looked, and the faster beat our hearts. It was settled that I was to try for him. I was nervous and uncomfortable. He was very big: it was a long throw and the wind horrible: I could not reach him, and like a fool I got rattled and pulled off too much line: there was an agonised groan from my friend behind me when a great curl of it was slapped on the water exactly over the trout's nose. We looked at each other without speaking, and he silently walked away up the river, leaving me staring stupidly at the spot where the trout had been rising. Of course he was gone.

The next two hours can be passed over. The small fly rise came and went. I caught a trout on a No. 2 silver sedge and finally, at about a quarter-past eight, found myself gazing gloomily at the place where I had bungled. The wild wind had blown itself out and had swept the sky bare of cloud. Silence had come, and stillness. The willows, which all through the long summer day had bowed and chattered in the wind, were straightened and motionless, each individual leaf hanging down as though carved in jade: the forest of great sedges, which the gusts had swept into wave after wave of a roaring sea of emerald, was now calm and level, each stalk standing straight and stiff as on a Japanese screen. There had occurred that transition, that transmutation from noise and movement to silence and peace, which would be more wonderful were we not so accustomed to it, when a windy summer day turns over to a moveless summer night: when the swing and clatter and rush of the day is arrested and lifted from the world, and you get the sense that the great hollow of the air is filled with stillness and quiet, as with a tangible presence. They are peaceful things, these summer evenings after wild days, and I remember particularly that this was one of the most peaceful; more so indeed than my thoughts, which were still in a turmoil. I stood watching mechanically, and then, tempting fate to help me, made a cast or two over the spot where the fish had been. How easy it was to reach it now, how lightly my fly settled on the water, how gracefully it swung over the place. All to no purpose, of course, for nothing happened, and I was about to reel up when a fish rose ten yards above, close under my bank. It was one of those small movements, difficult to place. It might be a very large fish or a very small one. A wild thought swept through me that this was my big one: but no, I said to myself, it cannot be. This is not where he was rising. Besides, things do not happen like that, except in books: it is only in books that you make a fearful bungle and go back later and see a small break which you think is a dace, and cast carelessly and hook something the size of an autumn salmon: it is only in books that fate works in such fashion. Why, I know it all so well that I could write it out by heart, every move of it. But this is myself by a river, not reading in a chair. This is the real world, where such things do not happen: that is the rise of a half pound trout.

I cast. I was looking right into the west, and the water was coloured like skim milk by reflection from where the sun had set. My silver sedge was as visible as by day. It floated down, there was a rise, I struck, and something rushed up stream. Then I knew.

Above me was open water for some twenty-five yards, and above that again a solid block of weed, stretching right across. My fish made for this, by short, irresistible runs. To let him get into it would have been folly: he must be stopped: either he is well hooked or lightly, the gut is either sound or rotten: kill or cure, he must be turned, if turned he can be: so I pulled hard, and fortunately got his head round and led him down. He played deep and heavy and I had to handle him roughly, but I brought him down without a smash, and I began to breathe again. But then another terror appeared. At the place we had reached the only clear water was a channel under my bank, and the rest of the river was choked with weed. Should I try to pull him down this channel, about three or four yards wide, to the open water below? No. It was much too dangerous, for the fish was uncontrollable, and if he really wanted to get to weed he would either get there or break me: even with a beaten fish it would be extremely risky, and with an unbeaten one it was unthinkable. Well, if he would not come down he must go up, and up he went willingly enough, for when I released pressure he made a long rush up to the higher weed bed, whilst I ran up the meadow after him, and with even greater difficulty turned him once more. This time I thought he was really going right through it, so fast and so heavy was his pull, and I think he was making for a hatch hole above: but once more my gallant gut stood the strain and, resisting vigorously, he was led down. This proceeding was repeated either two or three times more, I forget which: either three or four times we fought up and down that twenty-five yards of water. By then he was tiring, and I took up my station in the middle of the stretch, where I hoped to bring him in: my hand was actually on the sling of the net when he suddenly awoke and rushed up. He reached the weed bed at a pace at which he was impossible to stop, shot into it like a torpedo, and I had the sickening certainty that I should lose him after all. To hold him hard now would be to make a smash certain, so I slacked off: when he stopped I tightened again, expecting miserably to feel the dead, lifeless drag of a weeded line. Instead, to my delight, I found I was still in contact with the fish, and he was pulling hard. How he had carried the line through the weeds I do not know. To look at it seemed impossible: and if he had reached them earlier in the fight, when he played deep in the river, before he tired and the pressure brought him near the top, I should have been jammed hopelessly. But the line was clear, and the fish proved it by careering wildly on towards the hatch, making the reel sing. I believe he meant to go through into the carrier, as fish have done before and after, but I turned him. However, we could not stay where we were. The hatch was open at the bottom, there was a strong draw of water through it, and if a heavy, beaten fish got into this, no gut could hold him up.

At all risks he must be taken back over the weed into the clear water. I pulled him up to the top and ran him down. Then, for the first time, after so many perils, came the conviction that I should land him. He was obviously big, but how big could not be known, for I had not had a clear sight of him yet. He still pulled with that immovable, quivering solidity only shown by a very heavy fish. But at last even his great strength tired. He gave a wobble or two, yielded, and suddenly he was splashing on the top, looking huge in the dusk. There ensued that agonising time when you have a big fish nearly beat, but he is too heavy to pull in, and nothing you can do gets him up to the net. At last I pulled him over it, but I lifted too soon, the ring caught him in the middle of the body, he wavered a moment in the air and then toppled back into the water with a sickening splash. A judgment, I thought, and for a shattering second I believed he had broken the gut, but he was still on. I was pretty well rattled by then and, in the half light, made two more bad shots, but the end came at last, he was in the net and on the bank.

How big was he? Three pounds? Yes, and more. Four pounds? Yes, and more. Five? He might be, he might. My knees shook and my fingers trembled as I got him on the hook of the steelyard. He weighed a fraction over 4 lb. 8 oz. I walked up to find my friend and asked him to weigh him, too. He made him a fraction under 4 lb. 9 oz. And that is my biggest fish on the floating fly.

Big Secret Trout

BY ROBERT TRAVER

Many astute readers know by now that Robert Traver is the pen name for the late John D. Voelker, associate justice of the Michigan Supreme Court. Voelker wrote the best-selling novel Anatomy of a Murder, *made into a successful film starring James Stewart, that vaulted the name Robert Traver to international fame.*

For fly fishers, however, two other Robert Traver titles reveal a man whose reflections and memories of being on trout streams seem far more interesting and poignant than courtroom dramas. Trout Madness, *from which this selection is taken, and* Trout Magic, *edited and first published by Nick Lyons, are fly-fishing story and essay collections that rank among the finest of all time. Recently, Lyons Press republished several Traver stories in a new collection,* Traver on Fishing.

In "Big Secret Trout," the word "backing" never reaches the printed page. Even so, the spirit of this encounter in which big trout are played in tense, almost desperate moments, makes this a tale not to be missed.

No misanthropist, I must nevertheless confess that I like and frequently prefer to fish alone. Of course in a sense all dedicated fishermen must fish alone; the pursuit is essentially a solitary one; but sometimes I not only like to fish out of actual sight and sound of my fellow addicts, but alone too in the relaxing sense that I need not consider the convenience or foibles or state of hangover of my companions, nor subconsciously compete with them (smarting just a little over their success or gloating just a little over mine), nor, more selfishly, feel any guilty compulsion to smile falsely and yield them a favorite piece of water.

There is a certain remote stretch of river on the Middle Escanaba that I love to fish by myself; the place seems made for wonder and solitude. This enchanted stretch lies near an old deer-hunting camp of my father's. A cold feeder stream—"The Spawnshop," my father called it—runs through the ancient beaver meadows below the camp. After much gravelly winding and circling and gurgling over tiny beaver dams the creek gaily joins the big river a mile or so east of the camp. Not unnaturally, in warm weather this junction is a favorite convention spot for brook trout.

One may drive to the camp in an old car or a jeep but, after that, elementary democracy sets in; all fishermen alike must walk down to the big river—*even* the arrogant new jeepocracy. Since my father died the old ridge trail has become overgrown and faint and wonderfully clogged with windfalls. I leave it that way. Between us the deer and I manage to keep it from disappearing altogether. Since this trail is by far the easiest and closest approach to my secret spot, needless to say few, secretive, and great of heart are the fishermen I ever take over it.

I like to park my old fish car by the camp perhaps an hour or so before sundown. Generally I enter the neglected old camp to look around and, over a devotional beer, sit and brood a little over the dear dead days of yesteryear, or perhaps morosely review the progressive decay of calendar art collected there during forty-odd years. And always I am amazed that the scampering field mice haven't carried the musty old place away, calendars and all. . . . Traveling light, I pack my waders and fishing gear—with perhaps a can or two of beer to stave off pellagra—and set off. I craftily avoid using the old trail at first (thus leaving no clue), charging instead into the thickest woods, using my rod case as a wand to part the nodding ferns for hidden windfalls. Then veering right and picking up the trail, I am at last on the way to the fabulous spot where my father and I used to derrick out so many trout when I was a boy.

Padding swiftly along the old trail—over windfalls, under others—I sometimes recapture the fantasies of my boyhood: once again, perhaps, I am a lithe young Indian brave—the seventh son of Chief Booze-in-the-Face, a modest lad who can wheel and shoot the eye out of a woodchuck at seventy paces— now bound riverward to capture a great copper-hued trout for a demure copper-hued maiden; or again, and more sensibly, I am returning from the river simply to capture the copper-hued maiden herself. But copper fish or Indian maid, there is fantasy in the air; the earth is young again; all remains unchanged: there is still the occasional porcupine waddling away, bristling and ridiculous; still the startling whir of a partridge; still the sudden blowing and thumping retreat of a surprised deer. I pause and listen stealthily. The distant blowing grows fainter and fainter, *"whew"* and again *"whew,"* like wind grieving in the pines.

By and by the middle-aged fisherman, still gripped by his fantasies, reaches the outlet of the creek into the main river. Hm . . . no fish are rising. He stoops to stash a spare can of beer in the icy gravel, scattering the little troutlings. Then, red-faced and panting, he lurches up river through the brambles to the old deer crossing at the gravel ford. Another unseen deer blows and stamps—this time across the river. *"Whew,"* the fisherman answers, mopping his forehead on his sleeve, easing off the packsack, squatting there batting mosquitoes and sipping his beer and watching the endless marvel of the unwinding river. The sun is low, most of the water is wrapped in shadow, a pregnant stillness prevails. Lo, the smaller fish are beginning to rise. Ah, there's a good one working! Still watching, he gropes in the bunch grass for his rod case. All fantasies are now forgotten.

Just above this shallow gravel ford there is a wide, slick, still-running and hopelessly unwadable expanse of deep water—a small lake within the river. I have never seen a spot quite like it. On my side of this pool there is a steep-sloping sandy bank surmounted by a jungle of tag alders. On the far opposite bank there is an abrupt, rocky, root-lined ledge lined with clumps of out-curving birches, rising so tall, their quivering small leaves glittering in the dying sun like a million tinkling tambourines. But another good fish rises, so to hell with the tambourines. . . . For in this mysterious pool dwell some of the biggest brown trout I know. This is my secret spot. Fiendishly evasive, these trout are not only hard to catch but, because of their habitat, equally hard to fish. The fisherman's trouble is double.

A boat or canoe invariably invokes mutiny and puts them down—at least any vessel captained by me. My most extravagant power casts from the ford below usually do the same or else fall short, though not always. The tall fly-catching tag alders on my side discourage any normal bank approach consistent with retaining one's sanity. (Hacking down the tag alders would not only be a chore, but would at once spoil the natural beauty of the place and erect a billboard proclaiming: BIG TROUT RESIDE HERE!) Across the way the steep rocky bank and the clusters of birches and tangled small stuff make it impossible properly to present a fly or to handle a decent trout if one could. The place is a fisherman's challenge and a fisherman's dream: lovely, enchanted, and endlessly tantalizing. I love it.

Across from me, closer to the other side and nicely out of range, there is a slow whirl-around of silky black water, endlessly revolving. Nearly everything floating into the pool—including most natural flies—takes at least one free ride around this lazy merry-go-round. For many insects it is frequently the last ride, for it is here that the fat tribal chieftains among the brown trout foregather at dusk to roll and cavort. Many a happy hour have I spent fruitlessly stalking these wise old trout. The elements willing, occasionally I even outwit one. Once last summer I outwitted two—all in the same ecstatic evening. Only now can I venture coherently to speak of it.

I had stashed my beer in the creek mouth as usual and had puffed my way through the tangle up to the deep pool. There they were feeding in the merry-go-round, *both* of them, working as only big trout can work—swiftly, silently, accurately—making genteel little pneumatic sounds, like a pair of rival dowagers sipping their cups of tea. I commanded myself to sit down and open my shaking can of beer. Above and below the pool as far as I could see the smaller brook trout were flashily feeding, but tonight the entire pool belonged to these two quietly ravenous pirates. "Slp, slp" continued the pair as I sat there ruefully wondering what a Hewitt or LaBranche or Bergman would do.

"They'd probably rig up and go fishin'," at length I sensibly told myself in an awed stage whisper. So I arose and with furious nonchalance rigged up, slowly, carefully, ignoring the trout as though time were a dime and there were no fish rising in the whole river, dressing the line just so, scrubbing out the fine twelve-foot leader with my bar of mechanic's soap. I even managed to whistle a tuneless obbligato to the steady "Slp, slp, slp. . . ."

And now the fly. I hadn't the faintest idea what fly to use as it was too shadowy and far away to even guess what they were taking. Suddenly I had *the* idea: I had just visited the parlor of Peterson, one of my favorite fly tiers, and had persuaded him to tie up a dozen exquisitely small palmer-tied creations on stiff gray hackle. I had got them for buoyancy to roll-cast on a certain difficult wooded pond. Why not try one here? Yet how on earth would I present it?

Most fishermen, including this one, cling to their pet stupidities as they would to a battered briar or an old jacket; and their dogged persistence in wrong methods and general wrongheadedness finally wins them a sort of grudging admiration, if not many trout. Ordinarily I would have put these fish down, using my usual approach, in about two casts of a squirrel's tail. Perhaps the sheer hopelessness of the situation gave me the wit to solve it. Next time I'll doubtless try to cast an anvil out to stun them. "The *only* controlled cast I can possibly make here," I muttered, hoarse with inspiration, "is a *roll* cast . . . yes—it's that or nothing, Johnny me bye." If it is in such hours that greatness is born, then this was my finest hour.

Anyone who has ever tried successfully to roll-cast a dry fly under any circumstances, let alone cross-stream in a wide river with conflicting currents and before two big dining trout, knows that baby sitting for colicky triplets is much easier. For those who know not the roll cast, I shall simply say that it is a heaven-born cast made as though throwing an overhand half-hitch with a rope tied to a stick, no backcast being involved. But a roll cast would pull my fly under; a decent back cast was impossible; yet I had to present a floating fly. *That* was my little problem.

"Slp, slp, slp," went the trout, oblivious to the turmoil within me.

Standing on the dry bank in my moccasins I calmly stripped out line and kept rolling it upstream and inshore—so as not to disturb my quarry—

until I figured my fly was out perhaps ten feet more than the distance between me and the steadily feeding trout. And that was plenty far. On each test cast the noble little gray hackle quickly appeared and rode beautifully. "God bless Peterson," I murmured. Then I began boldly to arc the cast out into the main river, gauging for distance, and then—suddenly—I drew in my breath and drew up my slack and rolled out the fatal business cast. *This was it.* The fly lit not fifteen feet upstream from the top fish—right in the down whirl of the merry-go-round. The little gray hackle bobbed up, circled a trifle uncertainly and then began slowly to float downstream like a little major. The fish gods had smiled. Exultant, I mentally reordered three dozen precious little gray hackles. Twelve feet, ten feet, eight . . . holding my breath, I also offered up a tiny prayer to the roll cast. "Slp, slp . . ." The count-down continued—five feet, two feet, one foot, "slp"—and he was on.

Like many big browns, this one made one gorgeous dripping leap and bore down in a power dive, way deep, dogging this way and that like a bulldog shaking a terrier. Keeping light pressure, I coaxed rather than forced him out of the merry-go-round. Once out I let him conduct the little gray hackle on a subterranean tour and then—and then—I saw and heard his companion resume his greedy rise, "Slp, slp." *That* nearly unstrung me; as though one's fishing companion had yawned and casually opened and drunk a bottle of beer while one was sinking for the third time.

Like a harried dime-store manager with the place full of reaching juvenile delinquents, I kept trying to tend to business and avoid trouble and watch the sawing leader and the other feeding trout all at the same time. Then my trout began to sulk and bore, way deep, and the taut leader began to vibrate and whine like the plucked string of a harp. What if he snags a deadhead? I fretted. Just then a whirring half-dozen local ducks rushed upstream in oiled flight, banking away when they saw this strange tableau, a queer man standing there holding a straining hoop. Finally worried, I tried a little more pressure, gently pumping, and he came up in a sudden rush and rolled on his side at my feet like a length of cordwood. Then he saw his tormentor and was down and away again.

The nighthawks had descended to join the bats before I had him folded and dripping in the net, stone dead. "Holy old Mackinaw!" I said, numb-wristed and weak with conquest. A noisy whippoorwill announced dusk. I blew on my matted gray hackle and, without changing flies, on the next business cast I was on to his partner—the senior partner, it developed—which I played far into the night, the nighthawks and bats wheeling all about me. Two days later all three of us appeared in the local paper; on the front page, mind you. I was the one in the middle, the short one with the fatuous grin.

Next season I rather think I'll visit my secret place once or twice.

Ju-Ju Travel

BY DAVE AMES

I can tell you straight-up, without flinching, that one of the reasons I like to read Dave Ames so much is because he makes me feel like young again. And I am not a young man.

In this one, Dave Ames launches a bonefishing trip with the kind of youthful exuberance I still try to latch onto whenever I can and I distinctly remember having all the time when I was a lot younger.

Dave Ames' True Love and the Woolly Bugger *(Greycliff Publishing, Helena, Montana, 1996), from which this selection is taken, is a collection of tales you do not want to miss. I don't know whether to call this Montana veteran a "guide who writes" or a "writer who guides." Actually, it appears to me he is so adept at both that he can be called anything he likes.*

An Invitation: Top Ten Reasons To Go Bonefishing

10. You have to go—the bonefish won't come to you.
9. It's cold here. It's warm there.
8. Adrenalin—it's legal, and it's free.
7. Bob Marley and the Wailers.
6. Thong bikinis.
5. Snook and tarpon.
4. Banana daiquiris.
3. It's a good excuse to get a new reel.
2. You get more frequent flier miles.

And the number one reason to go bonefishing:

$E = mc^2$, where E is your Ecstasy, m is your mind, and c is a constant equal to the speed of bonefish squared.

Bonefishing

I scanned through the trip details in the following pages of the invitation. Round-trip airfare (including inter-island shuttles) for under five hundred dollars. We would be camping on a beach, under the palm trees, next to a bar and restaurant. There were bonefish flats within walking distance. It sounded too good to be true.

"If there was a Hall of Fame for travel agents," I thought, "The Duke should be enshrined."

As usual, I was broke. Although the trip would be cheap, it wouldn't be free. I had never before been bonefishing, but had always wanted to try it. I would just have to sell something.

I won't miss the truck. I'm still not sure about my soul.

That's Ju-Ju.

It all began with the highest winds yet, gusting to thirty knots. Duke and I were hunkered back to the wind on a weathered cypress dock, deep in the heart of the Caribbean, watching the sun rise, sucking coffee, waiting for our guide.

"There he is." Duke pointed to Garfield's red boat smashing through the whitecaps.

I watched the boat wallow through the wave troughs up to the dock. "I'd hate to see you get seasick on your birthday," I said.

The Duke threw his fishing bag down into the boat. "Fish till you puke," he replied.

"Goddom it!" Garfield called up from his boat. He spoke Carib, a staccato and melodic blend of several different languages, including English and Reggae. "Diss win' fury lok all bad hell mon."

"It sure is," said Duke.

"Heymon?" Garfield spit sentences like bursts of machine gun fire on full automatic. "Dat cas' might be dere no way dis day?"

"It will be all right," said Duke.

"Goddom mebbee?"

"No worries mon," replied the Duke.

I stared blankly at the two of them. It sounded familiar, like something I should be able to put together, but all I picked out was a whizzing bullet of a word here or there. It was so very, very fast. I turned to look at Duke. "What's going on?" I asked.

The wind caught the brim of my hat as I lifted my head, and it sailed off the dock. Duke jumped into the boat, then plucked my hat from the swells. "Garfield wants to know if we can cast in this wind," he translated.

I set the wet ball cap firmly back on my head. "We'll have to try. It's too early to go sit in the bar."

"Crazymon." Garfield laughed with delight as we roared off to sea. "Dem fly whack de head dis day, I see dat."

We were fishing a submerged volcano in the lee side of the Lesser Antilles. Unlike the other towering islands in this archipelago, we fished a land low and flat, a classic coral atoll crowning the peak of a sunken mountain, pulverized by hurricanes through the millennia into an ellipse of white sand and powdered shells now inching only twenty-six feet above the water, a land basically neither more nor less than a huge tidal flat. A good place for bonefish.

It is also a good place to sink a boat. The island is nearly surrounded by the most dangerous coral reef in the Caribbean—if statistics can be believed—for it is littered with the bleached skeletons of more shipwrecks than any other in the arc of islands stretching from the Florida Keys to Venezuela. Shipwrecks (like grizzly bears) can help keep a wilderness in character, and only 120 full-time inhabitants now populate the twenty square miles of this island. The developers and cruise ships haven't made it this far. It's too dangerous.

Much of the shoreline remains in a near natural state. Mangroves. Dunes, Cactus and thorny scrub. It is a harsh, desert land where life is dependent on the fresh water found only briefly during and after the intermittent rains, and in the faint light of the morning star as we bashed through the waves, it was desolation so beautiful it made me feel like dancing.

"Bonefish don't need no steenking condos," I yelled over the wind.

Duke nodded. He knew what I was thinking. Bonefish grew up in the family of the most primitive of living fish with hard skeletons, and shared the seas with the last of the dinosaurs. We bounced along through a tropical land in many ways similar to the Montana of 250 million years ago, when the Madison Limestone was forming.

Perhaps, even now, I wondered, the rich mineral veins of the next Montana were being formed in volcano beneath the boat. Perhaps, in the next Gondawana-like shift of the continental plates, Africa and South America would re-join, pushing the accumulated rock layers in this shallow sea into high cliffs sheltering a mountain trout river full of futuristic stone flies, and someone would find the gold, and put in a mine, and maybe kill the bugs first then the trout.

That's Ju-Ju. What comes around in the cosmic cycle, goes around. You can run, but you can't hide. Find the underlying patterns to life, and you'll catch more fish. Understand the patterns, and you'll have more fun. Happiness is the insight that comes from accepting your place in the circle of life.

Some days it all seems so clear; for me, those moments of clarity come only when I am as far into the wilderness as I can get. I was on the very brink of understanding that blue-sky morning when Garfield suddenly threw the wheel to the right. I was hurled against the bulkhead, and the boat swerved sharply toward the deeper water.

Garfield pointed and called, "Mud mon."

"My God," said the Duke. "My God." He grabbed up his rod. "It must be a quarter of a mile long."

I stared wildly at the ocean. My moment of clarity was utterly gone. I didn't see a thing.

Bonefish, at times, feed in large schools, sucking water through their gills and snorting it through their mouths, blasting holes in the sand, then digging with body and tail down after crabs and shrimp and clams like a herd of piscine Rototillers. The silt they kick up creates what is known in bonefishing vernacular as a "mud," and the experts call it easy fishing.

That much, I knew.

It sounded good in the book, but out here in the ocean—in bonefish central—it wasn't easy at all. I couldn't even *find* a mud that was supposedly as long as a city block. Garfield cut the engine and we drifted in the swells. I searched frantically for the phantom mud. The Duke was now casting hard into the wind. I had absolutely no idea what I was supposed to be doing.

"Where the hell is the mud," I shouted.

"We be in de mud mon."

"We're IN the mud?" I was about to panic. "We ARE?" I wanted to catch a bonefish so badly that I was leaping up and down with excitement. "I don't see a thing!" I screamed over the wind.

Garfield smiled. "No worries. Jus' cas' mon."

I ripped line from my reel. We cast furiously from the pitching boat, hurtling before the wind, blown so fast that even the heaviest of our flies had no chance of getting down to the bottom feeding bonefish.

"It's too deep," yelled the Duke, "We need sinking lines."

In the next instant the dark green water filled with the quicksilver of flashing fish. "Jocks! Strip fas' mon. Dey fight good ass all bad hell."

We were into a school of jacks, blue runners, predators feeding on bait fish, which in turn were feeding on the muddy smorgasbord of the sea now being served up by the rooting bonefish. Garfield jerked his lure back in quick bursts. A blue runner smashed his epoxy bonefish fly. He set the spinning rod in a holder in the gunwale, the fish still on, slashing, attracting other jacks within casting distance of our flies.

We sailed through the mud three times, shake-and-bake streamer fishing for jacks up to about two pounds, no bones about it, biding our time, waiting for Garfield's sixth sense to tell him—on this particular day—when the bonefish would begin feeding on the flats. The sun was well off the horizon and the tide was coming when Garfield said: "Dis coul' be de time."

He opened the throttle wide, and the boat fishtailed through a tight figure eight over the school of mudding fish. "Godda be makin' dem fishes to movin'," he explained, then as he turned the boat toward shore he ordered, "Siddown now, mon."

A few minutes of racing and the green water went white. The water was only a few feet deep when Garfield cut the motor, and held a finger to his lips. He poled quietly through the shallows, and slipped the anchor over the side. A pair of black-tipped sharks swam past, every few feet leaving swirls of sand as their tails swept the bottom like brooms.

"What fly should I use," I asked, not thinking about sharks as long as my leg.

"Try dis firs'." Garfield handed me a fly about two inches long, with a gold mylar body, orange marabou tail, soft grizzly hackle wings, and a long tuft of white bucktail.

I looked it over uncertainly. "What is it?"

"De bonefish special." It did not look like much of anything I would have expected to swim by my feet, but then, a royal wulff does not look like any mayfly I have ever seen either. When in doubt: don't argue with the guide. I tied on the special.

"Spread ou' mon," said Garfield. We scattered, Duke and I on either side of Garfield. "Now slow walk wid de current, bit fasser den de tide, den dose fishes don' smell troubles til too domn late for dem."

We began walking. There is nothing—not friends, not books, not lawyers, guns, or money—nothing that can prepare you for this moment when you realize a dream, for this moment when you first stalk a flat scanning for bonefish. Every nerve ending is completely alive, and you are awash in the beauty. It is an incredible experience. There is nothing that can prepare you for this moment because bonefish in the water, for all intents and purposes, are invisible.

"Dere dey are mon," hissed Garfield, pointing, "Two tree dozen bones righ' dere."

I strained to see in the surface glare, but came up empty.

"Got 'em," said Duke.

Where? Damn it, Where! I still didn't see anything that could possibly be a fish.

Duke was leaning hard forward, bent at the waist, peering intently at the water. He false cast once, twice, and shot line out into the blankness of the sea. Duke stripped in line slowly, then stood up and said, "They were too far away."

"Goddom fish. Dey turn bad scare."

"Did they smell us?"

"No mon, dat dere coul' be de scare bird." He pointed to the dark shadow on the bright water of a low-flying seagull.

The Duke nodded his assent. "So, what do you think? About twenty fish in that school?"

"Yah mon, bout dot."

"All right." The Duke took a deep breath. "That was fun. Let's go find some more."

Twenty bonefish? Where? Where!

We turned, and started slowly down the flat. I looked as I had never looked before, thinking, *I want a fish so bad,* turning each little clump of turtle grass into a fish, each little sparkle in each little wave into a fish, thinking, *this is fishy water,* pulse racing, staring into the glint and the glare and the ripples in the sand until I was adrift in the shimmering reflections, mesmerized, an unlit powder keg of nerves with a short fuse.

Garfield tapped me on the shoulder. "Dere dey are mon," he hissed.

I'll admit it. I was a mite startled when he unexpectedly slipped up behind me and lit the fuse.

"Don' jump mon!" Garfield grunted under his breath. "Cas'! Now!"

"Cast?" I wondered if my hair had turned white. "Where! I haven't seen a fish yet."

"Jus' cas' mon, hurry now."

He pointed. I eyeballed the angle of his arm, and flopped out a cast.

"Good mon. Jus' wait. O.K. mon, strip slow, strip slow. Stop now. Stop. Dey chase it."

"Oh," I thought suddenly calm, "so those are bonefish."

I had the strip, but not the stop, and seven bonefish had materialized at my feet. A fish followed my fly, watching it creeping through the sand, the fly now so close that my tippet was in the rod guides. I froze, crouched low with my butt on the bottom, my breath caught up in my throat. The bonefish that had been following my fly then turned away; and swam confidently past like I was just another errant mangrove. When the last fish passed, I turned to cast. The bonefish caught the movement, and the school vanished like a puff of smoke in a strong wind.

The entire episode—from first sighting to final disappearance—had taken only a few moments. These fish give you as much of a chance to present a fly as lightning gives you to leap aside; and at times, the cast to an approaching bonefish happens so quickly that it doesn't seem as if it happened at all.

"What h-h-happened?" I sputtered. It was so fast: There had been no time to think.

Garfield just smiled, ear to ear, a huge goofy grin with his big red tongue flopped to the side, shrugging wide with open shoulders and outstretched arms, a grin that started in the soles of his feet and ended in the roots of his hair.

It was a great grin worth a thousand words, a shrug every guide should master, a grin explaining why in the same feeding lane some trout will take a nymph, some a pupae, and others only a #23 spent-wing midge tied on a hook hand forged in Kenya just after sunrise on the winter solstice.

"There are some things," said the grin, "that just are."

I took a deep breath. Now that it was over, I was twitching like a puppet on a string. I took another long, deep breath, and exhaled slowly. "Did the bonefish take the f-fly?" I asked.

"No, mon, not dis time," said Garfield.

"Should I switch flies?"

"Coul' be, mon, but better you don' move de fly so fas'. De bait he don' outrun de fish—de bait he try hide quick bury in de san'."

Bones so close, I thought, *I could have touched them.* I swallowed hard to get my heart out of my mouth. Garfield was probably right, but as I looked at the fly, it just didn't feel right, and if you can't fish with confidence, you can't catch fish.

"Garfield," I said, "I have a feeling."

He nodded. "Goddom right. I see dat by da way you jump."

I was hearing from a familiar friend. The animal within (that bundle of fur hidden deep in our most ancient web of nerves that can still sniff the evening wind for an approaching storm) was calling out. That little voice of intuition has often been all that stood between me, a day of fishing, and a skunk dinner—when the animal calls, I answer.

"Tell me mon," said Garfield, "Wot you t'inking 'bout?"

"I think we should match the hatch," I replied. Throughout the morning small brown crabs had been scuttling about the bottom, disappearing in tiny puffs of sand as we drew near. Bonefish eat lots of crabs, up to nearly half of their diet according to some studies.

I tied on a McCrab. Originally designed as a permit fly, the McCrab is a realistic imitation of a crab, with legs of knotted rubber bands and bead-chain eyes. It is also heavy with lead and bulky with clipped deer hair, and even under the best of conditions it casts about as well as a carburetor.

Garfield eyed the heavy fly doubtfully.

"You cas' dat beeg t'ing in dis wind?"

"It won't be pretty, but I can do it."

"You try dat cas' firs'."

"Here goes," I said, and hauled a hard back cast into the wind. I leaned into the forward cast, putting everything I had into it, powering forward to shoot as much line as possible, painting a long, wide casting stroke then snapping with my whole body as the loop unrolled.

Garfield whistled, long and low.

"You right. Dat not pretty."

I could only groan.

"You bleedin'." Garfield shook his head.

I had been knocked nearly senseless. The speeding crab took me smack-dab in the center of the soft spot at the top of the brain stem in the back of my head. I fought nausea and swayed in place, gathering courage for another cast, finally trying a modified roll cast with a tail wind assist.

"Dat good 'nough mon," shrugged Garfield.

I shook my head. Good enough seemed too generous a description. "You think so?"

"What I really t'ink is bes' you don' kill you dead dis fine day."

We turned and resumed our slow stalk. The wind, the tide, and the sun were all to our backs. With the sun well up and behind us, the task of spotting fish would never be easier. Even so, that did not mean it was easy. You have to remember that to a beginner bonefish are invisible, and only occasionally reveal themselves in one of several ways.

The best is the silver flash of tailing fish, when the sun sparkles on the translucent tails of feeding fish in shallow water. Tailing fish are generally the easiest to see, and since they are preoccupied with feeding, also the easiest to approach and catch. Tailing fish are an avid bonefishman's wet dream.

Sometimes there will be nervous water, water that is somehow different, water that bulges or moves or flattens or chops or vees. It is a mirage, a piece in a wet, sandy puzzle that is oddly out of place. It is as much a feeling as a vision—like nymph fishing for trout.

Sometimes in bright sunlight you will see the dark shadows of bonefish flitting across a sandy bottom, once in a while you might actually see a fish.

Usually a first-time bonefisherman won't see any of this, and nothing is all I had seen when Garfield again whistled low under his breath.

He pointed urgently with both hands at the water dead ahead. Duke looked. He saw. He cast. I still hadn't seen any fish, but I was getting used to it. I flipped my line up and out, and then the loudest sound on the flat was the Duke's reel screaming as a hooked bonefish raced for safety. In the time it took for me to look up at Duke his fish was already the length of the fly line away.

"He take it mon," hissed Garfield.

"I know," I said, "Look at all the backing that fish pulled off! And he hasn't even slowed down yet."

"NO MON! YOU!"

"Me?" I thought. I turned to where my line was moving slowly upstream into the current. It had to be a fish. I set the hook with a hard strip strike. It came up solid. I had done it! And I hadn't even seen it. Whatever 'it' was.

The hooked fish darted in tiny circles, staying with the school, not yet quite sure what the problem was. I cleared the line, all ready for the run. I couldn't wait for that legendary bonefish run. Then my line went slack. "No, No, NO!" I yelled. "What happened?"

Garfield scratched his chest and looked at the sky. "He don' have it good."

I pulled in my line, and checked the hook. "It's still sharp. What went wrong?"

"Coul' be dat fly domn beeg. Bonefish got de tiny mouth."

"Is it too big for bones? Should I change it?"

"Mebbe not dis day. Dem fishes was after dat crab fly."

"I don't have any smaller crabs."

"Maybe jus' pop dem bones. Hit dem harder de nex' time."

"O.K. mon." We waited for the Duke to land his fish. It was enormous.

"Maybe eight pounds," he said, holding the fish out as I snapped the obligatory hero shot with my camera. "Wow. These are big Fish you have here Garfield."

The Duke released that bone in the shallow water, and then another, before we worked our way back to the boat and the next flat at the head end of a long sand spit. Here, the bottom was rough with hummocks, and spotted with clumps of coral and undulating turtle grass. The mottled reflections would make finding the fish that much more difficult.

"Now how am I going to see these fish?" I asked. There was frustration in my voice.

"No worries mon," replied Garfield. "I coul' be you eyes."

We slipped overboard, walking the ridge of the flat, calf deep in the shallowest of the water. Garfield had the midas touch on this day: We found fish everywhere he stopped, and it could not have been more than two minutes before his shrill whistle cut through the wind. I followed his pointing finger, and for the first time I saw—off to the side and already nearly past me—four dark shadows.

"Ai–i–i–i," cried Garfield.

I had changed casting directions to put the fly ahead of the advancing fish. The back cast was closer to the guide than the forward cast to the fish, but it didn't seem to matter, because as soon as the fly hit the water the bonefish jostled each other in a leisurely race toward a crab dinner. I stripped the fly back in slow bursts. A coil of line hung down into the water from the rod. I had pulled in ten feet of line when I finally felt the take.

"Remember, mon," whispered Garfield. "Pop 'im good."

The line tightened as the bonefish swam away. I counted one, two and hit the fish like I was skid-and-release woolly bugger fishing on 1x for autumn brown trout. I wanted that hook to pierce deep into that bony mouth. I wanted that fish to know who was boss.

I never was very good at upper level management. One nanosecond later the dilithium crystals glowed as the bonefish went into warp drive. The line whistled as it exploded from the water, leaving a wide arc of spray glistening in the sun. The slack was whipped into a loop that lassoed the tail piece of the rod as it shot past, and the line twanged to an abrupt halt.

Something had to give. It wasn't the fish.

"Hey, wot hoppen?" said Garfield as the line went slack.

"The leader snapped." I held up the rod, and loosened the loop of line from the butt.

Garfield shook his head. "I tole you, you won' stop dese fishes."

"That's three strikes," I thought, wondering if that meant I was out as we trudged back to the boat through the chop. "Damn," I said. "damn!"

"O.K. my frien'," said Garfield, looking over at me in his yellow shirt. "One other chance dis fine morn' you get."

It was the last chance before Africa, at the east end of the island, where centuries of pounding waves from the Atlantic Ocean have dumped out a long shallow shoal of broken coral. The square bulk of a wrecked freighter squats firmly on the nearby reef, just past the two rounded piles of empty pink conch shells, tens of thousands of shells discarded by commercial divers, rising now since the last hurricane in huge mounds like pink breasts each the size of a Trailways bus from the sea.

We cruised through the deeper aquamarine water between the symmetrical breasts and the shoal, just off the foaming white seam delineating the edge of the dark olive flat. We rounded the point of the island into the wind, and the waves were larger: so much larger that the largest of the waves began breaking over the bow into the open boat.

"Dere dey are," called Garfield.

We jumped up. At least one hundred bonefish were gliding through the shallows along the edge of the flat. You couldn't miss them from our perch high in the boat. Garfield raced past the fish, and water now poured in over the bow as we crashed through the waves.

"Where's the bail bucket," I yelled. Garfield just laughed.

"No worries. You get dat fish now. We cut dem off at de pass," he yelled back, John Wayne in dreadlocks, a testament to the power of satellite television and the New World culture.

We wallowed in the surf as Garfield cut the engine. Three-foot high waves crashed about us on the shoal. Duke crouched in the bow, rod in hand, poised for a leap into the shallow water just beyond the breaking waves. The wind and the surf roared. We surged past jagged heads of living coral, and Garfield dropped the anchor. Literally.

"Bad t'ing, mon," he cried, "De rope loose."

The loop at the end of the anchor rope had pulled free from the stanchion. There was nothing now to hold us back, and we were driven quickly out of control toward the jagged shoal.

"Here they come," said the Duke, who had never taken his eyes off the fish. He was focused, in the zone, ready to catch his fourth bonefish of the morning, and completely unaware we were about to become the latest in a long line of shipwrecks on the island.

"Jump Mon," cried Garfield, and the Duke leaped for the foaming line of surf at the edge of the flat. He came up just short, and crashed down on a coral head jutting up from the deeper water.

There is something you should know about the Duke. He is a big boy. He was a pulling guard on his college football team, and was invited to training camp as a free agent by the Dolphins. When he hits something, it stays hit. The reef never stood a chance.

The fragile shell of coral burst on impact. The Duke plummeted through sea fans and staghorn, buried waist deep in living reef. The highest of the waves lapped at his chest. The fish were close, and moving fast. He was ready. He began his cast. Then he screamed.

In frustration. The sea birds had built a nest in his reel when his back was turned, and he watched, helpless, line hopelessly tangled, as at least a hundred bonefish darted past twenty feet away. He leaned forward, arms raised, fingers clenched, as if he might go after them with only his bare hands and teeth.

Meanwhile, back at the boat, I hung backwards off the bow, fending away the coral with my feet. Garfield fired up the outboard, and edged in reverse away from the crashing line of surf.

Garfield laughed again. "Jump Mon! De waves is bad here."

"Are you crazy?" I yelled, looking at the Duke in his cocoon of coral. "Get closer!"

"Dis de bes' I coul' do you."

I looked at the surf. "No way," I yelled. "Get closer!"

"Coul' be prolly you see dere more fishes. Now *hurry* mon!"

More fish. Some things you do because you want to, and some things you do because you have to. I jumped, rod held high, out into the deep blue water, and hoped for the best. A curling wave snatched me up like driftwood, then dropped me gently on the flat and ebbed away.

"Huh," I thought. I put my hat back on. "That was easy."

"Fish down to de conch pile," yelled Garfield over the roar of the Evinrude as he sped away.

Duke had clambered from his hole, and was inspecting himself for damages. "Not a scratch," he said, "I went straight down."

"Lucky." We watched yet another shark swim by. They were everywhere.

"I kept waiting for the pain," he said, "and it never came."

"I still can't believe you jumped."

"I didn't even stop to think about it." The Duke poured the water out of his boxes of flies, then added, "It wouldn't be the Third World, without a little adventure now and then."

"So far, so good," I agreed. "There sure seems to be a lot of fish on this island anyway."

The Duke was already looking down the flat. "Let's go find out."

We shuffled down the flat, leaving a light cloud of green silt in our wake. The sun was now off to the side, and the surface glare was much worse. It had already been a long day. The adrenaline was wearing off. The bottom shimmered like a hypnotist's crystal. My eyes were tired. I hadn't admitted it but I was done fishing, and was just walking, when the Duke whistled.

"Bones! Twelve o'clock high."

My torpor evaporated. I scanned the flat. Nothing. "Where?" "Where?"

"Just past that little mangrove twig. Tailers."

And then I saw the tails. There were four fish, cruising haphazardly about one hundred feet in front of us. All the tails were big, but one tail soared majestically above the others, gleaming huge like the sail on a silver-plated wind surfer.

Life isn't fair. Duke saw the fish, but the fish turned toward me. I was to get the cast at these fish, three large fish and then Moby, a great white whale of a bonefish, a fish that to this day remains the largest bonefish I have ever seen. And it happened on my first day of flats fishing.

That's Ju-Ju.

"Huge fish," whistled the Duke. "Take him."

And finally, for the first time that day, tuned in and turned on, I found the zone. Action, reaction, and a sweet cast later the fly dropped gently in the waves, where the surging current swung the fly just so in front of the rooting fish. The biggest fish turned like the wind on a mountain lake, his pointed tail spearing up shiny in the air as he went nose down to suck in the crab. BAM, I set the hook.

Bonefish swim, at top speed, at about thirty-five miles an hour, or fifty feet per second. Twelve seconds later that fish was two football fields away. It was a run better by at least two kilograms of purest grandeur than any other I had ever known, and in about the time it takes to pee your pants the fish had ripped out nearly all of my backing.

The fish could easily have spooled me, but he stopped in the shallow water just above the blue water trough at the end of the flat. The conch pile breasts glowed pink in the sun just across the deep channel, rising from a shallow reef that represented safe haven for the bonefish. There was just one problem with the escape route the bonefish had picked, and it had sharp teeth.

The deep blue water trough between the bonefish and the relative safety of the shell mounts was barracuda country. The bonefish was loathe to venture past the drop-off into the deeper water; because a hooked bonefish is a bonefish in trouble, and barracuda can smell trouble.

The fish held for the moment and I worked down the flat, slowly gaining lost line. I know now that I should have been running Moby down at flank speed, taking backing as quickly as possible, but I was in a daze, blown away like dust by the power of that first run.

Therefore I wasn't anything even remotely resembling ready when the fish blitzed down into the deeper water, run number two, a moving target intent on escape, every second fifty feet closer to the conch piles.

"He'll cut the line on the coral," I yelled. I tried to stop him, and palmed the reel. It was like trying to stop a bull elk with a band-aid. Pop, just like that, the fish was gone. I crumbled butt first to the bottom of the sea. Sitting head in hands, sea salt burning my chapped lips, I stared into the shiny water. The waves lapped at my armpits, and mud oozed into my shorts as I sunk deep into a well of abject dejection. The Duke came over, fingering at the collar of his XXL T-shirt.

"I farmed him," I mumbled. "I can't believe I farmed him."

"Your learning curve," he said, "was steep today."

"What a fish," I cursed softly to the sand.

Garfield roared up, ready to take us back to camp.

"Goddom it," he yelled, "I tole you. You can't stop dese fishes."

"Goddom it yourself," I mumbled down into the waves.

"You need a beer," said the Duke, looking down to where I sat in the mud. "Bad."

Cocktail Hour

When you need a beer, bad, you don't want anything to get in your way. Fortunately, it was downwind all the way back to camp; more importantly, we were camped beside a bar.

"I'm buying," I said when we pulled up to the dock.

We walked the fifty feet to Neptune's Treasure, and sat at a round table on the stone veranda, in the cool shade of a grove of coconut trees. Beers and mixed drinks were an American dollar, we kept a tab, and poured our own on the honor system. The ocean lapped at our feet. Palm fronds rustled in the languid sea breeze. Sailboats swayed in the chop.

Just as there are times to drink and times to drink too much, there are places to drink and places to drink too much. We were in the right place at the right time.

"Now, this," said the Duke, toasting the azure sky with iced gin and olives, "is camping."

"Happy birthday," I said. I leaned on the beat-up guitar I had borrowed.

"Feliz cumpleaños a tú," sang Juaníta, Gloria, y María, the singing sisters of San Juan, in the tight three-part harmony that only family does best.

The girls were off-duty lounge lizards, cruise ship entertainment for the blue hair and polyester crowd, and as far away from the luxury liners as they could get in one day. They were on vacation. It showed.

"It you birt'day?" asked Garfield, "How man'?"

"Forty-seven," lied the Duke.

"Tell you wha'." Garfield smiled at the girls and stood up. "I come back later, we go into town for birt'day party."

Garfield left, and the singing sisters went to get ready for dinner. I just couldn't sit still. I exchanged the guitar for a pair of pliers and a knife, and began prying on the end cap of the reel seat on my brand new saltwater fly rod.

The Duke looked over. "What are you doing?" he asked.

"This end cap is stuck." I gave the seat a vigorous twist. "I couldn't get my fighting butt in today." I squeezed the pliers and gave a mighty yank. "These fish are so big I'm going to need it."

The Duke looked puzzled. "Those end caps just pop off," he said. "It shouldn't take a pair of pliers."

"Finally," I replied. "There it comes," and with one last jerk, I wrenched free the end cap. Jagged chunks of coca-bola wood and hardened glue clung to the metal. Something was wrong. Very wrong.

"Hey," said the Duke. "That's my rod."

Uh-oh. Same case, different rod. I had been using Duke's six weight instead of my eight, and I had just ripped off the end of his reel seat. Even by the standards I set for myself, this was pretty stupid. I couldn't believe it—all morning I had been casting carburetors in a typhoon with a six weight noodle of a rod.

"Send me a bill," I said. "What can I say but I'm sorry."

At least the Duke understood what I was going through. This wasn't his first rodeo. "The needle," he replied, "went in deep for you today."

I nodded. He had hit the nail right on the head. I was trembling, beside myself with excitement, only partially aware of my surroundings, newly addicted to a sport that is as habit forming as cocaine, and way more expensive. I was hooked. I was a bonefish junkie.

"Now," I said, "I'm going to have to get a job."

"Good luck." Duke bent low to light a cigarette in the wind. "Just promise me one thing."

"What's that?"

"Don't try and fix any more of my fly rods."

And then, after a dinner of fresh swordfish, it was Saturday night in the islands. We rode with the girls in the back of an open pickup, over sea shell roads, through the dark of a new moon, to the only village on the island, next stop oblivion.

"Dat de Banana Well," called Garfield. The stick walls of the only dance hall in town bulged in and out under the deafening beat of steel drum music. A six-foot fluorescent banana glowed yellow above the door. We walked in to one of the all-time great bar scenes.

The wet air dripped with the musk of sweaty dancers. The pungent smell of exotic spices—of nutmeg and cinnamon and myrrh—hung in the air. So did an inflatable Budweiser blimp, grey, red, and slightly flaccid, dangling from the grass-thatched ceiling and festooned with blinking Christmas lights. A chaotic potpourri of sailors from their boats, and dark natives with flashing gold teeth and great round hoop earrings, were dancing up a white and African fury.

A thin young black man approached us, then lashed out with his right fist. Garfield quickly punched back, then they gently rubbed outstretched fists top together to bottom in the local variation on a handshake.

"De welcome coul' be fo' you mon," said the boy.

"Dis be Carlos," said Garfield, and introduced us all around, explaining that Carlos owned the bar. Sort of. Actually it was his father's bar, but his father was off island on a buying trip, and Junior was pouring a lot of free drinks.

Carlos leaned close above the din of music. "You one dem movie star?" he shouted.

"Me?" I pointed to the center of my chest. "In the movies?" I shook my head no.

"T'ing is mon you coul' be de look alike Don Johnson," Carlos said, and rubbed his chin.

I rubbed my own chin, which I had just shaved for the first time in twenty years as part of a Halloween costume. I sported a five-day stubble, but any similarity I had to *Miami Vice* reruns ended right there. It was ridiculous. I look like a movie star like a rabbit looks like a gorilla.

"Not me," I yelled back. I had to laugh.

"Oh." Carlos smiled at me. "I thought maybe coul' be you wid de beach movie mon."

"Movie?" I accepted the cold beer Carlos offered. "What movie?"

Carlos said it wasn't really a movie so much as a commercial, and it was being filmed by a Dutch cruise line. The film crew, knowing that sex sells, hoping to tantalize the folks back home in Amsterdam into a cruise, had been throwing money all over the island building a sea-shell-encrusted shower stall. The shower stall was open to the sea breeze from the waist up; when the cameras finally rolled the stall was to be full of naked actresses showering together against a tropical backdrop of sand, sea, and sky.

"Dat be one dem girls dere," Carlos said, pointing into the corner where your basic blonde Norse Goddess in a halter top lounged with one shoulder against a wall.

"Is that right?" I said, wondering if there were any bonefish flats in the vicinity of where the filming would occur, knowing it didn't matter: I'd fish there anyway.

"Well, coul' be mon wid dat face you fin' de work in de movies." Carlos waved a thin arm at the bartender and bought me another drink.

"I doubt it," I said, "But thanks." I didn't mind small talking the man who was buying, but I'd heard enough about my face. To change the subject, I asked, "Have you lived here all your life?"

"Now dat be de sad question." Carlos looked at his feet. "I be borned on de island, but leave soon jus' de tiny babe."

"You want to talk about it?" It was a rhetorical question. Carlos wore his heart on his sleeve, and it was clear that he wanted to talk. Carlos looked up, and immediately launched into a tale of faded love.

Carlos said his mother left his father when Carlos was too young to remember—when he was a baby not yet two years old. His mother took Carlos to Brazil, and remarried. His mother's new husband had raised Carlos as his own son for over twenty years, and nothing had ever been said to Carlos about his real father.

And then, about six months ago, Carlos and his mother had climbed aboard a bus in downtown Rio. On the back wall of the bus was a four-color glossy poster of a smiling man waist deep in the ocean, holding up a lobster in each hand, advertising a string of Caribbean islands. His mother had seen the poster and shrieked out loud.

"I know the picture," I said. I had seen it on the cover of a travel brochure: The happy black man, his wriggling red lobsters, the blue sea, and the blue sky comprised the quintessential celluloid portrait of everything a vacation in the islands was supposed to be.

"Dat man," mother told son, pointing at the poster, "Dat be you daddy true now back den."

The devout Catholic in his mother saw the picture not as an advertising photograph so good it had to be used, but rather as a sign from Jesus, and then, in the back seat of the bus, after all those years, in a tear-soaked confessional, the whole story of Carlos's true father finally came out. Carlos had come back to the islands to meet his biological father, and was now working the bar his father owned.

"So how do you and your father get along now?" I asked.

"Hey, not so bad. But be big differen' mon."

"I'll bet."

"Hey, how 'bout now some pizza? Coul' be cook up good in de house of mine?"

"No thanks." I politely declined. Carlos was kind of weird, and besides, I wanted to dance. "I'm just not hungry," I added.

I wandered away into the crowd. "Hey, wot Carlos want mon?" said Garfield, when I caught up to him.

"Nothing really." I shrugged. "He just wanted to talk. He said I look like Don Johnson."

Garfield laughed and said, "Dat be good bet. Bes' you know dat boy like boys."

"What?" Recognition dawned in my eyes. That was it. Carlos had been hitting on me. "He's gay?"

"You got all dat right boss."

I considered the ramifications of being gay on an island of 120 people. I didn't envy Carlos his life. One thing was certain: "I'm sure glad I didn't go out for pizza," I said.

The Duke was busy waxing all comers at the pool table out on the porch; Garfield and I looked around for the singing sisters of San Juan. It was a pretty party. We danced. We sang. We poured down the hut specialty—a vicious blend of rum, kahlua, and pineapple/coconut/papaya juice—by the pint. It is not a drink for the faint of heart, and later I melted down next to Juaníta in the fresh air outside by the pool table.

"Chew gonna faint?" She poked me with her index finger.

"I hope not." But then there was really no way of telling what a man high on the hut specialty was capable of.

"¿Que haces aquí?" said the woman on my left. "What are you doing here?"

She was from Colombia, traveling the Caribbean by sailboat with her husband, who was now juggling a pineapple, an orange, and a foil bag of potato chips under a palm tree by the rusted-out hulk of a car balanced on broken cinder blocks.

"Yo soy pescador," I replied, making casting motions with my free arm, the one that was not resting lightly across Juaníta's brown shoulders.

"A feeshermon, como Jesús, ¿No?" said Juaníta, digging a sharp elbow into my side. She had heard quite enough fish stories for one night, thank you very much, and was not in the least bit thrilled with the turn of the conversation. She didn't seem to mind the arm.

"¿Quieres sacar los sabalos?" said Miss Colombia.

"Tarpon?" That got my attention. "¿Dónde?"

"¿Sabalos?" The Duke, radar on, flaps up, zeroed in from twenty feet away. Sabalos was one of the few Spanish words he knew, but he knew it well. He took three giant steps still holding his pool cue and grabbed my arm. "Where?" he said, "Find out where."

I established, in pidgin Spanish, that Miss Colombia had been seeing tarpon at the government pier nearly every night at low tide.

"It's low tide now," said the Duke.

"It's three in the morning," I replied.

"Are you coming or not?"

Talk about a tough decision. It was a question of priorities, and while there aren't many native girls in Montana, there simply aren't *any* tarpon. "Juaníta," I said, "I have to go."

"Wot, chew nuts?" Juaníta leaped up, her dark eyes livid.

I didn't answer Juaníta one way or the other, because the truth is, I'm not sure.

The Best Rainbow Trout Fishing

He sometimes signed his letters "Ernie" when he wrote this piece of journalism for the
Toronto Star Weekly *in 1920. He was 21 years old then and just beginning to flex
the literary muscles that would make the name Ernest Hemingway internationally famous. At the time of his death in 1961, he was called "Papa." The young "Ernie"
had disappeared many, many years before, and with him went the passion for hiking
into the country to fish cold, pure streams for trout. Beginning in the 1930s, "Papa"
went after only the big stuff—marlin, tuna, sharks.*

    *As an avid reader of Hemingway, especially in rereading him in the anthol-
ogy* Hemingway on Fishing, *published by* The Lyons Press *in 2000, I am struck by
the talent he displayed in this little piece. But I am absolutely filled with enchantment
and wonder over the short story, "Big Two-Hearted River," and the Spanish trout fishing scenes in his first novel,* The Sun Also Rises.

    *I can only wish that "Papa" had gone back to the rivers in his prose from
time to time. I'm sure he remembered them all. But when he was writing, he never
went back to them. He never went back to being "Ernie."*

Rainbow trout fishing is as different from brook fishing as prize
fighting is from boxing. The rainbow is called Salmo iridescens by
those mysterious people who name the fish we catch and has recently been introduced into Canadian waters. At present the best
rainbow trout fishing in the world is in the rapids of the Canadian Soo.

    There the rainbow have been taken as large as fourteen pounds from
canoes that are guided through the rapids and halted at the pools by Ojibway
and Chippewa boatmen. It is a wild and nerve-frazzling sport and the odds are
in favor of the big trout who tear off thirty or forty yards of line at a rush and
then will sulk at the base of a big rock and refuse to be stirred into action by
the pumping of a stout fly rod aided by a fluent monologue of Ojibwayian

profanity. Sometimes it takes two hours to land a really big rainbow under those circumstances.

The Soo affords great fishing. But it is a wild nightmare kind of fishing that is second only in strenuousness to angling for tuna off Catalina Island. Most of the trout too take a spinner and refuse a fly and to the 99 per cent pure fly fisherman, there are no one hundred per centers, that is a big drawback.

Of course the rainbow trout of the Soo will take a fly but it is rough handling them in that tremendous volume of water on the light tackle a fly fisherman loves. It is dangerous wading in the spots that can be waded, too, for a mis-step will take the angler over his head in the rapids. A canoe is a necessity to fish the very best water.

Altogether it is a rough, tough, mauling game, lacking in the meditative qualities of the Izaak Walton school of angling. What would make a fitting Valhalla for the good fisherman when he dies would be a regular trout river with plenty of rainbow trout in it jumping crazy for the fly.

There is such a one not forty miles from the Soo called the—well, called the river. It is about as wide as a river should be and a little deeper than a river ought to be and to get the proper picture you want to imagine in rapid succession the following fade-ins:

A high pine covered bluff that rises steep up out of the shadows. A short sand slope down to the river and a quick elbow turn with a little flood wood jammed in the bend and then a pool.

A pool where the moselle colored water sweeps into a dark swirl and expanse that is blue-brown with depth and fifty feet across.

There is the setting.

The action is supplied by two figures that slog into the picture up the trail along the river bank with loads on their backs that would tire a pack horse. These loads are pitched over the heads onto the patch of ferns by the edge of the deep pool. That is incorrect. Really the figures lurch a little forward and the tump line loosens and the pack slumps onto the ground. Men don't pitch loads at the end of an eight mile hike.

One of the figures looks up and notes the bluff is flattened on top and that there is a good place to put a tent. The other is lying on his back and looking straight up in the air. The first reaches over and picks up a grasshopper that is stiff with the fall of the evening dew and tosses him into the pool.

The hopper floats spraddle legged on the water of the pool an instant, an eddy catches him and then there is a yard long flash of flame, and a trout as long as your forearm has shot into the air and the hopper has disappeared.

"Did you see that?" gasped the man who had tossed in the grasshopper.

It was a useless question, for the other, who a moment before would have served as a model for a study entitled "Utter Fatigue," was jerking his fly rod out of the case and holding a leader in his mouth.

We decided on a McGinty and a Royal Coachman for the flies and at the second cast there was a swirl like the explosion of a depth bomb, the line went taut and the rainbow shot two feet out of water. He tore down the pool and the line went out until the core of the reel showed. He jumped and each time he shot into the air we lowered the tip and prayed. Finally he jumped and the line went slack and Jacques reeled in. We thought he was gone and then he jumped right under our faces. He had shot upstream towards us so fast that it looked as though he were off.

When I finally netted him and rushed him up the bank and could feel his huge strength in the tremendous muscular jerks he made when I held him flat against the bank, it was almost dark. He measured twenty-six inches and weighed nine pounds and seven ounces.

That is rainbow trout fishing.

The rainbow takes the fly more willingly than he does bait. The McGinty, a fly that looks like a yellow jacket, is the best. It should be tied on a number eight or ten hook.

The smaller flies get more strikes but are too small to hold the really big fish. The rainbow trout will live in the same streams with brook trout but they are found in different kinds of places. Brook trout will be forced into the shady holes under the bank and where alders hang over the banks, and the rainbow will dominate the clear pools and the fast shallows.

Magazine writers and magazine covers to the contrary the brook or speckled trout does not leap out of water after he has been hooked. Given plenty of line he will fight a deep rushing fight. Of course if you hold the fish too tight he will be forced by the rush of the current to flop on top of the water.

But the rainbow always leaps on a slack or tight line. His leaps are not mere flops, either, but actual jumps out of and parallel with the water of from a foot to five feet. A five-foot jump by any fish sounds improbable, but it is true.

If you don't believe it tie onto one in fast water and try and force him. Maybe if he is a five-pounder he will throw me down and only jump four feet eleven inches.

The Night of the Gytefisk

BY ERNEST SCHWIEBERT

The occasions when I've had the opportunity to fish with my friend Ernie Schwiebert have been far fewer than I would like, but they qualify as memorable experiences in every way. In Iceland, on the storied Brodheads in Pennsylvania, I have watched Ernie dissect salmon and trout water with the skilled cuts of a master surgeon. Ernie doesn't merely fish a stream: he strips it bare, from the outer layers of skin to the marrow of the bones. No secrets can remain hidden long from his detailed analysis. It's all very simple, really. Ernest Schwiebert finds where the fish are, figures out why they're there and what they're doing, then proceeds to catch them. Or maybe I've got it backwards. Perhaps he figures out what they're doing first, then finds them. In any case, as likely as not when you look his way on the stream you'll see the bowed, straining hoop of his rod.

In recent years, Ernie has not been writing many magazine fly-fishing pieces of the kind I once published so happily in the magazines I edited, but his literary output has remained nothing short of prodigious. He has been doing magazine pieces on the New Mexico years of the artist Georgia O'Keefe, Russia's Saint Petersburg, and the great castle hotels of Ireland. He is currently putting the final touches on book manuscripts on Alaska, its fishing, and amazing ecology; the legendary Umpqua and its steelhead, and the salmon rivers of Russia. He is also preparing definitive new updated editions of his classic Matching the Hatch *and* Nymphs *for publication by The Lyons Press.*

The Night of the Gytefisk is from Ernie's collection of stories, A River for Christmas, *published by The Stephen Greene Press, Inc., of Viking Penguin, Inc., in 1988. In this tale we'll be journeying as close as most of us will ever get to Norway's legendary Alta, home of record-breaking Atlantic salmon and the Aberdeen Proving Ground where reel drags, backing, and fish-playing skills are tested to their limits.*

kree-jah! the terns screamed. *Skree-jah!*

The midnight sun hung low on the northern horizon, strangely bright at two o'clock in the morning. The ghillies decided to stop for lunch. No one fished except in the twelve-hour twilight that passed for night. The boatmen skillfully worked our slender Karasjok riverboat ashore, and its graceful Viking-shaped prow grated on the gravelly shingle. Such boats have been used by river Lapps for centuries and are perfectly suited for salmon fishing.

It was quite cool for July, and a brisk wind riffled the great pool at Steinfossnakken. The ghillies built a fire on the beach, and I studied the midnight sun on the waterfalls that spill like Yosemite from the escarpment at Sautso, their plumes a thousand feet above the river. Cooking smells of bouillon and hot coffee eddied on the wind, and we sat on the mossy boulders, listening to the muted thunder of the Gabofoss Rapids a mile upstream.

Skree-jah! the terns cried.

The graceful birds were catching *Metretopis* flies that were hatching from the river, and I watched their hovering and fluttering before they dropped like ospreys to seize the mayflies with a rapier-swift strike of their beaks. Grayling worked softly to the hatching flies. The grayling ran between two and three pounds, but we were after bigger game. Three salmon lay gleaming in the boat, wedged crosswise to ballast its slender lapstrake hull. The best had been taken at Mostajokka, bright with sea-lice and thirty-three pounds. The smallest went twenty-one, less than average for the river. When it had cartwheeled awkwardly on its first eighty-yard run, the ghillies had laughed contemptuously and called it a grilse.

The thick sandwiches and hot soup warmed our bodies, and we sipped coffee laced with cognac, watching the river. Two wiry Lapps went past in the mail boat, bound for the Sautso camp at Sirpinakken. The Lapps waved and we waved back. We were in no hurry, with three fine salmon in the boat, although we would fish another two hours before reaching the middle camp at Sandia.

It was my second night at Sandia, and in the morning, the mail boat was scheduled to ferry me upriver to Sautso. The Sandia camp had been built for the Duke of Roxburgh in 1873, its simple log frame almost unchanged in more than a century. There are two bedrooms with private baths. Its sitting room has a fireplace, and four trophy fish between forty and fifty pounds. The trophies were taken by the Duke and Duchess of Roxburgh, and the room has become something of a shrine. The fishing house at Sandia sits high above the river, with a grassy clearing that reaches down from its porch to the boat landing.

The river itself begins in the treeless snowmelt plateaus and escarpments of the Finnmarksvidda, two hundred miles above the polar circle in Norway. It lies eight hundred miles north of Oslo, at the latitude of Point Barrow in Alaska. The valley floor is thickly forested, while the Finnmarksvidda is a granite highland that bears the lakes and grinding scars of the Pleistocene glaciers that shaped most of northern Europe. These arctic barrens are a world of scattered taiga and immense tundra moors, pockmarked and scoured with dark peat-stained tarns. The river gathers in the lichens and pothole seepages below Kautokeino, the settlement that is considered the capital of Lapland. The district shelters a number of Lapp encampments, with their pyramidal log roofs and storehouses on stilts and turf cabins. The settlements are permanent sites where the Lapp herdsmen winter with their reindeer. They migrate with their herds each spring, carrying their skin-covered pole shelters on the treks. The Lapps are patient and hardy. There is both wry humor and sadness in their coppery faces, deeply wrinkled by the weather at such latitudes—it is a swiftly vanishing tribal way of life.

The river rises slowly in its lacework of glacial ponds and burns, mixing and gathering until it finally spills into a series of deeply scoured gorges, fifty miles north of Kautokeino. Its first twenty miles are lost in steep-walled faults and chasms, filled with the spilling of countless waterfalls. Salmon are thought to spawn in these headwaters, using the labyrinths of impassable cliffs and rapids. Below the little gorge at Sautso, the river changes completely.

Between Sautso and its estuary, the river is a symphony in three movements. Below the first tumbling chutes at Svartfossnakken and Bolvero, its moods are almost pastoral, sliding into the two-mile mirror of smooth water below the fishing-camp at Sirpinakken. Such *pianissimo* passages change swiftly at the Velliniva Narrows, eddying into the deep half-mile lake that ends in the Gabofoss Rapids. The river plunges wildly through truck-sized boulders there, dropping almost eighty feet in less than a quarter mile.

Downstream from the Gabofoss portage, the river gathers itself again. It spills into the swirling amphitheater at Steinfossnakken, and its famous Sandia beats begin. The Sandia beats are a stairsteps of boulder pockets and brief holding-lies, rather than salmon pools in the classic sense. These reaches of river spill into brief, connecting rapids before swelling and spreading into another pool. Sandia ends in the moss-walled gorge above Battagorski, where the river fights its way through cottage-sized boulders. The river has claimed many lives here, its angry music filled with brass and kettledrums and cymbals.

The forests become dense at Battagorski, thriving on the sheltered valley floor. There is a magnificent salmon pool there, deep and smooth flowing above the great boulders that hide in its Stygian currents. It is a favorite midnight-lunch pool. Twenty-five summers ago, I watched Sampson Field hook a heavy salmon at Battagorski. It took a Silver Durham with a strike that wrenched his two-handed rod into a tight circle. The fight began as a stubborn tug of war. The ghillies worked hard to hold the boat against the strong current, and Field leaned back into the fish. It was sullen and strong. It did not jump and it steadily forced the boat downstream. The oarsman was sculling hard, his face tightening into a grimace of pain, watching the mossy boulders slip past. The current hissed past their longboat, its stern trailing a thickly eddying line of foam, and it drifted inexorably toward the rapids.

The big salmon was winning. It forced the boat into the swiftly gathering currents and bulled off into the chutes downstream. We still had not seen the fish and scrambled to follow in a second boat. The salmon was still taking line. It was exciting to follow down the rapids, watching the boatmen fight to stay alive and stay with the fish, and changing priorities in the wild chutes. The war lasted almost a mile, until it ended in a rocky backwater and the ghillie waited like a heron with the gaff.

Field pumped the fish close. The ghillie stared into the dark tea-colored currents and spume. Suddenly his shoulders tightened and he struck, swinging the great fish aboard. It was dispatched with a priest while Field rummaged through his tackle bag for the scale.

Twenty kilos! he said excitedly.

Forty-four pounds, I said and shook hands with him. *Congratulations!*

It was some fight, Field nodded.

Battagorski is a huge pool, its eddying depths brooding and mysterious, tracing fingerprints of foam. Its salmon lies mark the beginning of the classic Jøraholmen beats. These lower pools include such famous water as Gargia and Bradstraumen, where I watched the Duchess of Roxburgh boat a forty-six pound cockfish in 1963. Bradstraumen is also the pool that surrendered a forty-nine pound salmon to Charles Ritz in 1954, fishing as a guest of Herbert Pulitzer, and Ritz wrote knowledgeably about the river in his book *A Flyfisher's Life*. Ritz fished two seasons at Jøraholmen and its sweeping salmon pools, where the river finally winds through a valley of farmsteads and forests to the villages at its mouth. The estuary itself is unimpressive. Its shallows spread across a series of gravelly channels a hundred miles south of Hammarfest and its North Cape. Bossekop is the village at its mouth, its cheerful houses a brightly painted collage of color scattered along its hillsides. The fjord itself is more sprawling than scenic. It was not always so peaceful, because its sheltered moorings held German pocket battleships forty-five years ago, during the bitter convoy campaigns between Reykjavik and Murmansk. The river is the finest salmon fishery in the world.

It is the storied Alta.

The Alta has been fished since the Duke of Roxburgh first sailed his yacht into its fjord in 1862 and discovered that the river teemed with big salmon. Roxburgh shared its sport for many years with the Duke of Westminster, who was famous for both salmon fishing and his liaisons with the French couturier, Coco Chanel. Roxburgh built the Sandia and Sautso camps in Victorian times, but in earlier seasons his parties fished from steam yachts moored off Bossekop. The beats were fished in rotation, splitting the rods into four groups. Each party was patiently ferried and poled to Sautso, where they camped and floated back to their luxurious quarters on the yachts. When the first party reached the middle beats at Sandia, the second was ferried past them to the upper river, and the third group soon followed. These parties poled and portaged along the river throughout July, fishing back from Sautso to the comfort and cuisine of the yachts, stopping at rough camps along the river.

It was a time of great wealth and privilege.

Alta has been fished in our century by a parade of celebrated anglers. The Duke of Windsor and his equerry, the Earl of Dudley, were regulars on the river more than a half century ago. The Duke and Duchess of Westminster fished it steadily until his death in 1953, except during the Second World War, when German forces occupied Norway.

The Roxburgh family fished the river for more than a century, except for the war years, and the late Duke of Roxburgh had fished it every summer since childhood. The family seat was the Floors Castle at Kelso-on-Tweed, which commands the great salmon pool where the Teviot joins the Tweed. Roxburgh fished its spring runs from early childhood, sailed to fish the Alta for an entire month each summer, returned to shoot grouse in the highlands, and fished the autumn salmon run on the Tweed in Roxburghshire.

It's been wonderful, Roxburgh admitted over supper at Jøraholmen on the Alta. *It's been a life spent rather well, I think.*

Death duties and other changes in British life eventually ended British control of the river at midcentury. Anglers like Admiral Edward MacDonald, Herbert Pulitzer, Charles Ritz, Tony Pulitzer, Seward Johnson, Carter Nicholas, Anderson Fowler, Edward Litchfield, Robert Pabst, Ted Benzinger, Ralph Strauss, Roger Gaillard, R. R. Donnelly, Sampson Field, Peter Pleydell-Bouverie, Peter Kriendler, Robert Graham, Thomas Lenk, James Graham, Ogden Goelet, Cornelius Ryan, Robert Goelet, George Coe, Lee Wulff, General Lawrence Kuter, Charles Vaughan, General Thomas White, Walton Ferguson, Warrington Gillett, Sir Thomas Sopwith, Nathaniel Pryor Reed, Sir James Pearman, Earl Worsham, Philip Kingsland Crowe, and Admiral William Read—who successfully flew an NC-4 flying boat across the Atlantic before Lindbergh—became pilgrims to the Alta fishery over the past thirty-odd years.

Its fishing is unique. Twice in the past century, the river surrendered more than thirty fish to a solitary angler in a single night's sport. The Duke of Roxburgh took thirty-nine in 1860, and James Harewood killed twenty-six 16 years later. Major Courtney Trotter caught twenty-nine weighing 615 pounds in 1925. The following season, the Duke of Westminster boated thirty-three salmon weighing 792 pounds in twelve hours. Such catches averaged approximately twenty-three pounds. Sampson Field holds the modern record, with seventeen fish from the storied Gargia in a single night—all taken with flies and averaging just under thirty pounds, and the Alta surrendered eleven salmon weighing better than forty pounds that season.

Charles Ritz has written about such sport in *A Flyfisher's Life,* and I have heard him sing its praises from the little bar just off the rue Cambon, in his famous hotel at the Place Vendôme in Paris. *It is simply unique!* Ritz insisted excitedly with Gallic gestures and staccato speech. *There are no mountains except the Himalayas, no oceans to equal the Pacific, no fish like the Atlantic salmon—and there is only a single Alta!*

Ritz was right. Like a rock climber who has not tested his skills against Dhaulagiri or Annapurna in Nepal, and like the hunter who has not seen the Serengeti, the salmon fisherman dreams of fishing the Alta. Although I had boated a half-dozen fish over twenty pounds on three brief visits to Jøraholmen, I had been awestruck by a brace of cockfish weighed at its ghillie's hut that weighed over forty pounds in 1963. Those trophies had been taken by the Duchess of Roxburgh and Peter Pleydell-Bouverie, who had served with the British Western Desert Force, elite commando troops that gathered intelligence behind German lines in Africa. The Alta has the smell of history.

Valhalla! Ritz insisted over lunch with Robert Pabst and Ralph Strauss at the River Club in Manhattan. *It's the Valhalla of salmon fishing—and once you have tasted it, nothing in your life is the same!*

My first night at Sandia was something of an accident. I had been fishing the Reisa, and it had been so poor that we decided to leave three days early. When I arrived at Bossekop, there was a message telling me to come immediately to Sandia. Its party was a rod short, since one of the fishermen had become ill, and I had been asked to fish out his last day. It was not so much a day of fishing I had been offered, since the salmon I might catch belonged to the river owners and were worth considerable money. The night's fishing proved wonderful. Although I felt a little like a Danish trawler, I took ten salmon averaging twenty-three pounds with a ten-foot Garrison that had belonged to the late Paul Hyde Bonner.

The boatmen arrived after lunch to ferry me farther up the river to Sautso, and we motored upstream through famous pools like Ronga and Mostajokka to the foot of the boulder-strewn portage at Steinfossnakken. We changed boats there. The ghillies carried my duffle and baggage between them on a heavy pole, past the wild torrent of the Gabofoss rapids to the lip of the Gabofoss waterfall itself. I carried the tackle and a small duffle of fly-tying gear. Gabofoss thundered past in its chill explosions of spray, its roar blotting out all thought and other sounds, filling the morning with its icy breath. The rocky trail was traversed slowly, and finally we reached the Sautso stillwater.

We spooked a great fish lying off the upper boat mooring, and its wake disturbed the rocky shallows. The old boatman stood looking at the towering cliffs, squinting into a surprising midday sun.

Sautso is a paradise, he said.

Several terns circled and screamed, capturing salmon fry in the shallows. We rested before loading my baggage into the second Karasjok longboat and started upstream toward the Sautso camp, crossing the smooth flowage that lies between Sirpinakken and the Gabofoss Rapids.

The Sautso camp stands astride the small tributary at Sirpinakken, under the thousand-foot escarpments across the river. Its fishing house is simple and rough. It was also built by the Duke of Roxburgh just after our Civil War. There is a sitting room with log walls sheathed in wainscoting, two bedrooms with rudimentary baths, a small kitchen, and quarters for a cook and serving girl. The ghillies sleep in a Lapp turf cabin near the river. The sitting room wall had a pale pencil-tracing of the fifty-nine pound salmon caught by Admiral William Read at Steinfossnakken in 1962. It had been taken with a 3/0 hairwing Abbey dressed for the admiral at William Mills & Son. The salmon tracing was primitive and faint, in great danger of fading away. I reverently retraced its muscular outlines on the wainscoting with black fly-head lacquer, like the delicate brushwork in Japanese calligraphy.

The afternoon was still bright when the cook informed me that supper was scheduled for seven o'clock. Fishing would start at eight. Black curtains kept the light from the sleeping quarters, but I slept only fitfully, dreaming of giant salmon. Sleep proved difficult all week with the day's clock turned upside down. Supper is actually breakfast, since the fishing starts at eight and lasts until midnight, when the ghillies break to eat lunch, drink coffee, and plan tactics for the rest of the night. The midnight break is welcome. Depending on the night's sport, the fishing can last until five o'clock. Whisky is also welcome after an entire night on the river, and a wonderful cold buffet is always waiting too. Breakfast is transformed into an early-morning supper, and the anglers sleep through the morning until the late afternoon. Clocks are set for three o'clock, leaving a leisurely time to prepare tackle and dress flies. Cocktails come again at six, with dinner at seven o'clock, while the ghillies prepare their Karasjok longboats for another night's fishing.

The dice cup was brought out over coffee. We rolled dice, and my boat was awarded the upper river from Toppen, where the river finally escapes its impenetrable gorges, to the pretty pool called Dormenin. It is among the few wadable pools on the entire twenty-seven miles of river. We carried my tackle to the boat after supper, and I clambered eagerly aboard, trying hard to conceal a wildly swelling sense of excitement.

The motor caught quickly and we circled out. We traveled upstream swiftly, hand-lining the longboat around the Svartfossen Rapids and past the rocky chutes called Bolvero and Jagorski. Toppen lay still farther, flowing smooth and almost still between low cliffs that rise straight from the river. The ghillies put me ashore on the rocks and lined the boat farther upstream to the last mooring. They secured it there. The boatmen built a fire, brewed a pot of fresh coffee, and filled their pipes.

We pulled the boat over the fish, they explained in Norwegian. *We must give the salmon time to forget us.*

The coffee tastes good, I nodded.

Finally we doused the fire and started fishing. We clambered down through the boulders and pushed off, rowing furtively upstream. We waited quietly and I checked my tackle again. Leader knots are critical on fish averaging between twenty and thirty pounds. The pool seems quite deep, its secrets hidden in tea-colored depths. The ghillies had selected a big Orange Blossom, a silver-bodied hairwing dressed on a 3/0 double. Alta is a big-fly river. The current was swift and smooth against the opposite wall of rocks. It was a roll-casting place with another cliff of rhyolite behind us, and I had to loop the big fly only thirty-five feet to cover the fish. Their lie was tight against the cliffs. The boatman at the bow rowed patiently, measuring the current's speed and letting our boat drop about two feet downstream between each successive cast. It was obvious that he used outcroppings and other benchmarks to calibrate his work. It required great strength and discipline, mixed with intimate knowledge of the river. His skills were remarkable.

The fish were holding in a classic lie. I worked through ten casts against the cliffs, locking the line under my index finger with the rod-tip held low, pointing toward the fly as I patiently followed its swing. Our salmon tactics were basic.

But the Alta boatmen have evolved some footnotes over the century. The ghillie seated at the stern works a single scull to sweep the boat's stern with the fly-swing. The fisherman stands at the middle of the boat, bracing his legs against a cross-thwart shaped to cup his knees.

When the fly-swing came around toward the stern, I lifted the rod over the ghillie to extend its teasing half-circle, letting it work well behind the boat. The boat's stern followed smoothly, controlled perfectly by the ghillies, and deftly came back into line. My pickup was roughly parallel to the boat, and I false-cast once, changing direction into the final cast itself. It was beautiful fishing teamwork, rhythmic and metronome smooth, and I have not seen its equal elsewhere.

Before picking up each cast at the end of its fly-swing, I let it hang there swimming in the current a few seconds. Several six-inch pulls followed in a retrieve of about ten feet. Sometimes a fish following a swinging fly will take it when the fly-swing stops. Sometimes a fish will follow through its entire swing, circling under the fly when it stops, and take when its final retrieve is started back toward the boat. The ghillies believe the big Alta fish follow a fly surprising distances, and experience on the river confirms their judgment.

Salmon fishing is discipline and patience. Anglers must cover half-mile riffles with hundreds of patient, concentric fly-swings. The mind drifts and daydreams with the steady drumbeats of muffled oarlocks and casting, and I had started to think of other things when there was a big swirl.

Laks! said the ghillie softly.

The fish had rolled at the fly without taking, and the boatman stroked hard to hold our position, helping me repeat the cast.

He comes again! the ghillie hissed.

The entire current had bulged when my fly worked past, and there was literally a bow-wave showing, but there was still no weight. The fish had still not touched the big Orange Blossom.

Did you feel anything? he asked. *Did you feel him?*

No, I said.

Cast back to him again, he whispered.

Sometimes a fish can be teased into taking by changing the fly-swing. It was possible that my fly was swimming through too fast, perhaps faster than it seemed. The third cast dropped and settled into its swing, and I slowed the teasing rod-tip, stripping about six inches of line into its bellying quarter-cycle.

It slowed the fly just as it reached the salmon's lie, until it seemed to hang momentarily, and the fish was hooked.

There had been no warning, no bulging swirl when the fish rolled to follow. Its weight was surprising. The rod had simply snapped down as the bellying line sliced back against the current, and there was a tail splash when the fish bored deep and sounded.

Good fish! I thought wildly.

Several times it threatened to leave Toppen, working deep under the boat and bolting back into the shallows at its tail. Each time we patiently worked it back into the pool. It was almost thirty minutes before we finally controlled its strength. The boatman worked us back against the cliffs, between some sheltering rocks, and I pumped the salmon close. The ghillie in the stern reached with his gaff, deftly wrestling a thirty-pound henfish over the gunwale, and dispatched it. He washed the priest and laid our prize across the boat.

Det var findt! he grinned.

We rested the pool again, holding the longboat among the rocks while the boatmen smoked their pipes, and I ate a little Toblerone chocolate. We took a second twenty-pound fish farther down the pool, landing it easily after its first run threatened to reach the rapids.

Below the broken quarter-mile at Toppen lies the Jagotku Pool, the swift boulder-filled chute where the late Joe Brooks took a forty-pound cockfish, sharing a rod with his host, Warrington Gillett. The boatman walked our craft down the shallows while I waded and fished through Jagotku. It did not seem a likely holding-lie. But when the fly worked past a giant boulder, almost skittering across the choppy spume, a third salmon slashed out to seize it. The fish fought well but did not try to reach the chutes farther downstream, and it surrendered almost meekly. It weighed twenty-two pounds, and the boatmen came running to help just before I tailed the fish myself.

We laid the fish crosswise in the boat and decided to stop fishing. It was almost midnight, and it was getting overcast and cold, although it was still surprisingly bright. The fire on the rocky bar felt good. The boatman gathered more firewood while the ghillie laid out the midnight supper, making fresh coffee and heating a thick cauliflower soup. There were smoked reindeer and sausages and dill-cured salmon, and we finished with thick rose-hip jelly and cookies. It was quite cold when we doused the fire and launched the boat again.

Svartfossnakken was next, a sprawling rough-water pool where the river turned sharply toward the west, gathering itself to plunge into the Svartfossen Rapids. Their currents looked fierce, tumbling through a long sickle-shaped curve at the base of the mountain. Huge boulders and scour lines high above the river bore witness to the volume of its spring spates. The rapids are almost frightening downstream. The boatman held us expertly above the chute, back-rowing with seemingly effortless skill, while I covered the pool. We hooked another salmon after changing flies, and the boatman fought to hold our position, while I tried to force the fish. It proved foolish and the fly pulled out.

The ghillies quickly saw that I was not unhappy, and we laughed together, deciding to rest the pool. It was already almost two o'clock. We had three fish in the boat, and that was considered par on the Sautso water.

We hooked a second fish at Svartfossen almost immediately. It was a smaller fish, perhaps twelve pounds, and I suspect it was a stray from the Eiby tributary on the lower river. It fought well, but unlike the others, it lacked the weight to use the river and beat us. The fish was quickly boated.

Grilse, the ghillie teased wryly.

The boatmen lined their way down through the Svartfossen Rapids while I walked downstream through the boulders to Dormenin. It was our last salmon pool that night. Dormenin is the only real greased-line pool on the entire Sautso water, and I changed reels while the ghillies brought the boat downstream. Fishing from the shore, I moved a fish twice from a shallow lie where I once saw Ralph Strauss lose an immense salmon when the knot failed at the fly. I tried the fish for thirty minutes, but it did not show itself again. Another fish rolled farther downstream. The boatmen arrived, and I got aboard to fish the place it had porpoised, where the pool slides into Ovre Harstrommen. It was cold and starting to rain, and we fished through without moving another salmon. Dormenin was the bottom pool of our first night's beat.

It had been a good night, and we were ahead of the three-fish average at Sautso, although the Eiby stray was small. The boatmen were pleased with our night's work. It was four o'clock and still dark and overcast. When we reached the camp at the Jotkajavrre tributary, the ghillies were studying the sky. The smooth expanse of the Sautso was lost in misting rain.

Russian weather, the boatman said.

It will be stormy, the ghillie agreed, *but tomorrow we have Gabo and Velliniva to fish.*

Good pools? I asked.

Excellent pools, the ghillie said. *Velliniva is our favorite.*

It was raining hard before we finished eating and went to bed, and we fell asleep to its steady kettledrum pounding on the roof. I had stayed up long enough to dress several big Orange Blossoms. With the black curtains drawn tight, I fell asleep gratefully, listening to the rain.

It was late afternoon when the serving girl awakened us, but it was still gloomy and dark. The overcast had settled between the ragged escarpments until it hung like a shroud, a hundred feet above the river. Our breakfast omelets and goat cheese and brislings were ready, and the ghillies sat unhappily in the kitchen, staring at the barometer.

Russian weather, they muttered.

It did not feel like a fishing night. *The barometer dropped right through the glass last night,* I said. *It's really low.*

Ja, they agreed sourly.

It was raw and cold when we loaded the boats. We traveled slowly upstream to the gravel-bar island at Dormenin, rigged our tackle in the rain, and started at Ovre Harstrommen. The boatmen looked dour and sat staring at the current. The night grew more gloomy, its overcast settling until great scraps of mist drifted through the trees. It was raining harder now. We shouldered into our ponchos and slickers, watching the tea-colored river. It was rising slightly and looked murky. The ghillie had pointed happily to a freshly tied Orange Blossom, the pattern that had killed well the night before, and insisted on knotting it to the nylon himself. Since the ghillies share in the salmon which are sold, they seldom trust knots tied by others. The boatman worked us patiently into position, his leather oar pads squeaking in the rain, while we fished the sixty-yard pool.

Nothing! I said quietly when we had fished it out. *Too gloomy for fishing.*

Perhaps it's a gytefisk night.

What's a gytefisk?

It's a really big cockfish, the ghillie explained. *Some nights we catch nothing, even on the Alta—but when we finally catch something on such nights, it is often a big gytefisk!*

And nothing else? I asked.

Ja, he nodded. *We get the gytefisk when others will not take the fly.*

Pray for a gytefisk night! I laughed.

Ja, they smiled.

We worked back to the top of the pool. The currents seemed like strong tea but were still clear enough for fishing. It seemed wise to change flies, selecting something like a bright yellow-hackled Torrish. It was obviously visible in the tea-colored shallows beside the boat, with its canary-bright throat and silvery body. The Torrish was dressed on a 2/0 double, and it had been given to me by Clare de Bergh over lunch with Charles Woodman in Oslo.

They had been fishing the Jøraholmen beats with Seward Johnson, Anderson Fowler, and Carter Nicholas two weeks before, and Clare de Bergh had outfished them all. She had boated thirty-seven salmon weighing 987 pounds, including a superb Alta cockfish of fifty-seven.

Every bloody one took the Torrish, she laughed and handed me the fly. *You take the last one and try it.*

I'll try to dress copies, I said.

The dressing was a pale hairwing version of the Torrish that some anglers call the Scalscraggie. It had looked enticing in the Wheatley box, set among a covey of somber patterns like the Ackroyd and Black Doctor and Black Dose. The ghillie seemed lukewarm about my choice, but he took the fly and clinched it to the leader, preening its feathers and wing. We fished it carefully through Ovre Harstrommen without moving a fish. It was raining harder when we reached Nedri Harstrommen. It is a strong hundred-yard reach of water named for its heavy flow. The ghillies worked us expertly into position, and I stripped off line to cover the pool.

Good place? I asked in Norwegian.

Ja, they shook their heads. *We do not hook many salmon at Harstrommen—but the fish we hook are usually big.*

Gytefisk pool, I suggested.

Perhaps, they said.

It was almost prophetic. The line worked out into the darkness and rain, dropping the pale Torrish sixty-five feet across the currents in the throat of the pool. I lowered the rod and let the fly settle deep before it worked into its bellying swing. There was a heavy pull and the line came sullenly taut.

Fouled on something, I said.

It's not possible, the ghillie shook his head. *There's nothing out there.*

Gytefisk? I suggested.

The ghillies said nothing and looked grim. The boatman worked steadily to hold our position, and we stared at the throbbing line. It still felt snagged. The rod strained into a sullen circle. Both men seemed unusually concerned at the tenor of the fight, and suddenly I understood. The stalemate ended when an immense sow-sized fish cartwheeled awkwardly in the rain, landing with a gargantuan splash.

My God! I gasped.

The reel surrendered line in a wild series of ratchety jerks. The boatmen seemed almost stunned. The fish burst halfway out again in a huge gout of spray, broaching like a whale just off our boat, and fell heavily again.

Thirty kilos! the ghillie hissed.

The boatman nodded, pulling hard at his oars. Both men began chattering excitedly, more agitated than I had seen them with fish between twenty and thirty pounds, and we settled into the grim business of fighting such a fish in heavy water with a single-handed rod. The salmon shook its head angrily, turned almost majestically downstream, and gathered speed. The current was a powerful flood. The fish was strong too, ignoring any rod pressure we could apply, and it took a full hundred yards of backing with almost ridiculous ease. Its run was a little frightening, and I sighed with relief when it finally stopped. The fish still seemed like a snag. The boatmen used the time to maneuver into better position, and we crossed the middle of Nedri Harstrommen into the quiet shallows, a little below the fish. I worried about changing our angle so radically but dismissed those doubts when the fish began head-shaking. It moved upstream and shook itself angrily again.

The fish finally stopped, and I had just started to pump-and-reel like a tarpon fisherman when it turned and slowly left the pool. Its strength was still awesome. There was nothing we could do except follow, and it had simply shouldered us aside, floundering into the rapids downstream.

How big did you think he was? I asked.

Thirty kilos, they said.

But thirty kilos is over sixty-five pounds! I calculated its metric weight wildly. *Sixty-five pounds!*

Storlaks, the ghillie agreed.

The backing was dwindling too fast. Both ghillies worked desperately to follow, rowing and poling to keep the line free of the rocks. It was a wild half-mile trip with little control over the salmon. It escaped the pool downstream too, forcing us through the pools called Battanielo and Banas, until it finally stopped in the throat of Sirpinakken.

More swift water lay below, but it was tumbling and broken, and we came chuting through with the fish still hooked. The fight went better in the lake-sized shallows above our camp. The fish had started to porpoise, circling the backwater stubbornly, fifty yards out. It had finally seemed to weaken. The steady rod pressure forced it closer and closer, muting its weakening runs. I forced it into the Jotkajavrre backwater until there was line on the reel again, its dark green covering the pale backing. The fish circled closer still, until the leader knot was visible just under the surface. It foundered weakly and we gasped.

Thirty kilos, the ghillies were awestruck.

The fish bolted again weakly and stopped. It stripped off fifty feet and faltered, and I turned it back toward the boat. The boatman stroked patiently to hold our position. The ghillie slipped his gaff free, moved soundlessly into position, and sat waiting. The fish bulged to the surface, rolling and working its gills. It was floundering and beaten. The giant salmon was almost in reach of the gaff when it worked its jaws yawning until the fly came free.

Damn! I groaned.

The fish drifted just beyond our reach and the ghillie threw his gaff angrily. The boatman slumped exhausted at his oars, like a beaten sculler at Henley, and stared helplessly as the fish gathered its strength. It shuddered and turned back into the river, pushing a giant bow-wave like a half-submerged submarine. Alta ghillies are used to huge salmon and are usually so taciturn and laconic that their anger startled me.

The big cockfish was gone.

Our riverkeeper explained later that the biggest salmon killed on the Alta was a sixty-pound cockfish, and the boatmen were convinced that our fish was bigger, perhaps a new record for the river. The existing record-fish was caught by the Earl of Dudley, who came to the river while serving as Royal Equerry to the late Duke of Windsor.

Lord Dudley became one of the wealthiest peers in the United Kingdom before his death in 1969. He died in Paris and had lived abroad for many years, dividing his time between country houses in France and the Bahamas. The family seat was in Worcestershire at Dudley Castle, and its original title dates back to 1604. Dudley held extensive lands, but his family's great wealth lay primarily with its holdings of iron and coal, and the ancestor who developed a coal-fired iron smelter in the late seventeenth century. The earl was brusque and unpopular with the Alta ghillies, so intensely disliked that he is the only fisherman who was ever tipped into the river, belly flopping over the gunwale of his Karasjok boat at Kirkaplassen. The ghillies only smile when asked about Dudley's baptism, executed with a deft shift of balance.

The Earl of Dudley was a difficult man, the riverkeeper explained. *We have fished with dukes and kings and princes all our lives—and we know that equerries are little more than ghillies in the world of palaces.*

The great fish had easily won. It had carried the fight through several pools, down more than two miles of river, and it had fought an hour and forty minutes. My boatmen had wanted to share a new record fish and displace the Earl of Dudley. We sat quietly in the boat, trying to gather ourselves, knowing we had lost the salmon of a lifetime. It was starting to rain again, with mist hanging only fifty feet above the river. The night held little promise.

Let's quit, I suggested.

Nei, the ghillie shook his head stubbornly. *We hooked a gytefisk!*

Let's try another pool, I agreed unhappily.

Goddanieni lies just below the fishing camp, where a foamy current-tongue works two hundred yards along the rocky talus slopes under the Stein-fjeldet escarpment. Its eddies slide past a boulder fall into a similar holding-lie called Goddanielo. We worked patiently through both pools, because they had been quite productive a few days earlier, but the only fish was a two-pound breakfast grayling. The Sautso flowage is filled with such fish, but even its flotil-las of grayling were not dimpling to the swarming *Anisomera* midges that night. It was even more discouraging to find the grayling dour.

It's dead, I shook my head unhappily. *It's so dead the grayling are still sleeping too.*

We must fish the Velliniva, they said.

It's your favorite pool?

That's right, the ghillie smiled. *It's the best pool at Sautso—and we must fish it on such a gytefisk night.*

Let's go, I agreed.

Velliniva is not really a pool, but a beautiful hourglass narrows in the Sautso flowage. Ancient rock slides have pinched off the river, leaving immense puzzles of boulders in its bed. It was quite still and strangely quiet. The Gabo-foss waterfall was clearly audible downstream. The mist was clearing swiftly at midnight, and we built a cook fire in the trees. The river boils and slides past the truck-sized boulders at the throat of Velliniva, and there are broken ledges that stairstep across the current, forming its tail-shallows. It is the last taking-lie before the Gabofoss, at the bottom of the Sautso beats. Gabofoss is a place I have never liked. When a salmon is hooked there, the boatman cannot hold the boat by rowing, and the ghillie starts the outboard to tow the fish upstream. It seems foolhardy to row steadily only a single cast away from a chute that spells certain death.

Both ghillies often row simultaneously at Gabofoss, watching the chute warily to judge their remaining margin of safety. We finished our mid-night supper among the trees above Velliniva, and the night grew almost soft and mild. It seemed better for fishing. But we fished both Velliniva and Gabo-foss without moving a salmon and returned to rebuild our fire. We talked about giving up, sharing the last of our chocolate and coffee. The weather was getting better.

Let's fish through again, I said.

We always fish through Velliniva again, the ghillie smiled.

It was already two o'clock. The pool was a polished mirror, and it grew strangely warm. The overcast grew bright orange and gold, with a morning sky that seemed robin's-egg blue. Flies were hatching and the arctic terns were back. The pool had come to life swiftly.

Let's fish, they suggested.

Our fatigue was forgotten, and we drifted stealthily into position, dropping a quartering cast eighty feet across the current. The ghillie smiled and nodded, and I lifted the fly into another cast, mending line as it settled across the flow. The bellying fly-swing stopped on the third cast, and a huge swirl erupted just before I felt the salmon. There was a second bulge as the line tightened across the current, a swelling that carried swiftly down the pool, with a huge coppery flash in its depths.

It's not like the fish we lost, I babbled excitedly, *but it's big!*

Twenty kilos, they guessed.

The fight went well. Twice I felt the line rake huge boulders that had calved off from the cliffs into the narrows. The boatman rowed hard to work us away from the principal holding-lie in the throat of the pool, and the fish came slowly. It seemed well hooked. It jumped twice, and I thought I could see my fly firmly seated in its jaw. It came stubbornly when I pumped it away from the main currents, and it did not jump again. It spent its remaining strength running upstream against the line belly. The ghillie gaffed it cleanly in twenty minutes.

Twenty kilos, we confirmed.

It was a fine cockfish, just beginning to lose its polished sea armor to the first bronzish cast of spawning. It was sleek and hard-muscled and strong. It weighed just under twenty kilos, pulling my Chatillon scale to the forty-three pound mark. The ghillie bled the fish and laid it across the thwarts. It seemed like a perfect climax to the night's fishing, but the ghillies stopped me when I started to strip down my tackle.

We have our gytefisk, I said.

Nei, they insisted. *We have hooked two gytefisker tonight—they are taking well, and we still have two hours left to fish!*

Fine, I laughed. *We'll fish.*

Fifty yards below the lie where the first salmon had taken the fly, the currents had quickened perceptibly above the sunken boulders. The boatman pulled hard at his oars and changed his rhythm to hold us against the flow. Both men watched the pool intently. It was obviously the primary taking-lie, and I began to drop my casts closer together. Terns were busily working the shallows. The morning grew brighter until the cliffs were visible through the mist, strangely pink and violet, and it was getting almost warm. The overcast was gone, and the mist was burning off quickly.

Norwegian weather, I thought.

We were six casts into the pool before I dropped the Torrish well across the current, rolling a big mend before the line could settle and sink. I pointed the rod at the fly and held its tip low, teasing it with a subtle rhythm. The currents bulged behind the fly, welling up until a fifteen-foot circle drifted and died in the current, but I felt no weight until the fish flashed full length in the throat of the pool. It rolled powerfully, well hooked and strong, showing its guillotine-sized tail. It flashed again in the depths of the pool, bolting suddenly upstream until the line ripped through the water. When it jumped, writhing almost six feet from the river and falling straight back on its tail, I was almost certain that I had seen the bright-canary hackles of the Torrish.

My God! I shouted. *It's huge!*

It was another big cockfish, cartwheeling full length across the pool, until it fell with a heavy splash. The terns screamed in protest. The big fish jumped again, porpoising and splashing belly-down like a giant marlin. It held briefly in the heaviest current, shook its head sullenly, and bolted a hundred yards upstream into the Sautso stillwater. We followed it grudgingly to recover line and control our playing angles on the fish. The backing was almost entirely on the reel, when the big salmon turned back with sudden, explosive power and bulldogged angrily past the boat. The big Saint Andrews rattled and growled and shrieked, surrendering line as the fish gathered speed, and the pale backing blurred out through the guides.

We turned desperately to follow. The fish was still running wildly, and I was worried that it might foul the line in the boulders and ledges deep in the belly of the pool. It threshed powerfully through the ledge-rock shallows, riding their chutes into the stillwater below Velliniva. The fish had traveled a rough chute so filled with broken ledges that we did not follow and circled farther out to use a quiet channel. We negotiated it safely, lucky the fish had not stopped to sound among the worst rocks, and our luck still held. The fish had circled back while we were coming through with the boat, and the slack line had settled deep, fouling in a shoal of rocks. But the fish had largely spent its strength before it fouled the line. It lay resting in quiet water, too tired to break off. The boatman rowed furtively toward the stones while the ghillie probed and freed my line with his boat pole.

It took several minutes to work the line completely free, but the fish was still hooked and held quietly on the bottom. With the line untangled from the stones, it stirred itself to make a few strong runs that stopped. It was possible to turn the fish now. It flashed and writhed. I pumped it back until it rolled weakly at the surface, and I worked it close, holding my breath.

The big gaff sliced home. The great fish came wrestling in over the gunwale, and when the priest had stilled its struggling, we saw that it was bigger than our first salmon at Velliniva. It weighed more than forty-six pounds, and I stood beside the boat when we came ashore, staring in disbelief.

Gytefisk natt, the ghillies teased.

Kanskje, I agreed happily. *Men dette gytefisk natt var stor findt—tusen takk for alt!*

Ingen årsak! they said.

But our night at Velliniva was still not over. The ghillies brewed the last of the coffee, and we shared the cookies and Toblerone chocolate and last pieces of sausage. It was almost an anticlimax when we hooked another fish in the throat of Velliniva, and it steeplechased wildly toward Gabofoss. Its fight was explosive and berserk, too wild to last, and the fish spent itself quickly. Its last run lasted less than forty yards, circling almost blindly behind a shoal of rocks. It fouled the line weakly too, but it failed to break off, and the ghillie easily worked it loose with the boat hook. It tried to bolt again, but I snubbed and forced it back, until it floundered and circled our boat.

It's a pretty good fish too, I said.

Changing rod angles, I fought the fish in quickly. It seemed smaller and I forced it. The fish was still surprisingly strong, but it drifted weakly to the surface and the ghillie gaffed it. It twisted and writhed angrily. The ghillie deftly parried its struggles and killed it with a single blow. It weighed just over thirty-nine pounds. The ghillie laid it beside the brace of cockfish in the boat, and we sat quietly.

The ghillie scissored the Torrish from my leader and studied it. It had lost both junglecock feathers. Its hairwing was ragged and thin, showing the scarlet and bright blue and yellow hairs still left. The bucktail fibers were brittle and bent, and the canary hackles were matted with slime. Its dark ostrich butt was missing. Two long spirals of loose tinsel wound free of its body, and the working thread was worn thin, showing the hook. The fly had done its work, although I had never made copies, and I stood looking at the big cockfish in the boat.

Gytefisk night! I thought happily.

The ghillie climbed high on a mossy boulder, held the withered, brightly hackled Torrish above his head, and threw it out across the pool. *It belongs to the river now,* he said.

Headhunting

BY JOHN GIERACH

There are so-called "trout bums," and there are wanna-be trout bums. And then there is The Trout Bum, the man! His real name is John Gierach.

Beginning with his landmark book, Trout Bum, and continuing through too many titles to list here, John Gierach has been producing some of the most readable prose ever on the subject of fly fishing. And readers have literally beaten a path to the doors of the folks who sell Gierach books. Not because they want a lesson in fly fishing. They simply know they like John's style and want to go fishing with him. Even if it's only in print.

This particular Gierach gem is from The View from Rat Lake, published by Simon & Schuster in 1989.

We all want to catch big fish. That's one of the things nonanglers have straight about us. And the bigger they are, the better we like them. The International Game Fish Association even keeps world records on fish in several categories—including fly rod tippet classes—so we can see how big they get and how big a one can be landed on various strengths of monofilament—presumably for the purposes of comparison. Big fish are old, smart, wily, and secretive, or at least that's how we picture them. They have strong medicine, and, in a satisfyingly primitive way, we feel we can steal their magic by catching them.

But what *is* a big fish?

You can't go by the all tackle world records because those are the largest fish ever caught by sporting means, and it's not wise to adopt a scale that will make your own efforts look paltry. Except for a few real hotshots, world records have little practical meaning.

State records are more useful. You're still looking at monsters, but at least they were caught around home and make some relative sense.

"Relative" is the operative word here, and fly-fishermen are highly adept relativists. In our hands the question ceases to be "What is a big fish?" and becomes "Big compared to what?"

Judging from the stories of fishermen and the claims of guide services, any trout weighing in at 5 pounds is considered big in the overall scheme of things; big in the sense that if you are not impressed by such a fish, you risk being asked just who the hell you think you are anyway.

Using another form of measurement, any trout that's 20 inches from tail to jaw is big, even though he may not weigh 5 pounds. Some use inches, while others prefer pounds. The latter conveys more information. Some fly-fishers split the difference, measuring fish under 20 inches and weighing those above. That's because "18 inches" sounds better than "2½ pounds."

Based on the same stories and claims, a big largemouth bass (or a large bigmouth bass, if you like) will weigh closer to 8 pounds. To most of us who fish for both with a fly rod, a bass is a bigger fish than a trout, even though the world record largemouth at 22 pounds, 4 ounces is seriously outclassed by the world record brown at 35 pounds, 15 ounces and the world record rainbow at 42 pounds, 2 ounces.

For that matter, there are a lot of fly-fishers around who will tell you a brown is a bigger trout than a rainbow. But then, didn't I just say that world records weren't of much use in this context? Right, but how do you expect me to maneuver the discussion away from a 42-pound trout? After all, we're talking about big fish here.

What makes a bass a bigger fish than a trout is average size or, more properly, what is considered a keeper. This is a somewhat dated concept in circles where a keeper is now referred to as a "good fish," but it means the same thing: one you wouldn't be ashamed to bring home *if* you were to bring any home, which, of course, you're not going to do.

Around here a good trout is about a foot long. A good bass is more like 14 or 15 inches. If you wouldn't be happy to catch a dozen of either on a light fly rod, you are definitely out of my league.

"Big" is also a regional concept based on fisheries quality. On the Yellowstone River in Yellowstone Park, a 20-inch cutthroat is a big fish. A 20-inch rainbow from the Henry's Fork is also big, but, although it may be the biggest trout you take in a week's fishing, it's not the biggest one you can hope for.

Hope, as opposed to reasonable expectation, has a lot to do with it. An electro-shocking survey of a modest-sized brown trout creek might reveal the average fish to be 9 inches long, a few odd trout will push up to 15 or 16 inches, and the single old hen brown in the deep hole under the bridge weighs 9 pounds. Hope swims in the deep water in the Bridge Pool, feeding mostly at night. Some refuse to believe it's there. Among the believers are a few who think they've seen it. It's a fish that stands a good chance of dying of old age.

It's hard to argue with the idea that a big fish is the biggest one in the water you're fishing at the moment. In this context, a 14-inch brookie from a little beaver pond at 10,500 feet is the same size as a yard-long rainbow from the Madison River.

Late last summer I was fishing with A.K. and his old fishing buddy from Michigan, Bob Fairchild. We wanted to show Bob some huge Rocky Mountain rainbows, so we went and camped near a famous trout river. For several days, working in fairly crowded conditions, we caught fish that, in the context of this discussion, ranged from good to very good in a river where an 8-pound trout was once caught on a dry fly.

After a few days of this we took an afternoon off to get clear of the crowd. We drove up into the high country and hiked up a diminutive brook trout creek, a lonely little trickle that showed few signs of ever having been fished. It was up in there, a few miles from the truck, that A.K. landed a fat little 13-inch brookie that was clearly the biggest fish of the trip.

This relative-to-the-water-in-question concept gives rise to one of the most common sour-grapisms directed at famous big-fish anglers; you know, the guys with reputations as headhunters who are always pictured with enormous, ugly, dripping fish. "Sure," people say. "If I fished the places he did, I'd catch fish like that, too."

That's at least partly true. Most of us fish for the average fish. We go out during the day to cast poppers for bass, dry flies for trout, or whatever, looking to *catch some fish*. If we go to where the average fish are bigger than they are near home, well . . .

I'm as into this as anyone. I can stay home and fish the St. Vrain and the three forks and sometimes catch "big" 12- to 14-inch trout. No problem. Perfectly satisfactory. I use a light cane rod, tend toward dry flies, and have a fine time.

But then there are the relatively short trips to better Colorado rivers like the South Platte and Frying Pan. According to the last Division of Wildlife study I saw, the average trout in the Pan was 16 inches long, and there were plenty that were bigger. *Much* bigger.

I won't go so far as to say that the Henry's Fork is a better river than the Frying Pan—if for no other reason than that Bill Fitzsimmons, who owns the Taylor Creek fly shop on the banks of the Pan, would drive all the way down here to straighten me out—but I do make the obligatory pilgrimage to Idaho at least once a year. That's simply because fishermen must travel, it's part of the game, and when you go on the road you point your headlights in the direction of larger, rather than smaller, fish.

Being on the move is one of the charms of the sport, but you have to be careful to avoid the "never far enough north" syndrome. My father and I discovered this years ago in Minnesota. We lived in the southern part of the state, but drove north to fish in the summers. Way north, until we were far enough from home to feel the reality of a different place. We wanted to be up there where people went to fish.

Once we stopped in to see a friend of Dad's, only to find that he'd "gone north to fish." Dad turned to me and said, in his best allegorical tone, "Well, I guess you can never get far enough north." Then he gazed wistfully off through the trees in the general direction of the Arctic Circle, picturing his friend "out there" somewhere, standing on the pontoon of a floatplane catching fish. *Big* fish. Bigger than what we were catching, surely. I mean, he was farther north, right?

I remember that as one of those profound moments when you realize not only that your father is actually human, but that even the finest parts of life can hurt you; that it's possible to want too much of what you can't have. Dad died too young, but he was not a tragic character—quite the opposite, in fact. Still, he never did catch *the* big fish, and there came a time when I thought I could see that in his eyes. I'm not saying you shouldn't go. I think you should go as far and as often as you can, just don't go staring off into the trees like that when there are fish to be caught just five minutes down the road.

The other way to catch the big ones is to actually fish for them, which is something most of us don't do. We continue to hope for big fish while fishing for the little ones. Some honestly believe trophies are beyond their talents, but that is true only of the very worst klutzes. Most know how to catch big fish, but are just not up for it.

It's really pretty simple. First you gear up with a stout rod, a heavy leader, and some huge flies. By huge I mean bigger than the biggest ones you have now. Think of a big fish as a human being with a salary in six figures. If you toss a penny on the sidewalk to see what it will attract, you'll get kids and bums. A quarter will get you teenagers and the occasional adult, although the latter will glance around a time or two to make sure no one is looking before he picks it up. A dollar will get you most people, but a twenty-dollar bill will stop a Lincoln Continental in heavy traffic.

Next, find a good piece of water, ideally a lake or reservoir. All things being equal, a good lake will hold bigger fish than a good stream, with very large, productive rivers being the exception. Pick one close to home, because you'll be spending a lot of time there. If you must leave your own neighborhood, take the wall tent, Winnebago, or whatever you have in the way of portable luxury accommodations.

Dress warmly, because you'll be out all night and/or in the worst possible weather. Dead of the night, dark of the moon, and spitting rain is best.

Use a sink-tip or full sinking fly line to get deep and leave the #16 dry flies at home. Not back in the car, I mean at home where you can't get them if you weaken and decide to do a little real fishing, just to break the monotony.

Don't fool around wading and casting from shore. Get into a craft of some kind so you'll be mobile.

Finally, learn to sleep during the day and steel yourself for days, if not weeks, of dredging before you hook *the fish*.

Okay, maybe I'm being a little unfair, but that's how the real headhunters do it, day in and day out. It's not the only way to catch big fish, but it's how you make a career out of it. I can do it, but only for short stretches and only a few times in a season. Two straight days of kick-ass lunker hunting is about all I can handle, then I'm back to splitting the difference.

Splitting the difference means fishing all day like a gentleman on a good trout stream, taking a break for supper, and then coming back for two hours at night to cast a six-inch-long chipmunk fly to the stickiest logjam in the deepest bend pool in the whole river. Or maybe putting the bluegill rod away at dusk and coming back for a session with a 2/0, goggle-eyed bass bug and a jug of mosquito repellent. It must be done on occasion—especially when the conditions seem to beg for it.

Yet another way involves increasing your odds through precise timing. The prespawning congregation of fat, horney brown trout around the inlet to a lake may only last a week, but you can take your big fish then, and not just one, but several. A locally famous trophy hunter likes to go to the big reservoirs the night before the weekly stocking truck arrives. He says the big browns and rainbows eat the stockers like they were popcorn. They learn the stocking schedules and wait for the trucks.

Of course the hatches are the best; those few, famous, thick hatches and falls of large bugs that move the biggest fish to rise to the surface to dry flies. The most mythical of these is probably the hatch of the huge stoneflies on Montana rivers like the Madison and the Big Hole. The bug is the famous Pteronarcys something-or-other, known also as the giant salmon fly; the two-

and-a-half-inch long, orange and black dry fly. Yes, I've seen the bug. In fact, I have one on the desk here in a bottle of formaldehyde. (I got it out to measure it in the interest of accuracy; I was going to say three inches.) Over the years I've hit the ends or the beginnings of this hatch on two rivers in Montana and one in Idaho, but have never seen it in its glory. I've heard the stories, though, from fishermen who are normally calm and droll, guys who shook me by the lapels and swore it was all true, as if they'd just seen Godzilla grazing in a field east of town. "Twenty-four-inch trout on every cast," they said, "cars skidding in squashed bugs on the highway . . ."

Relax. I believe it.

An even more interesting question than "What is a big fish?" or "How do you catch one?" is, "What will you do with it?"

Mounting it seems logical, and there is something smug about having the evidence right there on the wall. Not only that, it gives you a gracious introduction to the story. You don't have to go out of your way to bring it up, you just wait for someone to say "Jeeze, nice fish," and there's your audience. Anyone who doesn't comment is probably a golfer and wouldn't understand anyway.

I have not been moved to have a fish mounted in recent years, but apparently that wasn't always true. My father swore that when I was just a tyke, no more than this high, I threw a fit because he refused to have a sunfish I'd caught in Wisconsin stuffed. "It wasn't even big enough to eat, and I threw it back," he said. "You raised hell for an hour."

What did I know? It was probably the fourth or fifth fish I'd ever caught and the first that wasn't a bullhead, but at the tender age of no more than five I knew what a mount was and I wanted one.

I still like mounts. I go out of my way to admire them (and not just to be polite, either) and have a special affection for old ratty ones that were caught by someone's daddy—who is now dead—forty years ago when everything, including the fishing, was better than it is now. But I don't have any myself.

There was a time when it was out of the question from an economic standpoint, and I'm not so sure that time has passed. I do now and then have a few extra bucks, but at five to eight dollars an inch, a 24-inch trout is worth two weeks on the road somewhere, during which time one might even catch yet *another* big fish.

I have a few photographs hanging around the place: the 8-pound rainbow from Kipps Lake, a 6-pounder from the nameless lake in Wyoming, etc. The 8-pound trout is my favorite because the photo was taken by Gary

LaFontaine, a big-time famous fisherman whose name drops loudly and who also knows how to make a wide-angle lens add several pounds to an already heavy fish. "Aim his head up toward the camera a little more," he said.

I have so far released all of my truly big fish, unless you count bluegills and crappies, many of which I have fried in beer batter and eaten happily. A.K. killed a 5- or 6-pound brown two years ago, but only because it had taken the streamer deep in the gills and was clearly bleeding to death. It was delicious, by the way. Don't believe what they say about big fish not being good to eat.

I could get all moralistic about this business of not killing large fish, but the fact is, I've just never figured out how big a fish has to be before it absolutely demands to be stuffed. I have also learned that they don't look as big as they really are when they're mounted. You need a real pig to raise discerning eyebrows.

I've only met one fisherman who seemed to have that under control. He asked me, more or less in passing, if I knew where he could catch a 16-inch brook trout. It seemed like a reasonable, but still slightly odd, request, so I asked what he was up to. It seems he already had a rainbow, a brown, a yellowstone cutthroat, a golden, and a grayling—all exactly 16 inches long—mounted on the wall of his den. "Specimens," he said. "Archetypal examples of the trouts (and grayling) of North America, not trophies."

I like that. It seemed rational, modest, scientific (but not *too* scientific); the well-bred answer to the problem of the trophy. I did actually have a suspicion about where a guy might catch a 16-inch brookie, but all I could bring myself to do was congratulate him on his finely honed aesthetics and wish him well. I'm a sucker for that kind of thing, but I'm not stupid.

So, how big should it be before you mount it? Hard to say. You could devise a rule of thumb, I suppose—if you didn't grunt when you lifted it in the net, it's not big enough—but that may miss the point. Unless you've got a wall full of stuffed fish, it should be a memento of a pinnacle in your angling career, and few of us are willing to admit that we've just caught the biggest fish we'll ever catch. With life as short as it is, that might be a milestone we don't care to pass.

Big fish are what we want, but they're like true love, success, lots of money, or maybe public office: we don't know *why* we want them, but we figure that will take care of itself if we ever connect. It will become obvious, won't it?

Maybe it's the quest that makes sense to us—the fragile balance between reality, possibility, and promise. The fisherman is privileged among human beings as one who can push his expectations with some hope of fulfillment. World peace and universal enlightenment are, I think, beyond us, but a fish that's an inch longer or an ounce heavier than the last one, well, shoot, that could happen.

Yet another problem with really big fish is that once spotted, they can't be hooked; once hooked, they can't be landed. As we all know, it takes tremendous fortitude to come away with anything like a straight face after being taken to the brink and then robbed of the satisfaction. Still, it's illustrative, possibly because it copies life in general so well.

Fly-fishing reveals character, and the bigger the fish the deeper the revelation. A potential wall hanger is not only a horrendous fish, it can also show your partners what you're made of.

Last summer A.K. and I were on our usual jaunt through Idaho and Montana when we hooked up with a gentleman named Bill Crabtree. Bill lives in Texas, but he spends several months in West Yellowstone, Montana, each year—at a place that's been in his family for several generations—to, as he puts it, "just sort of ease out a little, you know?"

One evening, after several days of fishing together, we decided to drive to a pond we knew of to see about getting into a big trout. Enormous fish live in this thing, but it's one of those places where you will probably not hook a fish, and if you do, you probably won't land it because it will be *too* big. For this reason, it's usually deserted, even though it's well known to fishermen in the area.

The main problem with landing the fish—over and above the usual problems one has with big, strong trout—is the weed beds. They're wide and dense and ring the shore, and the gooey, unstable bottom makes wading unfeasible. If you work from shore and get into even a decent fish, he'll take you into the weeds, tangle himself up and break you off. All the big ones have done this a hundred times and are real good at it.

The solution is to fish from a belly boat. That way you stand a better chance of keeping the fish out of the weeds, and, failing that, you can at least go in after him with some hope of coming out again.

You fish a place like this on occasion, not so much to catch trout as to see how much adrenaline you can generate and how much disappointment you can stand. When you're alone you can swear and scream and thrash the water with your flippers when you lose a fish, but in company a modicum of restraint is expected.

It was just coming on evening—the best time—when we arrived at the pond, having hauled our float tubes, flippers, and rods down from the road.

The smooth surface of the pond was unbroken by rise or boil, calmly reflecting the darkening sky and a range of mountains, but the knowledge of what swam there made the water seem to tingle with electricity. It was like the peacefulness of a hand grenade from which the pin has just been pulled. We rigged up slowly, with a studied casualness, although our eyes left the water only when necessary.

The first boil was unbelievably large. In most waters you'd assume it was a full-grown beaver, but not here. Here there were no beavers, probably because the trout have eaten them all. It caught us in various states of disarray: Bill and I were sitting on our tubes, half into and half out of our waders with rods still broken down. A.K. was still in hiking boots, but he had already strung up his rod and had a fly tied on—a #14 flying ant like the ones we'd seen on the water. A.K. always strings the rod first and he almost always starts with a dry fly.

He gave Bill and me a questioning glance. I shrugged and heard Bill say, "Hell, why not?"

A.K. worked out some line and cast ahead of the dissipating ripples that indicated the fish's direction. He barely had time to straighten the leader before one of the largest trout I've ever seen in the flesh swallowed the little dry fly with a great slurping and burbling of water.

A.K. set the hook, somewhat gingerly, and the fish shot to the deepest hole in the middle of the pond, tearing 6-weight line from the reel. And there he sat, immovable as a rock the size of a couch. The only sign of life was a petulant thrumming in the line. The fish wasn't scared, he was pissed.

"That was really stupid," A.K. said, half to himself. "Now what am I gonna do?"

Bill and I could think of nothing to say. Stupid, maybe, but there isn't a fisherman alive who wouldn't have cast to that trout from right there on shore. Anyone with the iron will it would have taken to suit up and get into the float tube first would be no fun to fish with.

He thought it over for a minute. It was painfully obvious.

"I'm gonna have to get into my waders and get into the belly boat and get the hell out there," he said. "Someone is gonna have to hold the rod for a minute."

Among fishermen there are moments of unspoken understanding; moments when there is no doubt whatsoever about what is going to happen next. It's enough to make you believe in fate.

A.K. looked over at Bill and me, who were both on our feet by then. Bill threw his hands in the air as if someone had just pointed a .44 magnum at his heart, did a smart about-face and walked off into the sagebrush and cactus. He knew what was about to transpire and he wanted no part of it.

That, of course, left the good old fishing partner.

A.K. gave me a silent look worthy of a Shakespearean actor. It said: this won't work, but it must be tried, and if the fish is lost it will be my own fault; I couldn't possibly blame you—but I will.

I wish I hadn't already put my flippers on, because the gravity of the situation called for something more dignified than for me to waddle over there like a duck and carefully take the rod.

A.K. was into his waders and flippers with one foot in the belly boat when I felt a ponderous wiggle in the line and the fly came loose.

It just came loose, honest.

A.K. froze in the unlikely posture of a man mounting a float tube. Bill was thirty yards out on the prairie, hands in his pockets, looking at the ground like a mourner at a funeral. The shadow of the mountains had swallowed the pond and a songbird twittered in that frantic way they have right at dusk—as if they haven't had enough to eat today and it's going to be a long, cold night.

And then Bill said, "I seen him break it off when you weren't looking."

The loss of a big fish, for whatever reason, reveals character. Much more so than the actual landing of a big fish, which only calls for a modicum of forgivably false humility.

Jay Allman and I were once fishing together on a lake known for its large rainbow trout; fish that were catchable, but that would come a few per day at best. And that's how they were coming to us. They were large enough— 5 pounds and up—that the usual suspicion that there were even larger ones in there was muted. This thought is never absent from the mind of the fisherman, and it is always true, but there are times when it doesn't matter.

We were both in belly boats, and my back was to Jay, but it was one of those clear, calm, profoundly quiet western days, and I could clearly hear the zzzzup of his line as he set the hook and the growl of the reel as the fish bored off almost casually. On this particular lake, the hooking of a fish was an event, so I turned and gave Jay the clenched-fist salute still popular with aging counter-culture types. He returned it with a nod of the head, as his right hand was engaged in palming the reel.

I turned back to the line of cattails in front of me along which the grapefruit-sized head and shoulders of a large trout periodically broke the surface, now here, now there, eating God knew what in no discernible rhythm or pattern. The problem at hand was simply to make a cast that didn't line the fish and spook him. If the fly was the right one and I happened to inadvertently put it in front of him, he might even eat it, at which point it would become an entirely different game that I could also easily lose.

This calls for some concentration.

It was probably five minutes later when I glanced over at Jay. He was playing a fish.

"Another one," I yelled. "Quit showing off."

"Same one," he said, not looking up.

Indeed. For a fly-fisher of Jay's caliber to spend five minutes playing a single trout meant one thing: my presence with the camera would be required. I reeled in and paddled over, harboring visions of a *Sports Afield* cover shot. Blue sky, puffy clouds, red rock hills, big fish. Perfect.

I stopped at a respectful distance to watch. The rod was bent nearly double, the white fly line vanished into a depth of clear water that was hard to judge. And on the end of that line was another nine or ten feet of leader. The fish swam in wide, deep, lazy circles, slowly turning the belly boat with it. Jay was nowhere near panic, nor was he in much control, either.

This was a big, big, big trout.

This was very serious business.

Now Jay adheres to the philosophy of land them or lose them, but don't mess around, so he was playing this fish to what he perceived as the limits of his tackle, trying to get it up off the bottom. It was working, but slowly.

Jay finally pumped the trout up to about six or eight feet, and we both caught a glimpse of him down there. We weren't really surprised at the nearly yard-long form because we'd both already taken some quite large fish there and none of them had been anywhere near this heavy or this tough.

It was about then that the rod went straight; Jay looked shocked for a few seconds, then bowed his head and sat there staring at the patch of orange material on the front of his tube where it says, "Inflate to 1½ psi during use; DO NOT OVERINFLATE" as if pondering the true meaning of the phrase.

After a minute or two of meditation, he looked up, smiled, and said, "Well, let's get another one."

That's all you can do. In fact, it's what you *must* do. It's one of the unwritten laws of the sport. There's obviously nothing to be gained by getting mad at yourself, and no one in his right mind would hold it against the fish.

After Dark

*If you happen to share my predilection for angling tales that "take you somewhere,"
which I mentioned in an earlier introduction, then Steve Raymond's book* The Year of
the Angler *belongs in your library. Published by Winchester Press in 1973, with illus-
trations by Dave Whitlock,* The Year of the Angler *takes you fishing with Steve
Raymond in places you don't want to miss.*

*In this absolute gem of a tale from that book, Steve shows me what I've been
missing by not embracing night fishing, something I've never been particularly fond of.*

Steve Raymond is also the author of other books, including The Year of the
Trout, *and two titles published by* The Lyons Press—Steelhead Country *and*
Rivers of the Heart. *He has been a reviewer and prominent editor of* Flyfisher *mag-
azine for more than thirty years and is a recipient of the prestigious Roderick Haig-
Brown Angling Heritage Award.*

James Chetham, writing in *The Angler's Vade Mecum* (1681), called night
fishing an "unwholesome, unpleasant and very ungenteel" sport, and a
practice "to be used by none but idle poaching fellows."

Without doubt there is more than a grain of truth in what he says, and
certainly the literature of angling is replete with tales of poachers and
perpetrators of other foul angling deeds who committed their crimes under
cover of darkness.

But if it is true that the darkest hours bring out the worst in men, it
also is true that they bring out the best of trout. Great trout, quiescent by day,
begin to prowl and feed at night, and hidden hatches set off explosive rises
from fish the daytime angler never sees. For those anglers whose intentions are
honorable and above reproach, the hours of darkness may provide angling of
an exciting, different sort.

I am not a night fisherman by regular habit, but occasionally when the day is warm and the wind gentle I will stay on the water long after the last light fades, and try to tempt the larger trout that come forth to feed at night. And occasionally, when I become aware of the presence of a large trout that will not take my fly by day, I make a special trip to try for him by night. More often than not these expeditions are successful, but successful or not they never fail to generate high excitement.

Night angling has a special quality. As the last light steals from the day, the earth changes suddenly in a confusing movement of dark and growing shadows. Familiar landmarks grow or shrink, become magnified in total size as individual details disappear, or dwindle into obscure and hidden shadows. A well-known place becomes suddenly mysterious and strange, forbidding and forbidden, and as total darkness descends all reference points slowly disappear until only the tops of the tallest ridges remain silhouetted dimly against the sky.

The stars begin their slow, silent climb to the zenith, and perhaps there is a pale moon with light enough to cast cold, silver shadows across the meadows or the mesas. The familiar life of day is gone and the creatures of the night take over. The rings from rising fish gleam briefly like spreading circles of molten steel in the ghostly evening light, and the swallows that fed on the daylight hatches are replaced by silent, plunging bats.

The night fisherman knows a different world. Normal daytime sounds subside so that one may hear the soft, close rush of wings from a bird in hidden flight. The bullfrogs talk to one another more freely than by day, and the loud slap of a beaver's tail echoes through the wild. The moon trades its cold light with the clouds, and occasionally meteors flash overhead with a last quick burst of dying flame. The stars wheel in their silent orbits—bright Rigel and mysterious Betelgeuse, and the Arab mourners plodding eternally after a casket traced in stars.

It is a time to pause, to look up in awe and wonder about the nature of things; a time that teaches humility in the face of evidence that the angler is only a small fisherman on a small water, an infinitesimal fragment of life hurtling through the void from an unknown source to an uncharted destination, with only his fragile faith to guide him.

But if it is a time for contemplation, it also is a time for action. There comes the sudden sound of a heavy rise, and the angler wheels blindly toward the sound and casts into the night. His fly rides an invisible wave and tensely he waits for the sound of a take or the sudden jolt that will tell him the trout has seen what he cannot see.

And then follows the struggle with an invisible opponent, a silent battle between a man who cannot see his quarry and a trout robbed of the sanctuary of familiar obstacles now hidden in the dark. And when it is over the angler is either flushed and trembling with the excitement of victory or filled with the pangs of defeat and wonder at the size of the unseen thing that defeated him.

My first real try at night fishing came on a warm September evening in central British Columbia. We were camped in the bottom of a great granite canyon with ancient Indian pictographs painted on its walls. The canyon held a pair of lakes, twin jewels of sparkling clear water with shallow, sandy shoals that sloped off into unknown turqoise depths.

I had spent the day fishing one of them, and in the shallow water behind a large weedbed I had found trout rising freely to a hatch. I had taken and released many on a dry fly, but most of them were small and I was frustrated because I could see much larger fish moving in and out of the shallows to feed. The larger fish refused everything I tried, wet fly or dry, and so I waited to fish the evening rise in hopes they would be less cautious then.

The light went quickly off the water in the deep canyon, and the sky changed from blue to deep purple. But there was no hatch and no rise, and I watched and waited as the last light disappeared without seeing a single ring on the placid surface of the lake. The next day we would have to leave and return to the city, and I badly wanted at least one more good fish before we left, so I determined to wait even until after total darkness had fallen. I had with me a small flashlight to aid in changing flies or leaders, and I settled down to wait.

It was quiet in the darkness, except for a gentle stir of breeze that set the tules rubbing against one another and pushed small wavelets at my boat that made a tiny lap-lap sound as they struck its windward side. And then, far back in the weeds, came the heavy splash of a feeding trout. It was far beyond casting range, and hopelessly hidden in the weeds, and so I waited further. Far off came the sound of another splashing rise and I sensed rather than saw the great, mothlike sedges that were beginning to flutter awkwardly from the surface of the lake.

Another heavy splash, this one close by, just at the edge of the weedbed from the sound of it. I cast quickly toward the sound, and as I felt the line strike the water in the darkness there was another explosive rise, and I struck instinctively. There was immediate, furious resistance from a fish so strong I thought for a moment I could not hold it on the light tackle. It ran along the edge of the weedbed and my reel screamed an angry protest. I felt the backing splice slide out through the guides and heard a great crash in the darkness as the fish leaped and fell back into the water.

Then it was a long and silent struggle as the fish turned and plunged and vainly sought the sanctuaries it used by day. It was confused in the darkness and turned away from the weedbed where it would have broken me off quickly, and I held it as firmly as I could so that it would not stray again out of the deeper water into which it had blundered.

Time passes quickly in the darkness, and it seemed a very long time indeed before all the line was back on the reel and only the leader extended beyond the tip of the rod. The trout circled the boat once, then again, and in the starlight I caught a glimpse of silver and stabbed at it with the net. The surface erupted as the net closed around the trout and I lifted it clear, struggling and twisting in the mesh. And then it lay quivering in the bottom of my boat, illuminated by the wavering beam of my flashlight, a great old trout of many summers, with broad silver flanks that bounced the light back into my eyes.

It had been as exciting a fight as I had ever had with a fish, and though I had waited for darkness with some reservations about the ethics of it all, I felt now that no trout ever had been more honestly taken or had struggled more nobly than this one. And as for the ethics of the matter, if the trout was somewhat handicapped by the darkness, the angler had been handicapped even more, and is not the taking of fish under difficult circumstances indeed the essence of the sport?

For me, the answer was affirmative, and with that question having been resolved my path has led to other nighttime waters.

I suspect all anglers are night fishermen in their hearts. Who among us has ever fished who did not look forward to the evening, the long, drawn-out death of the day when, as every angler knows, the trout grow less cautious and the fishing more rewarding? When does evening end and night begin? What is less honorable about fishing when the darkness is nearly total than fishing when a little light remains? What separates the night fisherman from the man who stays to fish the "evening rise"?

It is, of course, a matter of definition, and each angler has his own idea of the best time to fish and the best time to quit fishing, whether it be at five o'clock or midnight. Perhaps the most eloquent answer was that given by the great angling pioneer Thaddeus Norris, who said:

"Of all places, commend me, in the still of the evening, to the long placid pool, shallow on one side, with deeper water and an abrupt overhanging bank opposite. Where the sun has shone all day, and legions of ephemera sported in its declining rays; the bloom of the rye or clover scenting the air from the adjoining field! Now light a fresh pipe, and put on a pale Ginger Hackle for your tail-fly, and a little white-winged Coachman for your dropper. Then wade in cautiously—move like a shadow—don't make a ripple. Cast, slowly, long, light; let your stretcher sink a little. There, he has taken the Ginger—lead him around gently to the shallow side as you reel him in, but don't move from your position—let him tug awhile, put your net under him, break his neck, and slip him into your creel. Draw your line through the rings—cast again; another and another—keep on until you can see only the ripple made by your fly; or know when it falls, by the slight tremor it imparts through the whole line down to your hand—until the whippoorwill begins his evening song, and the little frog tweets in the grass close by;—not till then is it time to go home."

And so it is, in the sweet of the evening.

Three springs ago, I spent an evening among the rushes at Dry Falls Lake, at the head of the great coulee where eons ago the Columbia River plunged over in a mighty falls many times the height and width of Niagara. Now there is nothing left but the huge, silent, eroding walls of stone, and the rich lake that fills the old catchbasin where once the river fell.

It had been a bright, hot day, with the temperature well up in the 80s and the sun peering brightly into the depths. The fishing had been poor, as it usually is under such circumstances, and now I was waiting for the light to die beyond the coulee rim.

The light was a long time fading from the water, but slowly it did so and the great rocks reached out with shadows to replace the brilliance of the day. And as the shadows deepened, the trout began to move into the shallows to feed, with a steady march of rises to the shore.

I cast toward the rises and strained in the gathering darkness to see my fly. It was hopeless; my eyes were not keen enough to pick out the tiny dark pattern and separate it from the dark water on which it rode. So, holding the fine point of the leader up to the twilight in order to see what I was about, I tied on a larger pattern with hackle fore-and-aft and cast it out. This one I could see, with its dark bulk riding on stiff hackles as it waited for a trout to notice it was there.

I teased the fly with my rod tip so that it crept across the surface, and quickly it was gone, swallowed up in a rising wave by a trout which had it and was quickly away. There was no need to lift the rod; the tension came immediately as the fish began a powerful run. My reel on this occasion was an especially noisy one, and the echo of its ratchet rattled off the coulee walls as the trout took all the line and the backing quickly followed. He jumped, sixty yards out, and when I thought of the fine, 6X tippet on the leader, I had no hope that I would ever have him.

The trout turned and came back a little way, and once again I had some line on the reel. But then it was off again on another run, this one perpendicular to the first, and took the line around a clump of tules growing in the shallows. I slacked off to keep tension from the line and avoid a break in the leader.

For a long moment, nothing happened, and I stood there holding slack line. And then I saw the tip of my floating white line in the faint light beyond the tules, moving slowly through the shadows. The trout was still on. There was only one way I would ever get him out of the spot where he had gone, and risky as it was I had to try it. I threw a great loop in the line, almost as if I were mending an upstream cast. The loop cleared the tops of the tules and fell in open water on the other side. I reeled in, tightened, and once again felt the resistance of the fish.

From then on it was a long, slow, delicate fight, the trout tired from its two long runs and I afraid to be heavy-handed because of the light leader tippet. Finally the trout was kicking feebly in the shallows and I had my net under it. It was a rainbow, one of the prettiest I have seen, clean and bright with a sharp dividing line between the silver of its sides and the gunmetal gray of its back. I removed the hook from the gristle of its jaw and eased it back into the water, holding it for a long time until it regained strength enough to swim slowly away.

It was pitch dark when I started back, and I heard the faint call of the vanguard of a flock of Canada geese, winging their way north after a winter spent on the flats of Tulelake in California's northern hills, or in the grain-rich fields of the Sacramento Valley. Soon the flock was directly overhead, and though the great birds were invisible against the night, their haunting calls filled the great stone amphitheater with sound, echoing and re-echoing long after the flock itself had passed. It had been a satisfying day, rich with sensations of sight and sound and feel.

I have spent nights on many waters, gazing up at the Southern Cross while the gentle trade wind rippled at my shirt, or watching the silent flicker of the Northern Lights play across the horizon of a Canadian lake. I have fought a losing match with a great brown trout that took my fly on the darkest of all nights, and a winning contest with a giant rainbow that fell upon my fly in the middle of a night hatch where hordes of insects swayed and brushed lightly against my face and hands, all unseen. I have thrilled to the cry of a cougar and the lost, lonely call of a loon, the wildest sound in all of nature; and I have fought silent battles with unseen trout while coyotes howled in the hills.

The night is not to be feared; it is to be felt, touched, sampled and explored. It is filled with exciting secrets forever hidden from the day. It is a frontier, to be tried and tested and won, and I commend it to all anglers.

The Finest Trout in the River

BY HENRY PLUNKET-GREENE

In many ways similar to John Waller Hills' A Summer on the Test, Henry Plunket-Greene's Where the Bright Waters Meet *is an engaging chronicle of fishing English chalkstreams in the years 1902–12.*

Greene was a classic opera singer who loved flyfishing with a passion. As we mentioned in the introduction to this book, his favorite water was the enchanting little Bourne, and he wrote about his experiences there with a keen eye and great feeling. Greene's title is from a lovely poem by Tom Moore:

> *There is not in this wide world a valley so sweet*
> *As that vale in whose bosom the bright waters meet.*

Where the Bright Waters Meet was first published in 1924, revised and enlarged in 1936, and was published in the United States by Nick Lyons Books/ Winchester Press in the 1980s.

It might naturally be supposed that if one had the fishing of a trout-stream like the Bourne one would not leave an inch of it unexplored, but it was a fact that up to this time none of the rods had ever taken the trouble to investigate the top quarter-mile of the water. Savage and Sharkey had somehow got it into their heads that there was nothing worth troubling about above the "lagoon" immediately beyond the viaduct, and as they lived close to the top of the fishing, all the rest of us, myself included, had tacitly accepted this as a matter of fact. Nowadays the whole of this region is a vast watercress bed, and anyone looking out of the window of the train, when passing over the viaduct, would never realise that there was, or ever had been, a river there at all; but in those days there were two streams above, as well as below, the bridge, meeting a little way up and stretching as one, for a quarter of a mile to the end of the fishing.

We had all of us come on occasions as far as the hatch below this final stretch, but, in the belief that the water above was a blank, had always turned back when we got there.

On August 31st of this year, the last day of the season, I found myself at this hatch at about six o'clock in the evening. I had got four fish averaging 1¼ lbs., but it had been a bad rising day, cold and windy. At six o'clock it suddenly turned warm and calm, and I was sitting on the hatch smoking a pipe before going home, when I thought that, just for fun, I would walk up to the end of the water. I expected nothing, and had half a mind to leave my rod behind and saunter up with my hands in my pockets. I got over the fence and strolled up on to the bank unconcernedly, and, as I did so, from one weed-patch after another there darted off a series of two-pounders racing upstream like motor-boats. I dropped like a stone, but the damage was done. I just sat there cursing the day I was born and myself, not only for having lost the chance of a lifetime—for the iron-blues were beginning to come down thick—but for having left this gold-mine undiscovered and untouched for two years—and to-day was the last day of the season! If there had been any handy way discovered of kicking oneself physically as well as mentally I should have been unrecognisable when I got home. Every fish was under the weeds long ago, and I might just as well pack up my traps and clear out.

There was an old broken-down footbridge about a hundred yards above me, and I thought that I would go up to it and explore the reach beyond, more with a view to the possibilities of next year than with any hope for the present. I got down from the bank and circled round through the meadow till I got to it, and was just picking my way across its rotten planks when under my very feet I saw a small nose appear, followed by a diminutive head and the most enormous shoulder I ever remember to have seen in a chalk stream. I froze stiff where I stood, except that my knees were shaking like aspens, for there right underneath me was gradually emerging the fish of my life. I do not mean to say that I have not caught bigger fish before and since, but this was a veritable star in the dust-heap, a Cinderella stealing out of the kitchen that we had all despised, and the romance of the thing put him (*pace* Cinderella) on a pedestal of fame from which I have never taken him down.

It was agonising work, for he swam up in the most leisurely way at a rate of about an inch in every five seconds, while I was straddled across two rotten planks, either of which might have given way at any moment, and had to pretend that I was part of the landscape. He was immediately under me when he first showed up and I could easily have touched him with my foot. What fish will see and what they will not see will ever remain a mystery! It was then about half-past six (old time), the time of day when one's visibility is most clear, and yet he took not the smallest notice of me. He just strolled up the middle of the stream contentedly as though he were having a smoke after dinner. I can still feel my joints creaking as I sank slowly to my knees and got my line out. It fell just right and he took no more notice of it than of a water-rat, I tried again and again, lengthening the cast as he moved up, and at last he rose towards it, examined it carefully and, horror of horrors!, swam slowly after it downstream through the bridge under my feet! It would have been laughable if it had not been so tragic. There was I pulling in the slack like a madman, and leaving it in wisps round my knees, scared lest he should see my hand move; and he passed me by without a word and disappeared into the bowels of the bridge.

I just knelt there and swore, trying to look over my shoulder to see if he had gone down below. There was no sign of him, and the situation was painful in the extreme, for my knees were working through the rotten woodwork, and if I tried to ease myself I should either bring the bridge down with a crash or anyway evict Cinderellum for good and all.

I bore it as long as I could, and was just going to give it up and scramble out anyhow, when I saw that nose slide out again beneath me, and my old friend started off on his journey up-stream once more.

I began on him with a shorter line this time, and he took the fly at the very first cast like a lamb. If he was a lamb as he took it he was a lion when he had it. Instead of running up-stream, as I hoped and expected he would do, he gave one swish with his tail and bolted down through the bridge, bending the rod double and dragging the point right under. It was done with such lightning speed I had no time to remonstrate. I threw myself flat on my stomach and got the rod sideways over the bridge, and then the fight began. I was on one side of the bridge, and he was half-way to Southampton on the other. He got farther and farther downstream, going from one patch of weeds to the next, and digging and burrowing his nose into the middle of it, while I just hung on, helpless, waiting for the end. He quieted down after a bit, and finding that he could not rub the annoying thing out of his nose on the south side he determined to explore the north, and he began to swim up towards me. I must have been a ridiculous sight, spread-eagled on the rotting planks with splinters digging into my legs and ants and spiders crawling down my neck, vainly endeavouring to hold the rod over the side with one hand, to wind in the line with the other, and to watch him over my shoulder all at the same time. Fortunately, I must have been invisible from below, but the moment he got under the bridge he saw the rod and tore past me up-stream with the reel screaming.

But now we were on even terms and there was a clear stretch of water ahead, and I was able to play him to a finish. I was really proud of that fight, for, in addition to the cramped style which I was compelled to adopt, it took place in a stream ten feet wide, half-choked with weeds, and I got him on a 000 Iron-blue at the end of a 4x point. He weighed 3¾ lbs. when I got him home, and I have always bitterly regretted that I did not get him set up, for, with the exception of an 11¾-pounder in the hall of Longford Castle, caught in the Avon by one of the family on a "local lure" (the name of which neither fork nor spade would dig from me), he was the most beautiful river-trout in shape, colour and proportion I ever saw.

A Guide's Advice

BY MALLORY BURTON

Mallory Burton's very active life as a flyfisher has included some hard time as a trout guide on western rivers. As you might expect, she has seen a lot of folks come and go with fly rods in their hands, and several of them have become more or less immortalized in her engaging book, Green River Virgins and Other Passionate Anglers, *published by The Lyons Press in 2000.*

Stephen Bodio has written of Mallory's prose, "Mallory Burton knows more than fish and streams and tackle; she knows the hearts and minds of the humans who are happiest when they are waist-deep in a wild river."

Amen to that. Mallory's experiences and observations are as refreshing as the mountain streams whence they came. This tale is one of my favorites, pointing out that it may be true indeed that "a good man is hard to find," but a good brown trout is even harder.

I've rowed for women before. A few were fluffs—good-natured types who attempted a couple of casts, fussed dutifully over their husbands' fish, and went back to reading their novels. A few were outright maniacs, fishing like troopers from dawn to dark-thirty, so jazzed about the river I worried they'd cash in their return tickets for one more day on the water. But most of the women I take out on the river these days are just dedicated anglers, outfishing the men in the boat because they can take a guide's advice without their egos getting in the way.

Rebecca Sheffield, well she was a different type altogether. And she had reasons all her own for being on the river. She booked the trip six months ago. I remember taking that call. Andy, the owner, usually handles the bookings for the shop, but he was off bonefishing somewhere—hard to pin that guy down—and I was filling in. There wasn't much happening that day. I had a fire going in the woodstove and the coffee on. Usually you can count on a few of the regulars to come by for a chat, but that day nobody showed up. I'd spent most of the day sorting out the fly bins, so I was happy to take a few calls.

The conversation stood out among the others because it was so sparse, so impersonal. Most clients are anxious to chat it up, to pick your brain with questions about the water conditions and the bugs and gear. Ms. Sheffield just asked for a solo day trip on July 15. You would have thought she was booking the trip for someone else. Or maybe she fished so often, the whole thing had become routine. I hadn't been working out of Andy's shop for very long, and I wasn't all that familiar with his clientele. On the off chance that she was one of our repeat clients, I asked her who she'd like to float with.

"Are you free?" she asked.

"According to the book, I am."

"I'll fish with you then." I jotted her last name in the book.

"I'd be happy to take you out. I'm Paul Martin by the way."

She hung up.

Middle of March we had one of those freak Montana snowstorms that pretty well shuts down the town. Andy thought it might be a good time to put together some of the mail orders that were piling up and confirm a few trips. He'd only been back from Belize a couple of days, and I remember walking in out of the cold and thinking how out-of-place the guy looked in his own shop. I don't mean to suggest there's anything funny looking about Andy. He's a good-looking guy, tall, strong enough to handle a boat no problem. But there he was with this tan in the middle of winter, hair sunbleached, and these clean, clean fingernails. Strictly Hollywood. Dye his hair black, stick him on a horse, and he could be the Marlboro Man. Didn't even get my boots off and already he's down to business. That's the easterner coming out in him, I guess.

"Who took this one?" he wanted to know. There was a big red line under Sheffield in the book.

"I did. A woman. Not very friendly. You know how those easterners are."

"Coming alone?"

"Assume so. She didn't mention anyone else."

"Let me know how it goes."

"Want me to call her and confirm?"

"No. Don't worry about it. I'm just curious, that's all."

We never did confirm the trip, and we didn't hear from her again until last night, when she called from her motel. I suggested we meet at the shop in the morning, around eight.

"Perhaps you could pick me up here," she said. "On your way out."

She was obviously new at this, or maybe she just didn't like any fuss. Meeting at the shop was a big part of the ritual, all the guides and the clients trading stories and sizing each other up.

"No trouble at all. How're you fixed for gear?"

"I don't have any flies," she said.

I laughed. "That's the beauty of fly fishing. You can have your vest stuffed full of fly boxes and still never have exactly the right fly."

"I don't have any," she repeated.

"Better bring lots of money, then," I warned. "The Beaverhead willows have been known to eat a few flies."

"Of course," she said.

As it turned out, Rebecca Sheffield looked like she could afford to lose a few flies. Maybe a lot of flies. I couldn't say why. Maybe it was her New England accent and reserve, or the way she held herself, so straight and confident. She wasn't flashy, but she was attractive, classic even. Her straight brown hair was pulled back off her face and tied with a thin ribbon. She didn't wear perfume or jewelry. She was fine-boned, but square-jawed and long-legged, which gave her an athletic appearance. You could picture her in jodhpurs sailing over a stone fence or stalking through a meadow with a bird dog heeled at her side and a little Browning bent over her arm.

"Ms. Sheffield," I said, as she came over to the pickup.

"Rebecca," she said. We shook hands.

We loaded her gear and headed out on the old highway. Rebecca sat quietly, looking out the window.

"We'll put in near the Tash ranch," I told her, "and float all the way back into town. The shuttle vehicle's parked near the city dump. You might say we're floating Tash to trash."

Rebecca raised her eyebrows. "You might," she said.

★   ★   ★

If Rebecca wasn't a sparkling conversationalist, at least she had boat manners. She stayed clear while I loaded and launched the Avon. And I didn't have to keep an eye on her. Some clients wander around in the sage, and you have to remind them about the snakes. Rebecca just stood in one spot on the bank, staring out at the water. She rinsed the soles of her wading boots before she stepped into the raft.

I got a good look at the single fly rod she had brought as we shoved off. It was a custom job on a top-quality blank, set up in a style that was popular maybe two, three years ago. It looked familiar, quite a bit like the rods that Andy used to build when he first opened the shop. I wouldn't have been surprised to see his logo on the shaft.

"Nice rod," I said. "How's it fish?"

"I don't know," she answered. "I've had some casting lessons, that's all. The rod was a gift."

"Well, most of the casting's close in here," I assured her. "If you can manage thirty feet with any accuracy, you'll catch fish. Don't worry."

"I won't," she said. I didn't doubt it for a minute.

On those rare occasions when I take out a solo trip, I like to float the lower third of the river. The fish are a bit smaller there, but more plentiful, or maybe just more visible. The banks are closer together, making it difficult for two anglers to fish simultaneously without getting in each other's way. But it's perfect for one client. The willows are overgrown, and the casting distances are short.

I shipped the oars and let the boat drift through the first bend. The river narrowed to twenty feet, the overhanging trees barely allowing the boat's passage. I grabbed a handful of silvery-green willow branches and pulled us through, hand over hand. The willows' exposed roots were bleached the color of barnwood. They reached down toward the water, casting shadows that were nearly indistinguishable from the long, dark shapes of the trout lying in their shade. As the boat approached, the shadows of the willows slowly dissolved. The shadows that were fish bolted from their cover and fled downriver ahead of us. The river took another turn, and the boat emerged from the willows. A dozen fish suddenly streaked from beneath the undercut bank and raced downstream.

About this time, the more romantic clients start murmuring rubbish about the "African Queen" or some other exotic river saga. The more practical ones just grab for their rods. It's generally all I can do to convince them that the better water is yet to come—that we've still got some rowing to do if we want to catch the hatch just right.

If Rebecca had seen any of the fish we kicked out, she gave no indication. She sat motionless on the front casting seat, every inch as cool and deep as the river.

After a few hundred yards, the channel widened enough to allow a reasonable casting margin. I pulled in behind a gravel bar and rigged Rebecca's rod. The leader was old and brittle; it came apart in my hands. I replaced it and tied on a small dun. I shook out the leader and handed her the rod.

"Try a few casts," I suggested. "Just to see how it feels."

Rebecca Sheffield was what you'd call a natural. Though her first few casts were stiff and awkward, she soon eased into the timing, placing the fly within inches of the targets I pointed out.

"You've had some casting instruction?" I asked her.

"A friend taught me," she answered. There was a long pause. "His dog used to sit behind me and catch my line when it dropped too low."

I'd pictured one of those yuppie casting clubs or a week at a fly-fishing school. The idea of Rebecca casting into the grass with a dog minding her backcast hadn't entered my mind. I chuckled, and Rebecca turned to look at me.

"I still have the dog," she said. "Sometimes we practice."

I shoved off, and the boat drifted down the center channel. I aimed it at the shore and nodded at Rebecca.

"Go ahead. On the far side, as close to the willows as you can without hanging up."

Rebecca fired the fly just short of the willows.

"That shadow under the white stick up there, it's a fish," I told her. "Drop the fly in the fast water and let it drift over him." Rebecca's cast was right on the money, and he came for it. "That's you," I said. "Lift."

The fish was on. Rebecca kept her rod high and mechanically reeled him in. I netted the fish with a triumphant swoop and held it up for her to see. Rebecca sat quite still. She looked surprised and mildly annoyed, as if catching a fish was something she had never really intended to do. She didn't show the slightest inclination to handle the fish. I dipped my hands in the water and removed the trout gently from the rubber mesh.

"Your first fish. Want a picture?" Rebecca shook her head. "Want to release him then?" Her back stiffened, and she turned away.

"You do it," she said.

Maybe nobody had floated this stretch of water in a long while. Maybe there'd been an invisible hatch or an imperceptible change in weather. I'd never seen so many fish in the water or so many brought to the boat. The wind tossed her fly into deep pockets. The willows spit her flies back at her. The fish were everywhere they were supposed to be, big fish. They came up for dragging flies and streaked out for short casts. The fish apparently loved Rebecca, in spite of her indifference. Or maybe that was her secret. Sometimes when people tried too hard, forced their hands, things had a way of not working out.

A client who was excited about catching fish on a day like that would have lost concentration, botched more casts, sent more flies into the willows. Someone whose heart pounded at the sight of a trout coming up for a fly with its big white mouth wide open would have involuntarily jerked that fly away. Not Rebecca. She made her casts and carefully observed the fish as they came for the fly, setting only when the fish had turned with it.

Just after noon, we pulled in for lunch on a small island, beaching the raft in a backwater. I opened the cooler with some apprehension. If a dozen eighteen-inch fish before noon didn't impress her, I didn't figure she'd be too thrilled with a box lunch from a local greasy spoon. But if Rebecca minded the food, she didn't say so. She tried a little of everything and took the beer I offered her. She seemed to relax a bit, as if she preferred lounging on the grassy bank to the strain of fishing. We talked, and though she seemed reluctant to talk about herself, she showed an interest in the shop, the length of the season, and the other guides.

"Why do you do this?" she wanted to know.

Because if you do it long enough, it becomes more than just a challenge or a sport or even your job. Because the river seeps slowly into your life and washes away everything else. It slowly takes you over, until the only way to do it is to live it, to be on the river every day. I didn't think Rebecca was anywhere near understanding that.

"I'd rather be out here from May to September than stuck behind a desk all year, trying to find a few days to get away," I explained. That sounded kind of lame, but it seemed to satisfy her. She was quiet for a while, and then she started in again with the questions.

"You seem so independent. How do you like working out of a shop?" she asked.

I shrugged. "Andy's a good guy to work for. He's fair with the guides, and I've got a chance of buying in."

She nodded, agreeing with the business end of it, I suppose. "The owner's . . . wife," she said carefully. "Does she fish?"

"Andy's not married," I replied. "Used to be, I hear, but he never talks about it." Except to say one night between bottles of tequila that he'd been a fool for running out on his beautiful wife. But that wasn't really any of Rebecca's business. "Don't know much about him really," I continued. "He's from back East, like you. He dropped out for a year or so a while back. Fished everywhere there is to fish and eventually ended up here."

I couldn't help wondering what Andy would think of Rebecca. The local girls didn't seem to interest him much, though they were all over him like flies. He wasn't a small-town kind of guy. Rebecca wasn't my type. But she was a match for him, all right, New England accent and all. And she sure could fish, even though she didn't seem to get too excited about it.

Rebecca drew up her legs and rested her chin on her knees. She looked up the side channel where a small feeder spring, overgrown with wild cress, tumbled into the backwater.

"It's beautiful here," she said. Maybe there was hope for her yet.

"Finish your beer," I suggested, getting to my feet. "We'll walk around the island and nymph a couple big ones out of the fast water."

"You go," she said. "Take your rod. I'd just like to sit a while." She took a charcoal drawing pencil from the inside pocket of her vest, tore open a paper lunch bag, and spread it flat on a stone. As I walked away, she began sketching the boat and, behind it, the river. I almost forgave her, about the fish, I mean.

I walked quickly around the island, where I took a pair of decent browns out of the side channel. The wind came up after a bit, and I figured it was time to get back to my client. I cut back through the willows rather than taking the long way around. It took me a minute to locate Rebecca. She was on her feet, at the edge of the backwater, fishing across to the opposite bank. I crouched in the willows, watching her strip in line and send out cast after cast. The wind was playing havoc with her line, and she was losing patience, dropping her backcast and muttering to herself when the casts fell short.

The fish that she was working lay across the slough, in a pocket two feet long and less than a foot deep. A tree branch had fallen across the mouth of the pocket, causing a small jam of sticks. The big brown hugged the backside of the pocket, surfacing occasionally to take an insect in the swirling foam. The fish lay so far under the willows, she'd have been hard-pressed to get a clean shot at it with a gun, let alone set a fly in front of it. I smiled. So that was it. Rebecca liked to play the long shot, the impossible fish. If only she'd told me at the beginning of the trip. I'd have put her onto some real tough customers.

It was an impossible cast, but somehow she managed it. Her line lay across the branch, and the fly drifted back into the foam. The fish came, taking its time. The big brown opened its jaws. A huge half-circle of white closed on the fly, and Rebecca sucked in her breath. She set the hook as the fish turned. The line skidded down the length of the branch and miraculously came free. The monster felt the hook and bolted downstream. She didn't have a prayer of holding him if he got into the fast water. I stumbled out of the willows, hollering instructions.

"Follow him!" I yelled. "Run!" She ran, without a backward glance, racing the fish downstream. I splashed into the river beside her. She had good tension on the fish. He hadn't taken much line yet, but he would when he hit the fast water. I glanced at Rebecca. Her face was flushed, and her eyes were bright. She stared into the water intently, watching for any movement of the trout. The fish hit the current, and the reel screamed. Rebecca reached instinctively for the spinning reel. I anticipated her movement and grabbed her wrist.

"Do you want this fish?" I asked. She nodded. "Then let him run. He'll come back when he's ready. Just give him some room."

I released her wrist and looked down at her. She met my eyes, then raised her hand and deliberately jammed the reel. The line pulled straight, and the fish was gone. We stood there, in the river, glaring at each other. I seriously considered breaking the rod over her attractive head.

"I thought you really wanted that fish," I said finally.

"I did," she said. "But not on those terms."

She handed me her rod and walked back to the boat. I should have realized then that she wasn't talking about the stupid fish.

Considering the circumstances, Rebecca was remarkably pleasant for the remainder of the float. She said she'd had enough fishing for one day; she just needed some time to think. She settled back in the boat and demonstrated a quiet interest in the scenery and the wildlife. As we floated through the bends of the river, the tension in her face gradually faded. We checked Poindexter Slough on the way back, but I couldn't get her interested in wetting a line there. When I dropped her at the motel in the early afternoon, she insisted on paying for the whole day and tipped me generously. Still, I couldn't help feeling I'd let her down.

"Come back to the shop with me," I suggested. "You can meet Andy and we'll go for a drink."

Rebecca frowned and shook her head. "I don't think Andrew . . . Andy . . . would appreciate that," she said softly.

There was something in the way she said his name. It took a little while for it to sink in. And then I understood that I was looking at my boss's former wife.

Well, that explained a lot of things, like why she'd broken off a brown that any fly fisher would have given his casting arm for and why Andy hadn't shown the slightest glimmer of interest in anyone else. But it raised a lot of new questions, too, like how much of all of this was up to me, the guide. But springing it on me like that, she didn't give me much time to think.

"You never know," I said. "Maybe he would. You took a chance coming all the way out here. It's a long shot, but so was that fish back there."

Rebecca shook her head. "You were right," she said. "Andy's got to run. Maybe he'll come back when he's ready. Back home he was always saying that he needed more room. I thought it was me, but it isn't. It's this . . . this Wild West town, the fish, the willows, the canyons, the sage, that big, big sky. This is what he meant."

She opened the door and stepped out of the truck.

"Do you want me to tell him you're here?" I asked, knowing I would, regardless of her answer.

She slammed the pickup door and leaned back in the window. She pulled the ribbon from her hair and shook it loose. Her eyes were shining, and she smiled for the first time that day.

"Tomorrow," she said slyly. "When I'm gone. Just tell him I wanted to see what this crazy fly-fishing thing was all about."

I figured if I timed it just right, Andy would be pounding down her door about the time those long legs of hers stepped out of the shower.

"Will do," I promised. "Anything else?"

"Just out of curiosity," she said. "How big do you suppose that brown was?"

Spring Creek Encounters

BY NICK LYONS

Despite the depth and range of his considerable talent as a writer, Nick Lyons faced a rather daunting task when he set out to write an intimate portrait of the idyllic fly-fisher's life he lived for several weeks one summer on a fertile spring creek. The Montana creek was legendary for its big, finicky trout. And it was very, very private—guarded and patrolled. A postcard from such a privileged location is one thing; but an entire book on the day-by-day experiences on a river the reader can never fish—ever!—presents minefields of challenges for the prose if it is to become engaging.

Published by The Atlantic Monthly Press *in 1992,* Spring Creek *is indeed an engaging book, filled with reader reward for those who find gratification in what the late Arnold Gingrich called "The Fishing in Print." All the great and enduring tales of the great outdoors have always shared a common strength: the sharing of an exhilarating or emotionally moving experience—capturing what Hemingway called, "the way it was."*

In this excerpt from Spring Creek, *Nick will take you where you cannot go alone. And you're going to enjoy his company.*

As the days moved on into late July—a string of long bright days, like stones in an Indian necklace, fishing and painting—the fishing changed yet again.

Some of it grew easier. There were grasshoppers in the fields now and it was fun to wade wet, in khakis and sneakers, up the West Branch, casting a Jay-Dave Hopper right up against the far bank and chugging it once or twice. The fish struck explosively. Sometimes, for a fraction of a second, you could see a fish just before it struck—a bright flash of auburn and white, bolting from beneath the undercut banks, angling up and out toward the fly. It sent shocks through me. And sometimes, when there were grasses but not thistles on the opposite bank, I'd cast onto the shore and tug the fly off, so it dropped with a splat, the way a grasshopper would, coming down out of the grasses.

I found it extremely pleasant to walk up the river on a blistering after-noon, the sun brilliant—opalescent, violet, even through double-strength Po-laroids—and the spring water cold and sharp against my legs. There was a happy randomness to grasshopper fishing.

Sometimes, coming along the inside, slack edge of a bend, I'd spook fish from beneath the undercut banks, from no more than six or seven inches of water. At first I thought it a freak that fish of such size would position them-selves where the water was so shallow and there was virtually no current to bring them food. I could not remember having read of another river where big trout would make their stand in such places. And these were among the biggest trout in Spring Creek—fish well over twenty-four inches, sometimes at least thirty, broad and very dark, so sure of themselves that they moved slowly and steadily into the deep water in the shank of the bend, fish the size of a muskrat, fish that never failed to shake me silly.

It was natural to fish up the West Branch bends from the slack side, casting to where the current traced the far bank. It was logical for big fish to be under the deeper banks, where food would come in a continuous belt to them, where they were protected from predators by the broken water and had more depth in which to maneuver. And I got many truly fine and large fish from that current line and even from the center current of a bend, where large fish frequently busted up from the depths for a meal as substantial as a grasshopper.

I took two of the largest fish I'd taken from these West Branch bends—from a large pool whose path must have been changing. The water came down a narrow chute and once must have swept off to the right, creating a large half-circle of a pool. Over the years, the far arc of that pool had silted up and vege-tation had begun to grow in some sections—all of which forced the current to make its turn more sharply, with less dallying in the far pool. Working my way up toward that bend on a day in late July, about 2:00, I saw several swirls at the surface just where the heavy current hit the slack eddy. There was a defined seam, where the eddy pushed upstream and the headlong current swept down, and the fish was rising smack along that line.

I had been fishing a #16 Elk Hair Caddis in the pool below, where I'd found two fish rising to a tan caddis, but there were no flies in the air—and the size of the surface disturbance suggested a fish feeding on larger fare. Stupidly, I changed to a grasshopper without changing my 6X leader. The fish slammed the big fly on the first cast and I snapped it off at once.

A few minutes later I tied on another hopper, this time on a thick 4X tippet. On my second cast along that seam, in virtually the same spot, a second fish, at least the size of the first, came up, smashed the fly, and bolted directly downstream. It was a powerful brown and I wondered for a moment whether it wasn't the same trout, which might not even have felt that first hopper break quickly in its lip. Even with the heavy leader this time I could not turn it. I had to follow the fish three bends downriver before it slowed and gave in—a bright, brilliant fish, better than two feet long, no sign of my first hopper in its lips.

After kicking out four or five alligators from the inside slack banks, I often stopped well below a pool and fished that unpromising bank with great care. I'd start sometimes at the bottom and fish it a foot or two higher with each cast, but the water was so thin and placid that I spooked the fish before I put a fly over them, and abandoned this scheme. Later, I fished these banks just below the point of the bend, trying to get a long float in that slack water—but I gave that up, also. In the end, I came to think that those fish were virtually uncatchable, that they might move into the center current to feed on a heavy hatch of a fly as big as the Green Drake, or even to the far bank, but that they did not feed regularly when they were in that spot and could not be caught. Bill Willers, the trout biologist, later told me that he thought such fish might be social rejects—too big and slow to compete with stronger fish along the other bank. I don't know. I only know they scared me silly and I never came close to raising one.

I found other fish that could not be caught—at least not by me—and I liked their presence in the river. They represented a kind of ultimate challenge, a chance for me to grow.

I never caught a fish in the long deep stretches of the upper end of the East Branch. In these mysterious headwaters you could see dozens of truly large trout but I spooked every last one of them before I got within casting distance.

The toughest—and most frustrating—of all spots for me was the exit slick to the Second Pond on the East Branch. Here all the food from the broad pond, several hundred feet across and more lengthwise, funneled down into a slick some forty feet across. The water ran over white sand here and was no more than several inches deep most of the way across. When the larger trout from the pond moved into this area to feed, they were more skittery and paranoid than the Paranoid Pool trout: huge black forms, constantly in motion, wavering back and forth like the shadows of sun through clouds, watching always upstream and, with the merest break of the surface, taking some insect from the top. I could not catch these fish. I did not once come close to catching them. I tried crawling on my belly through thistle and high grasses but when I got to a casting position they were gone. I tried going to a spot and then sitting still as a heron for twenty, then thirty minutes. Yes, the fish came back—and then, as I raised my arm to cast, they'd take flight.

I tried many times to put a fly over them without their scattering first, and always failed. They seemed to me the most difficult trout I'd ever seen and in the night I dreamed of how they might someday be caught: by waiting great lengths of time, until they got to feeding heavily on a substantial hatch; by using a small—perhaps six-foot—rod that cast a smaller shadow, and by casting far above them, so the line never traveled above them; by casting a very loose line, with a great many S curves in it, so the line would not drag. You might have to wait four or five hours, or a day, or two days to get a couple of really good chances. That's the kind of fishing this was—and I was not quite ready for it. I was closer than I had been several weeks earlier, but the Second Pond Slick was miles beyond me.

When I reported all this to Herb he chuckled and said that it became a bit easier when the water was ruffled and the sky overcast—but not much. When the fish got down into the slick they knew how vulnerable they were; they were there to feed, but always with an eye for danger. Herb had taken some fish from the Second Pond Slick—but not many. Doug Ewing, who had gone to pieces when the big flat exploded, had taken the largest fish he'd ever taken on a dry fly—a twenty-nine-inch brown—from the slick.

I got several of the harder trout to rise in other tough places as the last week began: in the Third Bend Pool of the East Branch and even in the Paranoid.

The Third Bend Pool is the first bend below the impossible slick. There is a run of some three hundred yards—narrow and swift—and then the East Branch makes a right-angle turn. Beyond the outer rim of the current there is a slack flat area about eight feet wide by twenty feet long, created where the run bounces off a couple of knots of shrubs. Dermot Wilson liked this pool, Herb told me, and could sit for hours watching it. The fish—one, sometimes two—were in the slack area. You either had to cast directly upstream to them, across flat water, from the left-hand bank—as Dermot did—or, from the right, across the brisk main current. The logic of fishing from the left side was of course to remove the problem of drag; but the fish were always in the upper end of the slack water and that meant casting across fifteen feet of thin, shallow water. I could not do it with sufficient delicacy and must have put ten free-rising fish down either by lining them or having line and leader fall too heavily on the water behind them, where the slightest movement sent ripples throughout the entire flat area.

I tried from the right but the main current invariably dragged the fly before a trout had a chance to see it—and drag here meant a fish down for half an hour.

Then one day I found a single fish high in the water, wolfing every PMD that came down. You could see its snout come up out of the water and the white of its mouth open widely. The fish was high on the hog and had lost all caution. And, from the shadow it cast on the white sand bottom, it was a perfectly huge fish.

I got so excited that my first cast from the right-hand side was fifteen feet too far and I stopped it abruptly in midair, so that a great clump of loose line fell on the current while, miraculously, the fly and only the leader flipped left of the current and landed a foot above the great trout. Pure serendipity. I could not have duplicated that cast if my life, quite literally, had depended upon my doing so.

I was standing at a spot from which I'd actually made several astonishing casts, none with brilliance aforethought. From that spot I'd cast to the cove thirty feet above the backwater that day with Datus—and raised an impossible fish. I had accepted Datus's compliment of having raised the fish on my first cast, and then, a moment later, had lost the trout.

I did not lose the trout that rose to my miraculous plop cast into the slack water. The fish turned instantly when the fly came over it, took the #17 PMD in a rush, and bolted like a bonefish up the run toward the pond. Shocked, I let it take out all the slack line, got it on the reel, and began to gallop upstream after it, the fish already thirty feet into the backing. I made a tremendous commotion as I turned the corner brusquely, barely keeping the line out of the grass, and stomped noisily up the fast heavy run after the great fish. It never jumped. The fish just went hell-bent for the great pond and never turned, straight up the center of that fast run, with its sharp gradient. Then, in the difficult slick, and ninety feet of fly line, fifty feet of backing, me, and the gradient urging it back, the great fish hesitated for the first time and the current began to tug it back. I reeled madly, let slack line come between me and the fish, saw it slipping downstream in the center of the river toward me, began to strip back line with great ripping motions, lost contact again, regained control, lost control again, and saw the great brown trout slip downriver not two feet from my boots. The fly was still in the corner of its mouth. The fish was three or four inches longer than two feet—and fat as a bass. I'd never had a fish that size take a dry fly.

And then, from below me, it turned and headed up the left bank, going under the bank, coming out, going deeply under again as I put as much pressure on it as I dared. And then it was in a tangle of willow roots. I felt only dead weight. Quickly I waded to the bank, saw it a few feet up into the mass of roots, touched it with the fingers of my right hand, and it was gone.

By fluke or by skill, I was raising more and more of the tougher fish. On the inner rim of the Paranoid Pool—an impossibility within a difficulty—I saw a huge snout rise up and then descend. We were reconnoitering the lower water and I had taken three good fish from the flattest water. I felt up to it.

The fish required a directly upstream cast, through the current that came down between me and the fish. But every time it came up and I pitched to it that way, I lined the fish and it went down. What to do?

Gently I stepped a few feet to the right, cast directly above me, and then hooked the fly left—and the fish took it in a lurch.

In fact, what began to trouble me now were not the bigger, tougher fish that I did not catch but those that I did not fish for.

There is one that goads and taunts me to this day, a fish I saw from a high ledge on a rock cliff, gazing down into a run I'd never fished it looked so unpromising, though I always fished the pool above it. I was moving upstream to that pool after a morning in which I'd fished rapidly through a few miles of water, and from the forty-five-foot height of the cliff looked down and saw a mammoth fish, high in the water, sipping duns or perhaps floating nymphs. Had I been on the shore, I might not have seen it, for the huge fish barely kissed the surface. But from above, I could see its every movement, even when it chased a few six-inchers and dashed downstream for a few minutes. It always came back to the same spot, which seemed to have no particular features to recommend it: it was just in midwater. The fish was one of Spring Creek's thirty-inchers and it was in one of those rare—most rare—moments of ab-solute vulnerability.

What I should have done was perfectly obvious: mark the spot clearly in case I could not see the fish from the opposite shore, retreat the few hundred yards I'd just come along the ledge of the cliff, climb down, walk another hun-dred yards until I could cross, then come up the meadow on the opposite side and fish for this prodigy of nature.

But I was lazy.

It was late in the morning, past lunchtime.

Perhaps I could raise it from this side, from above; clearly it could not be fished from the base of the cliff directly below me.

Perhaps it would be there in the evening.

Or tomorrow morning, when the PMDs were on again.

But when I climbed down the upstream end of the cliff I could not see it again, tried three stupidly careless blind downstream casts, and then one thing led to another and I never saw the fish again.

Not ever.

And I'm made furious at myself every time I think of the entire episode.

One afternoon, the sun at high blaze, Herb asked if I'd like to fish the Back Channel with him. This was a relatively short piece of water, he said, and would take about two hours to fish properly. It was one of the toughest sections on Spring Creek and I had a suspicion he'd saved it until he thought I was ready for it. I was as ready as I'd ever be; we'd be heading East in three days.

After the East and West Branches of Spring Creek come together, the riverbed widens dramatically; in several places, spotted with bars or actual islands, it is three or four feet across. These are the great flats that provide such exacting fishing, large very slow pools where every feeding fish is immediately visible, and where the trout are cautious in the extreme.

The Back Channel runs behind one of these islands, taking a small portion of the main flow and winding it around a twisted island, festooned with wild rose, thistles, and rotted duck blinds.

We started on that bright hot afternoon where the Back Channel sweeps in from the left and enters the main river, fishing up to a deep right-angle bend pool that had one good fish flush in the middle of it, rising steadily in a classic sucking down of the water. As soon as he saw the fish, Herb found some trouble with his equipment, began to fuss with his reel, and insisted I try for the feeding fish.

The Pale Morning Duns were still on and I saw a dozen gold specks, a little flotilla, near the head of the run. By the slow nature of the rise, the deliberate breaking of the surface, it was clear the fish was taking the adult.

From where I had to cast, the distance was ten feet farther than I thought I could manage comfortably, so I begged off, said I'd rather wait and have the pleasure of watching him take the fish. No soap. It was my fish. So I tried a first cast and came down fifteen feet short, and rather hard. I pressed a bit too much and the next few casts collapsed in a heap. Then I double-hauled the line to where the fish was feeding but the line slapped the water and the fish simply stopped feeding. Well, there it was: my old incompetence coming back.

Some of Herb's passion for the most difficult fish, the most interesting fishing challenge, had infected me. I could not get the big one I'd seen from the cliff out of my mind; I kept thinking of the Paranoid and the Second Pond

Slick, and every tough chance I'd seen or tried or missed or failed to try. But I had none of Herb's great concentration of power, his precision casting—and I still gave up too easily.

I reeled in slowly, checked my leader and fly, put a bit of floatant on the fly with my fingers, and looked at Herb, who was still fussing with his reel. I did not think the fish would come back. The hot hard glare of the sun must have made it scoot to the bottom, and it would stay there all afternoon.

But in a few minutes the fish was up again. There were simply too many golden bonbons slipping by overhead.

"Show me how to do it, will you?" I called.

"Your fish," he said.

"Are you going to spend the whole afternoon playing with your tackle?"

"I sure the hell hope not. Go on. That fish can be caught."

The fish was rising in exactly the same spot, so I cast again, this time a foot above and to the left. It was a rather miraculous cast for me, I thought, and I was shocked that the fish did not agree. But I tried again, immediately, and made another lovely cast, and again the fly came down over the fish and he rose an inch or so away and instinctively I struck, ripping the water, putting the fish down again.

"That's it this time," I said.

"I intend to sit here until you catch that fish, Nick."

"I've had my chances."

"The fish can still be caught."

"By me?"

"By you. Take your time. Try another fly—maybe a very sparse Sparkle Dun. It will take me an hour to clear up this mess in my line."

I wasn't at all sure what he was doing, if anything practical, but he had his visor off and a little pile of paraphernalia on a rock in front of him now. I saw ointment and bug dope and several times he applied each, and then continued to fiddle with his reel or pretended to do so, and there was nothing to do but pursue this impossible fish. Well, if there was really no hurry, perhaps I'd just tuck in, take my time, figure out how to raise this fish, then take it.

I sat down on a little island, got out my fly box, and found a very sparse Sparkle Dun to replace the parachute I'd been using. When the determined trout started to feed again, ten minutes later, I cast at once, then again, the second cast falling just right—above and to the fish's right, so the fly got a foot and a half of good float before it came directly over its feeding position.

I leaned forward, tense.

And nothing happened.

"Thought that one was it," Herb said. I did not think he had been watching me or the fly. "Good cast."

I got three more decent floats, and then made another sloppy cast and the fish went down.

We'd been at the spot forty-five minutes now. I did not want to leave until I had hooked the fish. I was determined now to raise it. I watched the water near the bend carefully and saw a few more PMDs come down. There were also a few midges on the water, but no caddis. I felt sure that the right fly was a PMD, and that the dun would be best. The five or six different designs had each taken fish for me on both branches at various times, and the Sparkle Dun should have been the right fly. Perhaps there was something about the slant of the sun, the depth of the water here—or whatever—that simply did not allow the few patterns I'd tried to fool this fish. The water was deeper and the bright sun might actually make the surface more opaque. I thought I might try Talleur's cut-wing pattern. It was tied with a very blond body, only a few wisps of hackle, and the cut wings might provide a stronger silhouette here. So I tied one on.

On the first cast, above and to the right, the fly picked up the current, twisted slightly, then rode directly across the still-spreading circles of the trout's last rise and the fish took it in an instant and I smiled with jubilation.

"All right," said Herb, "let's go catch a few fish now."

After the deep bend pool, the Back Channel grew as small and shallow as a small carrier canal on a British chalk stream—perhaps twenty feet across, rarely more than several feet deep, over a light sand bottom. It was immensely difficult fishing and I barely caught one small fish. As soon as you stepped into the water, ripples went out for sixty feet; every cast seemed too hard; and the trout, everywhere, were skittery.

The channel is no more than four or five hundred feet and we were at the remotest section of it an hour later. Together we looked up a hundred-foot stretch of water—narrow here, with a glassy surface, little cover, none of the water more than eighteen inches deep. As we stood beside each other, scanning the water for a feeding fish, I kept thinking how the shallow water meant that the fish had a tiny cone of vision and a fly would have to float within inches of its lie if it were even to see the thing. There were no trees here, nothing to cast shadows, so the full light of the bright blue sky was over the water. Anything moving above the fish would scare them silly.

I took a small tentative step and the ripples and little waves went out forty-five feet ahead of me. I moved an arm and a fish from the far bank darted madly upstream. A very good fish, too.

I was still astounded at how many truly large fish in Spring Creek could be found in some of its smallest, shallowest water.

Ah, the sweet mad toughness of this.

Herb and I stood for five or ten minutes, still as poles, scanning the surface for a dorsal, a wake, a delicate rise. It would have been lunacy to cast without seeing a fish. But there seemed to be none. Herb lit a cigarette and watched the water. I tried not to move a muscle.

Then, where the current hit off a point some seventy-five feet upstream and made a slight but discernible ten-foot foam line, a fish came up with authority. There were still a few PMDs on the water and I had to think that they were what had brought this fellow to lunch. Up he'd come, every minute or so—not much more frequently than that. I imagined him a wise old dog of a trout, fat and territorial, not given to feeding binges any more, having a sweet tooth for these little sulphur bonbons, perhaps a Green Drake or two, always a hopper. The way he lolled just under the surface, dorsal out, and the steady, heavy way he moved, turning as he took a fly, suggested that he might be one of the Spring Creek alligators.

I could not even contemplate the cast necessary to take such a fish. I knew just enough to know that I would botch this one savagely. You could not cast directly over the fish or it would surely bolt for safety. If you cast to the right and hooked the line left—as I'd done for the first trout of the afternoon—the bulk of the line would fall on the shore, in the thistles. If you cast too roughly, by millimeters, no matter where the fly landed the fish would vanish. False casts would be disastrous. The water dropped off toward the left and some brush there would make all but some brand of steeple cast impossible from that side—and such a cast inevitably would come down too hard. And you'd get one cast, no more. The water was too thin, this fish too wary; like a Japanese brush painter, you'd have to catch it just right on the first try or try again some other time, on other paper. You couldn't correct a mistake. It had taken us a couple of hours to work our way around to this spot, I'd be leaving in a few days, and I was sure we wouldn't fish the Back Channel again this trip. Herb said it hadn't been fished in several years.

Five years ago I would not have thought twice about turning such a fish over to the better fisherman. During my first weeks I wouldn't have hesitated to do so. Now I thought twice—remembered my earlier success, my dozens of recent successes—and then decided to turn it over. I was a better caster now, a shrewder tactician, but this was out of my league.

Herb grumbled, I insisted, and then he said all right, he'd try it, and he stripped off a great number of coils of line, quietly, watched the water for five minutes and seemed to be looking for a rhythm in the fish's rises, found what he was looking for, hesitated for another moment, and (with one false cast to the side, over the land) made the most astonishing cast to a trout I've ever seen. I'd seen Herb make some spectacular casts; this transcended them all. As best I can reconstruct what happened—and I have replayed it a dozen times—he cast partially *underhand* (so that the line never rose more than a foot off the surface of the water, and thus could be laid down lightly); he cast far to the *left* across the stream (so the line never came near the fish); and then he hooked the line back to the right, so that the fly flipped over near the spit of land, several feet above the fish, caught the little line of current exactly, and came down over the place where the riseform had been just a minute before. I should add that there was, when he cast, a brisk downstream wind against us and that the cast was comfortably seventy-five or eighty feet.

It was a magical moment.

I let out an immense gasp of air.

And the fish came up as nice as you please and took the fly.

Later that afternoon I was treated to one more prodigy of technique. We'd come to the beginning of the channel and against the far bank there was a sweeping curve of perhaps 180 degrees—not fast but with a steady foam line that traveled about seventy feet from top to bottom, never more than an inch or two from the bank.

It was a fishy looking spot, with enough depth to hold good fish, and those undercut banks might well harbor something of astounding size. We had alternated fishing the last few runs and I'd just taken a decent fish on a parachute PMD. I'd seen him rising midstream, smack in the middle of a little broken water, and had nailed him on the first cast. The sweeping bend was Herb's pool and I waded carefully to the left bank to sit on the edge of the island and watch.

Tough fishing stretches you, provides you with skills and confidence for a thousand lesser moments—and it eggs you on to take great chances. It's not just courage that's required, of course, but some knowledge of the kinds of major tactics that can be necessary on a trout stream, and then a perfection of the skills needed to enact them.

Herb waded slowly up the silted area, away from the current, until he'd positioned himself where he was able to fish up to the top of the bend. His first cast was a bit short; it picked up the current a few inches from the bank but pulled out into the slack water about five yards downstream. His next cast, though, was perfect: it landed within inches of where the incoming water hit the opposite bank, picked up the current line, and floated downstream flush in the feeding lane. As it went, Herb manipulated the line so that he fed out an inch or two, carefully, as the fly headed into the farthest deep bend of the half-circle, going away from him, still drag-free, and then he took the line back in trifles as the circle turned and came closer to him. The fly floated without a trace of drag. When the float had gone twenty feet I leaned forward to see the bit of gold better; when it had gone forty feet, still in the foam line, still without drag, I began to hold my breath; when it had cleared the farthest point of the bend and started to come back, my chest was knotted with expectation.

But nothing happened.

Herb got two of the next three casts to float like that and I could not believe no fish came out to take the fly.

None did.

Sometimes they just won't come to play.

Steelhead of the Umpqua

BY RAY BERGMAN

First published by Knopf in 1938, Ray Bergman's magnum-opus Trout *still reads with a sense of mellow and engaging charm. I was delighted to see a new edition for modern readers published recently by The Derrydale Press. Even when describing routine encounters with ten-inch brook trout, Bergman's prose could cast a spell that held readers. And when the stakes were dramatically higher, as in this chapter, Ray Bergman's story-telling powers were equal to the challenge. Here, three icons collide: the renowned angling editor of* Outdoor Life; *the legendary Umpqua; and the iron-muscled steelhead fresh from roaming the ocean currents.*

Having been born and raised on the East Coast and not being wealthy, it took me a great many years to satisfy my desire to fish in waters west of the Mississippi. The first trip, with a five-year-old Model A Ford, took us to that river, from Canada to New Orleans, and out into the Atlantic as well: that is, to the island of Ocracoke, North Carolina. The next year, with a new car, we made a trip that brought us plenty of fishing in Michigan, Colorado, Wyoming, Missouri, Arkansas, and Mississippi.

During these years Clarence Gordon, of Oregon, had been corresponding with me. His letters about the steelhead fishing on the North Umpqua, in the vicinity of Steamboat where he had a delightful camp, painted such fascinating pictures that my wife and I couldn't resist them. We put aside other projects we had considered and surrendered to the lure of Oregon, California, and West Texas for that year. We have always been glad that we did. We feel that we owe Clarence a debt of gratitude for having hastened our first trip to the Pacific Coast.

A friend, Fred Gerken, of Tombstone, Arizona, also had a great desire to fish for steelhead, so the result was a meeting at the Wilcox Ranch on Encampment Creek, Wyoming. I'd become attached to this stream from a previous trip, and after ten days of splendid fishing there, we started for Oregon.

We went by way of the Columbia River Highway. My first glimpse of Mount Hood was enthralling. It fulfilled all my dreams of what a high mountain should look like. There were many forest fires raging at the time, and by some freak of the air-currents the smoke obscured the lower part of the mountain, but not the valley, leaving the peak suspended in mid-air—pointed, majestic, and fascinating. We'd seen higher mountains before but none more spectacular, for Hood rises from comparatively low country while the others rise from very high altitudes to begin with, thus losing much impressiveness. Next to Mount Hood, the Tetons hold my memory most. They are so rugged and jagged, and rise so high above the surrounding country, that they get your nervous system responding with inward heart quivers.

We had another thrill when we left Roseburg for the trip up the North Umpqua to Steamboat. The first few miles were not so much, but once above Glide it was as picturesque and tortuous a route as one could imagine. You felt sure you were going places, and you really were.

The river is wild and beautiful, and at first sight a bit terrifying. You wonder how you are going to be able to wade it without getting into difficulties. Despite this it isn't so bad once you learn to read the bottom. On the bottom are narrow strips of gravel that wander here and there and crisscross like old-time city streets. By walking in these and stepping only on reasonably flat, clean rocks or on other rocks where you can see the mark of previous footsteps, you wade with fair comfort and safety. The rocks of the routes between most of the good pools are plainly marked by the tread of many feet, and as long as you know what to look for you have no trouble. But do not hurry—watch each step closely unless you have the activity and sure-footedness of a mountain goat or a Clarence Gordon. When he gets to a hard spot he makes a hop, skip, and jump and lands just where he wants, while you gingerly and sometimes painfully make your way after him, arriving a few minutes later. He waits apparently patiently, but probably in his heart wishing you would move quicker. He finds it so easy it must seem ridiculous to him for anyone to be so slow and faltering. I once thought I was agile (I was, from what others tell me), but Clarence—well, just ask those who have fished with him.

Never having fished for steelhead, I decided to watch Gordon a while before trying my luck. From experience I know that you can learn plenty by watching someone who knows the water from concentrated fishing. The time of the year may make a difference in the places where the best fishing is found. At the season we have fished the North Umpqua, steelhead were found only in certain sections of the main channel. In addition, not all waters containing large steelhead were suitable for fly fishing. If of greater depth than six to eight feet, the trout were not much interested in a fly, although now and then one would take.

I fished first at the Fighting Hole, so named because it was all fast water and short, with white and fast water below, so that there was always a good chance of the fish getting out of the hole and into the rapids and thus taking you for a ride that often led to disaster in some degree. Usually this meant only the loss of the fish, but sometimes it meant the loss of a bit of tackle as well.

The first thing I noted was the way Clarence handled the fly. He cast quartering across and slightly downstream. When the fly touched water his rod tip began to dip and rise rhythmically about every three seconds. At the same time he retrieved a little line with his other hand—about a foot or two all told during the entire drift of the fly. On the first cast the fly did not submerge. Before making the next cast he soaked it thoroughly, and from then on it sank readily. He explained that in low, clear water a fly dragging over the surface was likely to spoil your chances. This was good trout-fishing lore. Many times I have soaked flies in mud to make them sink quickly for the same reasons when fishing for wary browns.

The Fighting Hole did not produce, so we moved down to the Mott Pool. This was a long fast run that terminated in a fairly wide basin. Almost at once Clarence hooked a fish. As it struck he let go the slack line he had been holding. The reel screeched as the fish dashed downstream. He broke water some hundred and fifty feet below and then started a dogged resistance. At this time Clarence gave me a little more information: "Most trout fishermen after steelhead for the first time make the mistake of stripping line when playing them. They do it with other fish and think they can do it with these, but you have got to play them on the reel: otherwise there is sure to be trouble." As I watched I knew this was true. As with Atlantic salmon, it would be certain suicide to your chances to attempt to play them by stripping. Those strong rushes—some as long as a hundred and fifty feet—those vicious tugs when like a bulldog they figuratively shook their heads savagely, would make it well-nigh impossible to handle them in any other way except on the reel. The slightest kink, the slightest undue pressure, and something would break.

Watching Clarence fight this fish was too much for my resolve not to fish until I learned something about the game. Besides, I had learned how to manipulate the fly; the rest would be the same as grilse or landlocked salmon—or at least so I thought.

The lower end of the Mott failed me. Clarence said it was probably because his fish had run into it several times and so disturbed the rest located there. I hooked a steelhead in the next hole—I think it is called the "Bologna" for the reason that when a fish goes over there it is gone; and as they usually do go over, it is just bologna to fish the hole; but I did not know it at this time. There was an irresistible vibrant pull at the strike, the reel screeched a few seconds, and then the line was slack. I had lost my first fish.

"You'd have lost the fish when he went over anyway," soothed Clarence. "It is usually over quickly in this hole," and then he told me why. "Going over" on the Umpqua means that a fish leaves the pool it has been hooked in and runs into the white water below. If this stretch of bad water is of any great length, a fish that "goes over" is usually lost. When it gets away the fish is said to have "cleaned" the angler.

It seemed as if the Umpqua steelhead had it in for me—at least I made a poor showing the first three days. I hooked five fish and lost them all. Three pulled out after a short fight, and two cleaned me out good and proper. I was in the doldrums. The only thing that cheered me at all was the fact that Clarence Gordon insisted my hard luck was due to bad breaks and not to poor fishing. "Besides," he said, "I have really been giving you the works—bringing you to places that always mean trouble when you hook a fish. Take that hole right here—I've never landed a fish here yet, and I have hooked plenty."

On the other hand Fred Gerken seemed to take the game with the greatest nonchalance and was making a record for himself. On the first day he used his four-and-a-half-ounce trout rod, thirty yards of line, and a 3X leader, went out on the Kitchen Pool, and took a five-pounder as if he were catching a one-pound rainbow. But he did not tempt fate by continuing the use of the trout outfit. The next day he assembled his nine-and-a-half footer and really went after business. Well did he uphold his grand start—a fish the second day, and no others were brought into camp. He did the same thing the third day, although he wasn't the only one. Phil Edson, of Pasadena, brought one in about four pounds bigger than Fred's. But still I had nothing to show. It was always excuses—this happened, that happened—well, you know how it is. To make it look worse my wife took a five-and-a-quarter-pounder at noon on the fourth day, and while she is a good bait-caster she had never done a lot of trout fishing. We started her out with the bait-casting rod, and she did not like it a bit. But to be a good sport she kept using it for three days. Then she rebelled—she wanted to fish with a fly like the rest of us. So I took her out on the Kitchen Pool to give her a little coaching. About a half hour of this and she decided she could go it alone. I had seen a steelhead jump at the lower part of the pool, so was only too glad to rush ashore for my rod. I had just reached the tackle tent when I heard my wife give a call. I rushed back and found her fast to a fish—I believe the very one I went in to get my rod for. As I say, she had not had much experience fly fishing, but she had turned the trick and handled the hooked fish like a veteran. She was proud of her five-and-a-quarter-pounder, but not as happy about it as I thought she had a right to be. I soon learned why. She said: "It was all luck. The cast that took him was the worst I made." I knew exactly how she felt. Dr. Phil Edson, a guest at the camp who had been an observer of the operations, remarked; "A sloppy cast—in the Kitchen Pool and a mid-day in a bright sun. That's something to make us think. Morning and evening, say the experts, and be sure to drop your fly lightly. I wonder what they will say about this?" (To my knowledge no one ever questioned this. They couldn't, as a matter of fact, because it actually happened.)

To make Phil's remarks even more pointed, immediately after lunch I slipped down to the Mott Pool and about halfway through hooked a fish. The singing of the reel was music to my ears. Nothing went wrong this time, and I had the satisfaction of looking up toward the end of the fight to see Fred, Grace, and Phil watching me. Phil was so anxious that I save the fish that he took off his shoes and stockings and with bare feet waded that treacherous water between us, just so that he could be on hand to help me land it in a most difficult spot. That is sportsmanship to commend. I shall never forget this spontaneous act of his as long as I live. It showed the real soul of the man, his unselfish desire to see that I got my fish. It was all very satisfying.

Now Clarence showed his angling acumen. For several days he had been planning his next move so that it would be most advantageous to me. He explained it, now that it was time to carry it through. It seems that when steelhead are not moving much, they become indifferent to flies fished repeatedly from one side of a pool. Mott Pool had been fished hard from the camp side for some time and was going a bit sour. But it hadn't been fished from the opposite side for at least a week—first because not many would tackle it from that side alone, because of the difficulty of wading, and second because Clarence always made an excuse when anyone mentioned going there. He wanted it to get *hot* before taking me there. Even after being taken to the other side by canoe there was plenty of rough wading before reaching the place from which you started fishing. If it hadn't been for Clarence showing me the bad spots and how to avoid them, I'd probably have floundered many times. As it was I never lost my footing.

When we reached the upper end of the hole that I was to fish, Clarence gave me some sage advice. "There are big fish here," he warned. "When one strikes, just keep a taut line and let him go. Don't strike back." Nothing happened until my fly drifted and cut across the tail of the pool. Here

I felt a tug but did not connect. But on the next cast I hooked a heavy fish. For the moment he simply held steady, then moved to the center of the pool. Once there he sulked for five minutes or more, and I could not move him. Suddenly he started doing things, and I have but a vague idea of what happened. The reel screeched, its handle knocked my knuckles, my fingers burned as the line sped beneath them as I was reeling in frantically to get the best of a forward run. At the end of this exhibition, in which were included several jumps, he started a steady and rather slow but irresistible run that made the backing on my reel melt away. Clarence was by my side looking at my reel drum. "He's gone over," he said. My heart sank. Then for some unaccountable reason, perhaps an unknown ledge below, he stopped running. I started to pump him—work him—and he came right along. I reeled as fast as I could, and still he kept coming. My spirits revived with this chance of success. By this time he was only thirty feet away. But the fish suddenly decided he had come far enough and started edging off sideways. I could not stop him. He made a short fast run into shallow water at the right, and then all I felt was a vibrant weight. "I'm hung up," I groaned. I walked from one side of the ledge to the other, I knocked the rod, gave slack line, did everything I possibly could, but he did not come loose. I could feel the fish, so I knew we were still connected.

It was partly dark by this time, and the water between me and the fish was treacherous. I had never waded it in daylight and could not attempt it in the dark. But Gordon took the chance even though he had never waded the place before. "The leader is caught on a board," he called. "There—he is all yours." I felt a tug, saw and heard a splash, and the fish was gone. "About a twelve-pounder," said Gordon. "It's a wonder the leader didn't break the instant you snagged." For this is what happened: the leader had finally frayed on the board and broken. The board had floated down from some bridge-construction work upstream.

And that night Fred brought in another fish. But fortune treated me better from then on. The very next evening I brought in two fish, one weighing seven and a half pounds and the other ten and three-quarters. The latter was the largest fish of the season, although a week after we left, Phil Edson took one of ten and a half pounds. From then on my luck ran better than average, but Fred's held true to form to the last day. At that time his score was seven hooked and seven landed—some record when fifty per cent is an excellent score. Clarence and the rest of us decided something must be done about it. The result of this conference was a trip down to the opposite side of Mott Pool. That night Fred hooked one he couldn't do much with, but even so he might have upheld the honor of his standing except for an unlucky break. The fish had been hooked lightly and pulled out. Anyway, he came in without his fish—the only day out of eight that this happened.

It is strange the way things sometimes happen. Dr. Dewey, of Pasadena, arrived at camp a few days before we did, took his limit of three fish two days in succession, and never lost one. But after that it was different. He hooked a number of fish, but something always went wrong. Some "pulled out," and one "went over." He tried to follow the latter, stumbled, and fell in. He came in wet, bedraggled, and muddy. He hooked a number of other fish on flies from which the points of the hooks had been broken on rocks, and of course he held these only a second or two. Twice his leader frayed on sharp rocks and broke at a critical moment. But this was good medicine. It taught him that it pays to inspect tackle frequently to avoid such needless losses. The complaints, "If I had only changed my leader," or "If I had only looked at my fly to see if the hook was all right," should never have to be made.

I experimented considerably with flies. I tried streamers, standard salmon patterns, and all sorts of flies that had brought me success in various sections of North America, but none of them produced. The best fly of all was the Umpqua. It had been designed especially for this stream. The Cummings was a close rival and often effective when the Umpqua would not produce.

From my own experience and from many talks with the fellows who fish the North Umpqua every season I gathered that only two sizes were needed—numbers 4 and 6. I used 4's most, but when a fish was missed I would change to a 6. Sometimes the smaller fly worked.

The day before we left Steamboat I concentrated on two pools, the Sawtooth and the Surveyor's. The Sawtooth got its name from the sharp-topped rocks that divide it. If a fish ever ran your leader over the center or saw-tooth rock, it was good-by to fish and whatever part of your terminal tackle below where it was cut by the rock.

The first time I had fished this pool both Clarence and Phil Edson were watching me. There was a suspicious smirk on their faces, but at the moment I didn't tumble to the reason. When I hooked a fish I could fairly feel their expectant joy in my downfall. I almost played directly into their hands too. I led the fish upstream, and only their uncontrolled chuckles put me wise that this might spell disaster because of the sharp rocks. In time I changed my tactics and landed the fish, and so spoiled their chance for a horse-laugh on me.

But on this last day I took my first trout from this hole with incredible ease. It was a fair fish, a bit over six pounds, and took the fly on my side of the sharp rock. By giving it the butt of the rod and showing no quarter I kept it from crossing the dangerous spot, and for some reason it gave up not long after. But the next fish gave me a taste of what a Sawtooth trout could really do. This one took in the center of the hole, on the other side of the sharp-edged rock. When he struck the shock was so great that it almost took the rod from my hands, and after getting hooked he quickly wrapped the leader around the rock and it cut through as if it had been a piece of cheese. It happened so fast that it temporarily dazed me. That was all the action I got from the Sawtooth that day.

At the Surveyor's Pool it was not necessary to make a long cast. The first one I made wasn't more than twenty feet, and a six-pounder took it at the very moment it touched the water. Landing this fish made me feel quite satisfied with myself. Two six-pounders in an hour was mighty good fishing no matter how you looked at it.

I rested the pool a half hour and then tried again. This time I had four rises that I missed, and then I connected with a fish that took slowly but surely. He was the heaviest one I had yet come in contact with. For twenty minutes I just held on. The fish didn't either run or tug; he simply bored to bottom and stayed there. Nothing I could do would budge him, even the taking of the line in my hand and pulling with that. But finally he must have become tired of the continual strain, because he suddenly started to kick up a general rumpus. First, he came direct from the bottom with express-train speed and continued into the air until the force of his rush had been expended. When he hit the water he did so broadside, making a splash that might have been heard a quarter of a mile. He then lashed the pool to a froth, made a few more less spectacular jumps, and finally came to rest out in midstream and near the surface.

It looked to me as if he had used up his energy, so I put on all the pressure the rod would bear, thinking he'd come in docilely. Vain hope. I couldn't move him any more than I could when he had been hugging the bottom. He just lay there with a wicked look in his eye and snapped the strength from my arm. Finally I had to release the pressure a bit. I couldn't take it. As I did this he started fanning his tail and his fins. I knew something was going to happen, but I didn't know what. I soon found out. Turning quickly he started downstream, and this time I could tell he was going places. There was no stopping him. I braked as much as I dared, burned my fingers as well as knocked my knuckles, but the line melted away. When I looked at my reel the end was near. He was in the fast water below the pool and gaining speed each instant, so I pointed the rod tip at him and prayed that only the leader would break. Then something snapped, and the strain was gone. The leader had broken at the fly, and the fish had "cleaned" me. The landing of the ten-and-three-quarter-pounder in the Mott Pool had been thrilling, but it did not affect me like this complete rout.

Now that time has lent perspective to the experience, I know that this particular incident was my most memorable angling adventure. And it is that way all
along the line. In every species of fish I've angled for, it is the ones that have got
away that thrill me most, the ones that keep fresh in my memory. So I say it is
good to lose fish. If we didn't, much of the thrill of angling would be gone.

The following year after this exciting incident found me on the way
to the North Umpqua again. This time we went through Yellowstone Park and
then took the northern route through Montana, Idaho, and Washington. It was
remarkably clear the day we drove down the Columbia River valley. Mount
Hood stood out so plainly that we decided it was the time to drive around her
base. The sight of this mountain did things to me again—put a lump in my
throat, a tremble in my nerves. Anyone who is fascinated by towering peaks
should never miss the Mount Hood ride. As much as I love fishing I'd give up
a day or two any time just to gaze at this pile.

But Mount Hood is capricious. After smiling at us for a couple of
hours she suddenly veiled her face with a reddish smoky cloud, and with the
coming of this cloud our spirits changed from gaiety and cheer to gloom and
depression. On the west side of the mountain it was dismal and oppressive, but
as we neared Oregon City the sun broke through the clouds and it was cheery
again.

The fishing conditions on the North Umpqua weren't very good. The
water was so low that the fish could not get over the racks of the commercial
fishermen at the mouth of the river. As a consequence there were comparatively few steelhead in the water, and the ones that were there had been fished
over so much that they had become decidedly wary and particular. It was
tough fishing, and no one could deny it.

On this occasion I had the good fortune to become acquainted with
Jay Garfield, of Tucson, Arizona. He and his wife had the cabin room next to
ours at Gordon's Camp. He had been fishing the river for about five weeks
straight and had been consistently successful, with a top fish of some eleven
and a half pounds.

Of course this might have been luck, but his success seemed too consistent to be the result of luck. As usual when contracting anything of this sort
I proceeded to discover just what there was to Jay's fishing that might account
for his good luck.

In this particular case the job was both easy and enjoyable. Jay is the
sort of fellow you warm up to as soon as you meet him, and he was not only
willing but eager to show me everything he knew about steelhead fishing. So
that I might get this idea about it at first hand, he asked me to fish with him.

The first place we tried was the Plank Pool. I had always fished it from the opposite side of the river, but Jay went to it from the camp side. "I like it best from this side," he said. "I think you have a better chance to fish it right. Besides, I have a special method which works best from this side."

So we waded across the bend just below the junction of the North Umpqua and Steamboat Creek. The spot was both fascinating and fishable, especially where the currents of the two streams united to form the Plank Pool.

Jay did not wade directly to the edge of the hole. He stayed back some distance from the edge so that he wouldn't alarm any fish that might be near his side and perhaps high enough in the water to see him. Then he made a cast up and across stream, dropping the fly so that it floated close to the ledge that skirted our side of the pool. As the fly drifted with the current he followed its progress with the tip of his rod, keeping the line on the verge of being taut and yet not pulling against it or giving the fly any action.

It was the old natural-drift method that I had used for brown trout for many years. Of course this lent added interest as far as I was concerned, because I hadn't expected anything of the sort. He got a follow on the first drift. I saw the flash of the fish, but Jay said it did not touch his fly. After that came at least a dozen drifts in the same current, but they were ignored. But he didn't seem to mind. He just kept working the edge of the ledge on our side of the current.

As usual, when the strike came it was unexpected. I was standing about fifteen feet below Jay and could see the lower part of the drift perfectly. One moment I saw the fly; the next moment it had disappeared and I saw a flash of color. At the same instant came the screech of the reel. Jay had hooked the fish and had proved that his method of fishing the Plank had real merit.

As I watched Jay fish other steelhead locations around camp I realized why he was a successful angler. He was painstaking, methodical, experimental, and extremely patient. He fished every inch of a pool, and if one style of fishing failed to work he changed methods. He never hurried a cast or a drift, never lifted the fly prematurely. Above all he never seemed to get discouraged, even when all his efforts drew blanks. He would not quit. He used Eastern brown trout methods on Western steelhead, and they worked. At the same time he did not neglect the regulation steelhead methods. So of course he caught fish.

As I watched him that old saying kept running through my mind: "The Colonel's lady and Judy O'Grady are sisters under their skins." It struck me that it was much the same with trout. Fundamentals of fishing for them remain the same regardless of the specific details necessary for individual species.

And Jay was fundamental and instinctive in his fishing rather than spectacularly skillful; hence he was a successful fisherman.

Because the Sawtooth Pool had fascinated me from the beginning, it was the first place I fished after watching Jay Garfield do his stuff. At first I fished it from the camp side of the stream. The regular method failing, I then tried the natural drift. A good fish rose when the fly skirted the tall of the left-hand glide, but I failed to connect. No other fishes resulting from my further efforts there, I decided to go to the opposite side, a good quarter-mile walk around. Here again I first tried regulation steelhead tactics. Because this didn't bring any results I changed to the natural-drift method.

Because the day was bright and the water clear and smooth-topped where I wished to fish, I knew I was up against a difficult proposition. I had to get closer in order to reach under the ledge with a sunken and naturally drift-ing fly. So I approached cautiously and crouched low and when in position to do the job stayed down on my knees, knowing that one little glimpse of me by the fish would ruin all chances for success.

The fly drifted along and sank out of sight as the undercurrent pulled it into the hole. I felt a peculiar slow tug and thought the fly had snagged. In-stead it was a steelhead, and when I exerted pressure he came out of the water with snap and action. While he was in the air the line went slack and I thought I saw my fly sticking from the side of his mouth. I had seen correctly. My fly was gone. And all because of a faulty knot. I had carelessly tied it to the leader with a simple jam instead of a turle. Because of such things we an-glers so often fail.

I was angry and disgusted with my carelessness and stupidity. I sat down, smoked a cigarette, tied on an Umpqua size 4, and made up my mind to try another natural drift even though I thought my chances were nil.

I misjudged the second cast and dropped the fly a few inches away from where the first started. This changed the drift. Instead of following the current, the fly started dragging across current almost at once and headed straight for the fissure in the rocks. I saw the danger of snagging and made an attempt to prevent it, but I was too late. I succeeded in jamming it well in the rocks.

It took a half dozen switch casts to release the fly, but this was finally accomplished. Then, instead of lifting it from the water to make another cast, I let it settle down in the pocket. What happened immediately is a question. My thoughts about it are confused and uncertain. All I can really remember is burned finger tips and the sound of a screaming reel. When full realization really returned, I was holding the rod tight and the line stretched out in the distance. Some hundred and twenty-five feet below me the fish had gone under a rock and snagged there.

I thought the fish was gone. Nevertheless I decided to handle the situation as if he were still there. So I reeled in, kept the line taut, and walked toward the place as I reeled. On getting there, I tried releasing the line by exerting pressure from all angles. I failed. The feeling of being inextricably snagged remained. I saw Clarence Gordon downstream. He was working toward me. I knew he would be with me shortly to aid me with his valuable counsel. But I became impatient. If the fish was gone, I might as well break the line or leader, whichever was caught; and if he was still on, I certainly couldn't get any place simply by applying pressure with the rod.

So I laid the rod on the ledge, where I stood and took hold of the line itself. At the greater pressure something gave away. I felt a pulsating throbbing and pulled some more. The fish was on, and these direct pulls on the line had dragged him from his stronghold. As he came free I dropped the line and grabbed the rod, and fortunately made a smooth connection. The fight was still on when Clarence arrived. Some minutes later I had the satisfaction of admiring the fish as he lay in shining splendor on the rock ledge.

Following this practice of careful approach and natural drifts netted me two more fish when I fished Fred Gerken's Pool, so named because the year previous it had been the one place that made it possible for him to make his record perfect for seven consecutive days. It was the next good hole below the Ledge Pool. The usual way of fishing this pool was to make a long cast from above and across to the Key Rock, and then to follow through with the regular dip-and-lift method of fly manipulation. I had fished it several times in this manner, but it hadn't produced for me even though it had for Fred; so after the Sawtooth experience I thought I'd try something different.

Instead of starting in from above I went directly opposite the rock, crawled on my knees to a fair-sized rock on shore, and from its shelter cast toward the Key Rock, letting the fly drift downstream, or rather across and toward me. Of course I took in the slack as it did this. About halfway across a fish took, hooked himself solidly, and made a rush back into midstream. He didn't fight hard enough to make me get off my knees, so I simply held on until he tired and then led him to a little landing harbor near the rock that was shielding me. Although I didn't have any real hope of rising another fish in this water after the disturbance of the fight, I thought I'd make a few more casts to make certain about this. In almost the identical spot I hooked a second fish, and this time not only did I have to get on my feet, but also I had to follow the fish downstream for considerable distance.

There were other incidents that proved the value of the natural drift in steelhead fishing, but this does not mean that it was better or even as good as the regular method. It simply gave me an extra chance at any piece of water and was better for certain locations and certain fish. On various occasions other anglers on the stream took fish with the regulation method after I had failed with the drift method. For instance, consider the following. Late one afternoon both Jay and I fished the Kitchen Pool with the natural-drift method. We did not get a rise even though we did see one fish jumping. After we left the pool we met Ed Dewey and told him about the fish we had seen but didn't get. He went back there and took it—or at least he took a fish, and we like to think it was the one we saw.

My own fishing for the entire stay on the river was about evenly divided, and I believe that adhering exclusively to either method would have reduced my final score. On the whole I think that many steelhead anglers get so accustomed to fishing far off that they often neglect the "hot spots" near by. The peculiar thing about this obsession is that whichever side the angler fishes from, the opposite side is the one he feels he must reach to get his fish. This is a natural reaction, but it isn't logical or sensible. Although the other side of the stream may look better, it doesn't necessarily mean that it is. The side you are on may be where your luck lies. So approach any bit of water with the utmost caution, and keep out of sight until you have exhausted the possibilities under your feet. Not that long casts aren't necessary for a complete coverage of the average pool. They are. But don't neglect the side you are fishing from.

And here is something else to think about. When fishing is good it doesn't matter if you fish far off and neglect the places nearby. You'll get all you want no matter where you fish. But when fishing is bad—when you are fortunate to get even one strike in a hard day's fishing—then the man who covers both sides of the pool and fishes them with varied methods is the angler who is most likely to answer: "Good," when someone asks him: "What Luck?"

Recommended Tackle for Steelhead

ROD. Nine to nine and a half feet, weighing from six to seven ounces on the average. Or you may try lighter-weight glass rods of less length. Some fishermen think they are tops. Recently I've been using some five-strip bamboo rods. I would think that an eight-and-a-half-footer of four and three-quarters ounces of this construction would be suitable for steelhead, salmon, and bass-bug fishing. It has the needed power without the extra weight.

REEL. This should be large enough to hold thirty or forty yards of fly line and three hundred feet of backing, in my estimation of about ten- or twelve-pound test, but not less than eight. The average steelhead rod will take a GBF torpedo-head or an HCH double-taper, of nylon. You might go one size smaller in double-taper when using a silk line. The eight-and-a-half-foot five-strip rod will handle the GBF nylon, but if silk is used, then HCF will be best.

LEADERS. Nine feet, tapered according to personal needs, desires, and the size of the fish one might hook, from .019 or heavier to .015, .014, .013, or .012. Often size .015 may be best, when the water is swift and the fish large. Sometimes .012 is best, when the fish are wary and the water low. The other sizes can be useful also, for in-between conditions. It is quite impossible for anyone to make an exact table concerning these things. There are too many variations involved, and to tabulate all the numerous complications would require the services of an experienced and understanding statistician.

All the Big Ones Got Away

Of all the scholars to stalk the dusty corridors of classic fly-fishing literature, John Mc-Donald is a towering and respected figure of diligence and exactitude in producing illuminating treatises on angling history. The pages of McDonald's books are peopled by fly-fishing luminaries such as Issak Walton, Dame Juliana, Theodore Gordon, G.E.M. Skues, and others. McDonald's research of the writing and fishing of the fly-fishing legends is presented in his classic books, The Complete Fly Fisherman: The Notes and Letters of Theodore Gordon *(1947),* The Origins of Angling *(1963), and* Quill Gordon *(1972).*

History, however, was not McDonald's only interest in angling: He was a fisherman. And just like you and me, he wanted to land the big one.

Scholar that he was, McDonald was no slouch when it came to telling a story himself, as you will soon see. This particular tale is from Quill Gordon, *and it reminds us all that angling's oldest cliché, "the big one got away," is always a bitter pill to swallow.*

Every day I see the head of the largest trout I ever hooked, but did not land.

—Theodore Gordon

Of course all the big ones got away, and we all know why. Lies, delusions. And, in violation of the law of sufficient reason, it's plausible. That's how the big ones got big. But see how the old story goes when you try to put it down chapter and verse.

To start, you have to untangle the question: What's a big fish? Every angler has his private scale. On mine, thinking of good, not big, fish which I have actually caught, I can say roughly that a fourteen-inch trout in a Catskill creek equals a two-pounder on the Yellowstone River equals a seventeen-pound salmon on the Restigouche. On the same scale, a two-pounder in a stream equals a much larger one in a lake; and a two-pounder caught on a fly representing an insect equals a much larger one caught on a streamer fly representing a minnow—all quite arbitrary according to one's own game rules and values. "Big" before fish is a peculiar word, suggesting, I imagine, for many anglers something outlandish in relation to the circumstances. I have seen Lee Wulff, who has taken the biggest fish in the world on the lightest tackle, catch a ten-inch trout on the Battenkill with sewing thread, to his evident pleasure. Joan Miller, who once caught a 900-pound swordfish off Cape Cod with spear and barrel, yelled "Oh my God!" when she hooked her first trout later in the Yellowstone—a nine-incher on a tiny Gray Wulff dry.

When I say that all the big ones got away, however, I have in mind for the occasion a formidable minimum on an objective scale: a four-pound trout caught on fly in a stream. The scale was set by Dan Bailey for the walls of his Fly Shop in Livingston, Montana. You can put a tracing of the outline of your trout on the wall if it meets these conditions, and few anglers who have qualified have disdained the invitation. Bailey set the scale remarkably well for that country, whose streams yield an extraordinary number of trout below four pounds and relatively few above, so that a four-pounder or better is an event to bring everyone running. Some anglers around there have caught numerous wall fish, and since so many are on the wall now, the rule is that a fisherman can add a new one only if it is larger than the one he has already put up, in which case the old one must come down. This rule can give the angler a tough choice: Does he want to take down his five-pounder caught on a big streamer fly and put up a four-pounder caught on a number 16 Quill Gordon? I have not had to face such problems; after more than twenty years of visiting the Fly Shop and fishing the Boulder, Yellowstone, Gallatin, Madison, Big Hole, and many other rivers, streams, brooks, spring creeks, and ditches of Montana, I am not on that wall.

I regret the omission for all the obvious reasons, and for another more obscure personal one. When Bailey and I shared a cabin beside a creek in the Catskills in the 1930s, we casually put our larger trout on the cabin wall. We traced the shape of the trout on a piece of paper and took it off in a line drawing in ink on the old faded wallpaper, writing in the name of the one who had caught it and the date, and attaching the fly to the nose of the outlined trout. Bailey put up the first one on July 14, 1935, a fifteen-inch brown which really looked impressive coming out of that creek; and we made a rule that the next one would have to be larger. It was two years before another went up, a sixteen-incher of mine, and thanks to Bailey's emigration to Montana, I had the honor of putting up the rest. There were only four in all—the largest one eighteen inches—when I abandoned the cabin in 1941, carved the whole thing out of the wall, and took it to New York to be framed.

That I never put a trout on the wall in Montana was not for lack of expert teachers. I have fished under the aegis of some of the best and most dedicated fishermen since Gordon. I have seen Bailey catch wall fish without particularly trying, that is, while fishing wet or dry, with tiny delicate flies or large Muddlers. Phil Fjellman, a habitué of the Yellowstone with whom I often fished, put fifteen trout on the wall while I went blank. Joe Brooks (*Trout Fishing,* 1972) a fabulous fisherman in all styles and a specialist in power fishing, a style he popularized for catching big fish in Montana, said to me one day in the Fly Shop, "I think you ought to be on the wall. Come with me."

Power fishing, or perhaps more correctly, power casting, is a mode of fishing that grew out of tournament techniques for casting long distances. It is widely practiced in San Francisco and around Miami. Some tournament casters never actually go fishing, but many do. Their techniques are now standard practice in steelhead fishing and saltwater fly-fishing. Visiting fishermen brought the techniques to Montana, and Joe Brooks had a lot to do with demonstrating that they paid off in big fish. Since then the style has become a vogue with a number of good Montana fishermen.

Power fishermen discard the old casting styles, familiar to Easterners, of holding the arm to the side. The key to the power style is the "double haul." If you are right-handed, you work your line with your left hand, giving it impetus with a sharp stripping motion when picking the fly off the water and again in the forward cast. The equipment includes the "shooting" or "torpedo" line, which weighs more near the forward end. When you go over to power fishing, you have to give up the versatility of traditional delicate styles for working varieties of water with small flies. And if you fish in the traditional style, you have to give up a lot of big fish, which you will see others taking in the big-fish season (September and October in Montana) with rods that are eight and a half feet, five and a half ounces or larger.

On the rivers I have fished, power fishing appears to be almost exclusively a man's sport. Yet this kind of casting does not take unusual strength with a floating line, and tournament-casting women—Joan Wulff, for one—get considerable distance. Perhaps one difficulty is the strength needed to stay at it with streamer flies for hours on end. Another is the real power it takes to drag a long sinking line out of the water.

In any case, this circumstance has not worked altogether to the disadvantage of women. Their mastery of the dry fly followed on its invention. And although far fewer women than men fish fly, six have put stream trout on the

Fly Shop wall since 1958. Debie Waterman, of the fishing team of Debie and Charles Waterman of De Land, Florida, is represented with a seven-pound brown from the Missouri, caught on a Silver Outcast or Renegade (an outcast from the Silver Doctor Salmon fly), and a four-pound, one-ounce brown from the Yellowstone, caught on a Muddler. As she had to choose one to stay up, I asked her which it would be. She replied without hesitation, "The four-pounder. The Yellowstone is more of a challenge." This preference reflects the impression that big browns are comparatively easy to find and catch in the rich trout grounds at the confluence of the Missouri and Beaver Creek near Helena, where they come down from the lakes to spawn. Consider also a further complexity in fishing values. Debie Waterman says, "I come to Montana to fish dry fly. The greatest catch of my life in salt or fresh water was a three-and-a-half-pound brown on Nelson's Spring Creek [a tributary of the Yellowstone] with a number 16 [fairly small] Cahill on a 6x [extremely fine] tippet."

Mary Brooks, of the far-ranging fishing team of Mary and Joe Brooks of Richmond, Virginia, is on the wall with a four-pound, fourteen-ounce brown from Yellowstone, caught on a Muddler. Sue McCarthy of Daytona, Florida, displays a five-pound, four-ounce brown from the Missouri, caught on a Muddler. Ann Prickett has a five-pound, thirteen-ounce brown from the Yellowstone, caught on a Muddler. Mrs. Winston Dine-Brown is represented by a four-pound, twelve-ounce brown from the Yellowstone, caught on a Dark Spruce streamer. And Patricia O'Neill has hung a six-pound, one-ounce brown from the Madison, caught on a Salmon fly (mysteriously named, as it represents rather realistically a large natural stone fly). Perhaps someone can figure out why four of the six caught their trophy trout on a Muddler. Although it is a big-fish fly, on one wall panel displaying sixty-three four- and five-pounders caught by men and women, only twelve were caught on a Muddler; on another panel containing six-pounders and better, very few were taken on a Muddler.

Joe Brooks and I went out together on a great pool of the Yellowstone, once called Paine's Pool—the only time I recall going out especially to try for a big trout. Joe lent me a powerful rod, a shooting line, and some large, bright-blue streamer flies from the Argentine, along with a couple of dark-brown patterns. A master of casting who has written authoritative books on the subject, he showed me how to get the wind-resisting streamers out to the edge of the fast water on the far side of the pool, where big trout often lie. I didn't catch anything worth talking about, but Joe, illustrating his teaching, brought in and released a great trout which he denied would go four pounds, though I knew better. The kick in this kind of fishing is in the great expectations and the suspense. But I had to say that I found it too repetitive, and Joe agreed with that. He is a generous and versatile fisherman who likes to work the water.

Certainly fishing in traditional ways excuses no one for failing to catch big trout; anyone who fishes long enough should get at least a few. But as it was, I amassed a record collection of ways to lose the big ones. Of course there are the routine ways of striking too soon or too late (these account for a normal number of my losses), inattention to damaged tackle (quite a few), entanglements in moss and other flora of the watery depths (quite a few), buck fever while casting to a big rise (a few), and the like. Altogether these mount up, but come to no more than most fishermen have experienced. Indeed, there is no normal way for me to account for all the big ones getting away. I like to think that I am absolved because the really big ones got away by being inspired and superbrilliant tacticians. I give just three examples, from the Madison River.

Here I was in the Bear Trap stretch of the Madison, a wilderness area where the great river narrows and the water crashes through a gorge—unfishable except in side pockets and eddies. I hooked a trout on a number 10 Bailey Grizzly in a large pocket and saw him only in the shape of the swirls he made before he plunged recklessly into the gorge and—upstream! It made as much sense for fish to go upstream in that water as it would for one to climb Niagara Falls. However, the maneuver gave me the advantage of holding for a moment. He then turned and raced down twenty yards or so with the torrent and should have kept on going. But he didn't seem to want to leave the neighborhood. Against the laws of nature, he turned again and streaked upstream through the middle of the gorge. Then this old Greek fish-god settled to the bottom under a great rock in front of me. I sat there above him for a long time before I concluded that he would outwait me. I then broke him off and went on my way looking for more natural fish.

Doubt unsettled me. How can one have an experience with nature contrary to its laws? Could the fish have been a phantom of my imagination? Did the swirls of its rise actually belong to a whirlpool in the pocket? Were line and fly dragged by an unseen current into the maelstrom, where one or the other caught on a rock at the bottom? Was the dash upstream my own doing as I raised the rod to get a tight line, and the dash down a result of my yielding to the pressure of the heavy rushing water? Was the return to the rock my return to a tight line? Descartes's aphorism, "I think therefore I am," ran through my head, and I wondered whether my doubt about the existence of the Bear Trap trout did not attest to *my* existence—a consolation of angling that I believe has heretofore gone unnoticed.

Again, I stood in late afternoon on the east bank of the Cameron stretch of the Madison—several miles of flat prairielike rocks and sagebrush cut through with winding roads, near the town of Cameron. I left my companions and went downstream, casting from the bank into the swift runs that pushed up and around protruding rocks close by. I caught several ten- and twelve-inch rainbows on a small, slender wet fly, which suggested that the fishing might be very good. The Madison here is wide, straight, and powerful, strewn with open and slightly submerged rocks. A fisherman in these parts usually keeps restlessly moving down or up, and on occasion across, if the opportunity appears. But crossing the Madison is a considerable undertaking when its depth ranges from knee to waist. Only in a few spots can it be done at all, and the angler can never be sure of making it all the way. I began to have eyes for better water on the other side, however, and looked for a possible crossing. Presently I found one that seemed feasible. Holding the rod high, I fished across inch by inch, the pressure of the current just short of carrying me away.

For this heavy water I had put on a number 10 Trude (a down-wing hair fly looking rather like a wet Royal Coachman), which tended to float a little before sinking. Three good strikes came, and though none held, I concluded that I had the right fly (no insect hatch was visible). When I reached the other side, I fished down again through some long streamy runs, and the fishing was beautiful. Cutthroats. Good ones, never jumping (they almost never do), but fast, hard runners. I lost track of time and distance, until the water turned black and its whitecaps crystal in the twilight. I looked for a ford, found none, turned back, and tried to remember the landmarks of the crossing: a fallen aspen on my side, a clump of willows standing alone on the other. Here they were. I relaxed and started carefully fishing across.

About a third of the way, balanced on my left foot against the force of the water and casting straight ahead, I let the Trude fall over the bulge of a submerged boulder, lifted the rod, and—it stopped. It seemed that a full minute passed, during which the powerful water rushed on while the fly stood still below the bulge. Then it started moving away from me at a right angle to the current, toward the other bank. I held the rod high with the line running and edged forward while I tried to find footing. But it wasn't necessary to follow, for the trout changed course in a sweeping, arc-shaped run downstream and back toward the middle of the river. At the end of the run he came out high and twisting, a great rainbow, I judged, from the way he danced on his tail. I stood still as he went under, moved slowly up against the current, leaped again and again, and rolled away, tearing the river into swirling black and white designs.

He was one of those trout over whom the fisher has at this stage no control whatever—every move an awesome phenomenon. He held again, and neither trout nor angler moved in the deep dusk, all but night. It was a long hold, giving me time to ponder a question. This was a very big fish—pounds greater, I imagine, than the wall's minimum. (I say that now, though the wall was not in my head then.) It was the kind of fish I would stay there all night with. If luck favored me I would eventually catch him somewhat downstream along the bank I had come from. But if I did that, I would be marooned in darkness on the west bank, with several square miles of rangeland around me. My companions would be at the car on the east bank, waiting, knowing nothing of this adventure. If only I had carried a flare! (The thought of carrying a flare had never occurred to me before that moment.)

I came to understand that I had no choice; I had to cross. I began a maneuver to get below him, but when I moved down, so did he, maintaining the same angle. We must have been together about a half hour when I took the only way out. I started moving across upstream from him, the worst position for an angler; but as long as I was on either side of him, I could go with him and turn him so that he couldn't break away. The critical point would come when I passed directly over him. I hated to reach that point; I felt like an astrologer before an eclipse. Would he know what I knew?

He knew. As the line came parallel to the main current straight above him, he rose, not forty feet away, carrying the entire line into the air. Against the white water I saw him full and entire, the biggest thing imaginable in the whole river. Wise old trout, like all my big friends and antagonists in the water, he came down, a launched torpedo, and shot straight downstream. I let the line run freely into the backing, knowing he was gone before he was off. As the line ran out, I pointed the rod down and straight after him, in a sign of resignation, for the snap which came in due course. So I wound up with the story and without the fish and did the talking at supper that night.

It is twenty years since I first met the king of the Madison trout, a brown, at Papoose Creek—the best-known big fish not on the wall at the Fly Shop. It was a clear August morning, too clear to be promising, and the salmon-fly hatch for which the Madison is celebrated—its great stone fly that brings up the big fish—was long past, when Pat Barnes, Dorothy McDonald, and I set out to float the river. The practice of floating the Madison has been criticized because thoughtless boatmen pass through water being fished by wading or bank anglers, and some of them are fish hogs. We felt innocent enough, since Pat is a scrupulously courteous as well as skillful boatman (and angler), and we were not out to kill many fish. Pat grew up fishing the Madison, taught school until recently in Helena, and spends all his summers in West

Yellowstone, tying flies and running an elegant fishing shop with his wife Sig, and guiding, not to speak of fishing. He knows the Madison the way a deer knows its woods.

We launched the boat about thirty miles downstream from the river's start in Hebgen Lake. It was a McKenzie River boat made to run rough water, with eight-and-a-half-foot oars for control among rocks. In the bow was a sort of pulpit against which one could lean and cast without losing balance. These features were a necessity, as we were soon running through rapids and around submerged rocks.

Of the hundred or so flies in my fly box I picked out a number 12 Royal Wulff dry, a variation on the classic Royal Coachman. Theodore Gordon never liked the Royal Coachman; indeed, he was positively irked by it. He knew of it as a renowned killer, but he considered it a lure and could not understand what its attraction could be when fished dry. His best guesses were that it resembled a "glorified ant" or that its colors aroused the trout's curiosity. "One thing sure," he conceded, "the trout can scarcely fail to see it." He had in mind the quieter waters of the East, where this fly might be seen too well. I have often found it an effective dry fly in fast, splashy water, where it throws off distinct glints of light—not, I imagine, with the effect of a lure but with that of some brilliant spinner. Fishing dry in the absence of a hatch, especially on Western waters, I sometimes begin the day by experimenting with the light effects of fancy flies.

As it turned out, the Royal Wulff was the only pattern I needed to use all day. Standing in the bow, I cast to one side or the other, twenty to fifty feet and slightly ahead of the boat. All day I saw that sparkling fly bobbing or gliding through marvelous waters. Floating the Madison introduces one to every conceivable kind of fishing water. It was a much better day than we had expected, and we began catching and releasing quite a few fish—Dorothy and I alternating with the rod. After awhile we approached the little tributary, Papoose Creek, which comes down from the east out of the Madison Range.

We left the main current for a channel between an island and the east bank, and with Pat braking the boat, I dropped the fly into a deep, slow run along the bank. At the confluence with Papoose Creek I saw a shallows, and beyond it the incoming flow of the creek. I dropped the fly just inside the flow, with some slack leader curled behind it. The fly moved naturally with the flow, and disappeared. I drew up and the line tightened. Pat held the boat. The king came straight up, clear of the water, framed against the bushes on the other side of the creek: a yellowing brown trout of enormous dimensions. We had a long time to look at him as he hung, seemingly weightless, at the peak of his jump. He fell back with a great splash and circled around the same point several times, while Pat maneuvered the boat backward and toward the bank. Then he came up again, giving us another full view as he turned completely over and dived nose first, with only a swish, into the water. I was so spellbound that, although I automatically held the line tight, I forgot I was fishing.

Two things then happened almost at once. Pat, who had kept his head, jumped into the deep water, clothes and all, to drag the boat to shore. Had I not been distracted, I should have followed him. In the next instant the king rose again sidewise, throwing himself out into the river. I came to, and saw I had to make a choice. Pat had assumed that I would play the fish from the shore, which would have been a sound move if I had left the boat when Pat did. But now the fish was off and running downstream, and in the split second of decision I yelled to Pat to come back in. The old king had benefited by the spell he had cast which put Pat in the water and left me in the boat. Pat was back in the boat in another moment and we were soon after him, but he had taken a lot of line. He was fairly far out and going swiftly downstream before we were moving with him and I was taking in line. Some 300 yards downstream were two boulders, the larger one about 100 feet offshore. But for those boulders the course of my angling life would be quite different—I should not be writing this story. The king knew his territory well. I had recovered a good deal of line when he went outside the big boulder and circled it. We couldn't make it quickly enough, and as we circled it the line slacked. When I reeled in, the fly was still on and the hook was bent straight.

We crossed to the other side. I listlessly dropped a new fly along the edge of a wide pocket. It disappeared and I drew up. A trout came out into the river; about five minutes later I lifted him out of the water and, deciding to keep him along with a couple of others, knocked him on the head and tossed him into the boat. That evening when we beached the boat seventeen miles downstream from where we had started, I laid our fish on the bank. Dorothy looked at them and said, "That last one was pretty good." I took out a pocket scale and weighed him: three and three-quarter pounds. With the Papoose measure in my mind, I hadn't thought much of him for size. Yet he was the largest trout I have ever caught.

The next day when I came into the Fly Shop, I looked at the wall for the largest stream trout caught on dry fly. There it was—a rainbow, ten pounds, three ounces, caught by a Livingston fisherman, Roy Williams, on a Grey Hackle Yellow dry fly in the Yellowstone River in October 1950 (a record that still stood in the spring of 1972). I studied this fish and compared him in my mind's eye with the lost king. Needless to say . . .

During the next two years, I went back to Papoose Creek several times with different companions. On one occasion Dan Bailey went along, only because he was willing to humor me. We got into the water, a couple of hundred feet above the confluence of creek and river and waded out to the shallows. Dan started fooling around a boulder below the island, waiting while I waded down the shallows and fished back in toward the bank until I came to Papoose. When I reached the creek, I heard a shout from Dan that told me he had a strike. I found him a few minutes later, aghast. "The waters parted," he said, holding his arms wide and laughing. "I was catching some little fish on a small Grizzly Wulff and this fine leader, not expecting anything else, when he rose beside that rock. All around, the river went dry behind his rise. He went straight across to the end of my line and never stopped."

The Fisherman Who Got Away

BY THOMAS WILLIAMS

Critically praised novels such as The Moon Pinnace *and seven others have earned the late Thomas Williams (1926–1991) the highest esteem among his literary peers. In addition, his book of collected short stories,* Leah, New Hampshire, *shows Williams as a master of that form. In his introduction to that book, the well-known novelist John Irving says of Williams: "He was an outdoorsman, a sportsman, a hunter and a fisherman, a conservationist and an environmentalist—and a man who built his impressive house of wood and stone with his own hands (and the help of his wife)." Before he lost his bout with cancer in '91, Williams was a college professor at the University of New Hampshire.*

Prior to being collected in Leah, New Hampshire, *"The Fisherman Who Got Away" was originally published in* Seasons of the Angler, *edited by David Seybold, published by Weidenfeld & Nicholson in 1988.*

A brook trout is the centerpiece of this tale. A very special brook trout.

Richard Adgate was at Romeo LaVigne's fishing camp on Baie Felicité, Lake Chibougamau, with two friends. They were three Americans of middle age, husbands away from their wives and families.

His wife had been unhappy about his coming on this trip, but he'd been working hard, and how often had he ever done anything like go off fishing for a week? He'd asked her this with a defensive stridency she'd of course detected, she, the woman he'd lived with for a quarter of a century. He could feel what she felt. She couldn't understand why on earth he'd ever want to escape her, she who considered herself fair-minded and good to him. That he wanted to go away with two friends—pretty good friends—why? The children were grown and gone now, and she could easily have come, but she hadn't been asked. How would he like not being asked?

And so it was like that, not something he thought about every minute, but there was an edge, an incompleteness that made him a little too surprised when on the broad lake a series of ponderous golden boulders as big as houses suddenly appeared beneath his keel when he thought he was in deep water. He didn't want to look down, to have the other world rise up like that to within an arm's reach.

He'd gone out by himself this afternoon in one of Romeo La Vigne's rental boats, a seventeen-foot aluminum square-ended canoe with a rock in the bow for ballast and a four-horse Evinrude motor. Pete Wallner's boat was a little crowded with three in it, and Joe Porter was getting a divorce and needed conversation, reassurance, or whatever; that was no good with three, either. It seemed unfishermanlike, Joe's constant preoccupation with his problem. Or perhaps it was that a real getting-away, a forever getting-away, was antithetical to the furlough of a fishing trip. "She" was the word constantly on Joe's lips. "She." Her name was Lois, but it was always "she," and in spite of the immediate unpleasantness, Joe was about to be free of her after all the years. There was a perverse sort of envy in his listeners, too, and Richard could only wonder what it would be like if there were no "she" to make him return, no tether of loyalty and pity and partnership.

In any case, here he was, Richard Adgate, a man no better and no worse in his frailties than other men, he thought, forty-nine years old and quite alone in the suffering of his wife's disapprobation. Her name, empowered by the years, was Nora.

He'd been trolling around a small island a mile or two from Romeo LaVigne's rather shabby log cabins, the only man-caused things in sight except for the Indian camp a couple of hundred yards farther on—log frames with bright red and blue plastic tarps over them. Pete, who had a Lowrance sonar, had told him that the depth dropped to forty feet about fifty yards out from the island, and then to ninety feet ten to twenty yards farther out, so he trolled a silver Mooselook Wobbler on lead-core line, with about six colors out, hoping to find that small plateau and not get hung up too often.

The July day was blue, clouds forming always to the southwest, growing, looking dark, but not amounting to a rainstorm. The little island was covered by the narrow spruce, virgin spruce less than a foot in diameter, so thick you couldn't push your way through them. So far he'd seen a scruffy-looking red fox, a beaver, a sharp-tailed grouse with five or six chicks (the first he'd ever seen), a vole, ravens, unidentified ducks, a killdeer. This was the boreal forest, chilled and stunted most of the year by the polar winds. But in July the air was mild. The lake was warm on the surface, but a foot down it was forty degrees, and the lake trout (*grise,* to the French) were not very deep.

After a while, with no fish taking the silver Wobbler, he reeled in, shut off the idling motor, and let the mild wind and little waves tilt him and move him slowly to the northeast, toward a distant, spruce-black shore.

He got his map from his pack and opened it along its folds to where he was, feeling the familiar small shock caused by a map's ideal, formulated authority, its precision reflecting the wide, moving actuality of the lake and the distant, oddly shaped hills. Magnetic north was nearly twenty degrees west of true north here, a knife-sharpening angle. He balanced on his spine in the canoe, above the depths of another inhabited world.

To the east, according to his map, was a narrow northward extension of the lake, a passage five or six miles long that opened into a large bay with many islands, where a good-sized river entered, with the symbol for rapids. Lake trout were fine, beautiful fish, but most of his life he'd been a brook trout fisherman, and only occasionally a troller. For him, the fish most familiar to his hand, least alien to touch, was the squaretail, the brookie, here called "speckled trout" or *moucheté*.

There were supposed to be large brook trout in the rivers hereabouts, especially in rapids. But up that long passage, into a place where no one else would be, miles away from anyone—did he really want to go there? Wouldn't those islands loom strangely, and the bottom rise up to startle him? The far bay had a name: Baie Borne; and the river: Rivière Tâche—he didn't know what they meant in French.

Along with his rods and tackle box, he had, in his pack, a sandwich, some chocolate, two bottles of Laurentide Ale, and all of the usual outdoors stuff: a compass, Band-Aids, nylon line, aspirin, binoculars, safety pins, toilet paper, bug repellent—things gathered over the years. He didn't consider himself fussy or overcautious in these matters. When he went out in a boat, he wore a life vest, and when it might rain he wore a broad-brimmed felt hat and took along raingear. It was stupid to suffer the lack of any little thing. On his belt he wore his sheath knife and a pair of Sargent wire-cutter pliers.

He was drifting toward the entrance to the northern passage. He had a full three-gallon tank of gas. Why not go there? Because he was here in northern Quebec in some ridiculous way without permission, and because, for all his years and his knowledge of the water and the woods, there was still within him a small child afraid of the deep and the dark.

In his life he'd never jumped into new things, dangerous things. He'd always crept in, somehow, slowly and cautiously, and gotten to the danger all the same. Not that there could be real danger here, unless a storm came up, and even then it would be nothing serious. He could always run to shore and wait it out, no matter how long the storm lasted. Even if his motor conked out, broken beyond his ability to fix it, he had a paddle. It would be only time that he could lose. So his friends might worry about him—so what? But it did worry him that they might worry—a small threat of anxiety, a small twinge of that psychic nausea. It all seemed so demeaning that he decided he would have to go to the strange bay and the river. He liked to be alone. He did. He was always saying that he did. He started the motor and swung northeast, looking for the passage. Of course he might go in, and he might not.

The entrance to the passage toward Baie Borne was narrow, full of boulders, and had a definite current. He could see that the passage beyond widened and deepened quickly, however, so he throttled down and just made headway as he left the broad lake. He thought of those who explored caves—spelunkers (where did that word come from?)—who sometimes crawled into holes so narrow they'd have to bet upon a larger space ahead because they couldn't crawl out backward. A cowardly thought on a bluebird day. But he got through without touching and went on, at least for now, with dark hills rising on each side.

He didn't know how deep the water might be, but since he edged into this passage at trolling speed, he let out the silver lure, its long leader, and a couple of colors of line. One swath on the western hills had been logged, and the greener brush was a wash of light. On top, some birches had been left, their tall trunks against the sky like African trees—a view of Kenya that slowly passed. A small bay opened on his left and, yes, the map was disconcertingly true again. As he passed the bay's entrance, it silently let him by, its farther regions secret, not caring, set for eternity. A heavy cloud to the north, moving away, made his pathway dark.

His rod quivered—a snag or a hit. A fish, he knew as he picked it up, because it moved a little to the side, undulant, like a heartbeat, a small spasm of opinion. He shut off the motor and checked the star drag as he reeled, feeling the caught thing, the line alive between them. A pull from below answered the question of size; it was small, probably a lake trout. It came up against all of its will, no match for his eight-pound leader, the silver three-pronged hook in its flesh somewhere. He would see it soon.

The fish was dark and narrow—a small pike about fourteen inches, hardly a keeper. The brown eyes in the slanted skull saw him. The way to grab a large pike, he'd been told, was to put your thumb and middle finger into its eye sockets, squashing the eyes into the skull; this was supposed to stop their thrashing. He reached down and grabbed this one behind its head, the smooth body a muscle, and forced the tines of the hook down and out, a fragment of white cartilage, broken by a barb, flowing half-loose. His too-strong hands let the small pike go back down. As he let it go he felt a little magnanimous, slightly closer to the vision all fishermen would like to have of themselves someday—a distinguished older man with well-patched waders and a split bamboo rod, Yeats's wise and simple man, the paragon of dignified age who is usually observed in the middle distance as he performs each ceremonial fishing rite with understated skill. He always catches a fine brown trout and of course releases it, his sparse gray hackle glowing in the falling light, a tiny hatch, like reversed snow, haloing his old felt hat. Oh, yes, the classic fisherman, his aesthetics honed to the finest moral patina. With age was supposed to come wisdom that was not detachment, mastery that was not boredom, experience that never bred despair.

His canoe moved steadily north through the dark water. He hoped the northern cloud would soon pass and the water would turn a less forbidding blue again. Was he really going to go all the way to the river and its indicated rapids, or not? Looking back, the entrance from the lake had disappeared behind God knew how many hills. That the larger bay and its many islands would come up, inevitably, on map and in real distance, had some of the quality of the sudden boulders that had appeared beneath him in the broad lake.

The motor plugged on smoothly; the long bow moved ahead exactly where he had it go. He might troll, but decided not to because of apprehension about what he might catch. No, not apprehension, but because to catch something here might delay him too much. He would catch a Silkie, a monster half fish, half woman, both natures writhing with hatred as they died. He could see in the deep the golden scales on the thighs, the fish-belly-pale shoulders, the inward-turning teeth of a pike. If he trolled he would be mixing exploration, which was perhaps neutral with the gods, with the intent to do harm.

He leaned forward and hefted the gas tank; of course it was still heavy. He could go ten times the map distance with that much gas, and he knew it. If he were at home, he would be safe, though deprived of the opportunity to make this lovely, lonely choice. Of course his wife was home right now, her unhappiness a distant and unsettling power.

Rivière Tâche must be a mile or so farther, with rapids at its mouth, and in some wonderment at his deliberate progress he steered on toward it. Rocks here and there caused tan blushes near the surface of the water, between deep places where to look down was to see, hopefully, nothing but the dark water-gray of depth.

Across the wide blue of Baie Borne he moved, now over sand with patches of weeds here and there, and then into the positive current from the river. The spruce came nearer on each side, and ahead were rocks and some white water. The southeast wind was at his back, so he shut off the motor, the wind holding him against the current, and got his fly rod out of its tube. In his reel was a sinking line, an old leader, and a tippet he was too lazy or impatient to change. He was always nervous as he strung the leader through the eyelets, but he got the line correctly strung and chose for a fly a medium-sized Gray Ghost. His fingers trembled as he tied his knot and clipped off the tag end. The water was five or six feet deep, the rocks below darker, denser-looking than the boulders out in the bay. His canoe turned in the wind and current, and he tilted the motor up before casting. He would begin here and then go up toward the frothings of white water.

After the first cast, which was only a half-decent cast, in fact a lousy cast, with the leader dropping in a messy coil not ten yards away, he began to strip in his line, worrying only about getting a knot in his leader and not at all about a fish. But the line jerked out straight, and his supple rod bent. "My God!" he said. "It's a fish!" He wasn't ready at all; there was a sense of bad timing, as though he'd rather not have a strong fish on just yet, after such a stupid mess of a cast. But the fish was there, whatever it was. He should have changed the tippet; surely more than three pounds had already stretched it out. His nerves went down to the invisible tippet as he let out line, let it out and recovered it. Careful, now! The fish ran upcurrent, then held for a moment before running down along the far bank, not quite to a snag angled into the water—a complicated dead spruce. He just managed to decrease by tender force the radius of the fish's run down that bank. Then it stopped, and he kept what he hoped was a permissible pressure on it, and then just a little bit more, but he couldn't move it. He was afraid of the sudden emptiness of no connection. "Don't happen," he said. "Don't happen."

He didn't know what kind of fish it was, only that it was big and strong. If it was a brook trout, it would be the biggest one he'd ever seen, he was sure of it, a salmon-sized brook trout. It might be a pike, or a large walleye, or a lake whitefish—what else was here? With one hand, he freed his boat net from the paddle: presumptuous to think of netting a fish he couldn't even move. But then the fish came in a little, maybe just a foot or so; the canoe was moving, so it was impossible to tell. But the fish didn't like that, and pulled so hard, so suddenly, he knew the tippet had to break, and for a moment thought it had, a hollow moment, but the fish had come toward him, and now it veered away upstream, the line cutting the surface. He must keep the fish from winding the leader around a rock—just to the limit of what he could do with a three-pound tippet, which was probably good for at least five pounds, except that it was old, so God knew what strength it had. He mustn't get used to its holding.

He had to see this fish. He wanted to own it, to have it. What a will it had, what strength! But the long minutes with his rod quivering, line in and out in desperation, might be too worrying for him. He'd deliberately put himself into a situation in which he felt anxiety. Why had he done that?

Beneath the water, the cold muscles fought for life against this fragile extension of his touch. How sickening it must be to be pulled by the invisible—like having a fit, epilepsy, a brain spasm. What did the fish think pulled him so hard, and what part of him said no? He must know the fly itself was too small to have such power; everything he'd ever hunted and eaten told him that, but some force wanted to haul him away from the dark rocks to the ceiling of his world and out of it. Everything smaller than he that moved in his world was food, yet now this small thing he'd tried to eat was overpowering him, little by little, with a constant pressure that felt like death. What else must he know in his neurons, in his lateral canals, and in all the circuits of his perfect body, when he'd lived a life of caution, too, hunter and hunted both?

The wild thing deep in the current was so tenuously bound to him by his skill and desire. . . . By what skill? He was a nervous wreck, trembling and sighing. His line looped at his feet, a coil of it encircling the shank of the paddle. If the fish ran now, it would be all over, so he held the rod high and reached down to free the line. The bunched collar of his jacket pushed his hat forward, and because he hadn't thought to fasten the chin strap, a gust blew the hat overboard. He reached for it and nearly shipped water, came upright again and noticed that his tackle box, weighted by the open tray, had dumped lures and eyelets and split shot and all kinds of necessary little objects into the bilge. His hat floated away; the coil of line was still around the paddle. He saw, but didn't feel on his line, the fish as it came to the surface of the water in a quick, in-turning swirl. It was black on its back, deep in the body, spotted, with a flash of orange at the fins; every memory, every known subtlety of shape and behavior said trout, said eight to ten pounds, the fish of his life that would make this moment, for better or for worse, forever a brilliant window.

He did clear the line from the paddle, and miraculously the fish was still on. He hauled in line as the fish came straight at him. He'd meant to get a multiplying reel and make it left-handed, so he could reel all this line in—why hadn't he done that? Why hadn't he done that long ago, as Ray Bergman had suggested in his book. *Trout?* The stripped line slopped half in and half out of the boat, some of it among his spilled lures, so that he'd probably have a bloody Christmas tree of ornaments on it when it came up again.

Something shoved him hard in the back—a mean, hurtful sort of shove; the canoe had drifted into the bank, and it was a dead spruce stub that wanted to push him onto his face. The fish moved upstream again, well out from the bank, thank God. If he could just get hold of the paddle, or even that nasty stub, and push himself away from the bank. He couldn't see why the fish was still on. It could just run away if it wanted—take out his line and all his backing and easily snap the tippet. Of course the next thing the wise and skillful fisherman would do would be to capsize the boat.

Where was his hat? Over by a sand bar, beached by the wind. He could get it later, if there was going to be a later. His arms seemed to be pushing as well as pulling—pushing against his tendency to pull too hard—and were getting tired. He must keep the fish working against the pitifully small pressure he dared use. He knew he was never going to possess this fish, because it was too good, too beautiful for the incompetent likes of Richard Adgate.

For a long time the fish hung into the current. He managed to reach the paddle and to push away from the hostile bank—at least for the moment, though the canoe turned perversely in the current and wind, as if it, too, had an opinion about the outcome.

He had time to think that he was not enjoying any of this. His hopes were ridiculous; whatever gods of luck there were had chosen him for their sport

Yet the fish fought for its life, and did Richard Adgate want to kill to have it? He *had* to kill in order to have it—a soft hesitation immediately gone, banished as too stupid to consider. If only he hadn't been so impatient, and had put on a new leader, maybe six to eight pounds; this was no little midsummer trout brook in New Hampshire. What all this showed was a major flaw in his character, the story of his life. *Unprepared* was his motto.

But the fish stayed on. The wind had been coming up, blowing the canoe up into the current, but at least near the center of the river. Though he'd been turning and turning, he began to see a pattern in the fish's runs; it liked a certain oval area of water and never went to either bank or to the dead spruce. Maybe bigger monsters lurked there and kept it away, although what of its own element might frighten a fish this large he didn't want to think about. Maybe the fish was as stupid as he was, but you didn't get that large by being stupid.

Time passed, and passed, his arms aching, his nervousness institutionalized, solidified. He had a vaguely hopeful theory that the longer he kept the fish from its fish-business, the weaker it would have to become. Sure, just think of salmonoids as weaklings.

He found himself guiding, turning the living fish but thinking of other things. He wondered if he would ever be brave enough to camp out alone here, say on one of the small islands in this bay, alone in the dark night. Could he endure the blackness of that night, the silence of it, when even in broad daylight he was unnerved by the strange coves of a small bay seen in passing?

A rose-white slab glinted over there on the surface—a large fish rolled, and it was his fish, on its side for a moment, its tail giving a tired-looking scull or two before it sank down again. Then there were a few pulls, weaker shakes of the head, weak though irritated: What *is* this thing pulling on me all the time? And he thought all at once that he might actually bring the fish to the side of the canoe. Maybe. It had been on more than half an hour now.

The fish came, slowly. When it first saw the canoe, it ran, but not far, and he gently snubbed its run and turned it again. If he startled it too much, it would simply run away from him, because it was not really as weak as it seemed. Nothing was as it seemed. With the rod in his left hand, the line snubbed with his fingers, he sneakily got the big boat net handy, then went back to his gentle urging, turning, and soon the fish was next to the canoe. With desperate strength he took the net and scooped it up and into the canoe amidst all the spilled and tangled gear and line and who cared what. He was on his knees, his hands over the net and his fish. What teeth it had! It was a brook trout, all right, but changed by size into something oceanic, jaws like forearms, gill covers like saucers.

The Gray Ghost was deep in its tongue, the tippet not even in existence any longer. His metal stringer was in the mess in the bottom of the boat, and he clipped one hanger through the trout's lower jaw and another around a thwart into the chain—of course he would never trust it in the water. As if it understood, the trout thrashed itself out of his grasp, into the air, then came down thrashing on the mess of lures, eyelets, spoons, net, line, sinkers, flies, reel-grease tubes, spinners, hooks, split rings—all the picky little toys and trinkets a fisherman collects.

And it was all right. He could sit back, drift where he would, and look at the sky, which he did for a while. Then he paddled over to the sand bar and retrieved his hat, his good old felt Digger hat that had protected him from so many storms. Good old hat!

He took his De-liar from his fly-fishing vest and measured the fish: twenty-eight inches, eight and a half pounds. The beautiful great fish trembled, dying as it must, as it must. And with that flicker of sadness the world changed for him. It was seven o'clock on this subarctic afternoon, a crisp southeast wind raising a few whitecaps on Baie Borne, the bluest of waters. He pulled the canoe up on the sand and carefully cleaned everything up, put everything away, sponged out all water and slime, made everything shipshape and Bristol fashion.

On his way back through the long passage, he headed into the wind, his bow pounding across the larger waves, a Laurentide Ale in his hand. There lay the trout, monstrous, outsized, beyond dreaming of. It didn't matter that it was nothing he deserved, that because of his clownish errors he should have lost it six times. The knowledge of his fear and awkwardness would only heighten memory. All the rest of his life he would see the pure and desolate bay and the pulse of incoming river, its turbulence meeting the blue water. The black density of the spruce, on island and hill, grew vividly into the past.

But what if he'd lost this fish? Would the shadows fall across these hills in tones of lead? Maybe that alternate fate was past and gone, as were so many alternatives, large and small, to the course of a life. No matter now; he was brought back, for better or worse, along a line as sure and fragile as his own.

The Dreadnaught Pool

BY ZANE GREY

Monies earned from his long skein of highly readable westerns, with romantic names like Riders of the Purple Sage, *enabled Zane Grey to pursue global fishing adventures at a time when every trip was a pioneering venture. In the 1910s and 1920s, Grey was fishing places like Tahiti long before many people even knew where they were. Guides and facilities were virtually nonexistent.*

Grey's many books on discovering fishing around the world, from the Delaware River where he was raised to regions across oceans where no one had ever sport-fished before, are treasures to own and read.

One of my favorite anthologies of Grey's best hunting and fishing tales is Zane Grey: Outdoorsman, *edited by George Reiger and published by Prentice-Hall in 1972. It includes this story of Grey's favorite New Zealand trout pool, which was published in Grey's* Tales of the Angler's Eldorado. *The zest with which Grey pursued the huge gladiators of the deep like marlin and swordfish was matched by his enthusiasm to find and enjoy trout fishing with proper fly-fishing gear, instead of the heavy tackle and spinners so popular at that time.*

Hoka, our genial Maori guide, whom I had begun to like very well indeed, averred one morning that the trout had begun to run up the river. Both Captain Mitchell and I verified this. But to make these rainbows rise to an ordinary fly was something which would take the patience of a saint, not to mention a good degree of skill. The Captain finally did it, and so did I, but at the expense of infinite labor. We resorted to large Rogue River flies, mostly number four, and then to salmon flies number two, and finally we got to dressing our own flies. This was fun for me. Some of the outlandish lures I dressed up should have scared a rainbow trout out of his wits. Nevertheless they answered the purpose, and one of them, a fly so extraordinary that I could not make another like it, turned out to be a "killer." The only difficulty about large flies was that they were hard to cast. By diligent practice and strenuous effort, however, I at length achieved considerable distance, making an average of sixty feet, often seventy, and rarely even eighty feet. And when I saw that gaudy fly shoot out to such extreme distance I certainly felt exultant and vain.

We had word of another record catch of eleven fish at the mouth of the Tongariro. This was given us by Mr. Gilles, the nail driver, who stopped at our camp on an errand. He saw the fish and vouched for their weight; a fourteen-pound average, with largest weighing sixteen and one-half pounds. All caught on a fly at night! But no other information had been vouchsafed. I asked Mr. Gilles many questions about this remarkable catch, very few of which could he answer. He was himself a fisherman of long experience, and it was his opinion the trout were caught by the fisherman letting out a large fly or spinner a hundred or two hundred feet from the boat, and then drawing it back by hand until he had a strike. I shared this opinion.

By climbing to the bluff above the river, when the sun was high, we could see the big trout lying deep in the pale-green crystal water; ten-, twelve- and fifteen-pound rainbows, and an occasional brown trout, huge and dark, upward to twenty pounds. This was a terrible, although glad, experience for Captain Mitchell and me. To sight such wonderful fish and not get a rise from them! Alma Baker took it more philosophically, and considered the privilege of seeing them quite enough. Cap and I, however, wanted to feel one of those warriors at the end of a line. In the pool below camp we tried at sunrise, through the day, at sunset and then after dark. Flyfishing at night was an awful experience for me. I got snarled in the line. I continually hit my rod with my fly, and half the time it spun round the rod, entailing most patient labor. Moreover, I was standing through the chill of night in ice-cold water. Finally I whipped the big hook in the back of my coat. That gave me sufficient excuse to go back to camp. What joy the camp fire! Captain Mitchell returned presently, wet and shivering. He did not complain of the cold water, but he lamented a great deal over the loss of his best fly. He had snagged it on a rock and nearly drowned himself trying to rescue it.

★ ★ ★

Next morning while the rest of the party were at breakfast I stole down the bank and made a cast into the swirling waters. I made another, and when I tried to retrieve the line, lo! it was fast to something that moved. I struck, and I hooked a trout. For fear he might rush out into the swift current I held him harder than I would otherwise, and thus tired him out before he could take advantage of me. When I was sure of him, a fine seven-pounder rolling in the clear water, I yelled loudly. The whole breakfast contingent rushed pell-mell to the bank, and to say they were amazed would be putting it mildly.

That was a prelude to a strenuous day for all of us. Baker elected to fish the pools below camp, where he did not have to wade. Hoka took Captain Mitchell and me, accompanied by Morton, up the river.

"Only a little way, about a mile," said Hoka, with the smile that always robbed me of a retort. It was a long, long mile before we even got off the road; and even a short mile in heavy waders, three pairs of woolen socks, and iron-studded clumsy wading boots was always quite sufficient. I can pack a gun and walk light-footed far up and down canyons, but wading paraphernalia burdens me down.

Hoka led us into a fern trail, one of those exasperating trails where the ferns hook your fishing line and leader and will not let go. Then he arrived at a precipitous bluff under which an unseen river roared musically. It was not the Tongariro. The Captain naturally wanted to know how we got down.

"We go right over," replied Hoka, and with that remark he disappeared. He heard crashings in the ferns. Next I went "right over." I held my rods high above my head and trusted my seven-league eight-ton boots to the depths. When at last I arrived at a comparative level, I awaited to see what would happen to my comrades. I knew there would be a fall all right. Soon I heard what might have been a rhinoceros plowing down the ferny cliff; but it was only Captain Mitchell who arrived beside me hot, furious, forgetful of all save his previous pipe, which a tenacious fern still clung to. The real fun, however, came with Morton. Our genial cinematographer was burdened with cameras, also a pair of iron-hoofed boots that I had insisted he wear. I have no idea how Morton got down, unless he fell all the way. We heard him talking vociferously to the obstructing ferns. At last he arrived, red of face, and grimly hanging on to his load.

Hoka was waiting for us with his disarming smile.

"You came down easy," he said. "But this panel over the river will be hard."

"Huh! What's a panel?" I asked. "Hoka, I've begun to have suspicions about you."

He soon showed us the panel. It was no less than a rickety pole bridge, swung on wires attached to branches of trees, and spanning a dark rushing little river that must have been beautiful at some other time. Just now it seemed treacherous. How the current swept on, down, rushing, swirling, gurgling under the dark overreaching trees!

Hoka went first. He weighed seventeen stone, which in our language is over two hundred pounds; and I felt that if the panel held him, it would certainly hold me. He crossed safely and quite quickly for so large a man; I went next. Such places rouse a combative spirit in me, and that made the crossing something different. Nevertheless when I was right in the middle, where the thin crooked poles bent under my heavy boots, I gazed down into the murky water with grim assurance of what might happen if the poles broke. I got across, proving how unnecessary the stirring of my imagination often is.

Once safe on the bank I was tempted to yell something facetious to Morton and Mitchell, but I desisted, for this was hardly the place for humor. They reached our side without mishap, and then again we beat into the jungle of ferns and *ti* trees. It was hard going, but soon I heard the mellow roar of the Tongariro, and with that growing louder and louder I found less concern about difficulties. We came at length into an open thicket of *ti* brush, bisected by shallow waterways and dry sandy spaces, through which we emerged to the wide boulder-strewn river bank.

"This pool here is called Dreadnaught," said Hoka, pointing to a huge steep bluff strikingly like the shape of a dismantled man-of-war. It stood up all alone. The surrounding banks were low and green. After one glance, I gave my attention to picking my steps among the boulders, while Hoka kept on talking. "My people once fought battles here. They had a *pa* on top of this bluff. I'll show you graves that are wearing away. The skulls roll down into the river. My people, the Maoris, were great fighters. They stood up face to face, and gave blow for blow, like men."

At last I found a seat on a log, laid aside my rods, camera and coat, and looked about. The Tongariro ran sweeping down in the S shape, between bright soft green banks; a white swift river, with ample green water showing, and rapids enough to thrill one at the idea of shooting them in a Rogue River boat. The end of the last rapids piled against the hull of the Dreadnaught bluff. A little rippling channel ran around to the right, out of sight, but it must soon have stopped, for the high embankment was certainly not an island.

I began to grow more interested. The bluff had a bold bare face, composed of three strata; the lowest a dark lava studded thickly with boulders, the next and middle one a deep band of almost golden sand, and the topmost a gray layer of pumice in the top of which I saw the empty graves of the bygone Maoris.

The current deflected from the base of the bluff, sheered away and swept down through the pool, farther and farther out, until it divided into three currents running into three channels.

The lower and larger end of that pool fascinated me. Under the opposite bank the water looked deep and dark. A few amber-colored rocks showed at the closer edge of the current. It shoaled toward the wide part, with here and there a golden boulder gleaming far under the water. What a wonderful pool! It dawned on me suddenly. The right channel, or one farthest over, ran glidingly under the curving bank, and disappeared. I could not see the level below. Points of rock and bars of boulders jutted out from a luxuriantly foliaged island. The middle channel was a slow wide shallow ripple, running far down. A low bare gravel bar rose to the left, and stretched to where the third channel roared and thundered in a deep curving rapid. Here most of the river rushed on, a deep narrow chute, dropping one foot in every three feet, for over a hundred yards.

I had to walk to the head of the rapid to see where the water ran, heaping up waves higher and higher, down the narrow channel that curved away under another high wooded bluff. Most of the water of the pool glided into the channel, growing swift as it entered. Green crystal water! I could see the bottom as plainly as if the depth had been ten inches instead of ten feet. How marvelously clear and beautiful! Round rocks of amber and gold and mossy green lay imbedded closely, like a colorful tiling.

My gaze then wandered back over the head of the pool, where the Captain stood hip deep, casting far across into the current. And it wandered on down to the center, and then to the lower and wide part of the pool. What a magnificent place to fish! I made up swiftly for my laggard appreciation. I could see now how such a pool might reward a skillful far-casting angler, when the rainbows were running. After a long climb up rapids, what a pool to rest in! There might even be a trout resting there then. So I picked up my rod and strode down to the river.

A clean sand bar ran out thirty yards or more, shelving into deep green water. Here a gliding swirling current moved off to the center of the pool, and turned toward the glancing incline at the head of the narrow rapid. The second and heavier current worked farther across. By wading to the limit I imagined I might cast to its edge. I meant to go leisurely and try the closer current first. It was my kind of place. It kept growing upon me. I waded in to my knees, and cast half across this nearer current. My big fly sank and glided on. I followed it with my eye, and then gave it a slight jerky movement. Darker it became, and passed on out of my sight, where the light on the water made it impossible for me to see. I had scarcely forty feet of line out. It straightened below me, and then I whipped it back and cast again, taking a step or two farther on the sand bar.

My line curved and straightened. Mechanically I pulled a yard or so off my reel, then drew perhaps twice as much back, holding it in loops in my left hand. Then I cast again, letting all the loose line go. It swept out, unrolled and alighted straight, with the fly striking gently. Was that not a fine cast? I felt gratified. "Pretty poor, I don't think," I soliloquized, and stole a glance upriver to see if the Captain had observed my beautiful cast. He was so engrossed in his own angling, he did not know I was on the river. Then I looked quickly back at my fly.

It sank just at the edge of the light place on the water. I lost sight of it, but knew about where it floated. Suddenly right where I was looking on this glancing sunlit pool came a deep angry swirl. Simultaneously with this came a swift powerful pull, which ripped the line out of my left hand, and then jerked my rod down straight.

"Zee-eee!" shrieked my reel.

Then the water burst white, and a huge trout leaped in spasmodic action. He shot up, curved and black, his great jaws wide and sharp. I saw his spread tail quivering. Down he thumped, making splash and spray.

Then I seemed to do many things at once. I drew my rod up, despite the strain upon it; I backed toward the shore; I reeled frantically, for the trout ran upstream; I yelled for Morton and then for Captain Mitchell.

"Doc, he's a walloper!" yelled the Captain.

"Oh, biggest trout I ever saw!" I returned wildly.

Once out of the water I ran up the beach toward Captain Mitchell, who was wading to meet me. I got even with my fish, and regained all but part of the bag in my line. What a weight! I could scarcely hold the six-ounce rod erect. The tip bent far over, and wagged like a buggy whip.

"Look out when he turns!" called Mitchell.

When the fish struck the swift current, he leaped right before me. I saw him with vivid distinctness—the largest trout that I ever saw on my line— a dark bronze-backed and rose-sided male, infused with the ferocity and strength of self-preservation; black-spotted, big-finned, hook-nosed. I heard the heavy shuffle as he shook himself. Then he tumbled back.

"Now!" yelled Captain Mitchell, right behind me.

I knew. I was ready. The rainbow turned. Off like an arrow!

"Zee! Zee! Zee!" he took a hundred yards of line.

"Oh Morton! Morton! . . . *Camera!*" I shouted hoarsely, with every nerve in my body at supreme strain. What would his next jump be? After that run! I was all aquiver. He was as big as my big black marlin. My tight line swept up to the surface as I have seen it sweep with so many fish. "He's coming out!" I yelled for Morton's benefit.

Then out he came magnificently. Straight up six feet, eight feet and over, a regular salmon leap he made, gleaming beautifully in the sun. What a picture! If only Morton got him with the camera I would not mind losing him, as surely I must lose him. Down he splashed. "Zee!" whizzed my line.

I heard Morton running over the boulders, and turned to see him making toward his camera. He had not been ready. What an incomparable opportunity lost! I always missed the greatest pictures! My impatience and disappointment vented themselves upon poor Morton, who looked as if he felt as badly as I. Then a hard jerk on my rod turned my gaze frantically back to the pool, just in time to see the great rainbow go down from another grand leap. With that he sheered round to the left, into the center of the wide swirl. I strode rapidly down the beach and into the water, winding my reel as fast as possible. How hard to hold that tip up and yet to recover line! My left arm ached, my right hand shook; for that matter, my legs shook also. I was hot and cold by turns. My throat seemed as tight as my line. Dry-mouthed, clogged in my lungs, with breast heaving, I strained every faculty to do what was right. Whoever said a trout could not stir an angler as greatly as a whale?

One sweep he made put my heart in my throat. It was toward the in-cline into the rapids. If he started down! But he ended with a leap, head up-stream, and when he soused back he took another run, closer inshore toward me. Here I had to reel like a human windlass.

He was too fast; he got slack line, and to my dismay and panic he jumped on that slack line. My mind whirled, and the climax of my emotions hung upon that moment. Suddenly, my line jerked tight again. The hook had held. He was fairly close at hand, in good position, head upriver, and tiring. I waded out on the beach; and though he chugged and tugged and bored he never again got the line out over fifty feet. Sooner or later—it seemed both only a few moments and a long while—I worked him in over the sand bar, where in the crystal water I saw every move of his rose-red body. How I rev-eled in his beauty! Many times he stuck out his open jaws, cruel beaks, and gaped and snapped and gasped.

At length I slid him out upon the sand. I never looked down upon such a magnificent game fish. No artist could have caught with his brush the shining flecked bronze, the deep red flush from jaw to tail, the amber and pearl. He would have to have been content to catch the grand graceful contour of body, and the wolf-jawed head, the lines of fins and tail.

He weighed 11½ pounds. I tied him on a string, as I liked to do with little fish when I was a boy, and watched him recover and swim about in the clear water.

Meanwhile Morton stood there using language because he had failed to photograph those first leaps, and Captain Mitchell went back to his fishing. Presently a shout from him drew our attention. He had broken his rod on the cast.

The Captain waded out and approached us, holding the two pieces for my inspection. The middle ferrule had broken squarely, and the Captain anathematized the rod in several languages.

"But, Cap, you've had it for years. Even the best of rods can't last forever," I protested. "We'll take turn about using mine."

He would not hear of this, so I returned to fishing, with my three companions all on the *qui vive*. I thought to try the same water, and to save that wonderful space out there between the currents for the last.

★   ★   ★

As if by magic of nature the Dreadnaught Pool had been transformed. The something that was evermore about to happen to me in my fishing had happened there. There! The beautiful pool glimmered, shone, ran swiftly on, magnified in my sight. The sun was westering. It had lost its heat and glare. A shadow lay under the bluff. Only at the lower end did the sunlight make a light on the water, and it had changed. No longer hard to look upon!

I waded in up to my knees and began to cast with short line, gradually lengthening it, but now not leisurely, contentedly, dreamingly! My nerves were as keen as the edge of a blade. Alert, quick, restrained, with all latent powers ready for instant demand, I watched my line sweep out and unroll, my leader straighten, and the big dark fly alight. What singularly pleasant sensations attended the whole procedure!

I knew I would raise another rainbow trout. That was the urge, wherefore the pool held more thrill and delight and stir for me. On the fifth cast, when the line in its sweep downstream had reached its limit, I had a strong vibrating strike. Like the first trout, this one hooked himself; and on his run he showed in a fine jump—a fish scarcely half as large as my first one. He ran out of the best fishing water, and eventually came over the sand bar, where I soon landed him, a white and rose fish, plump and solid, in the very best condition.

"Fresh-run trout," said Hoka. "They've just come up from the lake."

"By gad! Then the run is on," returned Captain Mitchell with satisfaction.

This second fish weighed 5¾ pounds. He surely had all the strength of an eight-pound steelhead in his compact colorful body. I was beginning to understand what the ice water of the Tongariro meant to the health and spirit of a rainbow.

"Cap, make a few casts with my rod while I rest and hug the fire," I said. "That water has ice beaten a mile."

"Not on your life," replied the Captain warmly. "I've a hunch it's your day. Wade in; every moment now is precious."

So I found myself out again on the sand bar, casting and recasting, gradually wading out until I was over my hips and could go no farther. At that I drew my breath sharply when I looked down. How deceiving that water! Another step would have carried me over my head. If the bottom had not been sandy I would not have dared trust myself there, for the edge of the current just caught me and tried to move me off my balance; but I was not to be caught unawares.

Apparently without effort, I cast my fly exactly where I wanted to. The current hungrily seized it, and as it floated out of sight I gave my rod a gentle motion. Halfway between the cast and where the line would have straightened below me, a rainbow gave a heavy and irresistible lunge. It was a strike that outdid my first. It almost unbalanced me. It dragged hard on the line I clutched in my left hand. I was as quick as the fish and let go just as he hooked himself. Then followed a run the like of which I did not deem possible for any fish short of a salmon or a marlin. He took all my line except a quarter of an inch left on the spool. That brought him to the shallow water way across where the right-hand channel went down. He did not want that. Luckily for me, he turned to the left and rounded the lower edge of the pool. Here I got line back. Next he rushed across toward the head of the rapid. I could do nothing but hold on and pray.

Twenty yards above the smooth glancing incline he sprang aloft in so prodigious a leap that my usual shout froze in my throat. Like a deer, in long bounds he covered the water. The last rays of the setting sun flashed on this fish, showing it to be heavy and round and deep, of a wonderful pearly white tinted with pink. It had a small head which resembled that of a salmon. I had hooked a big female rainbow, fresh run from Taupo, and if I had not known before that I had a battle on my hands I knew it on sight of the fish.

Fearing the swift water at the head of the rapid, I turned and plunged pell-mell out to the beach and along it, holding my rod up as high as I could. I did not save any line, but I did not lose any, either. I ran clear to the end of the sandy beach where it verged on the boulders. A few paces farther on roared the river.

Then with a throbbing heart and indescribable feelings I faced the pool. There were 125 yards of line out. The trout hung just above the rapid and bored deep, to come up and thump on the surface. Inch by inch I lost line. She had her head upstream, but the current was drawing her toward the incline. I became desperate. Once over that fall she would escape. The old situation presented itself—break the fish off or hold it. Inch by inch she tugged the line off my reel. With all that line off and most of it out of the water in plain sight, tight as a banjo string, I appeared to be at an overwhelming disadvantage. So I grasped the line in my left hand and held it. My six-ounce rod bowed and bent, then straightened and pointed. I felt its quivering vibration and I heard the slight singing of the tight line.

The first few seconds were almost unendurable. They seemed an age. When would line or leader give way or the hook tear out? But nothing broke. I could hold the wonderful trout. Then as the moments passed I lost that tense agony of apprehension. I gained confidence. Unless the fish wheeled to race for the fall I would win. The chances were against such a move. Her head was up current, held by that rigid line. Soon the tremendous strain told. The rainbow came up, swirled and pounded and threshed on the surface. There was a time then when all old fears returned and augmented; but just as I was about to despair, the tension on rod and line relaxed. The trout swirled under and made upstream. This move I signaled with a shout, which was certainly echoed by my comrades, all lined up behind me, excited and gay and admonishing.

I walked down the beach, winding my reel fast, yet keeping the line taut. Thus I advanced fully a hundred yards. When I felt the enameled silk come to my fingers, to slip on the reel, I gave another shout. Then again I backed up the beach, pulling the trout, though not too hard. At last she got into the slack shallow water over the wide sand bar.

The fish made short hard runs out into the deeper water, yet each run I stopped eventually. Then they gave place to the thumping on the surface, the swirling breaks, the churning rolls, and the bulldog tug, tug, tug. The fight had long surpassed any I had ever had with a small fish. So strong and unconquerable was this rainbow that I was fully a quarter of an hour working her into the shallower part of the bar. Every time the deep silvery side flashed, I almost had heart failure. This fish would go heavier than the 11½-pound male. I had long felt that in the line, in the rod; and now I saw it. There was a remarkable zest in this part of the contest.

The little rod wore tenaciously on the rainbow, growing stronger, bending less, drawing easier. After what seemed an interminable period there in this foot-deep water, the battle ended abruptly with the bend of the rod drawing the fish head-on to the wet sand.

Certainly I had never seen anything so beautiful in color, so magnificent in contour. It was mother-of-pearl tinged with exquisite pink. The dots were scarcely discernible, and the fullness of swelling graceful curve seemed to outdo nature itself. How the small thoroughbred salmon-like head contrasted with the huge iron-jawed fierce-eyed head of the male I had caught first! It was strange to see the broader tail of the female, the thicker mass of muscled body, the larger fins. Nature had endowed this progenitor of the species, at least for the spawning season, with greater strength, speed, endurance, spirit and life.

"Eleven pounds, three-quarters!" presently sang out the Captain. "Some rainbow, old man. Get in there and grab another."

"Won't you have a try with my rod?" I replied. "I'm darn near froze to death. Besides I want to put this one on the string with the others."

He was obdurate, so I went back into the water; and before I knew what was happening, almost, I had fastened to another trout. It did not have the great dragging weight of the other two, but it gave me a deep boring fight and deceived me utterly as to size. When landed, this, my fourth trout, weighed 6¾, another female, fresh run from the lake, and a fine rainbow in hue.

"Make it five, Doc. This is your day. Anything can happen now. Get out your line," declared Mitchell, glowing of face.

The sun had set as I waded in again. A shimmering ethereal light moved over the pool. The reflection of the huge bluff resembled a battleship more than the bluff itself. Clear and black-purple rose the mountain range, and golden clouds grew more deeply gold. The river roared above and below, deep-toned and full of melody. A cold breeze drifted down from upstream.

I cast over all the water I had previously covered without raising a fish. Farther out and down I saw trout rising, curling dark tails out of the gold gleam on the water. I waded a foot farther than ever and made a cast, another, recovered line, and then spent all the strength I had left in a cast that covered the current leading to the rising trout. I achieved it. The fly disappeared, my line glided on and on, suddenly to stretch like a whipcord and go zipping out of my left hand. Fast and hard! What a wonderful thrill ran up and down my back, all over me!

"Ho! Ho! . . . Boys, I've hung another!" I bawled out. "Say, but he's taking line! . . . Oh, look at him jump! . . . Two! . . . Three . . . Four, by gosh! . . . Oh, Morton, if we only had some sunlight! What a flying leap! . . . *Five!"*

The last jump was splendid, with a high parabolic curve, and a slick cutting back into the water. This rainbow, too, was big, fast, strong and fierce. But the fish did everything that should not have been done and I did everything right. Fisherman's luck! Beached and weighed before my cheering companions; 9½ pounds; another silvery, rosy female rainbow, thick and deep and wide!

Then I forced Captain Mitchell to take my rod, which he would not do until I pleaded I was frozen. But what did I care for cold? I made the day a perfect one by relinquishing my rod when I ached to wade in and try again.

The day, however, had begun badly for Captain Mitchell and so it ended. He could not raise a trout. Then we left the rousing fire and strode off over the boulders into the cool gathering twilight. Hoka carried two of my trout, Captain two, and Morton one. We threaded the *ti*-tree thicket and the jungle of ferns, and crossed the perilous panel in the dark, as if it had been a broad and safe bridge.

My comrades talked volubly on the way back to camp, but I was silent. I did not feel my heavy wet waders or my leaden boots. The afterglow of sunset lingered in the west, faint gold and red over the bold black range. I heard a late bird sing. The roar of the river floated up at intervals. Tongariro! What a strange beautiful high-sounding name! It suited the noble river and the mountain from which it sprang.

Murder

BY SPARSE GREY HACKLE

The late Sparse Grey Hackle (Alfred W. Miller) once told me that he felt a little per-plexed by the fame this particular story had achieved. Not that Sparse didn't think the tale was very good, and deserving to be republished in as many anthologies as it has been, but I got the impression that it seemed strange to him that "Murder" had eclipsed so many other fine stories and essays he had written.

In my own view, there is no mystery at all about the popularity of this tale. "Murder" grabs and holds the reader in the finest story-telling tradition. The story is perfect in every way, with a likeable lead character, wonderful setting, conflict and drama, and a very satisfactory ending. An astute reader may note that a reel's "back-ing" is never actually exposed in this tale, and that's exactly the point: the angler has no intention of letting this fish get "into the backing."

Sparse was not a prolific writer, but when he left us in 1983 he had produced the wonderful book of stories, Fishless Days, Angling Nights, *which has been repub-lished by Lyons Press. In 1998, The Lyons Press published* An Honest Angler: The Best of Sparse Grey Hackle, *a collection of letters and short pieces edited by Sparse's daughter, Patricia Miller Sherwood.*

I f fishing interferes with your business, give up your business," any angler will tell you, citing instances of men who lost health and even life through failure to take a little recreation, and reminding you that "the trout do not rise in Green Wood Cemetery," so you had better do your fishing while you are still able. But you will search far to find a fisherman to admit that a taste for fishing, like a taste for liquor, must be governed lest it come to possess its possessor; that an excess of fishing can cause as many tragedies of lost purpose, earning power, and position as an excess of liquor. This is the story of a man who finally decided between his business and his fishing, and of how his decision was brought about by the murder of a trout.

Fishing was not a pastime with my friend John but an obsession—
a common condition, for typically your successful fisherman is not really enjoying a recreation, but rather taking refuge from the realities of life in an ab-
sorbing fantasy in which he grimly if subconsciously reenacts in miniature the
unceasing struggle of primitive man for existence. Indeed, it is that which
makes him successful, for it gives him the last measure of fierce concentration,
that final moment of unyielding patience that in angling so often makes the
difference between fish and no fish.

John was that kind of fisherman, more so than any other I ever knew.
Waking or sleeping, his mind ran constantly on the trout and its taking, and
back in the Depression years I often wondered whether he could keep on in-
definitely doing business with the surface of his mind and fishing with the rest
of his mental processes—wondered, and feared that he could not. So when he
called me one spring day and said, "I'm tired of sitting here and watching a
corporation die; let's go fishing," I knew that he was not discouraged with his
business as much as he was impatient with its restraint. But I went with him,
for maybe I'm a bit obsessed myself.

That day together on the river was like a thousand other pages from
the book of any angler's memories. There was the clasp and pull of cold, hurrying water on our legs, the hours of rhythmic casting, and the steady somnam-
bulistic shuffling that characterizes steelworkers aloft and fly fishermen in fast
water. Occasionally our heads were bent together over a fly box; at intervals
our pipes wreathed smoke; and from time to time a brief remark broke the silence. We were fishing "pool and pool" together, each as he finished walking
around the other to a new spot above him.

Later afternoon found me in the second pool below the dam, throwing a long line up the still water. There was a fish rising to some insect so small
that I could not detect it, so I was using a tiny gray fly on a long leader with a
5X point. John came by and went up to the Dam Pool, and I lost interest in my
refractory fish and walked up to watch, for there was always a chance of a good
fish there. I stopped at a safe distance and sat down on a rock with my leader
trailing to keep it wet, while John systematically covered the tail of the pool
until he was satisfied that there were no fish there to dart ahead and give the
alarm, and then stepped into it.

As he did so his body became tense, his posture that of a man who
stalks his enemy. With aching slowness and infinite craft he began to inch up
the pool, and as he went his knees bent more and more until he was crouch-
ing. Finally, with his rod low to the water and one hand supporting himself on
the bottom of the stream, he crept to a casting position and knelt in midcur-

rent with water lapping under his elbows, his left sleeve dripping unheeded as he allowed the current to straighten his line behind him. I saw that he was using the same leader as mine but with a large No. 12 fly.

"John, using 5X?" I breathed. Without turning his head he nodded almost imperceptibly.

"Better break off and reknot," I counseled softly, but he ignored the suggestion. I spoke from experience. Drawn 5X silkworm gut is almost as fine as a human hair, and we both knew that it chafes easily where it is tied to a fly as heavy as a No. 12, so that it is necessary to make the fastening in a different spot at frequent intervals in order to avoid breaking it. I kept silence and watched John. His rod almost parallel to the water, he picked up his fly from behind him with a light twitch and then false cast to dry it. He was a good caster; it neither touched the surface nor rose far above it as he whipped it back and forth.

Now he began lengthening his line until finally, at the end of each forward cast, his fly hovered for an instant above a miniature eddy between the main current and a hand's breadth of still water that clung to the bank. And then I noticed what he had seen when he entered the pool—the sudden slight dimple denoting the feeding of a big fish on the surface.

The line came back with a subtle change from the side-sweeping false cast, straightened with decision, and swept forward in a tight roll. It straightened again in front of the caster, whispered through the guides, and then checked suddenly. The fly swept around as a little elbow formed in the leader, and settled on the rim of the eddy with a loop of slack upstream of it. It started to circle, then disappeared in a sudden dimple, and I could hear a faint sucking sound.

It seemed as if John would never strike although his pause must have been but momentary. Then his long line tightened—he had out fifty feet—as he drew it back with his left hand and gently raised the rod tip with his right. There was a slight pause and then the line began to run out slowly.

Rigid as a statue, with the water piling a little wave against the brown waders at his waist, he continued to kneel there while the yellow line slid almost unchecked through his left hand. His lips moved.

"A big one," he murmured. "The leader will never hold him if he gets started. I should have changed it."

The tip of the upright rod remained slightly bent as the fish moved into the circling currents created by the spillway at the right side of the dam. John took line gently and the rod maintained its bend. Now the fish was under the spillway and must have dived down with the descending stream, for I saw a couple of feet of line slide suddenly through John's hand. The circling water got its impetus here, and this was naturally the fastest part of the eddy.

The fish came rapidly toward us, riding with the quickened water, and John retrieved line. Would the fish follow the current around again or would it leave it and run down past us? The resilient tip straightened as the pressure was ended. The big trout passed along the downstream edge of the eddy and swung over to the bank to follow it round again, repeated its performance at the spillway, and again refused to leave the eddy. It was troubled and perplexed by the strange hampering of its progress, but it was not alarmed, for it was not aware of our presence or even of the fact that it was hooked, and the restraint on it had not been enough to arouse its full resistance.

Every experienced angler will understand that last statement. The pull of a game fish, up to the full limit of its strength, seems to be in proportion to the resistance which it encounters. As I watched the leader slowly cutting the water, I recalled that often I had hooked a trout and immediately given slack, whereupon invariably it had moved quietly and aimlessly about, soon coming to rest as if it had no realization that it was hooked.

I realized now that John intended to get the "fight" out of his fish at a rate slow enough not to endanger his leader. His task was to keep from arousing the fish to a resistance greater than the presumably weakened 5X gut would withstand. It seemed as if it were hopeless, for the big trout continued to circle the eddy, swimming deep and strongly against the rod's light tension, which relaxed only when the fish passed the gateway of the stream below. Around and around it went, and then at last it left the eddy. Yet it did not dart into the outflowing current but headed into deep water close to the far bank. I held my breath, for over there was a tangle of roots and I could imagine what a labyrinth they must make under the surface. Ah, it was moving toward the roots! Now what would John do—hold the fish hard and break it off; check it and arouse its fury; or perhaps splash a stone in front of it to turn it back?

He did none of these but instead slackened off until his line sagged in a catenary curve. The fish kept on, and I could see the leader draw on the surface as it swam into the mass of roots. Now John dropped his rod flat to the water and delicately drew on the line until the tip barely flexed, moving it almost imperceptibly several times to feel whether his leader had fouled on a root. Then he lapsed into immobility.

I glanced at my wristwatch, slowly bent my head until I could light my cold pipe without raising my hand, and then relaxed on my rock. The smoke drifted lazily upstream, the separate puffs merging into a thin haze that dissipated itself imperceptibly. A bird moved on the bank. But the only really living thing was the stream, which rippled a bit as it divided around John's body and continually moved a loop of his yellow line in the disturbed current below him.

When the trout finally swam quietly back out of the roots, my watch showed that it had been in there almost an hour. John slackened line and released a breath which he seemed to have been holding all that while, and the fish reentered the eddy to resume its interminable circling. The sun which had been in my face dropped behind a tree, and I noted how the shadows had lengthened. Then the big fish showed itself for the first time, its huge dorsal fin appearing as it rose toward the surface, and the lobe of its great tail as it turned down again; it seemed to be two feet long.

Again its tail swirled under the surface, puddling the water as it swam slowly and deliberately, and then I thought we would lose the fish, for as it came around to the downstream side of the eddy it wallowed an instant and then headed toward us. Instantly John relaxed the rod until the line hung limp, and from the side of his mouth he hissed, "Steady!"

Down the stream, passing John so close he could have hit it with his tip, drifted a long dark bulk, oaring along deliberately with its powerful tail in the smooth current. I could see the gray fly in the corner of its mouth and the leader hanging in a curve under its belly, then the yellow line floating behind. In a moment John felt the fish again, determined that it was no longer moving, and resumed his light pressure, causing it to swim around aimlessly in the still water below us. The sun was half below the horizon now, and the shadows slanting down over the river covered us. In the cool, diffused light the lines on John's face from nostril to mouth were deeply cut, and the crafty folds at the outer corners of his lids hooded his eyes. His rod hand shook with a fine tremor.

The fish broke, wallowing, but John instantly dropped his rod flat to the water and slipped a little line. The fish wallowed again, then swam more slowly in a large circle. It was moving just under the surface now, its mouth open and its back breaking the water every few feet, and it seemed to be half turned on its side. Still John did not move except for the small gestures of taking or giving line, raising or lowering his tip.

It was in the ruddy afterglow that the fish finally came to the top, beating its tail in a subdued rhythm. Bent double, I crept ashore and then ran through the brush to the edge of the still water downstream of the fish, which now was broad on its side. Stretching myself prone on the bank, I extended my net at arm's length and held it flat on the bottom in a foot of water.

John began to slip out line slowly, the now-beaten trout moving feebly as the slow current carried it down. Now it was opposite me and I nodded a signal to John. He moved his tip toward the bank and cautiously checked the line. The current swung the trout toward me and it passed over my net.

I raised the rim quietly and slowly, and the next instant the trout was doubled up in my deep-bellied net and I was holding the top of it shut with both hands while the fish, galvanized into a furious flurry, splashed water in my face as I strove to get my feet under me. John picked his way slowly down the still water, reeling up as he came, stumbling and slipping on the stones like an utterly weary man. I killed the trout with my pliers and laid it on the grass as he came up beside me; and he stood watching it with bent head and sagging shoulders for a long time.

"To die like that!" he said as if thinking aloud. "Murdered—nagged to death; he never knew he was fighting for his life until he was in the net. He had strength and courage enough to beat the pair of us, but we robbed him a little at a time until we got him where we wanted him. And then knocked him on the head. I wish you had let him go."

The twilight fishing, our favorite time, was upon us, but he started for the car and I did not demur. We began to take off our wet shoes and waders.

"That's just what this Depression is doing to me!" John burst out suddenly as he struggled with a shoelace. "Niggling me to death! And I'm up here fishing, taking two days off in the middle of the week, instead of doing something about it. Come on; hurry up. I'm going to catch the midnight to Pittsburgh; I know where I can get a contract."

And sure enough, he did.

Autumn Brown on the Rose

BY CHRISTOPHER CAMUTO

Nick did not like to fish with other men on the river. Unless they were of
your party, they spoiled it.

*Every time I think of those sentences from Ernest Hemingway's classic fishing short
story, "Big Two-Hearted River," certain images come immediately to mind. If I'm in a
dark mood, I think of all those photographs you see every spring of opening-day mobs
of anglers encircling some flimsy pool where buckets of trout have obviously been
dumped. Most of the time, I'm in a good mood, and I think of the prose of Christopher
Camuto.*

 *Christopher Camuto is the Nick Adams of modern fly fishing. No fictional
character like Hemingway's Nick Adams in "Big Two-Hearted River," the very real
Christopher Camuto seeks out and relives the Nick Adams experience with deep passion. He walks to hidden creeks and streams where cold pure water—and trout!—
abound. He makes camp and he fishes, in peace and quiet and solitude. Later, when
he's back home, he writes engaging prose about what he saw and heard and felt on the
tiny streams among the folded hills.*

 Christopher Camuto's A Fly Fisherman's Blue Ridge, *from which this
selection is taken, is one of the most eminently readable fishing books published during
the 1990s (Henry Holt and Co., 1990). In every way, the book still today lives up to
the high critical praise that greeted it on publication. In fact, a new edition of* A Fly
Fisherman's Blue Ridge *was published in the spring of 2001 by the University of
Georgia Press.*

 Christopher is also the author of the book Another Country: Journeying
Toward the Cherokee Mountains, *published by Henry Holt in 1997.* Another
Country *is a stirring narrative tribute to the Appalachians, the wildlife and natural
beauty, the stalwart people.*

 *Christopher Camuto has taught at the University of Virginia and Washing-
ton and Lee University. He is the book review columnist for* Gray's Sporting Journal.

I doubt it will happen again. But every autumn I fish a certain stretch of the Rose River very carefully. Just to make sure.

After two years the picture in my mind is clearer than my effusive field notes or the oddly restrained narrative in my journal. Like most fishing stories, this one is simple enough, as much a matter of image as event.

A small Adams disappears in the middle of a pool. No splash. No orange flash of autumn brook trout. Just a tiny bubble, which replaces the fly, and a slowly expanding riseform. I set the hook by reflex against the angle of a line that is already suspiciously tight to the river. The dark bulge which replaced the fly quickly becomes a weight at the end of the line.

I remember the unusually heavy surges of the fish when I tried to set the hook. I thought I could feel the long, light tippet stretch, as if it were tied to something I could not move. I knew I wasn't snagged. Rock doesn't strain upstream, strumming the line against the current. And a sunken tree limb, though it will pulse in a lifelike way when hooked, doesn't mill sullenly in tight half circles at the bottom of a pool. I thought I could feel something shaking its head slowly from side to side, as if saying no.

In retrospect, that first instant seems full of details and decisions. I remember how the rod bowed parabolic each time I tried to set the hook. I remember sensing the weight of the invisible fish digging deep into the butt section of the fly rod. I remember tightening my grip on the cork and feeling a slight strain creep up my forearm.

The subtle disappearance of the fly, the extreme arc of the rod, the sullen, determined weight I could feel in my hand all registered together. As I got tight to the fish, I stepped up to the back of the pool and stood in the narrow channel that was the trout's only way downstream.

My move to block the channel was instinctive, though the instinct was learned. I knew not to give a large trout the river behind me.

One rainy spring I lost the two biggest brook trout I have hooked in the mountains when I let them get downstream of me. The first grabbed a bushy dry fly the current led under a log that arched over the back of a deep run. I had no choice but to play the fish on a short line at my feet. While I tried to keep the trout out of the tangle of branches from which it had emerged, it got into the fast water to one side of me and jumped past me over the ledge below which I was standing.

A week or two later another big brook trout passed me, this time in pocket water. This fish never showed, except as a tactic that worked. The trout sucked in a nymph in front of a boulder upstream of me. By the feel of it, the trout was large for the water, which was still running high, and I was still green.

After an upstream surge the fish turned, putting slack between us. By the time I got the line tended, the trout was twenty yards downstream of me, winding its way among undercut boulders through which it neatly threaded a leader that came pinging back in my face when I tried to clamp down on its modest run.

I can still see both fish as clearly as if I had photos of them on the wall—one flashing away in the air, flanks bright with color against a background of cold spring whitewater—a fly hung in the roof of its mouth, a tippet draped over its back—and the other invisible except as a tight, sharply angled line cutting through the water downstream toward the freedom of a broad riffle.

Those two large brookies, far better fish than I was fisherman, seemed to take the fishing hopes of the young year with them. For a month I pored over the water where I lost them and lost the best part of the spring fishing trying to hook them again. But I never found them. Even in my mind I can't hold them upstream of me. They are always over my shoulder, going away with the river.

So when I felt the big trout in the Rose turn at the end of its first upstream run, I stepped into the narrow channel of fast water at the back of the pool and took the river away from it.

I don't know how I knew it was a brown, but I remember I wasn't surprised when, after its first run upstream to the head of the pool, it came back to midpool and showed itself, an angry yellow arc in the olive water. It *was* shaking its head. The small gray fly hung in a corner of the trout's mouth, where it lodged when the fish rose and turned to take it. I watched the trout's eye, a large black pupil ringed with an amber iris that glowed as if backlit. That eye watched me from the head of a foot-and-a-half-long swirl of dark, red-flecked brown lathered with yellow. In ten years of fishing in the mountains, I had never encountered a trout big enough to return a stare. In motion, the fish looked golden.

Brook trout are sprinters and jumpers, strong for their size and energetic, if not particularly cunning, in the first few seconds on the end of a line. They go through their moves quickly, too quickly to follow with much more than a generalized response. You catch them, fairly easily in most cases, or you lose them in the irretrievable instant when, by instinct or luck, they jump your complacency or inexperience.

But the big brown in the water in front of me was in no hurry. Once hooked, the trout made three passes back toward me, showing its broad, dark back more clearly each time, as if to distract me either with the unexpected beauty of its presence or with its bulk. The trout must have had some sense that it was large for the river and had grown to be a creature worth reckoning with.

So the fish swam at first in circles that brought it in and out of view, a strange and wonderful sight in the small stream.

During ten years of fishing in the mountains, I had dreamed of jumping a large trout, a fish big enough to throw the brook trout fishing I had grown to love a little out of focus. And I had heard rumors of big browns in the Rose. This one seemed to have come out of the back of my mind. So I wasn't altogether surprised by the large trout slowly swimming circles in front of me, shaking its head confidently from side to side, as if to say no.

I was in no hurry either. I knew what I was doing. The brown had come out of one of those promising places in a small stream a fly fisherman learns to see. Over the years you casually study and studiously cast to thousands of such spots, until you come to understand the possibilities for life the river has created on its way down out of the mountains. You get an eye for where your luck might lie. In a small stream the trout are not hard to find, but for some reason the appearance of a trout of any size from beneath a log or a boulder, or from the depths below the only eddy in a stillwater pool, never ceases to confirm something best not taken for granted. When a drift brings such a spot alive, and you hook the trout you made appear, the mountain up which you were wading seems revealed.

The trout had three moves, and it played them in different combinations, trying to unlock the invisible force that denied it the river.

When it returned under the deep shadow of the undercut boulder along the left side of the pool, where for years it had held while feeding, something was wrong. It now took effort to hold in the secure place where it had watched for insects struggling in the bright flowing film above it. A thin, sunlit diagonal cut across the pool from downstream. The fly in its mouth was attached to another world.

When the trout surged upstream, it could not find a way through the shallow riffles above the pool. It did not seem to tire, but it sensed how its strength was pointlessly eroded by the effort of swimming against the river. The force that pulled at it from downstream followed it. It could not slip the current to suddenly take cover, or drop to the layer of dead water on the bottom of the river to dart to new ground.

The right side of the pool deepened under a greenstone ledge the river had sculpted into a cavernous recess of deep stillwater. Here at the bottom of the river, under the ledge where the water was dark, the trout had hid and waited out the worst dangers. No natural predator could reach it there. No kingfisher or wandering heron could break into the depth of the place. No raccoon could reach it or water snake surprise it. But now when it sought this refuge, the force that controlled it followed.

The trout ranged around the pool, resting at times near the bottom fifteen feet in front of me, sullenly shaking its head. Every move was a waste of energy. The pool seemed undone. Something had taken the river away.

I played the trout for nearly ten minutes, giving it line when it insisted, but never giving it back the river. I had little to do but stay tight to the fish, hold the rod angled high to tire it, and keep the leader from catching on the rocks between us.

Several times toward the end the trout came straight back to me, not in a rush, but as if to check. It must have had some sense of the long river behind me. The way out was downstream, but the threatening, controlling shape stood *there,* just where it needed the river most.

Finally the trout charged the spot. I stood there awkwardly, holding the rod as high as I could trying to get some line into play, but only managing to get part of the long leader out through the tip top. When the fish came close I waved my left arm to scare it back into the pool, a graceless tactic that worked. I hoped no one was watching.

The trout made a few more circuits of its former havens, trying to regain its place in the river. But the threatening shape kept pressuring it from a distance.

The trout came back once more, fatigued but composed. There was no thrashing about, no gill flaring. It swam in front of me again, shaking its head and making the graphite tip of the fly rod dance. The water stirred all around it. The trout knew where the freedom of the river was: there where the water funneled downstream, white and fast into other pools.

I beached the fish in the leaf-choked slack water just downstream of the lie where it had been rising. The trout had grown too large for the food available to it, a fact that showed in the disproportion between its head and body. For all the beauty of its color and markings, which mimicked more accurately than a brook trout does the oncoming colors of autumn, that deformation and the fish's size betrayed it as out of place in the small mountain stream.

This was undoubtedly a fish that had first come to the river miles downstream in a hatchery truck, pale and slack-muscled, with ragged fins and no sense of the world of greenstone and blue water, of fat mayfly duns that a river might offer it or of predators that might eye it in turn. The brown escaped the first season of fishing in the warm and silty stocked water that flows through the farmland bordering Shenandoah National Park, and that first fall started to move upriver. Eventually it passed through the little Rose River valley, a hundred-acre floodplain where an appealing ramshackle hamlet has established itself, and made its way into the dark hollow through which the river flows.

At some point in its unnatural history, the trout crossed the boundary into the national park. The trout must have adapted quickly to the change in jurisdiction. Silt and strange metallic and plastic refuse were no longer in the river. The bottom seemed a natural, undisturbed course of boulders and rubble, small stones, and sand distributed by the current. The river made sense: There were places to feed and hide and spawn; pools were shaded; even in summer, when the water warmed, there were deep holes with sunken layers of cool water.

The river was full of life. Brook trout swam in and out of view, keeping a wary distance. Dace and sculpin and other forage fish schooled defensively in the shallows. Crayfish crawled about. Snakes swam through pools. There were shadows along the banks at dawn and dusk that bent to the river and stirred the water. Insects moved along the bottom, and in the drift, and hatched in the sunlit film at the surface. After a year, the trout must have sensed in some rudimentary way the proportion, regularity, and fitness of things in the cold, clear water. You could live forever, it might have seemed, in such a place.

As the trout grew, it changed. Its muscles were strengthened by the constant play of current, and the fish took on the lean, efficient shape of a salmonid. Its bruised pectoral, pelvic, and anal fins grew out, repairing themselves into strong but delicately scalloped muscles that caught and released filaments of currents with imperceptible precision. The trout's caudal muscle strengthened and its damaged caudal fin grew out. The natural color of the fish emerged during its seasons in the mountain stream, and although it never acquired the final brilliance of a stream-born brown, this trout had become, by the time I surprised it, a wild autumn brown in all but name.

I killed the trout with a blow on the head with the handle of my fishing knife and opened and cleaned the fish on the leaves against which I had admired it. Its stomach was nearly empty. I found a few unidentifiable, half-digested nymphs and one bright green katydid, still alive, lodged in its gullet. I cleaned the white interior of the trout carefully, picking blood out of the vertebrae with the point of my knife, and rinsed the scum and blood off the fish and my hands in the stream. It was still early in the afternoon, and I tried to keep fishing, but I had no expectations left with which to fish.

I found the vague fishermen's trail and followed a spur of it back up to the fire road that follows the Rose, one of the old transmontane pikes that leads west up over the Blue Ridge and down into the Shenandoah Valley. By the time I got back down to the steel bridge, a mile above where I was parked at the national park boundary, the colors of the big brown were fading and its skin was starting to blotch, as if the beauty of the fish had been held in place by its life in the river.

Two days later I blued the trout for friends in dry white wine. The bluing took the death pallor off it. The big fish had to be supplemented with small, mushy supermarket rainbows, but the entrée was buttressed with new potatoes, steamed broccoli, and hot biscuits. Everyone had a taste of the big fish and too much wine. Nothing was wasted. I must have told some version of the story about catching the trout.

I would like to have a painting of the two of us, rendered impressionistically, showing a fly fisherman deliberately blocking that narrow channel at the back of the pool, holding a dark parabola over the water, a bright line cutting down across the scene toward where a large brown trout shook its head from side to side, as if saying no. The scene would look like the beginning of the end of the year.

The painting would have to imply that the trout was being played to death in the early afternoon, and that the fisherman, who loved the lives of trout, felt no guilt about the killing. The painting would not be about death but about life, about early autumn on the Rose and years of fishing in the mountains. The painting would imply all that trout and fly fishermen learn about rivers during their lives, as well as render the graceful and awkward moves they make when they confront one another across the gulf between their natures and assert, for better or worse, the prerogatives of their species. Somehow the way the artist rendered the dark, greenstone landscape, softened by the pale yellow and bright green of October in the Blue Ridge, against which fish and fisherman appear together, would put all that in perspective.

Of course, the following year the pool was empty. I passed over that stretch of river in the spring, self-conscious about the trout that wasn't there. But I fished it the following fall, approaching the spot far more carefully and dwelling on it with far more ingenuity than I did the day I stumbled onto the big brown. But nothing I could do brought another such rise. Last spring I greedily fished big nymphs and woolly worms through the pool when the blue water started to subside, but nothing stopped the leader in the water.

This autumn I came up the Rose on a day much like that day two years ago. Driving through Criglersville and Syria, where the fall fruit markets were in full swing, I tried to tell myself to treat the river evenly and not plan the day's fishing around the pool where the brown had appeared. But the memory of it was now a hole in the river, and the big trout haunted my autumn fishing as surely as those two lost brook trout haunted my spring. The brown, too, had somehow gotten away.

By October, Indian-summer days with a hint of autumn have become autumn days with a vestige of summer. Even though the woods are still full and green, an intermittent breeze flickers the yellow beech and hickory leaves that start the turn of the hardwoods and rustle slowly to the ground all day. The reds of sumac and ivy catch the eye. You see the turn before you feel it, spawning colors unmasked in the hardwood canopy that has, since June, been an undistinguished forest green.

This October the clear, distinct sound of the Rose came to meet me through the woods, fairly ringing over its stony bed. Its insistent current seemed to stir the changing landscape. As I watched the Rose through the yellow and green foliage, I thought of trout all over the Blue Ridge moving out of the pools where they had congregated during the dog days of summer, reoccupying the rivers and beginning to search out spawning sites. The cool, steady currents of autumn, which re-create the spring character of rivers in miniature, seem to ensure the continuity of life in the Blue Ridge. While deer and bear increase their browsing range, wandering steadily through the camouflaged woods, river creatures, for whom stillness is exposure, take a cue from the motion around them and prepare for the end of the year.

The diminished autumn rivers scale the eye to details and slight movements. The exposed streambed of the Rose, now full of tiny ponds and oxbows and the flora that takes brief hold in the moist niches left by the contracted river, is full of life again. I walk along, fly rod in hand, eyeing the river's interesting banks. A salamander poises for insects on a wet stone. The pale brown stripes along its back seem to emanate from its dark, protuberant eyes. It tolerates my close inspection at first, but then turns to crawl partway under a rock. It takes a touch of my finger, however, to send the salamander completely into hiding.

A hundred yards farther on, a dark brown snake with a bright orange ring around its neck is more visibly skeptical of my intentions. The foot-long reptile bunches its muscles and freezes, almost hidden on the dark stones and leaves. It keeps pace ahead of me as I follow it upstream along the edge of the river, turning toward me and tensing when I approach it too closely. While I am stooped over the ringneck snake, a kingfisher, chattering and swooping in shallow arcs over the river, flies past me headed downstream. When I turn back to the ground, the snake is gone.

The trout, too, sense my presence and move away as I approach. The Rose has been fished hard. My footfalls warn the bigger trout, which tuck themselves out of sight under rocks. My shape or shadow freezes some trout in the tails of pools until I move too close and send them fluttering upstream.

Although early autumn brings the rivers to life, I am still hung between seasons, and I fish most of the day in a fashion far too halfhearted for the demands of autumn water. The big pools on the Rose feel like empty rooms. The scant insect life fails to interest me—a smattering of caddis and stoneflies, and a few late-season mayflies. I have let my fly boxes deplete without sitting down at the vise and replenishing them for the season. My fishing instincts seem awry. Although I keep meaning to tie some well-balanced twelve- and fifteen-footers, I have been fishing with the same jerry-built leader for weeks, a leader that has grown, by fits and starts, to some odd, unbalanced length. The split upper of my left wading shoe is bound with duct tape. The tip of my fly line is cracked and stripped of finish and waterlogs quickly. I forget things, leave them in the truck or, worse, at home. In the autumn of a year I've fished hard, I'm content to be the kind of fisherman I wouldn't be caught dead with in April.

Where the gradient of the river increases, I scramble up and climb a greenstone staircase, sometimes pushing my gear on ahead and then boosting myself over a ledge to the brink of the next pool. Here the Rose is a series of short, deep pools joined by the spouts of pouring water that give the river its mellow autumn voice.

Trout are tucked under the lip of bright leaves log-jammed at the back of each pool. If you nose carefully over the ledge you can get close enough to touch them, but they are almost impossible to fish to. The large pools are beautifully lit and perfectly still, except at their throat and tail. I cast dry flies into openings the current makes between the endless stream of leaves.

In these weeks before spawning, when adult trout seem to hide, the juvenile trout are more noticeable than they are at any other time. Even the normally aggressive dace subordinate themselves to the young trout and parr which are warier and more predatory than they have been all year. Instead of milling about in schools, they stake out worthwhile holding positions. They hover under leaves like adult trout holding in the shadows of boulders. They hang effortlessly in the current, and have picked up the habit of drifting back to insects in the film rather than darting forward for them. They seem to have found both a sense of themselves and the rhythm of the river.

Along one stretch of the river I catch more of these young trout than anything else for my trouble. Lying in the palm of my hand, each parr is a clear impression of a trout, formally perfect, grown already to be what trout evolved into long ago, the shape of parted water. The bodies of the tiny trout are completely formed, concave and convex by turns, their weight feathered by a delicate array of tiny fins. These young trout are pale—a soft, watery green—but all the markings of an adult are clear and distinct. Each parr seems like the idea of a trout in hand.

I work my way through a bright stretch of river, nymphing carefully through the brown's old pool. But the spot is less important than I thought it would be. The Rose is becoming a river again. When the afternoon begins to slip quickly away, as autumn afternoons do, I fish harder, especially the deep, sheltered runs. But except for a few small trout, the river flows blankly around me.

An oval pool below a long cascade offers me the day's last chance. The pool resembles a muted version of a spring pool. The river splashes into it, flushing the fallen leaves from its surface. A well-defined current rumples the throat of the pool below the whitewater, broadening into a tongue of turbulence that reaches to its center. Eddies slowly circle toward its banks. I lean against a cool brow of greenstone and work out line over the pool downstream of me. I cast a fur ant above the tip of the tongue of turbulence at mid-pool, below which I know a trout waits.

Brook trout are not prolific. Relatively few—say several hundred—fertilized eggs will begin to chance life in the river from a pair of spawning trout. Some of these eggs will settle properly into their redd, a bowl-shaped nest of gravel. If the eggs remain undisturbed and are properly filtered by the river, they will produce eyes; some eyed eggs will become alevins, wisps of trout. A handful of fry will come of this, and of these a half dozen will become the parr that bide their time in the marginal places in the river, as much prey as predators. Finally a trout or two will swim into adulthood out of the austere, beautiful mating of *Salvelinus fontinalis* that took place three years before and sent a small cloud of milt and eggs to the bottom of the river.

Throughout the year a brook trout is a compromise between camouflage and display. In autumn, in preparation for spawning, the natural definition of the male is enhanced to overstatement, and the trout becomes in fact what it often is in impression, a beautiful exaggeration.

The olive and black vermiculation on its back becomes more highly contrasted, as if it had been redrawn with a firmer, heavier hand. What from above should hide the trout borders on becoming a badge of identification, especially when the fish holds above the new-fallen leaves that have sunk to the bottom of a pool and not yet lost their bright colors. The vermiculation melts into a field of pale green contoured with yellow ovals that evolve into circles toward the midline; the yellow circles give way, on the flank of the trout, to scarlet spots surrounded by blue aureoles.

All year long, there is a splash of orange with a hint of fluorescence along the pearl white belly of the trout. But in autumn that orange darkens and spreads toward the gill covers and toward the tail, bleeding into the fins, reddening them at their base, and putting a hint of rose in the end of the tail. The white line along the tips of the fins and the bottom of the tail become wider and brighter, and the black line that finishes the tip darkens and thickens. Finally two thick black lines, which seem to have been quickly stroked on with a coarse brush, form a startling border between those orange flanks and what is left of the white belly of the trout.

The trout I hooked in the flatwater just beyond the tongue of current in that perfect autumn pool never left the water. I slipped the fly from its vomer and admired the way the fish glistened like an animated jewel in my loose grip. An autumn brook trout in its spawning colors is perhaps the clearest sign of the beginning of the end of the year. The beauty of the fish is difficult to convey. Releasing one such trout, I want to see another immediately. Photographs can capture their form, detail, and color, but not the impression of the fish in the field—the strange, otherwordly life in it. On the other hand, impressionistic renderings sacrifice the actual appearance of the trout to some inadequate idea of it. There is so much artifice in the brook trout's natural appearance that most representations are defeated by inaccurate stylization.

The trout dropped to the bottom of the pool when I released it and darted away when I straightened up. The amber afternoon light, which had given the river an appealing olive cast, had drawn away while I fished. A cool breeze chilled my wet hands.

During October I try to revisit the rivers I fish in early spring. October is like March, a time of year with a foot in each season; the days run backward, from fall to summer. In the morning you can see your breath; by midafternoon you have worked up a sweat. Evening comes quickly. The nights are cold, and that more than anything changes the rivers and the trout. The shortening days warm the rivers less and less, and the year runs on.

The unfamiliar calls of migrating birds counterpoint the breezy rustling in the woods, which each day seems more insistently stirred by the winds that turn the pleasant uncertainty of autumn into the long gray stasis of fall. The woods are rich with mast—acorns, hickory, and beech nuts. Hurried change is everywhere. There is the season of camouflage, of shifting patterns that conceal form. An unseen fox squirrel, blanked somewhere along the branch of an oak, chatters a warning through the canopy. The graying flank of a whitetail slides into a stand of ash. A dark bear-shape merges into granite shadows.

Cool mornings laced with autumn gives way to warm afternoons, but by the end of the day, when dusk sends me down a trail strewn with another day's layer of bright, dead leaves, I can feel the missing minutes in the air and sense the insistent flow of the year around the deadfall of spent days. The sun slips behind the southern ridge of the watershed too soon. I look up for the missing daylight as I try to tie on a fresh fly so I can fish one last quiet pool. The shadows that hover around my cold hands make me wonder where the year has gone. I sense, not without regret, the season of long evenings coming on. Rivers still hold the afternoon light longer than the woods, but I end the days fishing a little in the dark.

When I see so many irreversible signs of the season slipping away, I fish more attentively, combing each river for one last good trout. Although the hard-fished pools are usually deserted, the small, dark mayflies of autumn stir some trout out of hiding. To fish well in late autumn, you have to fight the sense of hurry in the woods around you, the change suggested by the constant rain of leaves and the chill autumn winds and the weakened warmth of the bright October daylight. The pace of bringing good trout to hand is one-tenth of what it was in spring, and it feels strange to move along so slowly and studiously when the year seems to be hurrying away. I play each good fish I hook a little longer than I should.

As I make this autumn circuit of my spring rivers, final signs appear, each one of which brings the fishing to a halt. On the North Fork of the Moormans, I stopped to watch a female brook trout build her redd. Vigorous white winks in the tail of a pool called my attention to the laboring trout. Even from fifty feet away, I knew instantly what the odd flashing in the river meant. Digging a redd is the most strenuous thing a brook trout must do, and its instinctual exertion in behalf of the next generation is as solemn an event as the spawning run of salmon. The nest building dramatizes, perhaps better than anything else a fisherman sees all year, the intimate relation of a wild trout to a river. From a distance, I could only see the fish when it turned on its side to fan the fine gravel at the tail of the pool. When I crept closer, I could see the bowl-shaped depression forming underneath its solitary efforts. The male trout was nowhere in sight, but the female swam in circles around the redd, as if to mark the site as claimed, and then twisted over on its side to work the gravel into shape with its tail. When I tried to get closer, I spooked the trout and put it off its task.

As autumn lost its luster and fall came on, I seemed to move too clumsily to stay close to what I wanted to see. I came on two spawning trout in a little side pool in the Chapman Mountain stretch of the Rapidan that I fish through carefully every spring—they might have been trout I caught and slipped back into the river in April. I crawled to within five feet of them. The female held over the redd without moving anything but her fins and tail to steady herself in the slight flow. She was so still and so intent, I wondered what kept kingfishers from gathering more noticeably over the rivers this time of year. The male poised himself next to her, almost brushing her with his fins. He might hold in the same position for as long as thirty seconds, and then, without apparent cause, swim to the other side of her and hold there. At times he would switch sides more frequently, as if to establish his presence everywhere. Several times he held at right angles to her, almost touching her side. These ceremonial gestures continued until I turned my head to glance at the large pool adjacent to their spawning alcove. When I looked back, they had disappeared.

On the Staunton a few days later my presence also seemed to do more harm than good. Toward the end of a day on what was left of the river above its long cascades I came on a brilliantly colored trout. I got within arm's length of it before it noticed me. When it did, it swam to the leaf-choked head of the run it occupied. As I approached closer the trout jumped out of the water onto a mat of sodden leaves. The spawned-out trout thrashed on the leaves as it tried to bore ahead, intent on surviving another year. Its desperation and lack of cunning in trying to escape were startling. I wanted to photograph the trout, but its thrashing there on the leaves made me nervous. I thought I would put it back in the deep water at the back of the run from which I had driven it, but when I reached for it, the trout jumped violently at my uncertain touch and was gone.

If by the end of May I have had enough of trout fishing, by the end of October I am tired of watching the life of rivers. A year of mountain fishing will wear itself down. The vest and waders and fly rod begin to feel like props, and I'm not sure what I am looking for. The few bright, colorful weeks of autumn, which I distinguish from the bare woods of fall, compose an odd, fifth season in my mind. And in the field during those two weeks when an uncanny, almost unnatural light filters through the dying hardwood canopy in the afternoon, events in the field seem odd, as if they had happened in a brightly illustrated story.

Even so, this year I took one last autumn hike along the Rose River fire road, unencumbered with gear of any kind. I left the road at the trail that goes into Dark Hollow, a well-named, haunting place with a trickle of stream running through it that eventually flows into the Rose. I hiked the stream for a few miles just to spend the time and started back down as I began to lose the light. Along the way I stopped to watch reddish mayfly spinners laying eggs in a riffly stretch of the small stream. They had prominent yellow thoraxes and heads. I didn't remember ever having seen them before. I watched one hold six or eight inches over the river, which flowed quickly through the shallow riffle. I could see the yellow egg mass at the end of its abdomen and its delicate, elongated tails. I wondered if the tails lengthened during its egg-laying stage in order to help it sense the surface of the river from a safe distance. I wondered if it felt the water rushing under it.

The mayfly danced uncertainly over the river, eventually swooping suddenly to the surface and seeming to rest there, for perhaps as long as a second, while a portion of the egg mass broke off and drifted quickly to the bottom of the riffle. The mayfly did this several times in the same place and then flew off downstream. Other mayflies were performing this same hypnotic ritual.

It was, I wrote in my field notes, a common but wonderful thing to see. I have seen it before, as have all fly fishermen, and have often noted what a poignant picture of contingency is etched on the mind's eye by the sight of a lone insect mated for a moment to a river, finishing the work of its life with such strange ceremony.

Like the fire road along the North Fork of the Moormans, the Rose River road is a familiar way home, and on the way down the river in the evenings that familiarity comes to meet me halfway, like a friend. As I reached the road from the Dark Hollow trail, I remembered the large brown trout from two years before. I would not have mentioned the Rose by name, except that I suspect it will be years before another hatchery brown makes its way up river to grow large and wild among the native brook trout. Ten years, maybe, if ever, before another flyfisherman wades unaware into an early-autumn afternoon on the Rose to find himself tethered to a strong golden swirl with a black and amber eye.

However long it takes for that hole in the river to be filled with such life, I don't think I'll need to harass such a trout again. I won't need to come back down that old mountain road strewn with yellow beech and hickory leaves, feeling with strange, undeniable satisfaction the slack heft of the end of the year in the dead weight at my side.

The Point—A Hebridean Day

BY SIDNEY SPENCER

Forgive me if I seem to be emphasizing this bit of reading preference overly much, but it seems important to me: I like writing that takes me someplace. Fishing, hunting, on great adventures, to strange lands, even to war or back into history. Come to think of it, the movies I like are the same way.

One of the reasons Sidney Spencer's book Salmon and Seatrout in Wild Places *has occupied a spot on my bedside reading shelf over the years is this little story of tramping over the moors in pursuit of Atlantic Salmon and seatrout in the Hebrides, the remote, beautiful islands off Scotland in the Atlantic. Published originally by H.F. & G. Witherby Ltd. (61 Watling Street, London EC4) in 1968, the book today is listed as being out of print in the sources I use and is very difficult to come by. I can only hope that someday this book, along with everything else Mr. Spencer has written, will be reissued.*

The wind blew a gale from the west and the west, in the location I describe means the open Atlantic. The sky at the western end of the loch always holds that infinity of emptiness which is an ocean sky and in the Hebrides, illuminated by the lights of the Isles, reminds you that you are, it seems, on the very edge of the world.

But the light that comes in most places with the west wind is a good fishing light, perhaps the best of all, and so it was when he hauled the boat from its heather cradle to the water's edge. Hopes ran as high as the waves on the sand—beautiful salmon-taking waves. It was a rough day on the loch and just as we had foreseen. For this day had been planned even more carefully than days on this loch have to be planned because of its remoteness away across six miles of mountainside broken with peat hags and endless ravines on the higher route, or very wet low ground on the other. Connected with the tide by a very short shallow river the loch gets, with any appreciable rain and a rise in the scores of small feeders, an immense run of seatrout and with them a few salmon.

Abounding in rocky points and clean pebble and sand shores it provides, I think, with its huge stock of medium weight fish, the finest seatrout fishing I know. It is uncommon to come away with less than eight or ten adult seatrout, which may, but do not always, run up to 5 or 6 pounds; apart from the finnock which are counted for record purposes but returned alive, as all finnock should be. And this, of course, in a very short fishing day since so much time is used in walking to and from the loch.

Thus, while this El Dorado glitters in one's thoughts over there on the rim of the western sea, one does have some regard, rather more careful than usual, because of its very remoteness, for conditions. An east or north-east wind day is useless because for one thing you must then fish over the best shore from shallow into deep and for another any north in the breeze will produce a nasty jabble against the best rocky point of all. To arrive after a gruelling trudge across terribly broken ground and find conditions bad is maddening, so one picks a day some time forward but decides to go only if at 10 A.M. summer time on that day, when the wind of the day has settled in—things look good.

The day I describe was such a day except that the plan was designed to make use of a watcher's report that some salmon had been seen to run the river a few days earlier and could reasonably be expected to have settled in one or other or maybe all of the three or four known lies. Combine this circumstance with a good west wind, a nice broken light and cloud carrying the odd shower or two and you may justifiably be happy in anticipation as I have indeed said we were. True, the wave was a great deal heavier than I like for seatrout, but I was after the salmon the watcher had seen and as for wind and wave, I had for ghillie the head keeper Angus, a man of exceptional physique and the best boat handler I know. On such a day, fishing over known lies of very limited extent, the man at the oars plays an equal part with the rod. That boat and rod are one instrument is a fact far too little appreciated by many anglers and some ghillies.

It was lunch time when, rod up and Yellow Torrish on the tail and Dusty Miller on the dropper of the 8/5 cast, we pushed off after much pounding among the breaking waves. The Torrish normally does well on this loch and I had picked the Dusty for a dropper because I always think it fishes best in that position—and on this day, with plenty of sunshine, it should do well. The tail was a four (old scale) to steady the cast and the dropper a six, both larger than normal because of the big wave.

We drew first across a subsidiary bouldery point which often yields a fish but in spite of meticulously careful working, drew a blank. But we like a fish in the boat before going ashore for lunch and I personally find that sandwiches taste a lot better when you can look at a fish in the heather beside you as you sit under some peat bank out of the wind. So off we went across a narrow and very draughty inlet to try the main lie off the point which gives these notes their title. Here a thirty-foot bluff drops sheer into three or four feet of boulder-filled water—great round boulders these, gleaming golden under the marching waves rolling across the point. Perhaps an area twenty yards square forms the taking place and we edged down it foot by foot, Angus holding the boat head to wind, heaven knows how, while I fished, Hebridean fashion, off the stern. Further out and in deeper water than I expected, for fish often lie close-in under such conditions—the first fish made a little splashy rise like a trout and I left the fly where it was although I didn't think he had it. But he had, and I was in him—not a big fish as we saw when he jumped but a fresh one. We led him inch by inch it seemed up into that terrible wind and wave and presently put the net under a seven-and-a-half-pounder with the Dusty firmly where it should be, in the scissors.

'That boy's not by himself,' said Angus and I agreed. These fish tend to stay in small companies for some time after entering fresh water and if a take is 'on them' you are likely to do well if you concentrate on a known lie. And so it proved for the next drift down produced another rise to the second cast—a very slowly-moving fish this time. I saw a light brown, almost golden, nose and the whole length of his back before he turned down and the line tightened. He came like a lamb out into deep water and disturbed the lie not at all. Then he suddenly realized something was wrong and gave us an exhibition of aerobatics at the end of a very long line—fortunately upwind, since I doubt whether the light cast would have withstood much of that wave pressure if drowned. Anyhow we had him aboard after seven or eight minutes and again the Dusty had done its job and again the fish was ideally hooked in the corner of his mouth. A nine-pounder this time.

So far so good. We decided to give the lie a wide berth and wallowed away downwind into the lee and thence into deep heather behind a quiet sandy beach for lunch. It was not a long break. If anything it was blowing harder than ever and a blue-black squall with cold fimbriated upper edges to its cloud-mass filled the western sky. I took the camera out of its waterproof bag and snapped the fish lying at the water's edge.

Back upwind of the lie we fished over the same ground again without response but a few feet inside the unfished area a little fish sailed out from between two sunken boulders and went quietly back with the fly. When I felt him we led him steadily out and after some deep boring and cast-thumping he came up and was netted—another victim of the Dusty and about six pounds. Whilst Angus held the boat head to wind out in deep water I cut the dropper out of the cast and re-tied dropper and fly. Even a gut cast, better in this respect than nylon, is the better for retying—particularly at dropper and main cast knot, after it has handled a brace of fish. The squall was on us now and I fumbled at the blood knot with soft wet fingers while the cold rain poured off the brim of my fishing hat, the boat slammed down in the troughs and Angus grew impatient to be at them again. Obviously they were still 'on'. The light had gone and I wondered about changing the Dusty for a Black Doctor or a Thunder, but concluded that time was vital and the little pink-hackled fly certainly had been right so far.

We struck a blank patch this time down; from the centre of the lie down to the tail end of the jumble of boulders was either fish-less, or they had gone off, but well downwind from the normal taking area, when we were preparing to draw out and away again, I had a spectacular savage rise and to my surprise found the hook go home as firm as a rock. This fish would not be led— he simply was not having any of it. He went downwind as though the Norsemen who used to spear salmon in these waters were after him, and we were quickly into the backing. That raised no great problem of course and the boat was dropping down on him and I was recovering some line, when he suddenly veered off to the right, finishing close inshore on the shallows with dorsal fin and tail showing among breaking waves. He then came a bit deeper, went down still further and bored away upwind. I now had twenty or thirty yards of sunk line and the wind of that accursed squall putting a frightening pressure on the belly from the rod-tip. I felt, for perhaps a minute, that something had to give but it didn't and out in the deep, where he had gone of his own accord, we played him out and netted him, Angus making the longest reach with the big net that I have ever seen, and getting very wet in the process—it really was a rough day. Another nine-pounder and another on the same fly.

I said that I would like to get another just to make five. What magic there was in five I do not know, but to be honest we both knew that it was finished and sure enough a further careful fishing of the entire area failed to produce any response. We baled the boat and considered. The other side of the loch four hundred yards away contained one lie at the mouth of an entering burn and two others off small undistinguished points of broken rocks. But these places could not be attained by direct passage in that weight of wind and wave and the only possibility seemed to be to take the boat upwind along our present shore, round in the lee of the head of the loch and drop down the other shore to fish the lies I have mentioned.

We found a little beach and I went ashore to lighten the boat while Angus applied his wonderful strength to driving the boat upwind, and I trudged through heather and bog to meet him in quiet water at the loch-head. Here is good seatrout ground but a change to smaller flies and lighter cast for the small waves of this quieter place served no purpose. As we drifted down the far shore, having fished across the head of the loch, we caught the wind again; the light cast came off and the cast of the morning was mounted again.

The river mouth where we confidently expected to find a fish was passed and the first of the points without sign of a rise. The squally weather had gone but the day was dark with none of the broken light which, with a lively wave, always flatters the fly and makes it easier to show it attractively, particularly in the dropper position.

However, at the second point and virtually the last of our unfished salmon lies, I had a deep quiet boil, instantly effaced by the rolling wave and the fifth fish was on, and pulling hard and steadily close to the boat. We took him out to safer water and there he surged about making no attempt at any sort of real run and keeping down. We both thought there was something odd about this fish. He just pulled hard without head-shaking, without showing and without head-down boring, and it went on like this until he came in the wall of a wave ten yards away and we both saw the best seatrout ever to come out of the loch—thick shouldered and golden of back and every spot on him showing up through the clear water. When we had him in the boat we found that we had to cut out the Dusty, so firmly was it fixed just forward of the scissors. 'This one will take some beating,' said Angus. 'He's a good six pounds.' He was later shown to be right.

And that was the end of that day. We fished down to the boat landing, even then reluctant to give up over an acre of possible salmon ground, but the day was done and we knew it. The water rolled sullenly under unbroken dark skies. An eagle, swinging in effortless spirals on the flank of the nearby hill, looked strangely light-coloured in that light.

The rollers carried us till we grounded with the bow on dry sand. Boat secured and fish washed and laid in the heather, I took another picture with misgivings about the light and presently we breasted the hill above the beach and with the wind in our backs, set out on our two-hour tramp to the lodge.

From the highest ridge we paused to look back at the loch—leaden silver against the western shore that separated it from the ocean gleam beyond. That, we said, and I still think, was a grand day! Five rises and five fish—four salmon and a big seatrout, and best of all, it went as we planned. You know, or if you don't you soon will, that in fishing this seldom happens.

Playing the Fish

BY LEE WULFF

Although it has not been my intention to make this a "how-to" book, feeling as I do that well-told fishing tales inherently contain plenty of useful information, I am straying off that course a bit in this selection. I, for one, need all the advice I can get that will prepare me for those rare and priceless times when I might find myself trying to deal with a fish that has taken me deep "into the backing." And what better guide could one ask for on the subject than the late Lee Wulff, an experienced and respected authority whose name will no doubt endure beside the greats of fly fishing for all time.

In recent years, after his death at age 83 in the crash of his small plane after apparently suffering a stroke or some such incapacitation, Lee's book Bush Pilot Angler *was added to his long list of distinguished and highly readable works. His widow, Joan Salvato Wulff, continues to do fishing instruction and casting clinics and write articles and books for* Fly Rod & Reel, Fly Fisherman, *and* The Lyons Press.

This piece is from Lee's book Trout on a Fly, *published by The Lyons Press in 1986.*

Most people play fish by three simple rules. 1. Keep the tip up (which means that the bending of the rod will absorb sudden shocks); 2. keep the pressure on (which means that you're tiring the fish); and, 3. don't give slack (lest the hook fall out or lose its grip).

It's good to know the rules but important to know, also, when to break them. To teach how to play fish at our school, the first thing we do is to set up some rods with two-pound and four-pound-test tippets tied to the corner of the porch. The students are told that rods are designed to work best when the angle between the rod butt and the fish doesn't exceed 90°. When a rod is pulled back to a greater angle, like 135°, it is doubled back on itself under conditions that make it unstable and much more likely to break. Within the allowable angle, it is almost impossible to break a rod. If your rod is bent too far back, pull in line to bring it down to a good angle.

Students find that they have to strain to break a two–pound–test tippet and some don't have the strength to break a four or six–pound tippet by pulling with the rod. Then I ask, do you bend your rod that hard (a pull a little less than the breaking strength) when you play a fish, and, if you don't, why not? This maximum pressure, which few anglers know, can be called the "safe static pressure." It should be applied only when things are static and line is neither going out nor being taken in through the guides. This can happen when neither the fish nor the angler's rod is moving or when both are moving at the same speed in the same direction.

Few fishermen know how hard they can pull with their tackle before it will break, yet knowing that safe pull is one of the most important parts of playing a fish. Therefore, most fishermen, failing to use their tackle to its full power, play fish much too long and endanger the lives of those they intend to release. Every angler should hook his fly to something solid with the varying strength leader tippets he plans to use and learn their strength each season before he starts fishing. Most anglers find this too much trouble. I hope you won't.

The question "How hard?" is especially important when we consider the strike.

What to do when there is a lot of slack in the line and a trout rises to a dry fly, is one such concern. And the only answer can be, try to duplicate the conditions you're thinking of, on a pond or stream. Cast out so that your fly line and leader have in them the amount of slack you want to know about— and then strike, time after time, until you determine exactly how fast and how hard you have to strike in order to make your dry fly move *an inch or two*, just enough to set the point of your hook beyond the barb. When you've found the proper pressure for a particular kind of water, you'll know the answer. And if you'll make these tests with varying amounts of slack, you'll learn how to strike under a wide variety of slack conditions and to strike instinctively with about the right pressure.

One strike that will cut through the most slack is a combination of a haul with the line hand and a move, preferably to the side, by the hand with the rod. A rod is designed to absorb shocks yet a shock is what's needed to set the hook. Line doesn't have any "give" and will transmit a pull right on through its entire length. Lay a piece of rope on the floor. Even if it isn't stretched out in a straight line, if you give a hard yank on one end it will normally be transmitted right on through the entire length to make the far end jump toward you. If it jumps only an inch or two, that is enough to set a hook.

It is a good thing to practice to see how much of a pull you need on your line and how much strike with the rod to move your slack-floating dry fly far enough to hook a fish.

With wet flies a strike is not normally required but most of us do lift the rod a bit when we feel the fish to be sure that there's enough pressure given to set the hook. A strike that's too hard will make the hole of the hook's penetration bigger and start the process of weakening the flesh at that point. Many a fish has been lost, many minutes later, without the fisherman's knowing what caused it. Most fishermen strike too hard.

The next question may be, "But exactly how hard should the actual pressure at the hook point be in order to make it sink into the flesh beyond the barb?"

My answer would be, on the next few fish you catch and keep, put hooks of varying sizes into their mouths and pull on your leader to see how hard you have to pull to set the hooks. If you don't keep many or any trout, the next time a leg of lamb is going to be cooked in your kitchen, try sinking the barbs of various hooks into the flesh. Try where it's softest and try where it is toughened a bit by skin or sinew.

Your first reaction may be that this is a lot of trouble. And so it is. Learning takes thought, time, and effort. There is no way an oracle can let you kneel before him (or her) and touch you with his magic wand and give you knowledge of this sort. You have to acquire it and most of it is there to be acquired, in the best way, by working out your own answers.

Many fly fishermen worry about slack. If I bare my forearm and stick a #10 hook into it beyond the barb, how long will it stay there if I don't pull it out? Probably a week. Why, then, do we worry about giving fish slack? Obviously we don't have to worry unless, during the playing, the flesh around the hook's hold has been torn enough to let the hook fall out. Sometimes I will hook some trout in our pond and give them complete slack time after time without losing them. Even barbless hooks will hold when slack is given, *most of the time,* with the smaller ones holding better with slack than the larger ones.

Do I use barbless hooks?

Not often. Mostly when I have to.

Many fishermen today think that if they *don't* use barbless hooks the fish they release will die. But *all* of the fish I return to the water, and there have been thousands, swim away strongly when I release them and I know from many observations that they live. Why, then, must I use barbless hooks to be a good sportsman? Barbless hooks should be your choice, not your necessity or a requirement for being considered a sportsman. Since slack is a tool I can use to play fish faster and barbless hooks may not let me use it as well without the risk of a lost fish, the fish I play on barbed hooks can have a better chance of survival.

Because I have been making movies of fish since 1938, not just playing them but making them act, making them jump when I wanted them to, making them run or stop or rest to give me the particular shots I needed to tell the story on film, I've learned a great deal about controlling fish that most anglers haven't even thought about. It began in 1938 in Newfoundland with a salmon film I was making for the Province, which was then a British Colony. I had an assistant to do photography and I was the actor/angler. We went to a salmon pool with the sun slanting down on the water at 7:30 in the morning. Ralph sat on a rock at the side of the pool with the camera ready to go. Periodically he had to change the lens opening when clouds covered the sun in varying degrees and to change the distance setting when I waded farther from shore. He stayed right on the job. Eight-thirty passed. Then 9:00. At 9:30 he moved over to the lunch box to get a soft drink. Still no salmon had risen to take the fly.

At 10:00 Ralph went off to the bushes for just a minute and in that minute I hooked a salmon. It came whirling out of the water in a magnificent series of leaps and splashes and my call brought Ralph running back. Again, the salmon leaped and ran while Ralph looked up at the sun to set the lens opening and then asked, "Where is he?"

I pointed far down the pool and said, "Near that boulder." Ralph checked the distance setting and aimed the camera there and when he saw the fish jump started it running. As I'd advised he kept it running and the second jump of the fish was captured on film from beginning to end. The first jump was half over before Ralph had started the camera and, since it wasn't complete, I knew I wouldn't use it in the film. We got the landing of the fish in full detail, changing lenses for a closeup, and following the fish out to deep water after the release.

We had a good salmon landing on film but we had only one tired jump, far in the distance. It wasn't fair to the salmon and obviously we wouldn't attract many tourist-fishermen if that was all the action a Newfoundland salmon would give them. I had to think.

I am a salmon. I was born in this stream not far above this pool. I spent four years in this section of the river feeding on its insect life and grew to a six-inch length before drifting down to sea with the spring floods. Then I swam the ocean for thousands of miles, feeding on shrimp and capelin and other good-tasting and nourishing things. I saw whales and sharks and jelly fish. I was chased by seals. I saw cruise ships and rowboats. I saw nets and escaped them. Finally, after two years, during which I'd increased my weight to twelve pounds, I decided it was time to come home. So I looked at the sun and the moon and the stars and felt the swing of the ocean currents and headed back to this, my native river.

I struck the coast some forty miles away and swam along it, smelling the changes in the sea's salinity and poking in toward shore to smell each river. The moment I smelled this one I knew it was mine and came into it full of memories and feeling strange changes within my body. I worked my way upstream, pausing quite a while at a forks where the difference between the two flows was small, until I was sure this was the branch of my birth. Then I swam on up until I came to this pool.

I had a great feeling of being home, of wanting to rest here. I had a feeling, too, of great well being. I was filled with energy and strength. Yet something told me I'd need it all in the times just ahead and as much as possible should be kept in reserve. I hadn't felt any hunger, which was strange and lucky, too, for the salmon parr I'd seen, because they were smaller and easier to catch than the herring and capelin I'd been feeding on out in the salt water.

I must have swum around the pool fifty times, looking it over, before finally picking out a resting place. It was a lie at which I could feel the gentle flow of the stream yet not have to expend much energy to hold my position there. I had sunshine on the bright days to add a little warmth to the river water, which was a little cooler than the sea I'd just left. There was deep water beside me in which I could escape an otter, water deep enough to discourage an osprey. I'd found a great spot for rest and safety.

If some creature, like an eel, otter, or merganser, were to attack me, I'd use all my strength to escape. I'd swim faster than any salmon had ever swam before. I'd leap higher. I'd fight to survive because my instincts were telling me that important times were ahead for me—the best, the most important, days of my life. On the other hand, if a sea louse that had clung to my side when I had come in from the sea were to bite me I'd simply ignore it or, at most, try to scrape that side against a rock to dislodge it.

Just how wildly a salmon can react to danger had come to me dramatically the season before when, on the White Bear River of Newfoundland's south coast, I'd hooked a salmon. I had on a fifteen-pound-test leader and was using a sturdy nine-foot rod. I leaned back at the strike as hard as I dared. The result was electrifying. The salmon, startled and wild, made a leaping run like a sailfish that carried it not only to the far bank but six feet on into the alders that lined it. I left my rod with a rock on it and had to walk a quarter of a mile downstream to find a place shallow enough to cross; then I walked up the far bank to get the salmon, and, carrying it, followed the same course back to where my rod lay.

At any rate, when the next salmon for my movie rose, I simply gave the rod a little twitch to set the hook and then let the line go completely slack. As I'd figured out, the salmon simply drifted back to the preferred place he'd spent so much time choosing. I shouted for Ralph to come beside me. I pointed to a large white rock showing on the streambed and said, "The salmon is just about six feet ahead of that rock. We know where he is, so put on the telephoto lens and set the camera for slow motion." He did this. He pointed the camera at the spot indicated and when I heard it rolling I tightened up on the fish, which then came out in a beautiful series of leaps that were something any Newfoundland salmon could be proud of and that any salmon angler would love to have happen at the end of his own line. That was my first step in making fish act.

My best example of slack at the strike came when I was fishing for a striped marlin record on a fly for ABC's "American Sportsman" series. I hooked the record fish only to hear, over the intercom, "We've got camera problems." I was in a fifteen-foot skiff and I immediately gave slack, following behind the fish as he lazed along in the sun. He didn't know he was hooked. The slight drag didn't bother him because these big fish often have remoras (fish that attach themselves to the marlin and ride along with them until they feed, then feed, too) clinging to their sides which must add a drag similar to my slacked-off fly line.

It was a full five minutes before word came over the intercom that the cameras were ready. Now where was the fish? I reported that the fish was exactly 52 feet in front of the boat, something I could determine by the marks on my fly line. The camera boat came up into position and, when they waved that they were rolling cameras, I leaned back as much as I dared with the twelve-pound-test leader and the result was that the surprised marlin gave us the finest series of marlin jumps ABC ever got.

Slack is a great tool in the playing of a fish. It gives you time and time can be precious. Once, while playing a salmon at the Shellbird Island Pool of the Humber River in Newfoundland I had my reel jam up. I was close to shore and, angling over to it, I set the reel seat firmly into a crotch in an alder so that it would hold and, going back to my car, I drove six miles to the Glynmill Inn where I was staying, got another reel, came back and attached it to the line and landed the seventeen-and-a-half-pounder.

Does that surprise you?

It shouldn't.

Suppose you were alone out on the northern tundra where you can see for miles. You crawl out of your tent in the morning and see a grizzly fifty feet away. He stands up. Then he starts toward you. You run and you hear him breathing behind you so you put everything you have into the effort. You're breathing hard, starting to stagger. After a bit you can't hear him behind you so you take a quick glance back. You see that the bear is running off toward the horizon and there's not another living thing in sight, all around the horizon. What would you do next?

You'd sit down and rest. You'd be thankful that the bear had stopped chasing you and perhaps wonder what it was all about. The last thing you'd do would be to keep on running. Just so with a fish. What's happened to him when he's hooked is inexplicable. When its over, he'll rest where he is or in the nearest convenient place he can find good resting water. You can count on it if he's at all tired.

Drifting down an Oregon river in a McKenzie boat, while making a movie of steelhead fishing I hooked a good fish. The fish went down out of the pool and we followed through the rapids. In the middle of the fast water the cameraman signaled he was out of film. I sang out, "Throw out the anchor." The guide objected, saying we'd lose the fish. I insisted. The anchor went over and we slowed to a stop. The fish ran a short distance, then stopped and waited patiently until the camera was reloaded, and then we all went on down together to the quiet water of the next pool, photographing as we went.

If you have a hooked fish that heads for a snag, don't just try to stop him with a braking power that will break your leader. Let him go. Often a fish will go into a snaggy place and, once there, feel that he's safe until you give him a few line twitches that tell him that he still isn't free. If he decides to move to some place else, he's likely to come out of that snag the same way he went in and you can start playing him again. Recently, a fresh-water striper I hooked at Santee Cooper wrapped the line around a sunken branch. I bounced the rod lightly against the line a few times, then firmly, without result, and my companions said I'd have to break the fish off. But I waited a little longer and the fish apparently swung back around the branch, freeing the line.

Fish often position themselves near or in a snag or problem foliage. Even though the situation may look impossible, there may be a chance of landing him. If he's a good one, it ought to be worth wasting a fly just in the hope of hooking him. If you can drop a dry fly on a plop cast, with a lot of slack, into a spot where a big fish has taken a lie in under some branches, he may take your fly before the current tightens the line and sets up an unnatural drag. *Then* you can worry about how to land him.

Flies are expendable. When bushes hang down from the far bank over deep water, creating a lie where you know a good trout should be, why not take a chance? Drop your wet fly, nymph, or streamer (one you have a spare for) fairly well upstream of the trailing branches to give the fly a chance to sink a little. Just as it reaches the right spot give it a bit of motion. If you're lucky, you'll either get a strike or have your fly drift on through without getting hung up. If you aren't, you've just lost a fly.

I well remember a situation of that type. A good trout was rising under a low walk-bridge across a feeder of the Bitterroot in Montana. The bridge was ten feet wide, the stream about thirty. The fish was lying in the midpoint in the central flow. I knew I couldn't cast up under the bridge from my position downstream; the bridge was too low to the water. Instead, I cast up *over* the bridge, a long, high cast with a lot of slack, enough to let the fly drift free to the fish. His take and the immediate drag of the current on the leader set the hook. I ran up onto the bridge, reeling in but not putting any pull on the fish until I was at the upstream edge. I played him with my rod held low, to work him up into some quieter water, then moved on down to the stream bank for the release.

Think, when you're playing a fish, about what he can know and what his instinctive reactions will be. That way you can improve on the old rule of "tip up, tight line." Of course, that rule will work, after a fashion. Just how well I used to prove every once in a while at my fly-in salmon camp in northwest Newfoundland. Now and then a couple would come to the camp, bringing along a son or daughter of nine or ten. It was a wilderness camp and we had no nature trails or playing fields and the youngster would get bored. After a few days, I'd go to the parents and ask, "How would you like to have little Augustine catch a salmon?"

Their eyebrows would lift and they'd query, "Little Augustine?"

I'd nod and say, "I think she could manage it. It will cost you five bucks for one guide for one afternoon."

If they were beginners, they'd probably caught only one or two salmon in three days. They'd think a minute and then nod their heads and say, "Okay."

First we'd find out just how far Augustine could cast; this usually wasn't far. We'd give her instructions and put her in the bow of the canoe. The guide would keep shifting the canoe until Augustine—with her steady one-length, one-directional casting—was putting her fly right over a salmon. Every camp operator worth his salt has a few ready fish in special spots saved for paraplegics and politicians and it was to one of those we'd go. In a little while a fish would come up and take the fly and the rod would go down and the reel would scream. Augustine would look at the guide and when the line was slack and she could lift the rod easily, he'd nod and she'd start to reel in. When the line tightened and the rod was pulled down again, she'd take her hand from the reel as if it was red hot and it would scream again. When the fish stopped and she could lift the rod up again easily, she'd reel in again. The minute the fish pulled her rod down, she'd yank her hand from the reel and let him run free. (We'd have her in an open pool, free of snags.) In about fifteen or twenty minutes the tired fish would swim across the guide's submerged net and he'd lift the fish aboard. Playing a fish can be that simple—but most of the time there are problems and solving them can give an angler a great deal of satisfaction.

When I first used small rods many salmon fishermen said that big fish couldn't be played with them. Some insisted, "But you can't really pull hard with them." I'd reply that I could lower my rod and, by moving away, break a hundred-pound line if I wanted to. Then they'd say, "But what do you do when a fish sulks?" I'd reply that my fish didn't sulk if I was free to move. And they'd look at me with disbelief.

If a fish is hanging downstream in the current at just the right angle from the line, he can put terrific pressure on your tackle. If you took a piece of wood the same size and length as the fish, put a halter on it to give it the right angle, and let it hang in the same spot, it too would put a similar strain on your tackle. The stick is inanimate and doesn't have to spend any energy to hold its position in that flow. Neither does the fish. Hanging there in the current doesn't tire him out. But if the angler moves downstream and the pull comes laterally or from below, the fish has to move. Now he has to fight the current to hold his place in it. If the angler is below him, the fish not only has to fight the current but the pull of the tackle as well. That's tiring. Even though a fish may not be moving, if he is either fighting a strong current or fighting an angler's strong static pressure, he is getting tired fast. By using maximum static pressure on a sulking fish *from downstream,* you can make him move in a matter of minutes. And, moving, he will continue tiring.

Those of us who have played great fish in the sea on light lines realize that our tackle doesn't pull a fish around and tire him out because of his resisting. That can happen with a one-pound trout on a four-pound-test leader but not with a sailfish on a ten-pound-test line or a big trout on a three-pound test leader. The truth is that the fish tires himself by his own efforts to escape until, when he's tired, the safe static pull of the angler's tackle will move him to net or boatside. Just as with Augustine, smart anglers let the fish tire themselves out without a lot of effort on their own part.

Most of these techniques are important with large rather than small fish. When your leader is twice as strong as a fish's weight, the problem is not really great. It is simply a matter of using the rod's resilience to take up the shock of a sudden surge and give time to get your hand off the reel handle so the fish can run free. But it's the big ones we're most anxious to keep and to play well. Here's the method I use when it's important that I land the fish, not get pictures of jumps or other angling action.

At the rise I'll set the hook with a quick little snap of the rod—then give slack. Sometimes I'll even strip line off the reel to give the fish a chance to settle. Most of the time it is simply a matter of lowering the rod quickly—and I really mean very quickly—as soon as the hook is set. This doesn't come naturally and you may have to work on it. Then the first thing to do is to get rid of the casting slack between the reel and the first guide. I do that by holding the line as it comes in between my first two fingers, let it loop down, and then pass between the third finger and pinkie before going to the reel. If the fish pulls, the line will slide out readily between the first two fingers; meanwhile, as I reel in, the rear fingers will put enough tension on the line to wind it smoothly onto the reel spool. When the loop disappears the fingers are spread and the line is on a direct pull from reel to first guide. It is easy, sometimes, to play a fish by stripping line, letting the loose line fall to the bottom of the boat or to the water, but any fish I really want to land I play directly from the reel to avoid the embarrassment of having a knot form in the loose line that will catch at the first guide and cost me the fish.

The next considerations are, "Am I in the best position to play this fish? Should I move to shallower water?" If I need to move I'll be doing this while I'm taking out the casting slack, or I'll give slack as I move.

While playing my fish, I will control the drag by relaxing or increasing pressure on the fly line as I hold it back or let it slip through my fingers where they press against it just in front of the reel. The finger pressure gives me instant relaxation or increase of pressure. My reels have a click setting that is just enough to keep them from over-running, no more.

The angle of my rod varies the drag a fish has to pull against to move line. If the rod is pointed directly at a fish, the drag of the guides is at a minimum; I do that when I want a fish to run freely, perhaps on a very light tippet. If I hold my rod up high, the drag of the guides comes to a maximum. Between the angle of my rod and the pressure of my fingers, I can maintain excellent control. If the fly line goes out off the reel and the backing line passes between my fingers, I cannot use finger pressure on it without burning skin. Then I use my left hand to give additional drag by pressing a finger or fingers against the rim, if it is a rim control reel, or against the inside of the outer flange of the reel spool, made bare because the full fly line is off the reel. Using this system, I don't ever get finger burns yet have the best possible drag control on a fish's runs.

Having reached a good playing position, I'll put a little pressure on the fish. It won't be enough to send him off on a wild run but enough to make him uncomfortable and cause him to move a little. The moment the fish starts to move, I'll take off all pressure and let him run freely. He'll move a bit and stop. I tighten up and make him uncomfortable again; then, again he'll make a short run. If I held back hard it would be a long, wild run—which I don't want. Such a run could take him out of the pool or far away where I'd have to play him on a long line with a greater chance of having it foul up somewhere along the way. About the third or the fourth time that I make him uncomfortable, he'll realize that he's really in trouble and will put his heart into his effort to get away. But by that time he will not be as wild as if I'd pressured him at first. He'll be a bit used to the strange pressure on his jaw. He'll be a little out of breath from the short dashes he's already made. He'll be more docile than when he was first hooked. Then you work on him as much as your tackle will let you. Use static pressure when you can. Otherwise, use enough pressure to make him move in tiring moves. A few good runs and leaps and I'll find times when I can apply more static pressure. He'll grow tired.

A fish will resist being pulled to the stream bank as energetically as you would resist being pushed into a pool of sulphuric acid. He doesn't *want* to come into the air at the shore. If you'll wade out to a depth of water in which he's comfortable, two feet or more, you can control him much more easily. You can have a fish make a complete circle around you, then—and work at any angle in all 360°. You'll bring him to net or hand that much quicker, which will, in turn, give him that much better chance of survival if you're going to release him.

A fish to be released can be corralled in a net so that he can be unhooked without lifting him from the water or holding him with any squeezing pressures. Perhaps the best release is simply to grip the shank of the fly with longnosed pliers or a hemostat and remove it without ever touching the fish, either while corralled in the net or played to a point where you can reach the hook without a net. Beaching fish is effective if you're going to keep them;

they have to be tired enough to be kept headed up onto the beach and unable to turn aside until grounded; then, with a moderate pull, their own efforts will drive them up farther since they're not designed to back up well.

There is a second side to playing fish beyond just tiring them out. That is the psychological. If you can destroy their will to fight, you can subdue them more quickly. That's the reason why I let fish run on a completely slack line. They think they're free. They've just made a great effort and, suddenly, the pressure is gone. They swim a ways and relax. Then that pressure comes back again, telling them that they're not free. Each effort they make is more desperate and each time its failure hurts more. Finally they give up. They've been able to do their best and it wasn't good enough. You can break a horse. You can train a dog. You can break a fish's spirit, too.

Contrast these pressures with a steady pulling of the fish. Then the fish settles into a tug-of-war and keeps right on tugging until he's completely exhausted. Such fish have the least chance of survival. Tug-of-wars take a lot more time.

An important factor in playing fish is to remember from which side you hooked them. Since fish are almost always heading upstream, you'll know which side that is. If, during the playing of the fish, you find you've changed sides, play with minimal pressure. A change of direction can use the shank length of the hook as leverage to tear the flesh at its hold and help it tear free or work out.

Another important factor in playing fish is the amount of line out. Line has a friction when pulled through the water and it can build up with increasing current and increased length. Much as your guide may want to leave the canoe at anchor, when you're out into your backing, it's best to follow the fish. If you're on foot follow him. Get line back. You can con fish into swimming toward you when they're still strong *sometimes* but it isn't worth losing a good fish because you were too lazy to follow him or the guide was too lazy to move the canoe.

An important trick with such big fish as steelheads, when they're in a pool or run and you don't want them to go down through the fast water at the tail, is to *walk* them upstream. I cannot explain why this technique works so well but can assure you that it does. A tired fish, if you can get him to stop and rest above the tail rapids, can almost always be persuaded to move along a little with a steady pull. Start with light pressure and increase it *very* gradually until the fish starts to move. Then, maintaining that same pressure, walk upstream at a slow and steady pace. The fish will come along, I believe, because the pressure is steady. If you try to reel in so that *you* won't have to move, the pressure on the fish will be jerky because of your reeling and he'll come only a little way before he'll run again. The movement of the line caused by reeling, or by a quivering of the rod, will cause most quiet fish to run. But a steady pressure has walked a good many fish back up into quiet waters for an easy landing.

I've often heard it said that a fish *must* be kept in the pool if he is to be landed. That isn't always true. I've saved a lot of fish that went down into the heavy, rough water below such pools. Again, the important word is slack. Let them go. Wise anglers carry enough backing line on their reels to manage this. Complete slack should be given so there is no nagging pull to urge them on. A fish that has ascended a river on a spawning run can well ask himself, "What am I going downstream for? I just came up!"

As soon as they come to a good resting place, most fish will stop, perhaps to rest. The current will carry the slack line downstream behind them. It will usually hang up on the rocks and whatever else is causing the rough water. An angler following along can reel in and clear the line of these objects as he follows. More often than not, when the angler reaches the fish he'll still be on, resting there and perhaps doing a little wondering. Renewed pressure may send him off on another downstream run, particularly if he's too tired to want to buck his way up through the rough water just then. Again, the angler can follow his slack-running fish perhaps through two or three more stops until the fish reaches water quiet enough for a landing. How much better that is than to have held too hard and broken tackle in an effort to hold the fish in the pool.

On western streams, I've had good rainbows make a long run then go into overhanging bushes or willow roots along a bank. Once the fish starts his run he is on complete slack. When he goes into the snag, I walk toward him, reeling in but without any tension on the line. I've reached a place outside the snag and sometimes seen the fish. Sometimes he'll come out where he went in; occasionally he'll go out through some other passage. If there is no pressure, the line will simply follow along behind him. There's no drag or pressure to break a tippet or pull out a hook. And sometimes I've been able to pass my rod in the path of the line on through the snag to the other side where the fish went out and play and land him in the open water beyond. Once a rainbow took my line between two big rocks that just touched under two feet of water. Again, it was complete slack and passing the rod through the passage the fish had taken that let me keep him on and land him. Slack can be wonderful.

Playing a fish is a lot like driving a car in a road race. You can drive just so fast without going off the road on the curves and you can hold or pull just so hard without breaking your tackle. Playing time with given tackle is a measure of one's skill. It is satisfying to play fish well, particularly if the fish is to be released. The longer a fish is played the slimmer his chances of survival. Knowing that safe "static" pull and using it on a tiring fish is a key to survival for released fish.

If you *do* tire a fish out completely, hold him, headed upstream and upright, in a current to revive him. I've been saddened to see people pushing an exhausted fish forward and backward through the water, time after time. Pushing him forward *helps* him to breathe. Pulling him backward *chokes* him. If you can't find a reasonable flow to head him into, push him forward through the water continuously. If a straight line isn't possible, make a big circle.

An angler can take a special pride if, whenever he unhooks a fish to release it, it swims away strongly on its own. This can be managed no matter how fine the leader point or how large the fish.

That's part of the measure of the angler.

A Phoenix for Dan

BY FRANK MELE

In introducing the late Frank Mele's engaging book of fishing stories, Small in the Eye of the River, *published by* The Lyons Press *in 1996, Nick Lyons said, "He has brought an absolutely new voice to angling literature—delicate, elusive, speculative, searching, earthy, witty, and ultimately wise."*

Nick had first become interested in Frank Mele thirty years before when he chose Mele's story "Blue Dun" for his fishing anthology, Fisherman's Bounty. *Mele, who passed away in 1996, had an extensive career in symphony and chamber music as a violinist with the Rochester Philharmonic and later as a violist with the Pittsburgh Symphony and Modern Art String Quartet. He lived most of his life in Woodstock, New York, close to his beloved Catskill rivers, where he was as much an artist with the fly rod as he was with this music.*

Frank Mele did not write many stories, but those he did publish lived up to Nick Lyons' high praise in every way.

PHOENIX: *Mythical, beautiful bird which, every 500 years, consumed itself in fire, rising up from its ashes to new life.*

No angler worth his rod will be surprised at hearing that Dan's story was delivered, as it were, on the bank of a river; nor, that the campfire had a hand in it. It would have had to, as we shall see. Besides, where there is a campfire there is always a story; and sometimes, as in our case, an Equation,* too. Moreover, it was a great fire—the

---

* The now famous Equation establishing the quantitative Table of Variants in the relationship of Mass to Maneuverability—that is, in a fish. (See: *The New Mathematics*, Veritas Series, University of Bologna [NY] Press, 1949.)

sort that brings frantic calls to the forest ranger's telephone by an alarmed countryside.

The cause for this offense against the rules of responsible camping was old Dan Brenan, who made fly rods in the city, had been a camper much of his life, was an Adirondack historian, and should have known better, and who did know better, but whose spirit was irreconcilable to small fires when he was out of doors. And indoors, too, according to his patient wife, who had had to call the community firemen on more than one occasion when the flames in the fireplace had spread to the walls.

I suppose that this touch of pyromania may have been called a "quirk of character" by tolerant neighbors; but it would have been superficial, misleading, even demeaning. As it now appears in retrospect, a deeper meaning can be ascribed to the passion which, at evening, transformed that gentle craftsman and historian into nothing less than a ruthless Pharaoh commanding his slaves, the younger of us, to haul small trees to the site of his Pyramid; and never a glimmer of compassion for our hanging tongues and perspiring bodies. This, after having waded, literally, a mile of river, making innumerable casts under a broiling sun.

I think that, for Dan, the fire was the emblem of a soaring Spirit. Well back in his mind there may have been a nagging ambition to conjure up a phoenix of his own. If improbable, I must say in Dan's defense that the possibility of a phoenix sneaking out of an uncorked whiskey bottle into the fire, and soaring out its flames, is surely stronger on the banks of a river than anywhere else.

By this time I had become familiar with the rather unique pattern of Dan's camping. But at first one thing had puzzled me: Dan, a most knowledgeable angler, whose lore was well nigh endless, did not fish. After the tents had got erected and all was shipshape, Dan would solemnly take his favorite rod, a powerful, glossy black eight-and-a-half footer out of its tube, join its two parts meticulously, and fit it out complete with reel and leader. Then he would carefully lean "Black Maria" against a nearby limb, and there it would remain the entire weekend.

On this occasion, as the night advanced and Dan's fire "arrived," as it were, I finally asked the question I had suppressed so long.

"Dan, you don't seem to fish much, do you?"

The firelight seemed to emphasize Dan's resemblance to the farmer in Grant Wood's famous painting, *American Gothic:* the long, austerely set features, grim, expressionless, his wife and the pitchfork between them all of a piece out of a Puritan forge.

"I don't," said Dan. "And I do."

He meant, I thought, that it was enough for him to see us younger men go into the river. But a thought kept insisting that something had made him stop, had made it impossible for him to take Black Maria to the stream. Bill, the youngest of us, must have been thinking along the same lines.

"Dan, when was the last time you fished?"

Dan sipped his whiskey and began.

"On a river even bigger than this one, in another part of the country—it's a good while back, I suppose, as calendars go—but that day and that stretch of river are as vivid as if it were yesterday . . ."

A gleam or reflected fire from one of Black Maria's facets twinkled in the darkness as if the river-water of that memorable day had not yet dried. Dan continued.

"This river was known among us for the size and savagery of its trout, both rainbows and browns. It was, and perhaps still is, one of the most unique streams in the entire country because, regardless of its size, the trout, even the largest, would take a fly, and, happily for some of us, even a dry fly.

"I had decided to fish a reach of this river that had become famous on two counts. Just two pools above the one I selected, that great angling clergyman, Henry Van Dyke, had taken a seven-pound brown trout on a dry fly. The other concerned another, even greater trout, which had by now become a legend. He had broken many a startled fly fisher on a beat that extended well over a mile of river; and on more than one occasion, the savagery of his strike and the overwhelming strength and swiftness of the plunges that followed splintered the rods of men who, however experienced, had never known anything like it, and were left pretty badly shaken.

"By now this trout had been named Ulysses, because, like his ancient namesake, he was apt to turn up anywhere. Unlike other big trout, he was not content with being the boss of one or two of those huge pools. He was like a baron who considered the entire river as his domain. And that it was.

"It was a strange day, overcast, a day in which a fine drizzle seemed to be just barely suspended, falling sporadically and so imperceptibly as to keep me in perpetual doubt as to whether it was actually drizzling or not.

"Now, such overcast days, as you must know, are often productive, even though the scene is not as idyllic as one would wish.

"I waded slowly and very carefully out to a position that would permit me to cast my fly into the current so that, instead of inviting a dragging fly with the usual consequences, I should manage to bring off a number of good drifts.

"As I was settling myself I noticed a tiny whirlpool in the quiet water to one side of the edge of the current. I don't recall flies in any number in the air at the time, and so I was not too hopeful of interesting this fish with a dry fly, which, as you all know, is the only method that interests me.

"It was the time of the year which is probably the richest for trout in point of variety, size, and number of hatching flies: the Grey Fox was still show-ing, the Light Cahills had been coming in droves, the Dun Variant and Cream Variant were prevalent, as were any number of smaller mayflies and caddis, some peculiar to this river. Hoping it might be an inspired guess, I selected a large, number ten Multicolored Variant and tied it carefully to a leader point that was none too fine—actually a good bit coarser than usual.

"As I lengthened my false casts the little whirlpool appeared again. Aware now of a certain rhythm in that trout's feeding, I kept false casting to one side until it seemed about right to present the fly. It landed gently, a little to the side in the quieter water, and as it went by him, the fly, for some reason, did a pretty, slightly flirtatious little turn. As it did so, the water bulged, the fly disappeared, and I struck smartly, doing so against a force as unyielding as a log.

"The pool at that point was very deep, owing, I suppose, to the exten-sive watershed of that river and the powerful gouging of spring floods. The leader sank slowly out of sight, followed by a surprising footage of the line it-self: the sinking movement stopped, leaving the arched and quivering rod and tense line pointing to the inert force beneath.

"As I began to recover from my astonishment I realized that this trout—if, indeed, it was a trout—was sulking at the bottom like salmon often do, and it occurred to me to try a device used by salmon men for stirring up a sulking fish. I began tapping on the butt of the rod. It took a fair number of strong taps and, sure enough, I saw that the tension was easing on the rod. As the fish rose he began circling to my right in the quiet water and began to head downstream.

"As the line passed me, cutting the water with slow majesty, I caught a glimpse of a huge shadow going by. Now, I may have reacted in some way and the fish must have seen me because he made a sudden lunge and began to swim downstream, gathering speed. The end of the line now flicked through the guides and the backing began streaking out, dwindling ominously on the reel, which was screeching away like a pack of hysterical bluejays. At once, a hundred or so yards below, the current unfolded, the huge form of the fish broke water, fell with a sickening splash and plunged on.

"For a moment I dared to hope that some quirk or, perhaps, its hom-ing instinct would prompt the fish to turn upstream or into the slack water, but—and I knew it now—this was Ulysses, who, for all I knew, might be heading for the ocean."

At this point Dan's throat must have felt pretty dry because he stopped to take two sips of whiskey. Then he went on.

"Now, as I saw the backing melt away, I thought, 'Danny Boy, here is where we get off the train.' There was a sudden jolt, the line went taut as a fiddle-string for a split second and fell limp on the water."

It was a solemn moment for all of us listening there, one that called for a general sip, in salutation and mourning at once. But the story had not yet been told.

"Apparently," said Dan, "when he got to the end of the backing, the resistance at the breaking of the leader must have set the hook deeper and maybe hit a nerve or something. Stupefied, holding the inert rod trailing some two hundred yards of limp line and backing, I saw Ulysses jump clear of the water some three times, going even faster, if you can imagine it—and when he got to where the river turned sharply south he was going so fast that he didn't—he couldn't—"

"Dan! You mean . . ."

"Yes." Dan nodded solemnly.

"Good Lord, Dan! You mean he couldn't—make the curve?"

In those days the world was as young as the fledgling fly fishers sitting about the campfire we had erected for Dan. Now, even the crackling of the flames had submitted to the persuasive drone bass of the patriarch's voice. In the distance, well beyond the campfire circle, I could hear that great fish flopping heavily on that distant, gravelly beach, his powerful tail thrashing helplessly against the useless air. Or was it actually the current in the dark river below slapping against a boulder?

"Dan, did you go after him?"

"Well," said Dan, "it had all happened so quick that when I saw him down there, flopping like a frenzied seal, nothing much registered for a while. As I came to and began thinking about it he'd made his way back into the water. I can still see the waves he made as he tore into the shallows; and that big dorsal—like a flag, as he sank out of sight."

The fire had now settled, barely flickering over the glowing coals, when from its very middle there came a sudden upsurge of flame, followed by a puff of smoke that spread and soared towards the stars. In the silence I marveled. Could it have been Dan's phoenix, after all? Who knows?

Gallatin River

BY JOHN HOLT

Really talented writers, a rank John Holt holds with distinction, just will not be pi-geonholed, stuffed into a certain category and ordered to stay there. Just when you take a peek at the bookshelves and see John's name associated with definitive guidebooks to trout-fishing destinations, he pulls out his prose bag of tricks and starts dealing out col-orful language and engaging tales about fishing his favorite streams.

Holt's books are always entertaining as well as informative, and one of the most lively is Knee Deep in Montana's Trout Streams, *from which this selection is taken. Gallatin veterans will probably not think of that beautiful little river as a "big fish" stream, but Holt finds it can live up to that distinction by going to one of the late Charlie Brooks's nymphing techniques.*

John Holt is a dangerous man for me. Every time I read his stuff, I end up itching to call an airline and start uttering the magic words: Bozeman, Montana.

T he Royal Coachman was taking an awful beating on that special day of my dimming past. If the pattern was actually a living thing, you would feel sorry for it, but since it was nothing more than a twisted melange of feathers and thread, there was no need for sym-pathy in this particular situation.

The experience exploded on one of those July afternoons that Mon-tana travel brochures brag about. Temperatures in the eighties, a little bit of breeze pushing some white, fluffy cumulus clouds across the Gallatin Valley, and rainbow trout on every cast.

Drag-free floats. Bellied-up-in-the-current floats. Dragged-under-the-surface-and-drowned-like-a-rat floats. The fish couldn't care less; they were hitting anything that moved past their holding spots behind midstream boulders, tight against grassy banks, and out in the wide-open riffles. The Gal-latin River here above its junction with the Taylor Fork was maybe fifty feet wide and could be waded if some caution were exercised. In the bright midday light you could see the trout holding steady all over, just above the colorful gravel and rock streambed. The rainbows averaged ten inches, and a couple of sprightly little devils hit the fourteen-inch mark, but size was not a consideration. Playing the energetic trout on a light cane rod, watching their miniature leaps, and feeling their determined runs across the current—that was more than enough and remains so to this day.

I'll never forget that outing, my first on a Montana trout stream. It was almost twenty-five years ago, and I was just a teenage Bozo from Illinois out in the "Wild West." I didn't know much of anything about the state, and this ignorance was not a point of concern in my young, naive existence.

My life was changed forever and for the better that day. I realized that although chasing girls and a good time was the main point of high school, casting flies to trout offered charms and a disarming honesty of a unique, uncompromising nature. Women's ways are still confusing, especially those of my wife and daughters, but the fascination with trout remains a full-blown curiosity. I understand that this is somewhat pathetic, but every time I think of the Gallatin I get a feeling in my stomach that reminds me of a crush I once had in sixth grade on a little blond sweetie. Talk about layered emotion.

This fly fishing business has proved itself to be weird, powerful stuff. And the Gallatin River's attraction is such that I manage to make the 600 mile-plus round trip from the state's northwest corner to the valley (south of Bozeman) at least once a year. And except when heavy rains have muddied the Taylor Fork and the water in the river below or when my timing is off and I hit the stream during spring runoff, the fishing is always as rewarding as on that first riotous afternoon.

To hell with Tom Wolfe and his sorry routine about not being able to go home again. Every time I see the river, step into it, and cast a line out over it, time vanishes and I'm a kid again. I'm free, with no worries and no responsibilities. No other river I've ever fished has the power to work this transformation so completely. After a day here, I have real trouble pulling myself back into accepted reality. No river has ever given me more.

Trout hunting on the Gallatin can be somewhat better than quite good, as one fish and game study of the late 1980s on a lower section of water indicated. There were almost 800 trout per mile over eleven inches, many of them rainbows of around one foot and a number of browns in the pounds region. I've heard reports suggesting that the browns may on very rare occasions exceed ten pounds and that there are over 100 brown trout per mile in the lower sections. In the water I'm familiar with, browns are fewer in number, but I've caught a few that weighed more than three pounds.

The Gallatin has a number of different stretches, but the ones I know a little bit about are from the Taylor Fork down to Big Sky and from the Taylor Fork twisting up into the river's mountainous headwaters in Yellowstone National Park (some refer to this portion as the West Gallatin River, an unnecessary affectation that will not be acknowledged here). There's good water—the big brown trout type—below these two sections, and sometimes a landowner will let a person fish the river below Gallatin Canyon and not too far from scenic, uptown Bozeman. The parts I like, though more remote, are accessible to the common man from either road or trail.

Fishing this water has the virtues of simplicity and/or complexity, with the choice up to the angler and his level of trouting skill and personal preference on any given day. If you want to take things easy, tie on a dry line like the Coachman and work the obvious pocket water and riffles. If you are in an aggressive mood and feel up to some challenging work, put on a short, stout leader at the end of a full-tilt, quick-sinking line and a large nymph like Charles Brooks's Assam Dragon and probe the depths of some racy, deep run. Hard work often pays off in big, hard fish. The choice is yours.

When I started fishing the river I always went the first route. It was just a blast being able to catch a bunch of rainbows on dries with no more complications than finding a place to pull off U.S. Highway 191 and rig up. After chasing the noble carp (a species I truly do respect, but that's the makings of another fantasy) for so many years in the warm, turbid, and very polluted waters of southern Wisconsin, tying into trout with such ease was something too pleasant to resist.

But times have changed. Ten years back, 90 percent of my fishing was with dries, but today that 90 percent is spent beneath the water's surface manipulating, sometimes with the illusion of competency, nymphs, streamers, and wet fly patterns. This nonpurist transformation began when I first read Charles Brooks's *Nymph Fishing for Larger Trout*. This approach opened the door to a new range of unrealistic expectations. Being fooled by twelve-inch fish is a source of endless fascination, but there are times when measuring successful disappointments in increments of pounds rather than inches offers curious and fulfilling amusement. Many fly fishers who are extremely skilled with the dry fly scornfully refer to these methods as bait fishing. I find that unless the conditions are just right—dumb fish, obvious hatch, easy-to-read current—I rarely take many large trout on dries anymore. On the other hand, with nymphs I consistently catch trout over two pounds. I like touching fish that have a size and heft to them that is not commonly associated with their twelve-inch brethren. So much for salmonid polemics.

There is a nice, glassy run right by the highway and just up from the Taylor's Fork that always holds some entertaining rainbows. To fish this piece of turf properly you must cross well above it so that you cast into the water from just short of midstream. There are slightly frightening overtones attendant with this location, especially in the gathering gloom of dusk, as you are standing in fast water well over your knees right next to very fast water over your shoulders. Fall here and you'll stay wet for a long time.

With a six- or seven-weight sinking line, a four- or five-foot leader tapering to a delicate leader in 1X or 0X, the Assam Dragon #4 or Montana Stone #2, a lead twist-on or two (extremely delicate angling is going on here), and a nine-foot rod, the angler begins his exploration of the arcane. Actually this is not as awkward or difficult as it may seem, and the technique works very well on all similar water in the Gallatin and throughout Montana. Semi-master (that's as far as I've progressed) this routine and you'll take big fish on any river.

Starting at the head of the run, cast the contraption about twenty feet upstream, allowing it to sink to the bottom, and work right through the run. Keep the slightest bit of slack in the line, but not so much that you can't feel, see, and sense (this comes rapidly with experience) the nymph bouncing along the gravel and rounded rocks of the streambed. This is where the trout are holding in the benthic or slower water that is created by the size of the obstructions and the drag of the bottom. It is the only place that is calorically efficient for big trout to hold. Anywhere else and the energy expended to maintain a holding position in the current would outweigh any potential gain from a stream of aquatic insects whizzing by.

Many so-called authorities adamantly suggest that you strike at any deviance in the movement of the nymph through its down-deep journey. I disagree. When a good trout hits it will be a vicious strike as the fish zips up after the food and then powers straight back to cover. You'll know when it happens. The rod tip will often be jerked into the water. Sure, a few fish are missed, but many more are taken simply because each cast is fished more thoroughly.

At the end of the drift, allow the fly to swing in the current for a few seconds, the time needed to take out the belly that accumulated in the cast as it was fighting the many conflicting currents in the water column. On occasion a big boy will hammer the fly at this time, an enlightening experience that normally comes while I'm staring at a rock cliff or off into space with out-of-focus visions of the golden age of the Woodstock generation staggering through my head.

If you are right-handed and the current is moving from left to right, making the next cast is not difficult. Just strip in the line with your left hand

and lift the rod simultaneously with your right. Flip the works back upstream. It will look a little like attempting a hook shot in basketball. Basically, you are making a single haul of short dimensions.

When the current is moving from right to left, each cast is a reverse effort and made backhand, which would seem to be more difficult but is not. With a little practice, the cast can be made with consistent accuracy. The only difference seems to be that the nymph tends to land a little farther out and away from you.

Brooks suggests repeating this move many times, but a half-dozen efforts is my limit before lengthening the cast a few feet and repeating the procedure. After thirty-five feet of line is out, things take on dangerous overtones with lead and hooks flying all over the place, frequently into the back of my head. Time to move downstream a couple of yards and try again.

The first fish I took here using this method was on the Dragon and was just short of two feet. It was my first BIG trout. Up to that moment I had had little confidence in Brooks's teachings because I had taken only a fish or two—which I attributed to persistence and a casual conjunction with good fortune (qualities I've learned that most good fly fishers have in abundance). Right in the middle of the hundredth drift of the day, the line stopped dead in a current that was well over ten miles an hour. Convinced I was hung up on the bottom I yanked hard in an upward direction. The line razored upstream instantly, cutting through the dark green water, and seconds later a very large, upset rainbow rocketed above the surface heading for the moon. The sound that that fish made when it smacked back into the water was a big fish noise. No other words describe the sensation. When you hear the energy and power of that sound you're addicted. It's like lusting (well, maybe just hoping) for the scream of a reel as line disappears on a big run.

There were three more leaps and crashes and then a serious session holding dead still at the bottom just above the run. Fearing for the tippet's life, I gave the fish gentle treatment, but holding in the fast water tired him. After one quick burst upstream, without leaping, he was led to the net.

A friend of mine once observed that whenever a good trout is close at hand everyone says "Nice fish!" He's right, and I'm afraid that's all I could think to say to this specimen. "Nice fish!" That is what nymphing on the Gallatin can do for a person: put him into sizeable trout with a fair degree of consistency.

Some years ago when I still believed that backpacking possessed some redeeming values, a couple of friends and I strolled up the drainage to Gallatin Lake, which rests quietly at 8,834 feet. We got a late start and managed only three or four miles upstream, but we didn't care as we passed through splendid green hills of native grasses and sagebrush. Pine forest wandered up and away on all sides. Here and there in likely looking pools we cast Royal Wulffs and Adamses and took small rainbows of about eight inches. Enough, maybe six or seven, were kept for dinner.

We set up camp in a grassy meadow near a copse of aspen perhaps 100 yards from the river, which ran smoothly through this gentle stage of the valley. The Gallatin was not more than twenty-five feet wide here, and two of us took a couple more trout for sport while our companion, who liked to cook, started a small fire of downed and dry aspen twigs and sticks. (This was back when you were still supposed to be having a good time out in the country and a slightly smoking, crackling fire was an integral part of that scenario. I have had a gas stove for nearly twenty years that I've never used. When I camp I build a fire of wood or have a cold camp.)

At any rate, when we returned to camp, dinner was ready. The trout, mushroom soup, and fried potatoes tasted great. The evening was calm and the light was taking on an orange glow as we all just relaxed to our own rhythms and incoherencies—that is, until a large bull moose appeared with the obvious intention of passing directly through our campsite to the river to dine graciously on green grasses and sip delicately of the pure waters found there.

We'd made an error in location, and the moose, a species that has caused me more trouble than any grizzly, snorted and appeared ready to kill us. There was not a lot we could do, so we ran like hell into the trees, which proved to be a wise decision. The animal's rack was too wide to permit him access to our sanctuary. The moose went on down to the Gallatin and ate his fill. The sight of him slurping the grass and water while standing in the stream is still clear in my mind.

His repast took about two months, and then he came back through camp, stopping to look us over with alien appraisal (actually we were the foreigners here) before disappearing over a distant hill. We did not sleep well that night and were up and on the trail before dawn.

The path took us through dark forest and then across a meadow covered with wildflowers in reds, blues, whites, and yellows. A small herd of elk spotted us and bounded quickly away into the pines. We stopped for lunch. I set out on a brief walk that ended abruptly when I saw recent bear tracks in a snowbank and mud. The ones in the mud were much wider than my extended fingers and still filling with water. After informing my companions of this gentle discovery, we did what we normally do in situations bordering on complicated—we panicked and scrambled up the trail as fast as we could for as long as we could, pans, bottles, and cans of fruit cocktail clanging away in the mountain air. Two hundred yards later, nearly dead from the effort, we collapsed by the Gallatin River, now turned mountain stream. We were thirsty, and the ice-cold water tasted good. Our fear added some spice to the adventure. The bear failed to make an appearance.

Several hours of hiking brought us to open parkland beneath wild, snow-covered peaks. According to our map, Gallatin Lake was just half a mile ahead. And from what the honest-looking person at the fly shop in West Yellowstone had told us, every cast should yield a monster trout. Suspicion was already growing, because this person had also informed us that the trip into the lake was only an hour's walk that he and his family, including two toddlers, made each Sunday. We'd already invested five hours, but we figured that being out of shape and carrying heavy backpacks were adding to our journey's length.

The next day we started off with our rods but were soon slogging through waste-deep snow as a warm July sun baked our brains. Two hours later we were at the lake. It was very pretty, but we could see that the fishing was going to be somewhat difficult. Gallatin Lake was frozen solid. We'd been had by a fun-loving West Yellowstone local. The three of us had invested more time, effort, and money on fruitless endeavors in the past, however, so we were not upset—which could not be said for the person in the fly shop when we returned and dragged him halfway across a glass display case offering severely over-priced fly reels. He threatened to call the cops so we left town without even visiting Dinosaur Land or buying any Montana copper jewelry.

A couple of winters ago, while browsing through Steve Pierce's informative book, *The Lakes of Yellowstone,* I learned that Gallatin Lake was 19.5 acres with a maximum depth of forty-seven feet and was fishless. There are some very funny people in West Yellowstone, I guess.

Several times recently I've fished the meandering, somewhat wild-looking portions of the river that are accessible from the highway, as well as the lower parts we encountered on the ill-fated hike. I have always taken a number of rainbows (and a few whitefish) on dries and nymphs. Never has a fish been bigger than fourteen inches, but the effort has always been rewarding: relatively easy fishing in very nice country.

Some years back, when my family and I (they let me travel with them in odd-numbered years) were staying at a local dude ranch in the valley, my stepbrother and I fished under the guidance of an individual named Yellowstone Jack. The guy knew the water and knew how to take trout, but he was not prepared to deal with a sibling rivalry that has spanned decades and is at once timeless.

Yellowstone Jack helped us rig up and sent us on our way upstream at different points along the Gallatin. The fishing was good, and my stepbrother and I began catching rainbows immediately and with regularity, and we both became keyed into how the other was doing. This soon degenerated into tag-team fly fishing, with rapid casts to each piece of holding water, a quick set of the hook, and even quicker sliding of the hapless trout to eager fingers for a quick release. Then it was on again up to the next hole splashing and crashing as, I'm sure, frightened hordes of salmonids fled for their very lives before our mad charges.

This activity continued for a couple of hours (and no doubt rendered that stretch of the river worthless for several weeks). Returning to the beginning, we found Yellowstone Jack sitting on the tailgate of the pickup truck. I think "sardonic" aptly describes his facial set and attitude.

"You fellers fish like that back east?"

"What do you mean?" we replied, more or less trying to feign ignorance of our obviously boorish behavior.

"Let me phrase things this way," said Yellowstone Jack slowly. "That was the biggest load of bullshit I've ever seen on a river around here and I've seen a lot of it in my time."

Well, we felt pretty sorry after that, and ever since I've tried to behave myself on a trout stream. Yellowstone Jack's scorn was perhaps the best lesson (and the toughest to accept) I've learned on the Gallatin.

My fishing here pretty much mirrors my experiences elsewhere. There have been successes, fine times, mistakes, and slight humiliations. A steady learning curve that has applied to more than chasing trout.

The river is always changing, and each visit has its own unique set of variables. Once in November when the sky cleared and the temperature hit the seventies there were whitefish everywhere and not a rainbow to be found. It was a day when the water was moving perfectly clear and blue across the colorful rocks and I started believing that maybe this would be the one all-time magic year when winter would never come . . . and I knew all the time that the feeling was just good old-fashioned Gallatin River voodoo. And that, of course, was why I was there in the first place.

How to Catch Trout

BY CHARLES F. WATERMAN

A regular in the distinguished Gray's Sporting Journal, *Charlie Waterman has been writing great pieces for so long that I am constantly amazed at his staying power. Most word-slingers I read who meet regular deadlines sometimes go into a sort of slump. You can't hit a homer ever time up, right?*

Not Waterman. I finish every Waterman story with the feeling, "Man, I'm glad I didn't miss that one."

This essay from Gray's *February/March, 1999, issue gives Charlie a chance to deliver a little poke into the ribs of those who at times take their trouting a little too seriously. Even the editors at* Gray's *got in on the fun of this one. They presented the piece with the blurb, "A chainsaw runs through it and other socially suspect fly fishing adventures."*

I have fished for trout for quite a while, and I feel that seniority is an important qualification in this field, possibly substituting to some extent for Latin insect names and references to famous angling authors, many of whom use long words.

I have a lot of books on fly fishing for trout, the shelf being several feet long. There are only a couple I don't understand, although most of them slow me up here and there with the entomology part. I am not rebelling against technical angling, just telling of some triumphs and failures that did not involve scientific research. For example, there were the trout that kept running into my legs—things like that.

The rainbows that ran into my waders were not backcountry rubes. They lived in a gently flowing spring creek that qualified as a "technical" habitat and carried a great deal of vegetation, most of which waved decoratively in the current. When there was a hatch of mayflies the fish would form pods of feeders, and if you waded daintily, didn't fall down in three feet of water, worked upstream and cast a long leader with a 6X tippet or smaller, you could catch some pretty good trout. As you moved upstream you would cause feeding pods to scatter, and then you'd go a little farther upstream to another bunch. It was the second season fishing there before I realized they were the same fish that had just moved upstream to new stations—for me, a scientific breakthrough.

Let's repeat that these were spooky rainbows and some browns that would go out of business in a hurry if anyone with large feet walked within 50 feet of the shoreline on dry, grassy land. If you hooked a fish near the center of a feeding bunch you might put the whole squad into wild flight; some of those ultrasmart thinkers would dart downstream, and some of those would run into my waders. It has always puzzled me that a fish that carefully chose size-18 flies over the slightly bushier 16s could not go downstream in a 60-foot-wide creek without ramming into a pair of dark waders in three feet of clear water.

I have concluded that trout selectivity works in many directions and am a firm believer in the "stranger" theory as an important phase of technical trout fishing. The theory, of course, is that perceptive trout, having become bored with their everyday diet, however desirable it may be, sometimes prefer something a great deal different.

At best, introduction of a "stranger" fly generally comes after serious effort at imitating something the fish are taking. Standing in a stream that was basically a little too scientific for my tactics, I once watched several thousand mayflies sliding down a narrow run—enough so that they seemed to color the whole stream; I am tempted to say they formed a yellowish "blanket" for the creek, but that description has been used before. Anyway, they were so well matched by a size-18 Light Cahill that I managed to drift one down that run 40 or 50 times, and except for several sloppy casts it seemed to match the naturals perfectly. The fish were almost wallowing in natural flies, and since I couldn't be sure which insect was mine I may have failed to set the hook after a take or two—but who knows?

Anyway, I put on a big, nameless fuzzy thing that looked like a bundle of trash from under a fly-tier's bench, tossed it out, and there was a big silent bulge by an old log over against the bank 20 feet away. A surface vee moved toward the run where all the action was going on, and the risers seemed to form a corridor; at this point you may insert your favorite prose of a trophy-brown-trout fight.

I am a little sorry about this as there has been a long list of articles featuring freak flies and big trout, but then this one happened to me. The stranger approach certainly isn't new, but that stranger was much stranger than usual, a triumph of coarse reasoning over science and delicacy.

I have learned not to be smart-alecky when a coarse method proves more successful than an aesthetic approach, but there are some triumphs that had best be kept quiet—like the time my wife caught a large spring-creek trout on a 6X tippet and a size-18 dry fly.

It was dusk and almost night when Debie carefully worked the shallow tail of a pool and set the hook in something solid after a slurping take. I watched from a distance and thought of the tendrils of interfering water growth that would have shown plainly in better light. Debie had stepped out of the water and stood on an undercut bank, and for some reason she had no net. The hook came out just as the fish headed for the undercut, and Debie plopped down on her stomach and stuck an arm back in there, grabbing a brown trout that weighed slightly less than four pounds.

I don't know if that constitutes a legitimate catch, and I guess it should have been kept secret, but I blabbed it in print and received a stiff-necked insult from a man who believed in tradition and said that not even he could catch a big trout under such circumstances and that he was sure this woman business was a fairy tale. He dropped some famous fly fishing names for emphasis.

As it happened, very famous Joe and Mary Brooks witnessed the amphibious operation, so I reported that and heard no more from the traditionalist, but I have been told to lay off that type of story even if it's true. My wife explained she could do without that kind of publicity.

I began my skimpy Atlantic salmon fishing late in life with a boxful of traditional and expensive salmon flies chosen for me by a man who knew about salmon and salmon tradition. I took the flies to Newfoundland, where they were observed with awe by a canoe-poling, fly-tying guide who said his homemade flies had no name and were very crude.

After several days during which I raised not a single fish, even after I had humbly clutched some of the guide's flies, I noted that he unobtrusively caught salmon regularly and was truly sorry for me. He simply could not make me do it. I later realized I was not really that bad a salmon fisherman but that I was having a period of pretty bad luck.

On my last day, while I was casting unproductively over a pool full of unresponsive salmon, the wind came up and blew a good-size twig from a nearby tree. As it struck the water it was taken immediately by a burly salmon. I have never discussed this with salmon experts and don't intend to. I refuse to describe the tree in detail. On that day I had tried nearly all my ornate flies with the traditional names.

There are certain trout streams so technical that they are subjects of hushed discussion by serious anglers and generally require special flies and approaches. I had heard of Pennsylvania's Letort for a long time before I visited it, and when I finally got there I had the feeling better fishermen might be watching me from the bushes. I began my day in a spot where I could tell some good-size fish were working in clumps of vegetation, but I got no response through two or three fly changes. I was wading fairly deep—up around my waist—and was a little startled by a splash a few inches from my right elbow. While I was watching the spot, a rainbow trout appeared, made a splashy strike and sank again.

In a sort of parody of fly-casting, I took an unusual grip on my rod and somehow got my fly to strike the water a few inches from where my elbow had been. The rainbow came up and took it with a sloppy glub, put up a pretty good fight and accepted release calmly. I had the idiotic thought that the fish was a resident aid for confused visitors.

But that isn't all of the Letort story. I saw a pair of two-pound brown trout swimming upstream at moderate speed in tandem formation. Within a few minutes, two more fish of about the same size came by on the same route, and that procedure continued all day. I reported it to a Letort regular, who changed the subject then walked away. He did not want to hear details of twenty-some two-pound trout acting that way in hallowed waters. There were never three trout—always two.

Trout on "technical" streams establish forms of behavior accepted by technical anglers, and major changes in their operations are viewed with displeasure or ignored. I think of a good friend who ties beautiful flies, can call forth Latin names on demand and does a lot of watching while he fishes. He ruefully tells how he received chilly treatment on a technical Eastern stream, which he attended as guest of a pair of regulars.

Before the trip he had studied the insects to be expected, was told just what hatches might occur on the chosen day and was careful not to express opinions. He caught a lot of trout and was treated coolly on the way home as the regulars hadn't done too well.

"I flushed some grasshoppers on the way to the creek," he said, "and I used some big hopper flies. The fish were taking them instead of the tiny stuff. But I didn't learn anything, and I may not get invited back."

Some of the most delicate fine-tippet anglers are willing to change tactics. Harry Murray, who is famous as a delicate operator, has written of it and evidently prefers it. But as it grew dark on highly technical Nelson's Spring Creek in Montana one fall, he heard some violent splashing that demanded a special approach. Harry submitted a big hair bass bug, and the result was what you expect in a fishing story.

"But I broke him off anyway," Harry said.

Only partly a rebel. He hadn't changed from his fine tippet.

When fly rods began to probe salt water they were greeted as something new by those who thought of fly fishing and delicacy at the same time. But, of course, Atlantic salmon fishermen had been using big two-handed rods on big fish for a long time. The casting and fly manipulation were very important, but in the matter of playing fish there have been quite a few discussions as to just what is fair.

There was the lady angler on a big Canadian river who became attached to a really big steelhead that did the usual steelhead rough stuff with her leader and then, as it began to tire, did what heavy fish in heavy current tend to do: It began to go downstream with the lady following on the rocky, brushy and uneven bank. There has been some discussion of the matter because a burly, wool-shirted type appeared with a chainsaw and trimmed the landscape noisily, rapidly and efficiently ahead of the lady angler, backwoods Canadian types being noted for finding their way around with chainsaws. There have been complaints that alteration of a landscape is not in keeping with the spirit of fish playing, but chainsaws are not mentioned in the rules for angling contests. For lack of a chainsaw, I nearly drowned while attached to a stubborn steelie in a treetop while a very loud river muffled my screams for help that never came. At the time I was unconcerned with fish-playing ethics.

I didn't ponder the ethics of fish fighting when I found myself in a hurrying but fairly smooth section of British Columbia's Kispiox and felt a stubborn steelhead that didn't hurry but seemed to be in charge of the operation. It refused to jump, and when it finally seemed to be barely holding against the current I noticed that where it was holding was above a steeply slanting rapids largely filled with a tangle of uprooted trees.

Since it was obvious that any fish that got into this would be on his own very shortly, I suspended my fading dignity and screamed for help. A shouldery angler named Sam responded (no chainsaw) and went hand-over-hand through the trees and roaring near-waterfall until he reached the logical gap for an escaping fish. With the energy and tactics of a hockey goalie, Sam blocked the escape route, shipping only a little water into his waders and digging his cleats into bottom, brush and anything else available. I think of the World War I motto of the French: "They shall not pass!"

The steelhead did not pass Sam, holding just above him until it tired a little more and could be swung toward shore, where it was landed. It weighed more than 27 pounds, and I was only slightly disturbed by the expressed opinion of a top-notch lady steelhead angler who disapproved of fly rods and had observed the performance.

"It never jumped. It must have been sick," she said.

Rules of angling fair chase do not mention Sam or chainsaws. You run into such things when you get really technical.

An old-timer once told me that really big trout are caught only under freakish circumstances when rules of delicacy are violated. There was almost that situation once in South Dakota. I stalked a gentle stream near dusk and was completely unable to figure what the gently rising fish were taking. I tried all of the tiny stuff and then resorted to a loud and bushy "stranger," which didn't work either. Then I stumbled onto a deep, quiet pool with a huge rock above it that served nicely as an observatory. From here I could look almost straight down and see a bunch of really big rainbows that seemed to be feeding on some sort of nymph.

Then one of the biggest fish began to act strangely on the bottom and seemed to be in serious trouble until he disgorged my huge, bushy stranger, which I had left floating on the surface and forgotten.

Fishing reputations can be made in rather unusual circumstances. I was once invited to fish a very private stream noted for highly selective trout, and although I accepted with enthusiasm I had a mild case of the apprehensions, as invitations to such waters often cause me to appear even sloppier than I am while the native experts catch fish with proper aplomb.

This time they showed me the fly that was working, and they promised that a hatch of it would undoubtedly start within a few minutes, which it did. I was stationed some 50 yards from any other caster, and for the first time in an erratic trout career I found a tightly concentrated hatch taking place about 20 feet from me and confined to an area about 10 feet across. I don't know what could concentrate nymphs like that, but it went on and on.

After catching an unreasonable number of trout I shouted that I was in the hot spot and would like to relinquish it to somebody else, but no one accepted my invitation, the others obviously feeling that since a few flies were hatching all along the run I was obviously exhibiting superior skills instead of standing next to an unreasonable concentration of flies and fish.

Should I have explained that?

The Hat Trick

BY JOE BROOKS

When Joe Brooks wrote this stirring big-trout encounter in the 1950s, his name was already legendary among angling readers. But back then the Argentine pampas and bocas were new settings for fishing stories, known only to a few intrepid fly fishers and writers. Today Joe Brooks is gone, and the names Argentina, Chile and Patagonia are popular, commonplace fishing destinations that frequent the dreams and travel plans of countless anglers eager to experience something of the exploits they have read about by writers like Brooks, Schwiebert, and Haig-Brown.

Although I never had the opportunity to meet Joe Brooks, I have been told that he was the ultimate gentleman and sportsman, a description that certainly confirms the impression I get by reading his works. Joe Brooks writes with a sense of generous sharing, with action and detail so vivid they seem as if I am hearing about something that happened last week. Even when the tale is almost a half-century old, as is this one, Brooks' stories brought many North American anglers their first descriptions of the possibilities that awaited them on the streams at the bottom of the globe.

I opened my eyes and looked out of the car window at a perfectly formed peak sticking up into the sky, its top covered with snow and ice. We were in the foothills, and if I hadn't known otherwise, it could have been Colorado, Wyoming, or Montana. The desert-like vegetation of the Argentine pampas, through which we had been driving when I fell asleep, had changed to a thick, yellow-topped thorn. And there was lots of sagebrush.

During the night we had rolled along in a cloud of dust, the headlights now and then picking out a short-eared Patagonian hare, or the black-masked vizcacha that looks like a cross between a raccoon and a possum. Now, just at dawn, we flushed a Patagonian rhea, a variety of ostrich. With its ungainly three-foot-long neck held high, it went dashing over the slope above the road.

"They're smaller than the African ostrich," said Bebe. "The gauchos eat the eggs. Wings, too."

We saw a group of the wild-looking gauchos by the roadside soon after that. They sat comfortably on their sturdy horses, saddles padded with cojincillos of soft sheepskin. They were almost completely covered with ponchos made of vicuna wool. A gaucho can practically live under his poncho and keep warm even in coldest weather.

Each of these picturesque Argentine cowboys carried his bola wrapped around his waist. It consists of three woven thongs, each ending in a skin-covered lead ball. Holding one ball in his hand, a gaucho can whirl the other two balls around his head, and toss the bola at terrific speed. It will entangle a steer's legs and drop him. Bola-throwing gauchos are just as expert at snagging an ostrich.

Jorge, who was driving, looked back. "There's Lanin," he said.

"That mountain?" I asked.

He nodded. "You'll be looking at it a lot during the next two weeks. That mountain range in the distance is the Cordillera de los Andes It runs all the way from Panama clear down to the tip of Tierra del Fuego. Some of those peaks are more than 20,000 feet high, but the Lanin, which is the important one to us, is lower, about 12,500."

"Why is the Lanin so important?" I asked. "Is it a volcano?"

"An extinct one," he said. "But see that little cloud sitting right on the top, like a hat? When Lanin has his hat on, the wind will blow, and fishing will be good."

"No hat, no hits," said Bebe. "Today he has his hat on."

"It's because the rivers are so clear," Jorge continued. "You can see the pebbles on the bottom at 20 feet. So the best fishing is when it's windy, cloudy, or even raining. When it's bright you may as well take a siesta. The fish just won't hit then."

I looked at the Lanin and hoped he'd keep that hat on. But at the same time I had mental reservations about staying in siesta even on the brightest afternoon, not after travelling 6,000 miles to fish for the big Argentine trout Jorge had told me were here.

I had met Jorge Donovan in a tackle store in New York, and like all fishermen we started comparing notes. My home is in Florida, and I told Jorge about taking bonefish on flies. Within a week we met in Florida, and in a couple of days he'd landed a 7½-pounder and an 8-pounder.

"Wonderful!" he said. "But now you must come to Argentina and I will show you big browns and rainbows that will break you up. In some of the lakes, trolling, they get 30-pounders. But we'll stick to the rivers, because that's what we both like, and you'll get the biggest trout you ever caught."

And that's how it came about that I hopped a Pan American World Airways plane in Miami one day in January, and the next day was driving west from Buenos Aires with Jorge Donovan and his friend, Bebe Anchorena, two of Argentina's most enthusiastic fly fishermen. We were headed for the eastern slope of the Andes, where the rivers pour down to the plains from mighty, snow-fed lakes.

As we neared the Junin de los Andes, where we were to stay, we saw some Araucano Indians plodding behind wooden plows pulled by oxen. On the mountain slopes forests of Coihue trees rose as high as 100 feet. I was told that some of them were five feet through at the butt.

It was late afternoon when we reached the Hosteria Chimehuin on the outskirts of Junin de los Andes. It didn't take us long to whip into our fishing clothes, grab our gear and hightail it for the Chimehuin River. There was a good wind blowing when we stopped by the Elbow Pool.

"This is where you start," said Jorge. "There are 8- and 10-pounders in here."

I tied a four-inch-long streamer, a red and yellow combination, on my leader.

"What's that?" asked Bebe. "A feather duster?"

"You said big fish," I said. "And big fish like a big mouthful. Try one."

I handed each of them a similar fly. They looked sceptical but pocketed them and took off downstream.

I waded out to cast, starting with a short line that I lengthened a couple of feet each time until I was throwing about 60 feet. I cast across current and brought the streamer back in slow, foot-long jerks. Each time I'd strip, the feathers closed in on the hook. When I stopped, they flared outward. It made the fly look alive.

I made half a dozen casts. Then I spotted a long, dark shape behind the fly. With dorsal fin clear out of the water, that fish fell on the fly like an avalanche. He left for the tail of the pool so fast that I thought he'd pop his scales. He made the water smoke for 150 feet, then came out in a broadside, going away jump. He splashed back in and headed for some rocks on the far shore. He must have nicked the leader or run it across a sharp rock, because the fly line snapped back at me, minus the big streamer.

I just stood there for a minute. My first strike in this river, and I'd lost a 10-pounder!

I looked up at the Lanin. He had his hat on, sure enough. I tipped mine. "You know your business," I said to him.

A flock of bandurrias came flying my way from across the river. They were big, ibis-like birds, with long, decurved bills, and they greeted me with a series of startled honks that sounded like a bunch of kids blowing ten cent horns. They zoomed over the bank in back of me, flighting in to roost.

It was 8:30. I had another hour before dark, so I tied on another big streamer. On the third cast I had a hit that I felt through my fingers, up my arms, and down to my toenails.

This fish was dynamite. He rushed my way. Then he turned and I struck again, just in case the hook had loosened. That made him mad for fair, and what he'd done before was peanuts. For the next 10 minutes I was withstanding a series of explosions. Then he sulked deep in the current, letting the water hold him there. He was so quiet I began to wonder if he'd wrapped the line around something, or had lodged the hook in a log and left me holding the stream bottom.

I banged the rod with the butt of my hand. That sent shocks down to him and he began to move, slowly at first, then with increasing speed. He didn't like those jolts. I saw the line come up, fast, and he jumped a foot above the surface, looking like a slab of molded bronze. His spots looked as big as saucers.

Ten minutes later I skidded him up on the shore, jumped on him and got a good grip on his gills. Then I rushed him away from the river. I was taking no chances on a wild flop.

I was just putting him on the scales when Jorge walked up. "Nine and a half pounds," I said.

"Mine weighs only seven," said Jorge.

He held up a beautiful seven-pound rainbow he'd had in his hand all the time.

"Get any others?" I asked.

"I put back a couple of six-pound brownies," he answered.

On our way back to the car a bunch of teros gave us a fit. These birds, like the bandurrias, seemed to object to fishermen. They kept yapping at us with shrill, rasping sounds, circling round our heads in a storm of raucous noises. Crows, magpies, jays and other loud-mouthed birds are pikers compared to teros, whose vocal cords must be made of metal.

Bebe showed up at the car with a 7½ pound rainbow. It was beautiful, sleek and silvery, and had given Bebe a terrific battle.

Next morning we had good fishing weather again, which means it was raining. By the time we got to the river the rain had turned to mist, just enough to keep our faces wet. The fish were rising.

I started using dry flies in my pool. They kept me busy for three hours—rainbows and browns from 3 to 6 pounds, and a top fish that went 6¾ pounds. In all, I must have hooked 30 fish in that short time. At noon, Jorge and Bebe came back.

"Seven pounds," said Bebe, holding up a brownie. "He took a streamer."

"An 8-pound rainbow," said Jorge, showing his fish. "On a big streamer, too."

"A 6¾-pound brownie," I announced, and added by way of apology, "but he took a dry, and on a 2-x tippet."

"We'll go back to the hosteria for lunch and a siesta," they told me.

"I'll take the lunch," I said, "but I don't have any plans for a siesta."

Jorge looked at the sky. The clouds were gone, a bright sun beat down. "There won't be any fishing until at least 6 p.m." he said.

I didn't argue, but as soon as they had gone off for their siesta, I headed back to the river. Three days later I'd had enough of siesta-time fishing to convince me that Jorge was right. Those fish wouldn't hit when the sun was shining smack on the pools. It had to be cloudy, windy, or rainy, except for early morning or evening. But when conditions are right, the Chimehuin stacks up against any trout stream in the world.

The Chimehuin (pronounced chim-e-wee-an) flows out of Lake Huechulaufquen (which-u-lof-kin), winds 22 miles down the mountains to the picturesque little town of Junin de los Andes, and finally, after being swelled by two other feeder streams, joins the Colloncura 18 miles below. The entire river lies at a comfortable fishing altitude of about 2500 feet, and all 40 miles of it is loaded with trout. Any pool may have a 12-pounder, maybe one weighing 15 or 20 pounds. In a single day, a fair angler can count on landing several fish in the 7- to 10-pound bracket—and he'll probably lose flies and leaders to a couple larger ones.

It's a big river, with pools over 100 feet across and 600 to 700 feet long. But in most places it's easy to wade, with a gradual slope toward the deep water. Like all rivers, the fish often seem to lie on the far side. A long cast pays off.

While many trout are caught daily on spinning and bait-casting equipment, fly tackle takes more fish because of the lighter presentation of the lure in the extremely clear water. A big streamer or bucktail fished on a fine leader will catch more lunkers than anything else.

All the standard fly patterns in use in the United States—both wet and dry—do well in Argentine waters. Since it's difficult to buy flies in Argentina, you should go armed with a complete supply. The only tyer I encountered was Jose Navas, manager of the Norysur Club on Lake Meliquina. His Matona, a streamer, is one of the best to be had, and his nymphs are also real producers.

Most Argentine anglers use Atlantic salmon flies and standard wets. They catch fish with them, too, but the lunker trout, the real heavyweights, seem to prefer something like a five-inch-long bucktail or streamer.

Partly to handle the big flies, but mostly because of the constant wind, it's best to have a nine-foot fly rod and a matching GAF fly line. On some of the smaller streams, and for dry fly fishing on all the rivers, we used 8½-foot rods with GBF lines. But you'll ordinarily make a lot of roll casts and change-of-direction casts, and be bringing your rod tip down almost to the water to get your flies out in or under the wind. And that's when the bigger rod pays off. It doesn't always blow a gale down there. Perhaps for an hour or two, or even a day or two, you may fish in comparative calm, but I leaned back against the wind for so long that a couple of times I nearly fell backward into the river when there was a sudden lull. Yet it has to blow a lot harder than that to stop a trout fisherman. You soon learn to buy a Basque hat, which stays on, and to thank the wind for producing more strikes.

We had two weeks of unbelievable fishing. We fished the Chimehuin from one end to the other, using everything in our fly boxes—weighted nymphs, hairbodied dry flies, streamers, bucktails with five-inch wings. The fish liked most of what they saw. It was a slow day when there were no 8-pounders. Four- and 5-pounders were routine. The fishing was, as the Argentines say, "fantastico."

One afternoon just before dark I was fishing Elbow Pool when Bebe came rushing up my way. "Give me another of those big flies," he gasped.

I handed him a streamer. He grabbed it and rushed away before I could get out a word. After he disappeared around the bend, I decided I'd better wander down and see what was going on.

Bebe was fishing the pool above the rapids known as Garganta del Diablo, the Devil's Throat. He was casting a long line, retrieving the fly, casting again. You could tell from his actions that he was expecting a hit from a lunker. Then out in midstream something socked his fly and threw up a screen of water that just about blotted out the far shore.

Bebe's line jumped back his way. He examined the fly, muttered to himself, and started casting again. Nothing happened. A few more casts and it was too dark to see. Bebe waded ashore and walked up to me.

"He must have been 25 pounds," he said. "Fantastico!"

It started to snow on the way home that night and it got plenty cold. Fresh from Florida, I was shaking up a fit. I put my sleeping bag over two thick woolen blankets already on my bed. It was February 10, but that's the middle of the Argentine summer, like our August 10. Nevertheless, when I looked out the window the next morning, snow was all over the foothills and the high mountains were packed solid.

We couldn't see the Lanin to get a fishing forecast, as it was still cloudy and spitting snow.

"It will be a good day," said Jorge.

That day each of us took some 6- and 7-pounders and Jorge crashed through with a fine 9¾-pound brownie that liked the looks of a red-and-white streamer. Then, as if by magic, the clouds rolled back and showed a bright blue sky. Business was over until after the siesta period.

About 5 p.m. I was watching Jorge fish the boca. Right away he hooked a rainbow that looked to be 12 or 14 pounds. It smashed the pool into a thousand drops of water. It belly-whopped and jackknifed. It walked on its tail and stood on its head. It was a wildcat on fins. Then it showed us how fast a rainbow can run. For 200 feet it flashed through the water, then came up with another leap. The fished slowed then, and Jorge started following it down-stream, reeling just fast enough to keep on a heavy pressure. He walked faster, got in his backing and some fly line. Then he strained on the rod, turned the fish, and got him coming.

That "tired" rainbow shot toward us, went past a mile a minute, and 20 feet beyond us jumped again, head over caudal, his crimson sides a blaze of glory. But he tired fast after that, and Jorge led him gingerly across the shallows and slid him up on shore. He weighed an even 10 pounds.

After congratulations, I hurried off to start in a pool of my own. I passed Bebe in the Elbow Pool.

"I left the Garganta Pool for you," he said. "It should be good tonight."

As I waded in I looked at the Lanin. He had his hat pulled down over his ears. I made a cast. I had a hit, landed a 6-pounder and released it. I got a 4-pounder and put that back. Both browns. I moved further down.

It was tough casting here because of a high bank in back of me. The pool was 125 feet across where I stood. Seventy feet below me it spilled into the Garganta del Diablo, a quarter of a mile of rocks, boulders, and white water. Any hooked fish that reached that raceway was a goner.

Right in front of me the current slipped along at a neat clip, with only a couple of feet of wadable water before the bottom dropped off abruptly to a six-foot depth. A trout, I reasoned, would lie in front of that protruding rock out there on the rim, or between it and the shore. And right here the shore be-came a rocky ledge that shouldered right into the water. A great flow of cur-rent swept along that ledge and then busted into the white water of the rapids.

"It's a hopeless place to play a trout," I thought. (But it was a perfect lie for a big trout.) "Big fish like a big mouthful." I mumbled to myself as I searched through my fly box. A guy needed something like a five-inch buck-tail, a streamer, or what have you? And suddenly I saw it—a what have you. It was a big gray popping bug with yellow deer-hair tail. I tied it on my 6 pound test tippet, tried the knot and was ready.

"Here's your big mouthful," I said. "Come and get it."

I tossed the backcast high over some bushes behind me and made the forward throw, shooting the line at the same time. The big fly-rod bug hit 60 feet straight out. I let it float quietly, without imparting motion, until it began to swim in toward my bank. Then I stripped in slow, foot-long pulls making bubbles with the bug, but not pops. I wanted to attract trout but not scare them. Nothing happened.

I stripped five more feet of line off the reel and shot the bug out again. This time I jiggled it slightly as it floated. Before it started to swing my way I began to strip, bringing it fast across the tail of the pool, past the protruding rock, along the lip and in toward the ledge. I let it hang a moment directly below me, then started it upstream, without pops, with just a slight gurgle.

Suddenly, a great, wide-open mouth engulfed the bug, and the upper half of the mouth snapped down. As I struck I saw the head and shoulders of a great trout. I felt his strength for a moment; then he dived and I couldn't feel him at all. The line was tight, but there was no movement. I was sure he'd run me around a rock or a log at the submerged base of the cliff.

I began reeling fast as I walked down that way, keeping a tight line, taking no chances. I reached the ledge and my line went straight down. I could see the top of the 12 foot leader. I could also see a black cave under the ledge, about four feet down. If the fish was still on, he was in there. It looked hopeless.

"Well, here goes," I thought, and stuck the nine-foot fly rod as far out over the water as I could, away from that cave. "Maybe I can pull him out."

But I didn't have to. That trout shot out and up, clearing the surface not ten feet in front of me. He looked to be 25 pounds.

I almost fell in. One foot slipped down the drop-off and I pawed madly for a foothold. But automatically I held the rod high and survived the monster's jump.

He sulked then and gave me time to think. My only chance was to get him away from the boiling rapids of the Garganta run below me. I pulled back on the rod and began inching my way upstream. I walked him up for 100 feet, like a bull on a nose ring; and then, just as I was beginning to breathe again, he came halfway out and shook his head at me. His teeth looked as long as a crocodile's. He almost scared me. Brownies just don't come that big.

He liked it on top and kept thrashing around on the surface. He rocked the rod and threw buckets of water. When I dropped the tip to keep him from snagging the leader with his teeth, he took advantage of me and dashed downstream for the rapids. He didn't stop until he was right on the brink of the pool, and then I guess he stopped only because he didn't like the look of the rapids any better than I did.

I walked down to the cliff again and started all over. This time I worked him up 200 feet. I put more pressure on then and he came to the top. He peeped out at me and left on a faster run than the first, headed for the other shore. When he slowed, I turned his head upstream and his dorsal fin came out.

Then he began to give me the creeps. A hundred feet across the current and about 50 feet down, he began boring away from me with wide flaps of his tail. It was an Atlantic salmon trick, a wicked, line-swatting thing, and I had to admit it was a good move from the fish's point of view. I ran downstream, reeling fast, until I was opposite him, then I pulled hard on the rod and got him turned my way. He charged across and jumped not 20 feet out from me, mouth wide open, showing all his teeth. That leap gained him 35 feet of line and gave me 35 more gray hairs.

Once again he wound up on the lip of the pool and once again I went down and started him back. I was still afraid of those rapids. Even if he tired, I couldn't hold his dead weight out in the fast water with the tippet I had on. So I edged him upstream. Inch by inch, I walked him as far as I could, about 250 feet above the tail of the pool. There the tree limbs came down to the water so thick that I couldn't get under them, and the drop-off was so sudden that I couldn't wade around them. This was it. This was where I'd have to make my play. I pulled him my way, found that he was almost ready. He could make only a feeble flap now with his big, broad tail. I pulled some more and he came to the top and rolled over on his side. He was as long as my leg.

But now I had another worry. I had no gaff, no net, and the bank jutted up too high to beach him. I'd have to tire him completely and pick him out of the water.

He righted himself and started boring away again with slow flaps of his tail. Each beat might pull the hook out. It was brutal, I pulled the rod in toward my bank, held him for a second, then turned his head and reeled the leader halfway in through the guides to get him close enough to reach. But he turned and threw water all over me as he dashed for the deep.

I stopped him fast, this time, and pulled him on his side against a rock. As he lay there quietly, I slipped my fingers through his gills, lifted him, and ran up the bank. Halfway up he gave a convulsive flap with his great body and almost pulled me over backward. But I had a death grip on him and I kept going until I hit the path.

Then, at last confident that he couldn't kick himself back into the river, I laid him down and with shaking hands got out my scales. He weighed

18½ pounds. He was an inch short of being a yard long and had a girth of 22 inches. It had taken me three-quarters of an hour to land him.

I grabbed him up again, popping bug still in his mouth, and ran up the path toward the pool above, where I knew Bebe was fishing. I rounded some bushes and there he was, working upstream with a dry fly, his back to me.

I was so excited I wanted to shout, but I went quietly to within 15 feet of him. Then I shed my jacket and sat down on the bank, braced myself, and held up that great trout.

"Look Bebe!" I proclaimed. "Una marone grande!"

A Season Ends

BY NEIL PATTERSON

Neil Patterson's Chalkstream Chronicle *is far and away my favorite fly-fishing book of the 1990s. Published by Lyons & Burford in 1995,* Chalkstream Chronicle *is the detailed month-by-month account of living on a lovely English chalkstream, or spring creek as we say on this side of the ocean, a stream carrying sweet cold water pumped from Mother Earth at the same temperature 365 days a year.*

Neil Patterson shares his experiences and observations in a charming sort of Wind in the Willows *style, much as Kenneth Grahame might have done. Set in late September, as the trout season on the river is drawing to its close, this episode finds Patterson desperately needing one last trout to close out the season. He has promised his neighbor and former landlady, Lady McFarlane, a nice fish. To get it, he will find himself going deep "into the backing" in a most unusual way.*

The people in the Big House can sense the seasons changing. The snow comes in winter, the cuckoo comes in Spring, the leaves turn in autumn, and the fishermen's cars come, and go. With the end of September only a couple of weeks away, very soon the track down to the river will be silent and the river banks will be theirs again to walk around unchallenged. And at this time of year I can read a look in the residents' eyes, an expression on a face, a hand movement. It says: 'When are we going to be given our last trout of the season?'

It's a thought on The Hollow flyfisher's mind also, as the resolve of the trout remaining in the stream toughens, hard-baked by the sunshine of a long summer and latterly by a non-stop three weeks of clear blue sky, without a drop of rain.

I told Lady McFarlane I'd do my best when I met her walking back up the track with her dog as I was on my way down. I volunteered a trout, for she never asks for anything. Of all the people I give trout to, she's the one I most like giving to. But on that still, featureless afternoon, I'd need to be lucky to get any fish up to the glare of the unyielding September sun at the surface. If not lucky, then highly resourceful.

The river was viscous. The trout, set in it like flies in jam, glared glumly into the middle distance, stony monuments to the hardest month of all. Needless to say, the flyfishing had been interesting of late. Not a single nose pushed through the rubbery surface during the day. Instead, trout joined the shoals of roach and dace, to gawp at the nymphs of small olives skidding along weed fronds, flipping head-over-heels and tumbling upwards to the surface. But not in any great numbers. It was time to rethink my approach. If only for Lady McFarlane.

I think Vincent Marinaro got it right when he said that what Halford did with the dry fly was catch more fish—and what Skues did with the nymph was catch even more fish than that. As for myself, as you will have gathered by now, I prefer to fish the fly on the surface rather than beneath, for no other reason than that this is what I *choose* to do—and because I never feel handicapped doing it. One aspect of trout behaviour that consistently creeps into nymph versus dry fly debates, and that remains constant and beyond dispute, is the fact that on hot, dry summer days, a trout feeding on nymphs at a depth of anything from a foot down, and therefore in mid-water, is rarely inclined to interrupt a fly on the surface. If this was not the case, if nymphing trout were happily drawn upwards to inspect every insect that passed over them, there would be no need for nymph patterns, no need for nymph fishing, and G.E.M. Skues would never have received half the book royalties he did. He might even have kept his rod on the Abbots Barton beat on the River Itchen from which he was unceremoniously turfed off for his heresies.

As fly-life fades in the summer, many trout leave their once rich and reliable Spring food-bearing lies and move to feeding stations better-suited for gorging on the more plentiful subsurface food. These moves are a misfortune, not just for the dry fly man, but for the nymph fisherman also, because in the course of a normal day there are several occasions when it's better to lift a nymphing trout to the surface to take your offering. Quite simply because, by doing so, you immediately eliminate the problems that often make taking a trout on a nymph more demanding than on a dry fly.

Let me group some of these difficulties under three rough headings: the first is when it's better to get a nymphing trout to break the surface, so you can see and 'read' the take.

Probably the most common occasion it's necessary to do this is in slack water when, in order to cast your fly, you put yourself in a position where you can no longer see the trout, usually on account of reflected light. Under these conditions, because your nymph is moving at a slow, ponderous pace, the trout has ample opportunity to suck in your artificial and spit it out again in the time it takes a lightly-greased leader on the surface to travel an inch down-stream on the flow. This being the case, any leader indication is likely to be subtle and unpronounced and will seriously limit your chances at the strike.

A second example of another 'seeing' problem is experienced when fishing to a trout nymphing under the far bank. The difficulty here is that, be-cause of distance it's often impossible to detect a slight sideways movement of the trout, or tiny tell-tale openings and shuttings of his mouth, making the sig-nal to tighten both inaccurate and largely guesswork.

The next group of difficulties I put under the heading 'presentation'. There are three instances of this problem that spring to mind. Instance one is when, in the case of open shallows, trout are likely to be scared, rather than stimulated, by the unnatural arrival of a sub-surface food-form—a nymph from out of the sky—and in order to get round this problem you cast way ahead of the trout, with the result that when your artificial arrives at the trout it's well below the horizontal plane of his mouth. Or, as is often the case with low-lying trout you can't see, it snags on the river-bed.

Instance two is particularly common on the wild, weedy stretch of river on the way up to the Firs at the beginning of the Marshes where trout frequently lie in mid-water directly behind a log, or beside weed-beds, fallen trees and similar obstacles. In situations like this, even though you handle a rod with lunging accuracy, it's an impossibility to get your nymph high enough up in front of a trout to let it sink to his depth.

Instance three is the classic problem of successfully presenting nymphs to trout lying in mid-water beneath low bridges where, in the space provided, you are only able to manoeuvre an artificial a few inches above the trout and there-fore, as in instance two, not high enough up to get your nymph to his depth. And, if you are fishing blind, not allowing enough time for your leader to straighten and become an effective take-indicator. As with the two 'seeing' problems, if a trout could be lifted to the surface, all these difficulties could be overcome.

The last category of problems, I file under 'rules'. There are some beats of chalkstream that I have fished where, during September, the rule is strictly 'dry fly only'. And I hear that often in this month, even though the fly-life re-turns, the trout seem slow and reluctant to feed on the renewed source of sur-face food during the day. At no other time is it more essential to bring a nymphing trout to the surface, for if you are to make contact with a trout, this is the only place etiquette allows you to make your introductions.

With Lady McFarlane awaiting her trout, frying pan at the ready, and her potential breakfast staring into a weed-bed as if it were a television screen, the leading question remained: Is it possible to lift a trout up to a dry fly when it's basking in a food-bearing lie or feeding in mid-water in a blinkered nymphing state?

The answer, of course, is: yes. But not if you think conventionally. Not if you are of the opinion that artificials tied on anything larger than a #14 are not a sporting method of luring chalkstream trout.

The fact is, dry flies tied on sub #14 sizes imitate only one thing. The one thing guaranteed *not* to tempt a trout in a nymph-bearing lie to the surface. Even though, as is often the case, naturals may be appearing in respectable numbers.

Taking into consideration the sort of food that trout in such lies are on the look-out for, any such imitation runs the very real and dangerous risk of being unnoticeable to the point of being invisible. And even if it was to catch a trout's eye, it simply doesn't warrant the effort it would need to pull himself up to the surface when he can trap similar sized food-forms in his mid-water position.

With this taken into account, the sort of dry fly I require will need to do something a little out of the ordinary. Unlike most dry flies, it must in some way distract the trout from what he is feeding on (nymphs), and then sell him the idea of feeding on something at a different level. Clearly, to do this, the fly will have to be large, with a distinct 'presence' about it that will first of all distract the trout, then hopefully, interest him enough to make him feel a trip to the surface is worth his while.

Lastly, as an added bonus, the fly must appear trapped to reassure the trout that, having made the extra effort, it will not escape before he reaches it.

With this as a brief, we're speaking about something no smaller than a #12 hook, something that's not alien for a trout during the summer to find glued to the surface film. This left me with one, or perhaps two, very clear options. Not river flies, but land-born ones. The bluebottle, and the daddy-long-legs.

The bluebottle—and the green-bottle for that matter—is a fly that has been around for some time in the flyfisher's armoury, but appears to have been largely ignored by most angling writers and, more significantly, most angler's fly-boxes I've peered into. Exactly why is hard to say. Perhaps on grounds of respectability, the fact that it is humbly born in unpleasant places and is the end-product of the maggot, and therefore cannot boast the same pedigree as those insects reared on the clean gravels of the chalkstream.

If this is the case, the more's the pity. But I suspect it has never won the popularity it deserves because no one has ever seriously considered its potential. This is a situation I dearly wish to reverse because, over the seasons, it has taken a significant percentage of nymphing trout in situations where, for reasons given earlier, a nymph would have been the obvious choice.

The pattern I recommend is a mishmash of several patterns. But there are no rules. In fact, this is an artificial few professional flydressers tie correctly for, like the Grizzle Mink that starts my season, the more chewed-up the finished effect, the better. You won't find it the best of floaters. This is essential, for the fact that it half sinks, I believe adds to its 'trapped' appeal. But to make sure it doesn't sink out of sight, I advise you to keep one in your floatant bottle. This way, when you come to use it, you'll find it will have soaked up so much floatant oil that if it caught fire you'd need Red Adair to put it out.

The first of my bluebottle imitations, tied with a cork body, caught me many nymphing fish—and the attention of the angling press when I first released it onto the the poor unsuspecting chalkstream fraternity weaned on the Halford ethic. The following month, it prompted an article by Richard Walker to put my case in perspective.

I remembered putting off reading it at first. I was terrified. It was a good few days before I mustered enough courage to read it. I imagined that Walker would be attacking me for promoting the house fly as a serious addition to the ephemeropteran armoury. But everything he wrote turned out to be in defence of my observation. He went on to suggest two other flies that could be added to my 'big dries' category—the daddy-long-legs and the red sedge. He also suggested that instead of the cork for the body of my bluebottle, spun around with blue lurex, I should consider the employment of five or six strands of ostrich herl, twisted together over wet varnish on the hook (and then spun round with blue lurex), for this would work just as well. He also questioned the importance of wings. And, of course, he was right, on both counts.

I confess that until I'd taken my first half dozen trout on the bluebottle I had never had much faith in exaggerated or large flies on chalkstreams, apart from mayfly. It's hard to rationalize, but the bigger the fly, the more it seemed to give away my intentions. In short, I never believed for one moment that trout were foolish enough to be taken in by these big flies. But autopsies and my experience with the bluebottle—and for that matter, the daddy-long-legs—have altered my view, dramatically.

The daddy-long-legs, another damp location lover like the Spring hawthorn, lays its eggs in marsh areas, in decaying wood and fungi. For this reason, it is no surprise that we find it so close to the trout's heart if, that is, the way to a trout's heart is through its stomach. The daddy-long-legs larva has a rough, tough brown skin, and is known as a 'leather jacket'. But that is of no interest to a fisherman.

My imitation is simplicity itself to tie and incorporates two main materials. Garden-plant-binding raffia, and eight short lengths of brown nylon leader material that you might have lying around in the three to four pound category, knotted to form kneecaps on the legs. The combination of this, plus a couple of hackles, form the basis of a fly that sits in the surface film and is disturbingly attractive to even the most bottom-sucking trout. Trout cannot resist rising up and filling its mouth with this large leggy picnic. But it's not as easy as it sounds.

I have lost many a fish because I have not given special consideration to the size of the meaty chunk on the end of my line. For this reason, I have developed a unique style of striking. I call this the 'pause strike', for when a trout sucks in my mammoth offering, I drop the rod tip, let the line free from my left hand, and when the stream swings the loose line round forming a belly, I trap the line as it tightens between the forefinger of my right hand and the cork of my rod, letting the current wash the hook home. With a final uplift from my right hand to gather in any slack line, my trout now should be as well hooked as it ever will be.

Even with all the time taken during the 'pause strike' it is only rarely that I either miss the fish or I hook it in any place other than the jaw or the lip. I often wonder what a trout does with the daddy in its mouth to warrant such a delay in swallowing, for it seldom blows it out in rejection. Certainly not as many times as trout seem to do with imitations ten times smaller in size. Odd.

As a picture from Skues' *Nymph Fishing for Chalkstream Trout* eloquently suggests, bluebottles, like daddy-long-legs do lift nymphing trout to the surface more times than may be good for them. The picture is of an autopsy of a trout's stomach. The dish is filled with olive nymphs and a single bluebottle sits amongst them. For me, this is picture-proof that 'Big Dries', as Walker christened them, are dry flies no dedicated nymph fisherman should be without.

Lady McFarlane got her trout, in the end. In the bitter end. On the last minute of the last day, I crawled up the track for the last time that season, with the last trout of the season dangling from a stick. My mind was swimming with the trout I'd left behind. I was only able to leave the trout I hadn't caught because, as their home was also my home, I wasn't really leaving them.

The days were getting shorter, faster. The wheat fields were fixed solid in the landscape, like plates of gold. I had said my farewells to every trout I knew, every trout I'd missed, every trout I'd hooked and lost, or unhooked and released—with a very special nod of respect (and a final flick of a fly) to those I'd never been able to torment, no matter how hard I tried. Every inch of river bank had been trodden. Every corner had been investigated for the last time. Not a single watery, bank-side spider web, drenched by the first sodden autumn dews, had been left unbroken.

My last fish didn't come easy. The river was wriggling with rods, many of whom I hadn't seen since mayfly. One rod I had never seen before. He told me that he'd only come once all season. 'I had an hour to kill before the horse racing started. Anyway, I like the wet fly,' he told me, rushing back up in the direction of the Mad House and his car, at a gallop that would win him the 1000 Guineas.

Over-Here was in his element. It didn't matter that he couldn't see fishermen, he couldn't help but bump into them. Accidentally-on-purpose we didn't make contact. I got within hailing distance a couple of times, but every time I saw him he was being well looked after by one rod or other. It was a good job he'd said his goodbyes and gone home by the time I eventually managed to get my last fish to take a fly.

All week, the bank-side vegetation had been weighed down with large cinnamon sedges. On Cemetery by the Withy Bed where in the final hours I'd staked out a fish in the two-pound bracket, they were rattling away like Flamenco dancers. On The Hollow, these frankfurter-sized sedges start hatching late on in the season, usually in the last two weeks of September, and they keep on hatching well into October if the weather stays mild. One October they flew off the river and up in the air so thickly, that guns out on the first day of the pheasant season might have been forgiven for shooting at them. And it was a shotgun I was beginning to think I'd need to get this trout lying tucked under the bend on Cemetery. Out of last-minute desperation, I attached the largest fly in my box to the end of my line.

'Right,' I said, shaking a fist clenched round my frankfurter imitation, 'No more Mr Nice Guy'.

Rolling back my fingers, packaging the sedge pattern in the palm of my hand, I let the line whisk it away. Once behind my back, I shot it forward, squeezing the cork as if I was squeezing the trigger of a gun. The sedge hit the water with force, and my trout snapped out of its no-play coma and rose to the surface. A moment later with fear, with anger, with regret, with betrayal, the trout was buried in deepest weeds on one side of a dense bar of ranunculus. The side I wasn't on.

I went through all the normal, 'weeded-up' procedures. Walking above the fish and giving a yank, walking below the fish and giving a wrench, pointing the rod tip in the direction of the trout and giving the handle of the rod a healthy tap in the hope that if I couldn't haul the fish ashore physically, then I might be able to do it psychologically, using sinister sound waves to freak him loose. I began to debate whether or not it was worth trying to wade in up to my waist to unravel the nautical knitting. It was the last half-hour on the last day of the season, what the heck. But I had a drier idea.

With no bridge between me and the hatch pool a hundred yards below, and not enough line or backing for me to walk down that far, I stripped all the line and backing off my reel and, detaching the line from my reel drum and letting it run free through the rod rings, I tied the end to a log and threw it at the trout. Not a flicker. It didn't budge an inch, but the log drifted downstream, as intended, taking my line with it. I followed after it.

With all the line between the trout and the log paid out, the log jolted to a halt and swung towards the bank at the bend on the opposite side of the river awaiting my collection. I kept on walking down to the Meadow Steam hatch, crossed over and walked back up to the log, whistling with confidence. Lifting it out of the water, I untied my line, fed it back down through the rings, knotted it to my reel drum and wound on the line as I walked back up towards the trout. I was singing aloud by now.

The trout wasn't expecting all this. Out of the weed it slipped into my waiting hand, onto the dew-covered bank, and straight into Lady McFarlane's deepfreeze, the door shutting softly on the season.